Coping With Divorce, Single Parenting, and Remarriage

A Risk and Resiliency Perspective

Coping With Divorce, Single Parenting, and Remarriage

A Risk and Resiliency Perspective

Edited by

E. Mavis Hetherington
University of Virginia

 LAWRENCE ERLBAUM ASSOCIATES, PUBLISHERS
1999   Mahwah, New Jersey   London

Lawrence Erlbaum Associates, Inc., Publishers
10 Industrial Avenue
Mahwah, NJ 07430

Cover design by Kathryn Houghtaling Lacey

Library of Congress Cataloging-in-Publication Data

Coping with divorce, single parenting, and remarriage : a risk and re-
    siliency perspective / edited by E. Mavis Hetherington.
        p. cm.
    Includes bibliographical references and index.
    ISBN 0-8058-3082-0 (cloth).—ISBN 0-8058-3083-9 (pbk.)
    1. Divorce—Psychological aspects. 2. Divorced people—Psy-
chology. 3. Children of divorced parents—Psychology. 4. Single-parent   family—Psychological   aspects.   5.
Remarriage—Psychological aspects. 6. Stepfamilies—Psychological aspects. I. Hetherington, E. Mavis (Eileen Mavis), 1926–
HQ814.C665 1999
306.89–dc21   98-30550
                                                                    CIP

Books published by Lawrence Erlbaum Associates are printed on acid-free paper, and their bindings are chosen for strength and durability.

Printed in the United States of America
10   9   8   7   6   5   4   3   2   1

Contents

Introduction and Overview   **vii**

PART I: WHY MARRIAGES SUCCEED OR FAIL

1 Predicting the Future of Marriages   **3**
Sybil Carrére and John M. Gottman

2 Black Couples, White Couples: The Early Years   **23**
of Marriage
Terri L. Orbuch, Joseph Veroff, and Andrea G. Hunter

PART II: CHILD ADJUSTMENT IN DIFFERENT FAMILY FORMS

3 Multiple Risks and Adjustment in Young Children Growing   **47**
up in Different Family Settings: A British Community Study
of Stepparent, Single Mother, and Nondivorced Families
Kirby Deater-Deckard and Judy Dunn

4 Family Structure, Parenting Practices, and Adolescent   **65**
Adjustment: An Ecological Examination
Shelli Avenevoli, Frances M. Sessa, and Laurence Steinberg

**PART III: FAMILY FUNCTIONING AND CHILD ADJUSTMENT
IN DIVORCED AND SINGLE-PARENT FAMILIES**

5 Should We Stay Together for the Sake of the Children?   **93**
E. Mavis Hetherington

6 Father Absence and the Welfare of Children   **117**
Sara S. McLanahan

v

7 Children of Divorced Parents as Young Adults   147
   Paul R. Amato

8 Young African American Multigenerational Families   165
   in Poverty: The Contexts, Exchanges, and Processes
   of Their Lives
   *P. Lindsay Chase-Lansdale, Rachel A. Gordon, Rebekah
   Levine Coley, Lauren S. Wakschlag, and Jeanne
   Brooks-Gunn*

9 Protective Factors in the Development of Preschool-Age   193
   Children of Young Mothers Receiving Welfare
   *Martha J. Zaslow, M. Robin Dion, Donna Ruane Morrison,
   Nancy Weinfield, John Ogawa, and Patton Tabors*

**PART IV: FAMILY FUNCTIONING AND CHILD ADJUSTMENT
IN REPARTNERED RELATIONSHIPS AND IN STEPFAMILIES**

10 Contexts as Predictors of Changing Maternal Parenting   227
   Practices in Diverse Family Structures: A Social
   Interactional Perspective of Risk and Resilience
   David S. DeGarmo and Marion S. Forgatch

11 From Marriage to Remarriage and Beyond: Findings From   253
   the Developmental Issues in StepFamilies Research Project
   James H. Bray

12 A Social Constructionist Multi-Method Approach   273
   to Understanding the Stepparent Role
   Mark A. Fine, Marilyn Coleman, and Lawrence H. Ganong

13 The Dynamics of Parental Remarriage: Adolescent,   295
   Parent, and Sibling Influences
   *Edward R. Anderson, Shannon M. Greene, E. Mavis
   Hetherington, and W. Glenn Clingempeel*

PART V: INTERVENTION

14 Psychological Interventions for Separated and Divorced   323
   Families
   *Robert E. Emery, Katherine M. Kitzmann, and Mary
   Waldron*

Author Index   345

Subject Index   355

Introduction and Overview

This book is comprised of chapters written by some of the leading researchers studying single-parent families, divorce, and remarriage. Authors were asked to write chapters that were interesting and accessible not only to other researchers but also to nonresearch professionals working with children such as psychiatrists, pediatricians, social workers, clinical psychologists, family therapists, and educators. Hence, some of the more complex data analyses found in journal chapters are not presented in detail in these chapters. The chapters included in this volume are, for the most part, based on programmatic research and studies based both on large-scale surveys and on smaller studies involving multiple methods and multiple measures that include observations, standardized tests and questionnaires, interviews, and multiple informants. The conclusions of authors are sometimes not in accord, and in reading the chapters it is instructive to think about the strengths and limitations of different methodologies and the kinds of questions different methodologies are best able to answer.

The authors take a risk and resiliency approach in examining family functioning and child adjustment in different kinds of families. The interactions among individual, familial, and extrafamilial risk and protective factors are explored in an attempt to explain the great diversity in parents' and children's responses to different kinds of experiences associated with marriage, divorce, life in a single- parent household, and remarriage.

These topics have become increasingly important in the United States as demographics relating to marriage and childbearing have changed. Marriage is being delayed; cohabitation, births to single mothers, and divorce have increased. Although about 75% of men and 66% of women eventually remarry, the remarriage

rate—especially for women with children and for older women—has declined. Because the rate of divorce is even higher in remarriages than in first marriages, 1 out
of 10 children will experience at least two divorces of their residential parents before reaching the age of 16. More parents and children are going through a series
of transitions and organizations of the family associated with notable challenges
and changes in roles and relationships and life experiences that can undermine or
enhance the well-being of family members.

Although divorce, growing up in a single-parent family, and remarriage put children at risk for developing social, emotional, behavioral, and academic problems,
most children eventually emerge from these experiences as competent, reasonably
well-adjusted individuals. Many of the chapters in this volume examine the processes and factors that lead to children's vulnerability or resilience in dealing with
their parents marital transitions and with life in a single-parent family or a
stepfamily.

The volume begins with two chapters examining what contributes to successful
or unsuccessful marital functioning. Chapter 1, by Carrere and Gottman, reports
the work of the most innovative and important programmatic set of studies on
what makes marriages succeed or fail. It is notable for its use of multiple measures,
many of them developed in the Gottman lab, and a variety of methods including
physiological, observational, interview, and questionnaire. Chapter 2, by Orbuch,
Veroff, and Hunter, is an interesting companion to the previous one, because it
uses some similar measures, including observations and a marital history interview, to examine White and African American marriages. It is one of the few studies to use multiple methods including observations in the study of African
American families.

Part II of the volume uses large survey data sets to examine the adjustment of
children in different family forms. The first study, by Deater-Deckard and Dunn,
is British and examines the effects of multiple risk factors in diverse family types
on the adjustment of children. The second involves the reports by children of
their experiences in the family, school, neighborhood, and peer group and the influences of these experiences on adjustment. The Avenevolli, Sessa, and Steinberg
study is notable for its examination not only of family structure but also of social
class and ethnicity and in considering family functioning and child adjustment in
relation to other social systems.

Part III deals with families that are headed by a single parent because of
out-of-wedlock childbearing or divorce. Hetherington (chapter 5) attempts to answer the frequently asked question, "Should we stay together for the sake of the
children?" by examining family relations, parenting, and child adjustment preceding and following divorce and in high- and low-conflict families. McLanahan
(chapter 6) uses the results from several large nationally representative data sets to
explore why children in father-absent families are at risk for lower attainment than
those in families headed by two biological parents, and the relative contributions
of economic, family and neighborhood factors to the development of children in

father-absent families. In chapter 7, Amato takes a life-course perspective in examining the socioeconomic attainment, marital relationship, relationship with parents, and subjective well-being of young adult offspring from divorced families. In chapter 8, Chase-Lansdale, Gordon, Coley, Wakschlag, and Brooks-Gunn examine poor multigenerational African American families, the relationship between a young unwed mother and her mother, and the effects of the parenting by mothers and by grandmothers who do or do not co-reside on children's adjustment. Zaslow, Dion, Morrison, Weinfield, Ogawa, and Tabors (chapter 9) use data from the New Chance Demonstration program to study the effects of parent and child characteristics, parenting, and social support on the adjustment of children born to poor, disadvantaged teenaged mothers on welfare. Although the families in the Chase-Lansdale et al. and Zaslow et al. studies are fairly similar, those in the treatment group in the New Chance study had been involved in an intensive intervention involving education, job training and improving parenting and other life skills and health.

Part IV examines family functioning and/or child adjustment in repartnered families or in stepfamilies. In chapter 10, DeGarmo and Forgatch study the effects of repartnering and social support on parenting including problem solving and aversive discipline, and the subsequent outcomes for children. This study is unusual in including observations of mothers interacting with confidants to assess processes involved in supportive relationships. Next, Bray (chapter 11) presents the results of his longitudinal study of stepfamilies taking a family systems approach to examining risk and protective factors in family relations as families negotiate the unique challenges confronted in a stepfamily. In chapter 12, Fine, Coleman, and Ganong present their social constructionist approach to understanding the stepparent role. Their emphasis on the contribution of perceptual and cognitive processes to adaptation in stepfamilies represents an innovative theoretical contribution to the study of stepfamilies. Anderson, Greene, Hetherington, and Clingempeel (chapter 13) conclude Part IV by illustrating the differences associated with remarriages when children are young adolescents.

After the previous chapters, which have used diverse methods to study risk and resiliency in divorced, single-parent, and remarried families, we come to the final part and chapter of the volume, which deals with how to intervene in divorce in order to promote the well-being of family members. After reading the Emery, Kitzmann, and Waldron chapter (chapter 14), one must conclude that there are insufficient data from well-designed and controlled intervention studies to draw conclusions about the most effective intervention methods. Moreover, a chapter on interventions in remarriage was not included because there is an even greater dearth of high-quality intervention research in that area than in divorce. This is a topic that clearly warrants further study.

It is hoped that the reader will gain an understanding of the current issues, questions, research methods, and knowledge about divorce, single-parent families, and remarriage that we have gained through cutting-edge studies such as those presented in this volume. It also is hoped that after reading these chapters the reader will have a keener awareness of the great diversity there is in response to experiences in different types of families and the role that risk and protective factors play in shaping these outcomes. It is the diversity, rather than the inevitability, of outcomes for family processes and the adjustment family members in divorced, single-parent, and remarried families that is striking.

—*E. Mavis Hetherington*

PART I

Why Marriages Succeed or Fail

1

Predicting the Future of Marriages

Sybil Carrère
John M. Gottman
University of Washington

WE ARE INTERESTED in the causal processes that destroy marriage and those processes that build marriage. Our goal is to develop a theory that explains the different trajectories toward divorce and marital stability. As Karney and Bradbury (1995) pointed out, it is not enough to predict divorce or marital stability; researchers must be able to explain why marriages fail or succeed. Our research has discovered some of the pathways that lead to marital dissolution. However, causal factors in marital dissolution is not sufficient information to build a model of functional marital processes. Recent findings in our laboratory indicate that stable, happy marriages are based on a series of marital processes and behaviors that are more than just the absence of dysfunctional processes. Constructive activities build strong marital relationships and help the unions withstand the stressful events and transitions that can destroy weaker marriages. Our goal is to identify both those processes that make a marriage work and those that make a marriage dysfunctional. In this chapter we provide an overview of our research findings and theoretical formulations on the functional and dysfunctional dynamics of marriage.

THE METHODOLOGY OF OBSERVING COUPLES

We have been following 638 couples in our laboratory and in collaboration with Robert Levenson, Lynn Fainsilber Katz, Neil Jacobson, and Laura Carstensen. There are six different cohorts we are studying: a newlywed group of 130 couples (for the past 6 years); a group of 79 couples whom we first saw when they were in their 30s (for the past 14 years); two cohorts of 119 couples with a preschool child at the time of the first visit to our laboratory (for the past 11 and 8 years, respectively); a group of 160 couples, half in their 40s and half in their 60s the first time we contacted them, and half happily and half unhappily married; and a group of 150 married couples who were physically violent, distressed but not violent, or happily married (for the past 8 years). We collected the same core of Time-1 marital assessment data for all our cohorts. Each cohort had additional measures that were specific to the hypotheses associated with the research, but for purposes of this chapter we report primarily on the marital assessment procedures that these studies have in common.

The marital interaction assessment consisted of a 15-minute discussion by the wife and husband of a problem area that was a source of ongoing disagreement in their marriage. This interaction was videotaped with two remotely controlled, high-resolution cameras. The frontal images of the two spouses were combined in a split-screen image through the use of a video special effects generator. Physiological measures were collected during the discussion period and synchronized with the video time code. The couples were also asked to view a videotape of their problem-solving session. During the replay of the marital discussion the couples were asked to rate, in a continuous fashion using a rating dial, how positive or negative they were feeling during the conflict interaction. Physiological measures, video recordings, and data from the rating dial were synchronized and collected during this recall session. We followed these six cohorts over time to assess the stability of the marriages as well as marital satisfaction, health, and family functioning.

Physiological Measures

The peripheral physiological measures we indexed during the Time 1 assessment session were interbeat interval (i.e., the time between the r-spikes of the electrocardiogram; the heart rate is 60,000/interbeat interval), pulse transit time (i.e., the time it takes for the blood to get to the fingertip), finger pulse amplitude, palmar skin conductance, and activity (i.e., gross motor movement). Several of the most recent studies have included ear pulse transit time and respiration. In our study of newlyweds we assayed urinary measures of epinephrine, norepinephrine, and cortisol. We collaborated with Hans Ochs to collect blood assays of immune response in these newlywed couples.

Affect

We primarily used our Specific Affect Coding System (SPAFF; Gottman, 1996) to index the affect expressed by the couples during the marital interactions. SPAFF focuses solely on the affect expressed. The SPAFF system draws on facial expressions (based on Ekman and Friesen's facial action coding system, 1978), voice tone, and speech content to characterize the emotions expressed by the couples. The emotions captured by this coding system allow us to see the range and sequencing of affect the couples use during their conversations and problem-solving interactions. The positive affects include humor, affection, validation, and joy. The negative affects include emotions such as disgust, contempt, criticism, belligerence, domineering, defensiveness, whining, tension or fear, anger, and sadness.

Problem Solving

We used three observational systems to index problem-solving behavior by couples. We originally used the Marital Interaction Coding System (MICS; Weiss & Summers, 1983). The Couples Interaction Scoring System (CISS; Markman & Notarious, 1987) was later developed in our laboratory to separate the behaviors used in problem-solving sessions from the affect displayed. The Rapid Couples Interaction Scoring System (RCISS; Krokoff, Gottman, & Haas, 1989) is the most recent version of the problem-solving coding system and was created to assess conflict resolution behaviors more quickly. RCISS uses a checklist of 13 behaviors that are scored for the speaker and 9 behaviors that are scored for the listener at each turn of speech. We used the speaker codes to categorize the couples into regulated and unregulated marital types. These codes consist of five positive codes (i.e., neutral or positive problem description, task-oriented relationship information, assent, humor-laugh, and other positive), and eight negative codes (i.e., complain, criticize, negative relationship issue problem talk, yes-but, defensive, put-down, escalate negative affect, and other negative). We computed the average number of positive and negative speaker codes per turn of speech and the average number of positive minus the negative codes per turn.

Oral History Interview

The Oral History Interview is a semistructured interview in which the interviewer asks the couple a series of open-ended questions about the history of their marriage and about their philosophy of marriage. We started using the Oral History Interview in 1986. This interview was developed by Gottman and Krokoff and is modeled after the interview methods of Studs Terkel. The interviewer explores the path the relationship has taken from the first moment the couple met through the dating period, the decision to marry, the wedding, adjustment to marriage, the highs and lows of the marriage, and how the marriage has changed. Philosophy about marriage is examined by having the couple choose a good marriage and a bad marriage they know and describe the qualities of those marriages that make them positive or negative. Finally, the couple is asked to describe their parents' marriages. Buehlman and Gottman (1996) developed a coding system for this interview that assesses nine dimensions of marriage:

1. *We-ness versus Separateness* indexes the degree to which a couple see themselves as a unit or as individuals;
2. *Fondness and Affection* of each spouse for the partner;
3. *Expansiveness versus Withdrawal* measures how large a role the marital

partner and the marriage plays in each spouse's world view; it is the "cognitive room" an individual allocates to the marriage and to his or her spouse;

4. *Negativity Toward the Spouse* reflects the disagreement and criticism expressed during the interview by the husband or the wife;

5. *Glorifying the Struggle* taps the level of difficulty the couple has experienced to keep the marriage together and how they feel about the struggle;

6. *Volatility* indicates whether the couple experience intense emotions, both positive and negative, in their relationship;

7. *Gender Stereotypy* is a measure of how traditional or nontraditional the couple's beliefs and practices are in their marriage;

8. *Chaos* is linked to whether the couple feel like they have little control over what happens to them;

9. *Marital Disappointment and Disillusionment* tells us if the couple feels hopeless or defeated about their marriage.

PREDICTING THE MARITAL PATH

We have reached a point in our marital research, across three longitudinal studies, where we can predict with 88% to 94% accuracy those marriages that will remain stable and those marriages that will end in divorce. Some of our earlier studies focused on which couples would divorce (Buehlman, Gottman, & Katz, 1992; Gottman, 1994; Gottman & Levenson, 1992). The older research addresses what is dysfunctional in an ailing marriage, but we have now expanded our research questions to include the etiology of the dysfunctional patterns and what is "functional" in stable and satisfying relationships. Our recent research describes the origins and development of negative affective patterns of communication that predict divorce. This new body of work has also produced findings that reveal the role of positive affect and the nature of conflict resolution in stable and happy marriages. In this chapter we describe the indices of the trajectories toward marital dissolution and marital harmony.

THE CASCADE MODEL OF MARITAL DISSOLUTION

Gottman and Levenson (1992) developed the Cascade Model of Marital Dissolution based on research conducted with 73 married couples who were first brought into the laboratory in 1983. The Cascade Model of Dissolution was proposed, in part, to address the difficulty of predicting divorce in short-term longitudinal studies. Such studies usually have a low base rate of divorce. Gottman and Levenson identified behavioral precursors of divorce with a relatively high base rate of occurrence in marriage. The idea was to predict the entire cascade toward divorce, instead of focusing on only one dichotomous outcome variable. They created a Guttman scale (thus the term *cascade*) and demonstrated that marriages that are likely to end in divorce travel through the same series of stages. They proposed that, as the marital relationship moves along the trajectory toward dissolution, increasing numbers of these high base-rate variables are exhibited. The Cascade Model predicted the following trajectory toward divorce: low marital satisfaction at Time 1 and Time 2 (1983 and 1987, respectively) → consideration of separation or divorce → separation → divorce.

The data from the study supported the model. In the time period between 1983 and 1987, 36 of the 73 couples (43%) considered divorce, 18 of the couples (24.7%) separated, and 9 of the couples (12.5%) got a divorce. Structural equation modeling of the data indicated that the data were consistent with the Guttman-like ordering of the variables proposed by the cascade model (see Fig. 1.1).

Now the question became, what process variables in behavior, cognition, and physiology, the Core Triad, predicted the cascade? A balance theory motivated the search for predictors (Gottman & Levenson, 1992). The idea was that in the behavioral domain each couple finds a steady state, or a balance between positive and negative affect. With this in mind, the couples were categorized as regulated or nonregulated based on their RCISS data (see the previous discussion for a more detailed description of this coding system for problem-solving behavior). Regulated couples were defined as those for whom both the husband and the wife displayed more positive RCISS codes than negative codes. The nonregulated couples had at least one spouse who displayed either more negative than positive RCISS codes or who had an equal amount of positive and negative codes.

Gottman and Levenson found that the couples in the regulated and nonregulated groups traveled very different paths in their marriages, as indexed by behavioral, physiological, and cognitive markers. The nonregulated couples, compared with the regulated couples, reported more severe marital problems at Time 1 and lower marital satisfaction both at Time 1 and Time 2. These nonregulated couples also described themselves as experiencing poorer health in 1987 than the regulated couples. The physiology of the two groups of wives, but not of the husbands, differed as well. The nonregulated wives had greater sympathetic arousal as indexed by finger pulse amplitude and heart rate. Both of these physiological markers are associated with stress and subsequent risk for disease (cf. Cohen, Kessler, & Gordon, 1995). One can conjecture that the increased sympathetic arousal during the marital conflict sessions is indicative of the pattern of physiological arousal likely to be found in these maritally distressed wives and perhaps causally related to their reports of poor health in 1987.

The rating dial data, a cognitive measure, indicated that these nonregulated couples experienced the marital discussion as a more negative encounter. During the marital interaction sessions the nonregulated couples exhibited more negative emotional behaviors such as defensiveness and whining while also displaying fewer positive emotions such as validation, affection, and joy (SPAFF).

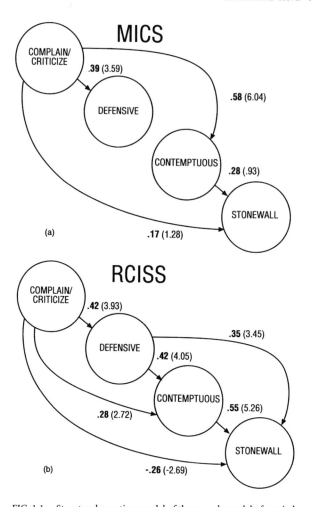

FIG. 1.1. Structural equation model of the cascade model of marital dissolution. From "Marital Processes Predictive of Later Dissolution: Behavior, Physiology and Health," by J. M. Gottman and R. W. Levenson, 1992, *Journal of Personality and Social Psychology, 63*, p. 227. Copyright © 1992 by the Journal of Personality and Social Psychology. Adapted with permission.

   We learned from building the Cascade Model of Martial Dissolution that there is a continuity between the processes of marital distress and separation and divorce. This work also laid some of the theoretical foundation for understanding which behaviors make a marriage dysfunctional or functional. We also learned that communication patterns with a greater proportion of positive to negative affective and problem-solving behaviors have a stabilizing and healthy influence on relationships.

THE FOUR HORSEMEN OF THE APOCALYPSE

The next research question was to ask if all negativity is equally corrosive. Further analyses of the data from the 1983 cohort of couples revealed a behavioral process predictive of marital dissolution. Using both the MICS and RCISS coding systems, Gottman (1993b) constructed structural equation models of this behavioral cascade toward divorce. In both observational systems, criticism led to contempt, which in turn led to defensiveness and subsequently to stonewalling (see Fig. 1.2). Stonewalling is a withdrawal behavior primarily observed in men but associated with physiological arousal in both spouses (Gottman, 1994). The descent through these four behaviors was predictive of divorce and lent further support to the idea of using a Guttman-like scaling model to delineate the stages of marital deconstruction. It was of particular theoretical import to learn that anger, considered a

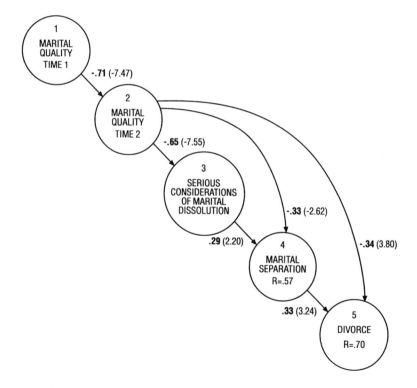

FIG. 1.2.   The cascade behavioral process models using (a) MICS coding and (b) RCISS subscales. From *What Predicts Divorce: The Relationship Between Marital Processes and Marital Outcomes*, by J. M. Gottman, 1994, Hillsdale NJ: Lawrence Erlbaum Associates. Copyright © 1994 by Lawrence Erlbaum Associates. Reprinted with permission.

dangerous emotion in marriage by many (e.g., Hendrix, 1988; Parrott & Parrott, 1995), did not predict marital instability.

THE DOMAIN OF PERCEPTION:
THE DISTANCE AND ISOLATION CASCADE

Another series of signposts indexing the trail of marital instability emerged from the questionnaires used in our research (Gottman, 1993b). A set of five questionnaires outlines the growing distance and isolation the spouses experience in the marriage and can be modeled using structural equation modeling techniques. This cascade has several stages:

1. Flooding, which is a spouse's sense that his or her partner's negative emotions are unexpected and so overwhelming that the individual will do whatever he or she can to escape from them;
2. a perception that the marital problems are severe;
3. a desire by the spouses to work out problems individually rather than together;
4. the creation of separate lives in which they are increasingly less likely to spend time with each other; and
5. loneliness within the marriage.

Men typically experienced flooding at a lower threshold than women. Specifically, men experienced flooding in association with criticism, but women were more likely to report flooding in association with contempt. These findings that men experienced flooding at a lower threshold were consistent with the observation that men are more likely to stonewall than women. In general, we found that once flooding started, the cascade toward loneliness led to an emotional divorce within the marriage and ultimately to marital dissolution. We also think flooding is the first step in building a set of negative attributions about the marriage (thus the tendency to see the marital problems as severe). These attributions may serve as a filter through which neutral or ambiguous behaviors by one's partner are interpreted as negative. As we describe later in the chapter, this conjecture is supported by our research with newlywed couples.

A TYPOLOGY OF DYSFUNCTIONAL
AND FUNCTIONAL COUPLES

The next step in developing a theory of marital stability and dissolution was to further distinguish the behavioral differences between the regulated and nonregulated couples. To this end Gottman (1993a) presented a typology of three groups of functional, stable marriages and two categories of unstable, dysfunctional marriages.

The SPAFF, MICS, and RCISS observational data from the Time 1 and Time 2 contacts with the 1983 cohort of married couples were used to determine these behavioral differences. Both speaker and listener behavior were evaluated. Gottman
classified the couples into stable and unstable groups by considering the balance between positive and negative behaviors. The stable couples had very different mixes
of behaviors but in all cases had more positive behaviors than negative. The volatile
couples had the greatest emotional expressivity with extensive negativity; however,
this negativity was balanced by laughter, a positive presentation of problems, and a
passionate, romantic marriage. These couples had fewer nonneutral moments than
other couples. Volatile couples worked to persuade their spouses of their perspective throughout the interaction. The validating couples had more neutral moments
and were more likely to be selective about their efforts to persuade their partners.
They tended to disagree, confront conflict, persuade (in the middle portion of the
discussion), and express support for their spouses. Conflict-avoiding couples were
the third type of stable marriages. These couples had the greatest number of neutral
interactions and rarely engaged in persuasion efforts. Conflict-avoiding couples
tended to minimize the importance of disagreement but seemed to make a trade-off
by having more emotional distance in their relationships.

Contrary to the hypotheses of Raush and his associates (Raush, Barry, Hertel, &
Swain, 1974), conflict avoidance by couples was not a dysfunctional process leading to marital dissolution, nor was the escalation of quarrels, as found in volatile
couples, likely to result in divorce. Each type of stable marriage had a different level
of emotional expressiveness that was associated with a particular balance of re-
wards and costs. However, in each kind of marriage there was a balance of positivity that outweighed the negativity and served to stabilize the marriage.

The two groups of unstable marriages, hostile and hostile/detached, were characterized as having more negativity than positivity in their interactions. Hostile
couples exhibited a high amount of conflict, listened attentively, and displayed
large levels of defensiveness (one of the four horsemen). In contrast, the hostile/
detached couples listened less to each other, engaged in reciprocal attacks, and had
bouts of defensiveness.

Gottman (1994) proposed that in hostile and hostile/detached marriages,
spouses were unable to accommodate each other to find an adaptive pattern of
interaction and thus stability. The partners in these nonregulated marriages had
mismatching patterns of conflict interaction that served to destabilize the relationship and move it toward dissolution.

MATHEMATICAL MODELING
OF THE MARITAL INTERACTION

In the early 1990s Gottman began a collaboration with James Murray, a leading
mathematical biologist (Murray, 1993). This collaboration led to the construction

of a successful nonlinear dynamic model of the parameters used to discriminate between the regulated and nonregulated couples (Cook et al., 1995). The mathematical model was a breakthrough for our work. Cook and his colleagues constructed a model, using the balance theory, to "explain" the Gottman–Levenson prediction. The model provided a theoretical and mathematical language for describing how spouses affect one another over time. Mathematical models also allowed us to simulate via computer the couple's interactions in situations other than those in which they were observed. This modeling technique allowed us to move beyond statistical summaries that provide a one-dimensional, static representation of the marital interactions to a dynamic, temporal, and multidimensional portrait of marital processes.

Cook and his associates were able to determine how individuals' affective behavior influenced the subsequent behavior of both their spouses and themselves within the 15-minute interaction. Using the 1983 data set of married couples, the investigators modeled data for the three types of stable couples (i.e., volatile, conflict-avoiding, and validating) and the two types of unstable couples (i.e., hostile and hostile/detached). In general, the stable couples had more positive uninfluenced set points. Uninfluenced set points can be thought of as the cumulative effect of the marriage on each spouse and that spouse's propensity to act in either a positive or negative manner. The uninfluenced set point is thought to be more stable and less open to the immediate moment-to-moment interactions taking place in the marriage. Cook and his associates found that validating couples had a linear influence over the whole range of their interaction. This means that when the validating couples were more negative than positive in their interactions, they had a negative impact on their spouse's behavior. When their behavior was more positive than negative, validating couples had a positive influence on their partner's behavior. Conflict-avoiding couples only influenced their spouses in the positive ranges of their behaviors. Volatile couples had no influence on their partners in the positive ranges of behavior but had a more positive uninfluenced set point than the unstable couples.

In general, the unstable couples had more negative uninfluenced set points. This is consistent with Gottman's (1993b) proposal that couples on a trajectory toward divorce, as indexed by the distance and isolation cascade, begin to have negative attributions about the marriage. These negative attributions are thought to act as a filter through which all marital interactions are viewed. Thus, having a cumulative perspective on the marriage as more negative (i.e., the uninfluenced set point) makes theoretical sense for these unstable couples. The unstable couples also had mismatched influence functions. Spouses were unable to accommodate each other in their patterns of communication and influence and as a result were unable to form one of the stable adaptations to marriage. Cook et al. (1995) found that in these mismatched, unstable couples, one partner was more suited to one style of marriage, such as a volatile marriage, whereas the other partner was suited to a different style of marriage, in this example, either conflict-avoiding or validating.

From the mathematical modeling of stable and unstable couples we developed a set of concepts to help explain what makes marriages last. Couples in stable relationships had a more positive perspective on their marriages (i.e., the uninfluenced set point). These couples tended to influence each other in positive ways. The exception was the volatile couples who appeared to overcome their negative influence on each other with a high rate of positivity in their conflict resolution interactions. Unstable couples had more emotional inertia in their marriages and had mismatched patterns of influence that appear to sabotage their efforts at conflict resolution and communication.

FUNCTIONAL AND DYSFUNCTIONAL PROCESSES IN MARRIAGE

Recently, we examined more closely the role of functional and dysfunctional interactive processes in marriages. The goals were to learn if some negative affects are more destructive than others and whether there are gender patterns associated with the longitudinal stability of marriage. We also wanted to see, among stable newlywed couples, if we could discriminate between happy and distressed couples on the basis of interactive communication patterns (Gottman, Coan, Carrère, & Swanson, 1998).

We explored seven types of process models to tease apart the functional and dysfunctional behavioral interactions in marriage: (a) anger as a toxic emotion, (b) negative affect reciprocity, (c) de-escalation of negative affect, (d) negative startups of marital conflict, (e) active listening, (f) positive affect models, and (g) physiological soothing.

Anger Is Not a Toxic Emotion in Marriages

Anger is thought by many to be a destructive force in marriage (e.g., Hendrix, 1988; Parrott & Parrott, 1995). Our perspective is that it can have a positive long-term effect in marriage (Gottman & Krokoff, 1989) and that the more corrosive negative emotions such as contempt and defensiveness predict divorce (Gottman, 1994). With this in mind, we used the SPAFF affect codes to distinguish between low intensity negative affect (i.e., sadness, anger, whining, tension/fear, and domineering) and high intensity negative affect (i.e., contempt, defensiveness, and belligerence) in characterizing sequences of marital interactions.

In our newlywed couples we found evidence replicating Gottman's (1994) findings that contempt, belligerence, and defensiveness displayed by both the husbands and wives were predictive of divorce but that anger was not implicated in destabilizing the marriage. The expression of low intensity negative affect by the wives (i.e., the sum of sadness, anger, whining, tension or fear, and domineering) predicted divorce but did not predict which couples would be satisfied or dissatisfied with their marriages at Time 2 (6 years after the initial marital assessment).

Negative Affect Reciprocity and Escalating Negativity

Negative affect reciprocity discriminates between happy and distressed couples (e.g., Gottman, 1994; Margolin & Wampold, 1981). We divided the negative affect reciprocity model into two categories: negative reciprocity in kind and escalating negativity. The first type of negative interaction sequence is one in which a negative affect is reciprocated with a negative affect of the same intensity, such as anger being met with anger or sadness. Escalating negativity is a behavioral sequence in which a low intensity negative affect is followed by a high intensity negative affect, such as a husband's sadness followed by a wife's contempt.

The newlywed wives in unstable marriages were more likely to reciprocate low intensity negativity in kind, compared with wives in stable marriages (Gottman et al., 1998). We also found newlywed couples whose husbands escalated their wives' low negative affect were more likely to get a divorce than couples in which the husbands accepted their wives' influence. However, negative escalation by the wife did not discriminate between couples who were divorced at Time 2, nor did negative escalation by the wife discriminate between couples who were unhappily married and those who were happily married at Time 2.

Negative Startups

The manner in which a conflict was started, and by whom it was started, also predicted the stability of the marriage. *Startup* is the escalation of conflict from one partner's neutral to the other partner's negative affect. For example, a husband may make a neutral comment followed by the wife's belligerent statement. This concept is part of the Negative Startup model which comes from the work of J. R. Patterson on coercive processes in families (e.g., Patterson, 1982). We found a higher rate of divorce among those newlywed relationships in which the wives more frequently used negative startups. This is consistent with the Female Demand–Male Withdrawal pattern described by Christensen and his colleagues (e.g., Christensen & Heavey, 1990; Heavey, Christensen, & Malamuth, 1995).

Active Listening

Our goal was to see if the practice of active listening, a technique recommended in many marital therapies (e.g., Guerney, 1977; Hendrix, 1988), was practiced by couples who remained happily married over the 6 years of the study. We found virtually no examples of active listening taking place among the newlywed couples. An average of 4 seconds was spent actively listening during the 15-minute conflict interaction. Instead, happy, stable couples argued respectfully but relentlessly.

Positive Affect

Our objective was to compare our ratio model of positive affect (i.e., stable marriages have a greater ratio of positive to negative affective behavior) with models of positive affect that would predict that positive affect either occurs randomly (noncontingent on a previous behavior) or is used primarily to de-escalate marital conflict in the newlywed couples (Gottman et al., 1998). In general, the amount of positive affect (i.e., the Ratio Model) used in the newlywed marriages not only predicted which couples stayed married but also which couples were the happiest in their marriages at Time 2. We used path modeling to compare the different models of postive affect. We found that positive affect was contingent and acted to de-escalate negative affect only among stable, happy couples.

Physiological Soothing

Previous research with Levenson (Gottman & Levenson, 1988) indicated that men were more emotionally flooded by negative affect in marital interactions and experienced greater physiological arousal than women. In these situations, men were more likely to withdraw from the marital conflict. We wondered if de-escalation of marital conflict among the newlywed couples, especially by women, served to physiologically soothe their husbands and, as a consequence, served a functional role in marriage.

Positive affect and de-escalation among these happy, stable newlywed couples were associated with both physiological soothing of the husband by the wife and self-soothing by the husband (Gottman et al., 1998). The use of humor by the wives in these satisfied, stable marriages soothed the husband's physiology, as did his own de-escalation of emotion and his use of affection and validation during the marital interactions.

This research with the newlywed couples was exciting because it helped delineate some of the functional and dysfunctional interactive processes in marriage. This research also indicated that some commonly held beliefs about marital processes may be wrong.

THE ROLE OF POSITIVE AFFECT

Up to this point, much of our discussion has centered on dysfunctional processes that dismantle marriages. We are also interested in the roles of positive affect and cognitions in marriage. It appears that the absence or presence of positive affect and cognitions has a great deal to do with the success or failure of the marriage.

Gottman and Levenson (1997) recently constructed a model to analyze the affective components predictive of marital stability and divorce among the couples first assessed in our laboratory in 1983. The model identified those affective behaviors (SPAFF) predictive of divorce early (average of 5.2 years) or later (average of 16.4 years) in the course of the marriage. Four negative affective behaviors (i.e., criticism, contempt, defensiveness, and stonewalling) were associated with early divorce at Time 2. Later divorce was associated with the absence of positive affect during the initial marital assessment in 1983. These data indicate that the presence of positive affect during marital problem-solving interactions, not just the absence of negative emotions, is associated with long-term stability. These two dimensions are not two sides of the same coin. The absence of toxic, negative emotional communication patterns during marital conflict does not mean that these couples are utilizing positive affect in their interactions. We suspect that when couples fail to employ positive emotions in their interactions, the interactions lack the warmth and support that serve to make marriage desirable. These marriages are the emotionally detached marriages indicative of couples further along the Distance and Isolation Cascade.

KNOWING AND CARING ABOUT ONE'S SPOUSE MAKES A MARRIAGE LAST

We learned that a good foundation for making a marriage last is built on the fondness and admiration of each spouse for one another. We also discovered that marriages could weather hard times when couples prioritize knowing about each others' experiences, feelings, and concerns. We interviewed several of the cohorts about the history of their relationships and about their philosophy of marriage using the Oral History Interview. Buehlman, Gottman, and Katz (1992) used the Oral History Interviews to predict, prospectively with 94% accuracy, the marital stability or marital dissolution of married couples with young children. Carrère and her colleagues (Carrère, Buehlman, Coan, Gottman, & Ruckstuhl, 1997) replicated these results with newlywed couples. Scores on the Oral History Interviews, conducted in the first year of marriage with 90 Seattle couples, predicted with 87.9% accuracy which couples would remain married or get a divorce during the first 6 years of marriage. A closer examination of the data for both studies revealed that those couples who remained married displayed significantly more fondness and admiration for their partners and allotted more cognitive room for their partners' world and the relationship's history.

POSITIVE AND NEGATIVE SENTIMENT OVERRIDE

Weiss (1980) hypothesized that reactions during marital interaction may be determined by a global dimension of affection or disaffection (i.e., Positive and Negative Sentiment Override, respectively), rather than by the immediately preceding valence of the stimulus. We extended Weiss's idea of Positive Sentiment Override and

Negative Sentiment Override and suggested that these global sentiments have their basis in everyday, mundane, nonconflict interaction. These overrides are determined by insider–outsider coding discrepancies as follows: In *Positive Sentiment Override,* a spouse can say something with negative affect (as judged by observers) and it is received as a neutral message by their partners (as indicated by their rating dial outcomes). In *Negative Sentiment Override,* a neutral message (as judged by observers) gets received as if it were negative.

Notarius and his associates (Notarius, Benson, Sloane, Vanzetti-Nelly, & Hornyak, 1989) found that distressed wives were more likely to evaluate their partner's neutral and negative messages as negative (suggesting the operation of a Negative Sentiment Override). Distressed wives, given a negative evaluation of their partner's antecedent message, were also more likely to offer a negative reply than were all other spouses. Notarius et al. (1989) found no evidence for the buffering qualities of Positive Sentiment Override.

However, Michael Lorber, an honors student in our laboratory, found that Positive Sentiment Override was important in marital processes. Lorber examined the impact of Positive Sentiment Override on repair attempts in our newlyweds' marital conflict interactions (Lorber, 1997). As described previously, negative reciprocity is a behavioral interaction pattern most likely to be carried out in distressed marriages. Efforts by the couples to repair the interaction and exit the cycle of negative communication are important to the stability of a marriage. Lorber's results indicated that husbands' Positive Sentiment Override was significantly associated with the success of repair attempts.

Research by Melissa Hawkins (1997), a member of our research team, shed further light on the nature of Positive Sentiment Override. She proposed that the Oral History Interview indexed the global sentiments the spouses held about each other and their relationships. These sentiments were thought to serve as a filter through which the partner's behavior was interpreted. Using the marital interaction data from the newlywed couples, she compared the objective SPAFF codes with the partners' rating of their spouse's behavior (rating dial). Wives who scored very high on the Oral History Interview rated their husbands' expression of anger as a neutral emotion, whereas the wives who scored low on the Oral History Interview rated their husbands' expression of anger as a negative emotion. Hawkins theorized that in these happy marriages the wives' prior experience with anger has been productive because these wives didn't escalate a low-intensity negative affect, such as anger, to a higher level of negativity. The result is that wives with positive sentiments may be able to engage in successful and productive conflict resolution. Hawkins proposed that although the expression of anger may not predict marital success (cf. Gottman et al., 1998), the manner in which wives perceive their husbands' anger may discriminate between distressed and happily married couples.

In our previous research we found that the Distance and Isolation Cascade indexed an increasing emotional detachment in the marriage as couples moved on a trajectory toward divorce (Gottman, 1993b). The Distance and Isolation Cascade was thought to reflect a set of negative attributions the couples make about their relationships. These negative attributions may be a filter, like Negative Sentiment Override, through which the behaviors in the marriage are viewed. If so, there should be some association between the Distance and Isolation Cascade and the scores on the Oral History Interview. Individuals who experience emotional flooding or severe problems in the marriage, who feel they need to work out problems alone, and who are lonely may also be people who score low on the Oral History Interview. This, in fact, was the case. Newlywed couples who scored low on the Oral History Interview also had husbands who felt lonely and flooded by their wives' emotions and wives who reported being lonely and leading separate lives from their husband.

PREDICTING THE DROP IN MARITAL SATISFACTION DURING THE TRANSITION TO PARENTHOOD

Alyson Shapiro, a graduate student in our laboratory, used the Oral History Interview to predict the course of marital satisfaction during the transition to parenthood with a sample of our newlywed couples (Shapiro & Walker, 1997). Most couples experience a decline in marital satisfaction during the transition to becoming parents (e.g., Belsky & Pensky, 1988). Shapiro hypothesized that the global sentiments couples held about their marriages could act as a buffer during this life event. Shapiro compared the 46 newlywed couples who became parents during the first 6 years of the study with newlywed couples who did not become parents during this same time period. She indexed marital satisfaction (Marital Adjustment Test; Locke & Wallace, 1959) each year of the marriage. She found that the wives who became mothers were more likely to experience a decline in satisfaction when compared with newlywed wives who did not become parents. There were no significant differences between the newlywed fathers and newlywed men who did not become fathers. A subset of the new mothers increased in marital satisfaction over the transition to parenthood. For these mothers there was a significant relationship between their marital satisfaction and Oral History Interview scores. Specifically, when both the husband and wife knew extensive information about their partners' interests, feelings, and behaviors (i.e., Expansiveness), the mothers' transitions to parenthood were more likely to remain maritally satisfying. This was also the case if the husband had expressed fondness for his wife and a sense of unity (We-ness) with her. In contrast, in those marriages where the wives experienced a decline in marriage during the transition to parenthood, both husbands and wives had expressed disappointment in the marriage during the Oral History Interview and felt that much of what took place in their marriage was outside their control (i.e., chaotic relationship). The husbands were also more likely to have expressed negativity toward their wives during the Oral History Interview in these relationships where the women were less happy with their marriages during the change to becoming a parent.

Shapiro's findings extended the impact Sentiment Override has on marriages from the more micro-moment of the marital interaction to the macro-marital process of weathering a pivotal developmental change in the relationship. This emotional reservoir of positive regard provides a fundamental foundation for a "sound house of marriage" that can withstand the challenges that life presents.

SUMMARY OF THE GOTTMAN THEORY
OF THE SOUND MARITAL HOUSE

We used our longitudinal studies to search for a process model of marriage. In addition to determining those processes dysfunctional in marriage, our goals were to answer two questions: What is the etiology of dysfunctional patterns? and What is "functional" when a marriage is working well (stable and happy)? Our research produced findings that expand our understanding of the role of the etiology of Negative Affects predictive of divorce, the nature of conflict resolution in well-functioning marriages, and the role of Positive Affect in stable, happy marital relationships.

We found the roots of dysfunctional marital processes in the patterns of affective behaviors couples use with each other and in the kinds of global sentiments spouses have about their partners. Our earlier work determined that the ratio of positive to negative affective behavior during the marital interaction discriminated between stable couples and couples later divorcing (Gottman & Levenson, 1992). Further analysis of these data revealed three types of stable couples, validating, conflict-avoiding, and volatile, and two kinds of unstable couples, hostile and hostile/detached (Gottman, 1993a). The stable couples had similar patterns of persuasion and influence (Cook et al., 1995), whereas the unstable couples were mismatched in their patterns of persuasion and influence and were more negative in their interactions overall.

Subsequent work by Gottman et al. (1998) also found gender differences in conflict resolution important in stable marriages. Marriages were more likely to last when husbands could accept influence from their wives and de-escalate the conflict and when wives used softened startup techniques in conflict situations.

We also learned that some negative emotions are more toxic to the well-being of the relationship than others. We found that anger is not a corrosive emotion as some have suggested (e.g., Hendrix, 1988), but the use of criticism, contempt, defensiveness and sometimes stonewalling in marital interactions is toxic (Gottman et al., 1998; Gottman, 1993b). The increasing distance and isolation in a marriage leading up to divorce appears to result from couples experiencing emotional detachment and loneliness. Thus, the trajectory toward divorce is one of increasing emotional toxicity and distance until there is no love left.

The good news is that Positive Affect matters. It is essential in conflict resolution strategies. We learned that Positive Affect can help physiologically soothe men so they don't withdraw from resolving conflicts (Gottman et al., 1998). Positive Affect was also instrumental in the long-term stability of marriage (Gottman & Levenson, 1997). The absence of Positive Affect, not just the presence of Negative Affect, predicted divorces later in marriages.

Positive Sentiment Override, positive global sentiments about the marriage, also was an important element in conflict resolution. It helped wives view their husbands' displays of anger more positively, and it predicted the success of husbands' repair attempts during marital conflict.

The level of fondness, unity, and cognitive room spouses have for each other was predictive of enduring marriage for couples whom we interviewed during the middle years of the marital life course (Buehlman, Gottman, & Katz, 1992) as well as for our newlywed couples (Carrère et al., 1997). The positive feelings and cognitions a couple exhibited toward each other and the relationship during the first year of their marriage also predicted which couples will make the transition to parenthood in a maritally satisfying fashion (Shapiro & Walker, 1997).

Couples who build a system of friendship, fondness, and admiration for each other and who infuse their marital interactions, especially the conflicts, with positive affect are the most successful in building a "sound house of marriage." Marital success comes through finding conflict resolution patterns of persuasion and influence that are similar in nature to those of one's partner. Marriages are more likely to remain intact when men can accept influence from their wives by de-escalating the negativity of the interaction and when women can soften the startup of the conflict. These are the ingredients for making a marriage happy and for making the marriage last.

ACKNOWLEDGMENTS

We thank Linda Crumley, Melissa Hawkins, and Mary McGonigle for their constructive comments on an earlier draft of this chapter.

REFERENCES

Belsky, J., & Pensky, E. (1988). Marital change across the transition to parenthood. *Marriage and Family Review, 12,* 133–156.

Buehlman, K. T., & Gottman, J. M. (1996). The oral history coding system. In J. M. Gottman (Ed.), *What predicts divorce: The measures* (pp. OHI1–OHI118). Mahwah, NJ: Lawrence Erlbaum Associates.

Buehlman, K. T., Gottman, J. M., & Katz, L. F. (1992). How a couple views their past predicts their future: Predicting divorce from an oral history interview. *Journal of Family Psychology, 5,* 295–318.

Carrère, S., Buehlman, K. T., Coan, J., Gottman, J. M., & Ruckstuhl, L. (1997). *Predicting marital stability and divorce in newlywed couples.* Manuscript submitted for publication.

Christensen, A., & Heavey, C. L. (1990). Gender and social structure in the demand/withdraw pattern of marital conflict. *Journal of Personality and Social Psychology, 59,* 73–82.

Cohen, S., Kessler, R. C., & Gordon, L. U. (1995). Strategies for measuring stress in studies of psychiatric and physical disorders. In S. Cohen, R. C. Kessler, & L. U. Gordon (Eds.), *Measuring stress: A guide for health and social scientists* (pp. 3–26). New York: Oxford University Press.

Cook, J., Tyson, R., White, J., Rushe, R., Gottman, J., & Murray, J. (1995). Mathematics of marital conflict: Qualitative dynamic mathematical modeling of marital interaction. *Journal of Family Psychology, 9*(2), 110–130.

Ekman, P., & Friesen, W. V. (1978). *Facial action coding system.* Palo Alto, CA: Consulting Psychologists Press.

Gottman, J. (1996). *What predicts divorce: The measures.* Mahwah, NJ: Lawrence Erlbaum Associates.

Gottman, J. M. (1993a). The roles of conflict engagement, escalation, and avoidance in marital interaction: A longitudinal view of five types of couples. *Journal of Consulting and Clinical Psychology, 61*(1), 6–15.

Gottman, J. M. (1993b). A theory of marital dissolution and stability. *Journal of Family Psychology, 7*(1), 57–75.

Gottman, J. M. (1994). *What predicts divorce: The relationship between marital processes and marital outcomes.* Hillsdale, NJ: Lawrence Erlbaum Associates.

Gottman, J. M., Coan, J., Carrère, S., & Swanson, C. (1998). Predicting marital happiness and stability from newlywed interactions. *Journal of Marriage and the Family, 60*(1), 5–22.

Gottman, J. M., & Krokoff, L. J. (1989). The relationship between marital interaction and marital satisfaction: A longitudinal view. *Journal of Consulting and Clinical Psychology, 57,* 47–52.

Gottman, J. M., & Levenson, R. W. (1988). The social psychophysiology of marriage. In P. Noller & M. A. Fitzpatrick (Eds.), *Perspectives on marital interaction* (pp. 182–200). Clevedon, England: Multilingual Matters.

Gottman, J. M., & Levenson, R. W. (1992). Marital processes predictive of later dissolution: Behavior, physiology, and health. *Journal of Personality and Social Psychology, 63*(2), 221–233.

Gottman, J. M., & Levenson, R. W. (1997). *The role of positive affect in long-term marital stability.* Unpublished manuscript, University of Washington at Seattle.

Guerney, B. G. (1977). *Relationship enhancement.* San Francisco: Jossey Bass.

Hawkins, M. W. (1997). *Sentiment override: The effect of perception on marital conflict.* Unpublished manuscript, University of Washington at Seattle.

Heavey, C. L., Christensen, A., & Malamuth, N. M. (1995). The longitudinal impact of demand and withdraw during marital conflict. *Journal of Consulting and Clinical Psychology, 63,* 797–801.

Hendrix, H. (1988). *Getting the love you want: A guide for couples.* New York: Henry Holt.

Karney, B. R., & Bradbury, T. N. (1995). The longitudinal course of marital quality and stability: A review of theory, method, and research. *Psychological Bulletin, 118,* 3–34.

Krokoff, L. J., Gottman, J. M., & Haas, S. D. (1989). Validation of a rapid couples interaction coding system. *Behavioral Assessment, 11,* 65–79.

Locke, H. J., & Wallace, K. M. (1959). Short marital-adjustment and prediction tests: Their reliability and validity. *Marriage and Family Living, 21,* 251–255.

Lorber, M. (1997). *Repair attempts in marital conflict.* Unpublished manuscript, University of Washington at Seattle.

Margolin, G., & Wampold, B. E. (1981). Sequential analysis of conflict and accord in distressed and nondistressed marital partners. *Journal of Consulting and Clinical Psychology, 49,* 554–567.

Markman, H., & Notarius, C. I. (1987). Coding marital and family interaction: Current status. In T. Jacob (Ed.), *Family interaction and psychopathology: Theories, methods, and findings* (pp. 329–390). New York: Plenum Press.

Murray, J. D. (1993). *Mathematical biology (2nd corrected edition).* Heidelberg: Springer-Verlag.

Notarius, C. I., Benson, P. R., Sloane, D., Vanzetti-Nelly, N. A., & Hornyak, L. A. (1989). Exploring the interface between perception and behavior: An analysis of marital interaction in distressed and nondistressed couples. *Behavioral Assessment, 11,* 39–64.

Parrott, L., & Parrott, L. (1995). *Becoming soul mates: Cultivating spiritual intimacy in the early years of marriage*. Grand Rapids MI: Zondervan.

Patterson, J. R. (1982). *Coercive family process*. Eugene, OR: Castalia.

Raush, H. L., Barry, W. A., Hertel, R. K., & Swain, M. A. (1974). *Communication, conflict, and marriage*. San Francisco: Jossey-Bass.

Shapiro, A. F., & Walker, K. (1997, April). *Marital satisfaction: Predicting changes over the transition to parenthood*. Paper presented at the the Biennial Meeting of the Society for Research in Child Development, Washington, DC.

Weiss, R. L. (1980). Strategic behavioral marital therapy: Toward a model for assessment and intervention. In J. P. Vincent (Ed.), *Advances in family intervention, assessment and theory* (Vol. 1, pp. 229–271). Greenwich, CT: JAI Press.

Weiss, R. L., & Summers, K. J. (1983). Marital interaction coding system III. In E. E. Filsinger (Ed.), *Marriage and family assessment* (pp. 35–115). Beverly Hills, CA: Sage Publications.

2

Black Couples, White Couples:
The Early Years of Marriage

Terri L. Orbuch
Oakland University
University of Michigan

Joseph Veroff
Andrea G. Hunter
University of Michigan

As THE DIVORCE RATE in American society skyrocketed, many concerned social scientists undertook research to discover the factors affecting both the psychological well-being experienced by couples as their marriages progress and the stability of these marriages over time. Some of these explanatory factors focus on changes in the interpersonal lives of these couples—how couples try to manage and regulate their interactions to maximize positive outcomes and reduce conflicts (Carstensen 1991; Carstensen, Gottman, & Levenson, 1995; Gottman, 1994; Markman, 1991; Markman, Renick, Floyd, Stanley, & Clements, 1993), how they express their feelings (Cowan & Cowan, 1994; Gottman, 1994; Veroff, Douvan, & Hatchett, 1995), and how they do or do not reinforce each other (Huston & Chorost, in press). Other factors focus on structural issues in these couples' lives—economic issues (Vinokur & Van Ryn, 1993), the addition of children to the family (Ade-Ridder & Brubaker, 1983; Belsky, Spanier, & Rovine, 1983; White & Edwards, 1990), the embeddedness of couples to networks (Timmer, Veroff, & Hatchett, 1996), and the structure of work–family connections (Orbuch, House, Mero, & Webster, 1996; Orbuch & Custer, 1995; Orbuch & Eyster, 1997a). An important recent analysis by Amato and Rodgers (1997) of a prospective longitudinal study reveals ways in which interpersonal problems experienced in marriage mediate some of the structural features found to be predictive of divorce. Thus, various interactive styles or structural characteristics can be considered risk factors portending

divorce or low marital quality and a number can be considered sources of resilience for a marriage.

   These factors affect not only the couples but also the children of these couples.
Previous research indicates that marital tension, conflict, and separation have adverse effects on children who are party to the disrupted marital life their parents
are performing; there are disabling long-term consequences of marital conflict and
divorce on children's development, well-being, and social and interpersonal relationships (Amato, 1993; Amato & Keith, 1991; Demo & Acock, 1996; Hetherington, 1993; Hetherington & Clingempeel, 1992; McLanahan & Sandefur, 1994;
Orbuch, Thornton, & Cancio, 1997; Seltzer & Bianchi, 1988; Webster, Orbuch, &
House, 1995).

   It is no wonder then that in the past two decades some important longitudinal
studies of marriage have emerged. Many of them are still ongoing. Much has been
learned from them about the dynamics and structural supports of marriage. However, most of this research has been constructed with the eye to establishing universal principles about family dynamics, and for the most part the studies ignore
the ways in which the particular social context in which marriages are embedded
shape the determinants of marital quality and stability. In this chapter, we concen-
trate on a longitudinal study of marriage, the University of Michigan's Early Years
of Marriage Project, because of its unique focus on the social context of marriage.
The primary objective of this longitudinal study was to get a better understanding
of the marital processes and determinants of marital quality and stability among
African American couples and White couples. Which ones survive? Which are resilient to stress? Given differences in marital cultures and in the contexts of marriage in the Black and White communities, we anticipated that the explanatory
factors affecting marital quality and stability would differ for Blacks and Whites.
Thus, this chapter does not focus as much on the universal dynamics of marriage
as it does on ways in which marital quality and stability depend on the social context of marriage. One context is of particular importance: How does being African
American in American society affect the way marriage progresses, especially in
contrast to being members of the dominant White society?

RESEARCH ON BLACK–WHITE DIFFERENCES
IN THE MEANING OF MARRIAGE

The high rates of divorce and separation are specifically pronounced for African
Americans. Yet little research attention has been given to Black American marriages. According to Billingsley (1992), relatively little attention has been given to
Black marriages because of researchers' inability to go beyond the pathological
approach to Black families, which relies heavily on single-parent families and teen
pregnancies within this cultural group: "Overlooked are the positive functions
served by marriage. Overlooked also are the patterns of diversity within and among

these families" (p. 205). Furthermore, Billingsley (1992) argued that given recent U.S. Census data, the thesis of the vanishing Black family is not supported and empirically untrue. In 1990, "a majority of African Americans lived in households; a majority of these were family households; a majority of family households were married-couple households; and a majority of married couples had young children of their own" (Billingsley, 1992, p. 207).

Structural Explanations

In general, social psychologists and other social scientists who study marriage have focused greater attention on the structural rather than interactional factors that underlie the risks of divorce or promote psychological well-being and stability of marriages. This structural emphasis is especially evident within the literature on racial differences in divorce rates. Marital quality and interpersonal processes within African American marriages have been scarcely studied and are not well understood (Tucker & Mitchell-Kernan, 1995)

Researchers have proposed various structural explanations of the differential rates of marital quality and stability between African Americans and Whites. One structural explanation focuses on the sex ratio of Black males to females (Lichter, McLaughlin, Kephart, & Landry, 1992; Staples & Johnson, 1993; Walker, 1988). The marriage market may be different for African Americans than for Whites because there is a smaller number of marriageable Black men than women. This situation increases the probability of unmarried Black females and decreases the number of possible husband–wife combinations (Staples & Johnson, 1993). The unbalanced marriage market also influences the degree to which Black men have a larger pool (either physically or psychologically) from which to choose a partner or mate, which may affect the selection of a mate or the likelihood that one stays within a marriage. The unbalanced marriage market is viewed as also contributing to Blacks' marital dissolution (Elder & Caspi, 1988; Hatchett, Veroff, & Douvan, 1995).

Another structural explanation is that African American couples face different structural obstacles and greater ongoing tensions and injustices than White couples. Such ongoing conflict with the external environment may carry over and affect the well-being and stability of African American marriages. African American married couples may also have more difficulties and obstacles to overcome given the unstable job market and lower earning power of African American males. In the 1980s Black women made significant gains in achieving structural resources, but Black men did not (Staples, 1991). There is also evidence to suggest that since 1954, unemployment among African Americans in general has been twice as high as among White Americans (Billingsley, 1988). Therefore, African American marriages may suffer disproportionately from the long-term effects of unemployment. In addition, although the results are inconclusive (Adelmann, Chadwick, & Baerger, 1996; Broman, 1993), socioeconomic factors such as lower average household income among Black families may also explain the higher rates of divorce and lower marital quality of Black marriages.

Cultural Explanations

Past research has given little attention to the role of cultural factors beyond structure affecting differential rates of quality and stability among Black and White marriages. We argue, however, that as social researchers we need to understand that marital relationships are embedded within the context of a racial and ethnic culture, consisting of norms and expectations that determine the meanings of various interpersonal or marital processes, such as conflict, parenthood, or decisions regarding the division of household labor. These meanings are important to understanding racial differences in divorce rates; the various meanings are not negative or deviant but integral to the organization and functioning of those marriages that endorse them (Walker, 1988). Thus, cultural norms exist and are significant to explaining marital quality and stability among both majority and minority cultures in American society. It is also important to note that there is considerable diversity in these cultural norms, both between and within cultures.

If we focus on cultural factors beyond structure, we might expect Black–White differences in marital processes for several reasons. First, Black and White marriages may not be affected by the same factors and in the same ways. Specific factors may be important to one culture but not critical to marriage in the other culture. For example, Orbuch and Eyster (1997a) found that husbands' participation in household responsibilities and childcare was related to marital well-being for Black wives but not for White wives. Broman (1993) also demonstrated that some of the large differences found in Black–White comparisons of reported marital quality (i.e., Blacks reporting lower marital quality) can be attributed to the degree of financial satisfaction expressed by couples, particularly Black wives, and the degree of spousal support. A path model revealed important indirect effects of race on marital well-being through these factors. The meanings of interactions and styles of behaviors within each ethnicity or race can help clarify the cultural context within which the well-being and stability of marriages are experienced over time.

Second, the underlying factors that determine marital quality and stability for Black and White couples may be similar, but how these factors get translated or expressed within marriage differ for the two groups. For example, a supportive social network is a significant predictor of marital stability for Black and White couples, yet this support may be expressed or embedded within different networks for Blacks and Whites: Stack (1974) found that neighborhood support is particularly important to the well-being of Black women raising their children. Neighborhood support might very well compensate for or perhaps undermine the social support experienced within the couple's own relationship. Thus, the expression of support and where it stems from may differ within the two groups, although the basic mechanism or factor is similar.

We might also expect Black–White differences in risk factors for marital instability and for resiliency factors that promote marital well-being because Blacks and
Whites may come to marriage with different family trajectories and histories (e.g.,
Black women may be more likely to be parents), which also have consequences for
how factors are related to marital processes. The normative transitions for the majority White culture (i.e., marriage, then parenthood) may not be normative for
other cultural groups. Adelmann et al. (1996), for example, argued that one problem with perspectives that rely solely on structural characteristics to explain marital quality for Blacks over the life course is the assumption of negative marital
effects of children. The satisfaction and well-being of African American marriages
may be less integrally connected than White marriages, to the presence or absence
of children. This may be true because Black couples spend less than a year together
before having a child and thus are more likely to enter marriage as parents, compared with White couples who spend an average of 2 years together before parenthood (Littlejohn-Blake & Darling, 1993). This emphasis on differential trajectories
and histories based on race and ethnicity can lead to either unique factors contributing to marital quality and stability in the two groups or separate illustrations
of the same underlying factors.

Finally, it is important to understand that Black women and men may organize
their lives differently from White women and men, specifically around issues of
gender and power. Studies find that Black couples are more egalitarian than White
couples in their attitudes toward women and gendered roles (Hunter & Davis,
1992; Hunter & Sellers, 1998; Kane, 1992; Orbuch & Eyster, 1997a). Hunter and
Sellers (1997) claimed that for African American men, one positive proactive
adaptive strategy to their experiences with the lack of structural opportunities has
been to value the input of both women and men inside and outside the home and
to adopt an egalitarian gender role ideology. Furthermore, much evidence suggests
that Blacks are more likely than Whites to criticize gender inequality and traditional views of masculinity and femininity (Collins, 1990; Hunter & Davis, 1992;
Hunter & Sellers, 1998; Kane, 1992). Given these differential views of women and
men and their import to the economic and psychological survival of the family, the
factors that influence marriage or the underlying representations of these factors
may differ for Black and for White couples.

In summary, the cultural context of early marriage and the interpersonal processes that transpire within these marriages may be different for Blacks and
Whites. Furthermore, the cultural context also filters ways that men and women in
marriage experience the power they have within the marriage. As Fine (1993)
stated, "diversity is sometimes narrowly used to refer to differences in family structure, as opposed to differences in how families function and operate both within
and outside of their homes" (p. 237). Explanations that focus on cultural factors
beyond structure are important for a better understanding of racial differences
and similarities in the quality and stability of African American and White marriages. Our recent work stems from a longitudinal study of early marriage and fo-

cuses on the differential meanings of marriage for Blacks and Whites with specific attention to the cultural context of those marriages.

THE EARLY YEARS OF MARRIAGE STUDY

Our own insights about the differential meaning of marriage and marital quality and stability among African Americans and Whites derives from a longitudinal Early Years of Marriage study. Since 1986, a research group at the Institute for Social Research has been collecting and analyzing data from an urban sample of couples, married for the first time in 1986 when they were first interviewed and then followed up again yearly in 1987–1989 and again in 1992 during their seventh year of marriage. This project started with 199 African American couples and 174 White couples who applied for marriage licenses in Wayne County, Michigan, during 1986. Only couples who were still married were reinterviewed. To be eligible for the study, both members of the couple had to be of the same race and in their first marriage. All eligible Black couples and a random sample of White couples were contacted and asked to take part in the study. Many different methods were used in both face-to-face and telephone interviews. Individuals were asked standard and open-ended questions in their interviews. Couples were asked to do two unusual tasks together: One was a narrative procedure for them to tell the story of their relationship (Veroff, Sutherland, Chadiha, & Ortega, 1993); the other was a behavioral observational procedure for them to resolve their differences about the important rules for a good marriage (Coon & Veroff, 1996; Crohan, 1992). Gottman (1994) employed similar procedures in his prospective study of marriage.

The major findings from this longitudinal study in marriage contrasting African-American and White couples' marital stability in the early years of being a couple are found in *Marital Instability* (Veroff et al., 1995). In this book, marital instability was examined by both an objective assessment of whether the couple divorced after Year 1 and a subjective assessment of how often each spouse thought about leaving the marriage. Veroff et al. (1995) explored the ways in which the determinants of marital instability are identical in African American and in White couples during the first 4 years of their marriages. These similarities, however, are few and far between. The authors have more to say about the ways in which the determinants are different in these two groups. In some instances the differences represent parallel phenomena in the two groups, but these phenomena are manifested in different ways. In other instances, the differences truly represent ways in which the contexts for marriage elicit different concerns in the two groups. These major findings in *Marital Instability* relevant to African American and White comparisons in the meaning of marriage are summarized next, after which we integrate other findings from the project that confirm or add to the conclusions about Black–White differences that *Marital Instability* provided.

Results Emerging from *Marital Instability*

First, we provide a summary of the differential meanings of marriage discovered for Blacks and Whites in *Marital Instability*. We carefully list results that were highlighted in the book, and in this chapter we expand on the interpretation of the meanings for marriage that these results on Black–White differences might have for the two different cultural contexts. In particular, this discussion emphasizes the issues of gender–power dynamics that inform our interpretations of interactional processes among Black couples and White couples.

There are four instances where identical variables are associated with marital instability in both African American and White couples: frequency of conflict, the wife having an affair, interferences experienced from wives' friends, and the experience of marital unhappiness among wives. These are all interactional risks for divorce, rather than structural ones. The structural risk factors that emerged were specific to one group or another but not general to both. When we look closely at the four instances of identical risk factors in the two groups, we note that beyond the expected finding that the more conflicted marriages are, the more unstable they are, the other common results to both groups have to do with wives specifically. This pattern of results suggests that any marriage, whether involving African American or White partners, will likely become unhinged when a woman takes an active stance about the difficulties in her marriage (e.g., having an affair, complaining to their friends) or is free to acknowledge her desperate feeling (e.g., reporting her marriage as unhappy).

There are also certain themes that are parallel in understanding marital risk factors in both African American and White marriages but have different manifestations. These themes implicate important interactive phenomena that are critical for stable marriages or gender–power phenomena that can destabilize marriages, or both. We list each theme in Table 2.1. We also list in the table how that theme is prototypically manifested in the two groups. We discuss each in turn.

Supportive Wives

The first parallel theme is that in stable marriages wives are supportive. This is clearly a direct interactive phenomenon but one that can touch off many concerns about what is appropriate behavior for men and women in marriage. However, this theme takes on slightly different channels in two subcontexts. For White stable marriages, wifely nurturance is found in whether the wife is judged to be cooperative by both the husband and the wife. This is not so for the African American couples, which suggests that being judged as cooperative for a White woman implies an overt kind of nurturant compliance to their husbands. Being cooperative in this way evidently can have other negative meanings for some African American couples, for whom a woman's collaborative style is important for understanding marital stability.

TABLE 2.1
Parallel Themes Found in Stable Marriages of Both African American
and White Couples With Different Prototypic Manifestations

Parallel Theme	Prototypic Manifestation in Stable African American Couples	Prototypic Manifestation in Stable White Couples
Stable marriages depend on nurturing wives.	Wives have collaborative style with their husbands.	Wives are rated high in being cooperative.
Stable marriages require compatibility in interpersonal interactions.	Infrequent fighting. Complementariness in openness to experience.	Infrequent fighting. There is sexual tension, and spouses share leisure activities.
Stable marriages depend on husbands having clear evidence of their achievement in society.	Husbands have highly educated mothers, have low anxiety, and are low in alcohol usage.	Hunsbands have high personal income and have jobs that are reported as not interfering with their marriages.
Stable marriages depend on harmonious integrations with social networks.	Little interference from friends and from husbands' families.	Little interference from friends.
Stable marriages depend on husbands maintaining some independence and control of their wives.	Wives have not had affairs.	Wives have not had affairs. Husbands don't complain about having no privacy. Wives are not high in alcohol usage.

We propose two explanations for the collaborative style of interaction for Black couples. First, this measure can be a much more subtle kind of nurturance. Collaborative style is a measure of how much a person in a joint storytelling situation dovetails her remarks with those of her partner. This collaborative style is not necessarily agreement but a meshing of ways of interacting. It may very well be that some Black men would be suspicious of a more direct nurturant style from their wives, a style that would immediately suggest that the wife be rated as cooperative. African American men perhaps need to be subtly nurtured by their wives, to feel comforted by their wives' way of interacting, because they feel vulnerable about their power in the family and hence can easily read their wives' cooperative efforts as conscious manipulations to make a go of a marriage.

Alternatively, this collaborative style of interaction may represent the significance and value that Black men place on women's independence and strength. Black men desire an active, equal, and supportive partner in their spouse. Given differences in structural opportunities for Black men compared to White men, a reliance on an equal partner rather than a submissive or cooperative one is critical to Black couples' marriages; Black families' survival is often dependent on two active partners.

Interpersonal Compatibility

It seems like a mere truism to state the second parallel theme as baldly as we did: Stable marriages require interpersonal compatibility. In both sets of couples the tendency to fight a lot, a mark of considerable incompatibility, is characteristic of unstable marriages, but each set also has particular kinds of compatibility that are important to marital stability. For the Black couples, there has to be a balance or a complementary orientation to experience; one spouse has to be cautious while the other is adventuresome. For Whites, compatibility in their sexual and leisure lives is important for stability. This set of findings leads us to suggest that sexuality is not centrally connected to the risk factors to be found in the marital lives of African Americans but it becomes a more figural risk issue for White couples. We also suggest that Black husbands and wives lead more independent lives as married couples than do White husbands and wives. Such being the case, some balance on each spouse's orientation to experience seems critical for Black couples, whereas sharing of leisure becomes more critical for White couples.

All these findings deal with interpersonal compatibility, which takes different forms in the two subcultures. Some separation and independence from each other might be more critical for compatibility to African American than White couples. This may be the case because African American couples have so many ways that their married life might be disrupted by external factors. Furthermore, as stated previously, there is greater gender parity, equality, and an appreciation of women's independence in Black than White marriages (Hunter & Davis, 1992). Thus, interpersonal compatibility takes on different forms in the two groups.

Male Achievement or Power

The third parallel theme noted in *Marital Instability* speaks of men having to feel accomplished. With the White husbands, the theme emerges directly. The higher White husbands' incomes are and the less interference their jobs create in their marital life, the more stable their marriages. We can read the first result as a stabilizer of men's call on power in the marital relationship and the second result as showing that the work demands on men should not disrupt smooth interactions in the marriage.

This pattern is not the case for the African American men, who showed more indirect evidence of the theme: the education of their mothers and whether they themselves were anxious about their lives or turned to alcohol. Black husbands with highly educated mothers, who were free from anxiety and were not heavy drinkers, were more likely to be in more stable marriages. In contrast to White couples, husbands' financial success during young adulthood did not have a significant impact on the marital stability of Black couples. This may reflect the occupation trajectories of Black men, who often begin their adult work lives with lower paying jobs and experience a slower climb to peak earnings than do White men (Davis,

1995; Lichter, 1988). However, because mothers' education is positively related to educational achievement in Black men, it may have an effect on men's achievement potential (Epps, 1985; Smith, 1991). Because educational achievement is related to occupational status, Black husbands with highly educated mothers may have better long-term prospects for occupational achievement and in turn may have less provider-role anxiety than the sons of less educated mothers. Indeed, despite the gains in occupational opportunity, Black men's worries about job security and financial well-being are well founded (Davis, 1995; Lichter, 1988). Being anxious and seeking illusory power through drinking, other significant risk factors for African American men, can be symptomatic of some men's concerns about how well they are providing for their families.

In addition, unlike White husbands, black men must manage race-related stressors (e.g., discrimination) that may undermine marital relationships (Johnson, 1990; Taylor & Zhang, 1990). Race-related stressors, particularly as they are manifested in employment, may be reflected in increased anxiety and alcohol use in Black males (Bowman, 1988; Williams, Lavizzo-Mourey, & Warren, 1994). According to Johnson (1990), findings support a direct relationship between Black men's perceived race-related job stress and strained couple interactions as well as the potential for separation and divorce.

Integration With Social Networks

The fourth theme, stable marriages being dependent on harmonious integrations with social networks, also has some common manifestations in both groups. Both sets of marriages find it hard to withstand interferences from networks of friends, but Black couples in addition find it difficult to remain stable when the husband's family is interfering. Thus, network interactions are implicated by these results.

Prior research suggests that integration with families and intergenerational relationships are more important to the well-being and stability of African American families than they are to White families (Stack, 1974; Taylor, Chatters & Jackson, 1993). It is not hard to suppose that the support that African Americans derive from their families seems especially critical for them to withstand the disruptive forces on marriages that occur in a racist society. Families can provide the interactive reassurance that helps one or the other spouses, but maybe particularly the husbands, to feel comfortable about their threatened position in the society that, in turn, has repercussions about a threatened sense of power in the marriage.

Husband's Independence and Control

The last theme reiterates the patriarchal ideal, that husbands in successful marriages maintain their independence and some control of their wives. In both groups a wife's affair was disruptive to the marriage, but a husband's affair was not consistently disruptive. A man whose wife has committed adultery has had a blow to the male ego, much stronger than the blow to the female ego caused by a philandering husband. In this way African American and White marriages are alike. However, White males, in contrast to Black males, seem to need even more reassurance about being in control of their own lives without overt need of their wives. Having no privacy is a complaint White but not Black husbands voice in unstable marriages. The image of the solitary male withstanding obstacles and also having adventures without the restriction of a family is a highly romanticized theme in our society. Witness the popularity of the *western* movie. This ideal perhaps has a stronger foothold in the lives of the majority White group. It is with that ideal in mind that we note that *Marital Instability* finds that stable White marriages depend on wives not being alcoholic, unlike stable Black marriages. One could suppose that when their wives are alcoholic, White males need to be especially caretaking. Being tied down like that might undo some of the husbands' autonomy.

These inroads into autonomy may not shake the African American marriages as much because these marriages may hold more cultural norms for independence among Black women as well as men. Black husbands already have the skills and ideology to deal with problems in the household should they come up as a result of a wife's drinking problem. We have clear evidence that only in African American marriages does stability have anything to do with the sense of power that wives have in controlling their lives (Veroff et al., 1995). Furthermore, we find that only in Black marriages is an egalitarian role orientation a positive force for marital stability. As we noted in the first and third themes, Black husbands are not threatened as much as White husbands are about their wives being more independent of them on a day-to-day basis, although having an affair is still a threat to their masculinity.

From our presentation of parallel themes noted in *Marital Instability,* we have suggested a number of ways in which the African American context for a stable marriage might be different from the dominant white context. We summarize these here:

1. Black wives are more likely to be collaborative in their interactions with husbands. In white marriages, direct cooperativeness is desired. This collaborative style may represent a subtle form of nurturance toward Black husbands or more likely the validation and significance of Black wives' independence and strength.

2. Given the differential structural positions between Black men and White men, there are other issues beyond direct financial take-home pay that may represent the accomplishments of the Black male in Black couples (e.g., anticipatory achievement given mother's education, fewer job-related stressors leading to anxiety). Among White husbands, financial success is paramount to a male's achievement.

3. For Black marriages, compatibility about sex and spending time together in leisure are not critical, but these issues are important in white marriages.

4. Integration with families of origin is a major support of a marriage for Blacks, but it is less critical for Whites.

5. There is an acceptance of parallel but relatively independent lives in the way Black husbands and wives conduct a marriage, unlike the norm for inter-dependence that is more important in White marriages but that makes White husbands feel defensive about their autonomy. This acceptance illustrates that unlike Whites, Black husbands and wives organize their married lives with greater attention to women's independence and equality.

Other Results from the Study

Many other results have been reported about Black–White comparisons from the Early Years of Marriage study. Most dovetail well with the interpretations we have discussed; some offer new insights about the different meanings of marriage in the two contexts. In all instances these findings confirm the general orientation we have taken in this chapter, that different cultural contexts as we find in White and Black subgroups represented in our urban American sample can differentially shape the gender–power dynamics that inform our interpretations of the interac-tive processes found in marriages at risk.

Supportive Wives. Further evidence for how important it is for Black wives to subtly manage their relationships in nurturant ways comes from findings that Acitelli, Douvan, and Veroff (1997) have documented. These researchers report that when African American wives indicate that they understand what their hus-bands are doing when faced with a conflict, their marriages are happier. They evi-dently translate their understanding into behaviors that permit their husbands' attempts to deal with their fights to be truly constructive. The results were just the opposite for the White wives. Their understanding correlated with marital unhap-piness. These findings suggest that the same type of understanding in the White wives gets translated into something that further exacerbates couples' conflicts. We conclude that Black wives subtly take their understanding into account in their interactions, whereas White wives perhaps feed that understanding into further confrontations about their conflicts.

A similar type of subtle support by African American wives was reported by Veroff, Douvan, Orbuch, and Acitelli (1998). They found that the especially happy African American marriages in the fourth year of marriage (i.e., those who have never thought about leaving the marriage and profess extreme happiness and sat-isfaction with the marriage) were ones with partners who had considerable over-lap in reported interests and hobbies. It is not so much that they share leisure time together but that they share interests. This finding was not apparent for happi-ness in the White marriages, although, as we noted previously, sharing leisure time was important for maintaining the stability of White marriages. We interpret this set of findings to mean that when a Black woman has an interest in what her hus-band is interested in, this interest may be totally sincere and thus positively con-veyed as caring for him. Why does this result not apply to White couples? We can only suggest that a White woman may be less sincere or less subtle in the way she conveys a mutual interest, so that the husband may think of her as being potentially manipulative. It has become part of the dominant White folklore that men and women do not share the same interests. When they do, or appear to, some men may be uncomfortable or suspicious.

Interpersonal Compatibility. The different meanings of interpersonal compatibility in the two contexts of African American and White societies have also shown up in other investigations with the Early Years of Marriage Project data. Veroff et al. (1998) have reported that, for couples who remain especially happy after four years of marriage, the presence of positive sex and the absence of negative sex seems more critical for White couples, and the absence of conflict seems more critical for Black couples. We have already noted that untroubled sexuality is more important to the stability of White marriages than it is for Black marriages. What these new results tell us is that enjoyment of sexuality is important for the especially happy side of marriage for the White couples as well. It is difficult for us to state that sexuality is unimportant for African American couples, but we can conclude that evaluating a marriage on the basis of sexual feelings is less paramount in Black marriages than in White marriages.

Henderson-King and Veroff (1994) have also found many complicated differential patterns for the effects of sexual feelings on various facets of marital well-being. In their analyses, sexuality does not drop out of the picture for African American well-being, nor is it always prominent in White well-being. Nevertheless, it does vary by race and also by gender, and they advocate that further analyses of sexuality need to be pursued differentially for African Americans and Whites. This finding alerts us in the future to consider in more depth the specific contextual meaning of sexuality in marriage for the two groups.

The fact that the absence of conflict seems particularly critical for Black wives to be especially happy in their marriages (Veroff et al., 1998) led us to consider the possibility that the meaning of marital conflict may be different for African American couples and White couples. Results from a study by Orbuch, Veroff, and Holmberg (1993) corroborate this possibility. Orbuch et al. (1993) found that Black couples were significantly more likely to present stories with couple conflict than were White couples. However, findings from this study also indicate that for all but the Black husbands, some conflict in telling their courtship story in the first year of marriage was predictive of less marital happiness in the third year. These findings confirm Kochman's (1981) work, which suggests that Black couples are more likely to conflict with each other in interaction as a general style of discourse, but it is not necessarily abusive or destructive and can be seen as playful and engaging. Thus, Black couples may display more conflict with each other, but the meaning behind that interactional style may differ for Blacks and Whites.

Crohan (1992), however, has also shown that for both Blacks and Whites, holding the following attitudes toward marital conflict have negative effects on marital

happiness: beliefs that conflicts should be avoided, beliefs that conflicts are un-
healthy, or beliefs that conflicts cannot be resolved. Therefore, a general shying
away from conflict resolution puts couples from both groups in jeopardy.

We had started our research into Black–White differences in the meaning of
marriage with an expectation that Black couples would be more immune from
conflict troubles in marriage than Whites, given the research by Kochman (1981),
which suggests that conflict may be taken for granted more in human interactions
in African American society. Our finding noted in Table 2.1 that infrequent fighting
was in fact a stronger predictor of stability in Black couples than in White couples
suggested something to the contrary. Crohan's (1992) analysis of conflict attitudes
also gives us few new insights about why we found this difference and why Black
wives are particularly happy when they experience infrequent marital conflict.

Our best speculation is that there are fewer barriers toward divorce in the
African American community in general, so that frequent fighting if seen as prog-
nostic of a problematic future can more quickly lead to divorce in an African
American couple. We indeed found that African American couples rated the following as a good reason for divorce significantly higher than the White couples:
fighting and arguing and financial problems. The White couples, compared to the
African American couples, rated the following statement higher as a good reason
for not divorcing: their families were opposed to divorce. Among African Americans, there may be a lower threshold for tolerance of fighting to preserve a marriage, especially if the fighting is about financial matters, which it often is. Our couples report fighting about financial matters as a very frequent source of difficulty.
There are no differences between Blacks and Whites in reported frequency of fighting about money matters, but Black husbands were more dissatisfied with the way
things were left after fighting about money matters than were White husbands.
This result suggests that fighting about money matters is hard to resolve for Black
males who perhaps feel especially vulnerable to their own anxieties about financial
matters. It is not hard to guess that the African American male's anxiety about being an adequate provider induces considerable marital conflict, which may be the
trigger for marital unhappiness and instability.

Male Achievement and Power.   There are also other pieces of evidence for
how the theme of masculine achievement as a force for marital stability and happiness may be differentially experienced by African American and White husbands,
and this evidence may cast a differential light on gender–power dynamics in each
group. Veroff et al. (1993) showed that couples' discussions of financial issues as
part of their story of their relationships correlates significantly with the marital
unhappiness of Black husbands but with no other group. So does mentioning issues dealing with children. It is not hard to interpret these findings to mean that
financial insecurity with regard to raising children in a family is a more prominent
issue for how a Black husband feels about his marriage than for the other groups.
So long stereotyped as an unreliable family person and provider, the Black hus-

band has a handicap in ever thinking of himself as an adequate achiever. Most White couples have inherited a legacy of financial support from their families if they are doing well. For example, many young White couples can count on their families for help in putting together down payments for a first home. Not so for most African American couples whose rise in the middle class has come with little financial backing from parents. For this reason we think financial insecurity remains a dominant anxiety for Black males in particular, even when and perhaps especially when their incomes rise.

Numerous studies (Broman, 1988; Hossain & Roopnarine, 1993; Taylor, Chatters, Tucker, & Lewis, 1991; Willie, 1985), including findings from the Early Years of Marriage Project, indicate that Black husbands are more egalitarian and more likely to participate in household and childcare tasks than White husbands (Orbuch & Custer, 1995; Orbuch & Eyster, 1997a; Sutherland, Went, & Douvan, 1990). African American husbands do not appear to be threatened or challenged when they participate in feminine tasks in the household. Furthermore, Orbuch and Custer (1995) found that although career wives may threaten or challenge both White and Black husbands, this threat is especially salient for White husbands who participate in traditionally feminine household and childcare tasks. Participation in housework seems to threaten their positions as dominant males in the family and is related to increased anxiety. For Black husbands, however, wives' work has adverse effects on well-being, but only if they are not able to justify the work as economically necessary for family survival. In general, whereas the balance of power for African American husbands is challenged by financial insecurities, that balance for White husbands is threatened by participation in traditionally feminine tasks in the home.

Orbuch and Eyster (1997a) argued that Black husbands in the Early Years of Marriage Project were more aware of gender inequality and thus less threatened by involvement in female-typed tasks at home than were white husbands. This argument is supported by Hunter and Sellers (1998), who contended that African American men are likely to support an egalitarian gender-role ideology because of their "unique social location—that is, their simultaneous experience of race oppression and gender privilege, in addition to less gender asymmetry in the economic and social organization of African-American families" (p. 2). Orbuch and Eyster (1997a) also provided evidence that African American wives have significantly greater resources (e.g., income and education) relative to their husbands than do White wives. This greater economic independence may explain why African American husbands' participation in home labor was positively related to marital well-being for African American wives but not for White wives. African American wives may expect their husbands' assistance at home.

Integration With Social Networks.   There has been additional support for the conclusion that the well-being and stability of African American couples depend significantly on the integration with their families, to a greater extent than for

White couples. Veroff (in press) found in Black males but in no other group evidence that integration with in-laws contributed to commitment to marriage by the seventh year. Timmer, Veroff, and Hatchett (1996) specifically found that among Black couples, a close relationship between the couple and the husband's family in the first year of marriage predicted greater happiness in the third year, particularly when the couple was stressed by a combination of low income and high family responsibilities with children. The husband's family among Blacks can act as a particularly important buffer for marital stability. Timmer and Veroff (1997) found in-law buffering much more prominent in predicting the risk for divorce in Black couples compared to White couples. Thus, we can conclude that the role of the extended family is more critical for the well-being of African American couples than for White couples. Any analysis of why African American young men and women are less prone to get married in the first place and more prone to divorce if unhappily married in the second place has to take into account the importance of Black extended family networks. These networks might give some support for not marrying if children are born out of wedlock (see Stack, 1974) and for divorcing rather than sticking it out when there is trouble in the marriage.

Husbands' Independence and Control.   The importance of independence for White men in maintaining their marriage is underwritten further in Veroff's (in press) findings that for only White men is not being very disclosing to their wives a factor that correlates well with their commitment to their marriages in the seventh year. Such was not the case for the Black husbands, although interdependence was not absent in White males' commitment. For both Blacks and Whites, Veroff found that the strongest predictor of commitment was how affirmed husbands felt by their wives. We had previously suggested that for White marriages there is an ideal of interdependence alongside the image of male independence. Thus, there no doubt is a defensive adherence to signs of independence in White husbands that may be critical to the balance of power in White marriages. Although these findings may appear in conflict with Gottman (1994), who found that husbands who engage in stonewalling (i.e., men who withdraw from conflict) are in unhappy marriages, we must remember that his measure of withdrawal is a behavioral assessment. In contrast, Veroff's (in press) self-disclosure measure is a self-report measure mostly dealing with talking about problems. The more husbands think they talk about problems, the more they may actually have been confronted with problems from their spouse.

The Meaning of Parenthood.   Findings from the Early Years of Marriage data also support the notion that the presence, absence, and timing of children have differential effects for Black and White marriages. Orbuch and Eyster (1997b) examined the stories that individual spouses and couples told regarding the experience of becoming a parent. They argued that African American couples are much less likely to think about if and when to have children than White couples are. In contrast, the themes of whetl.er the birth was planned and whether the couple desired a child when they became pregnant were salient themes in the birth narratives of White married couples.

Orbuch, Eyster, and Veroff (1997) also found that parenthood differentially affects marital quality for African American and White couples. White husbands and wives with children in the first year of marriage report less marital quality in the third year of marriage than do those couples without children. Furthermore, parenthood in the first year leads to a decrease in marital quality from Year 1 to Year 3 for White husbands and wives. This was not the case for Black husbands and wives. In the early years of marriage, children have negative effects on the quality of marriages for Whites but not for Blacks. We speculate that the meaning of children and its connection to the psychological well-being of marriages differ in the two cultures. We argue that any future analysis of the risk factors associated with divorce and lower marital quality must consider the different meanings of parenthood and children for African American and White marriages.

CONCLUSION

Recently there has been a growing interest in discovering what makes a marriage work amd the risk factors associated with divorce and low marital quality. Much of this literature has been geared toward developing universal assumptions about how to keep a marriage intact and happy. This vast literature advances the notion that two sets of factors affect the psychological well-being and stability of marriages over time: structural issues connected to the couple's lives and the interpersonal or interactional processes within the marriage. However, the literatures on African American and on White couples vary in their emphasis on structural or interactive processes. Specifically, studies of Black marriages and racial differences in marital stability are more likely to focus on structural processes.

Given this general approach in the marriage literature, the goals of this chapter were twofold. First, we focused on ways in which marital quality and stability depend on the social context of race and ethnicity, specifically the cultural norms and expectations associated with being African American or White in American society. Second, in examining the interactional styles of relating that may be important to predicting which marriages survive and which are more resilient to stress, we looked for similarities and differences in African American and White couples.

We spotlighted findings from one unique longitudinal study of marriage, the Early Years of Marriage Project at the University of Michigan. Our inquiry into the risks that are present in unhappy and unstable marriages identified few interchangeable factors but many parallel factors that take on different guises in the two co-cultural contexts. We identified five prominent interactional themes that we argued differentially express themselves in Black or White marriages: (a) supportive wives, (b) interpersonal compatibility, (c) male achievement and power, (d) integration of social networks, and (e) husband's independence and control. African Americans and Whites attach differential meaning to such interactional phenomena as wives' nurturance of their husbands, being independent or interdependent with one another, sexual relationships in marriage, marital compatibility, financial security, husbands' participation in household activities, resolving conflicts about money matters, and the meaning or experience of becoming a parent. All these phenomena and issues are significant risk factors for one group or the other, or both.

Our discussion and interpretation of these interactional risk factors in Black and White couples were informed by an examination of gender–power dynamics that differentially play themselves out in the two cultures. We argue that the experience of being male or female has a unique meaning depending on the cultural social context. These meanings are important to gaining a better understanding of the male–female interactional processes in Black and in White marriages that promote or inhibit happiness and divorce. As social researchers we need to examine marital interactional processes through both cultural and gendered lenses.

Similarly, even structural factors contributing to marital risks or resiliencies are best interpreted within a cultural and gendered context. Thus the meaning of parental status, income, educational background of mother, and social network ties is different in the two groups (and for husbands and wives), which leads to differential connections to marital risk in the two groups.

It would not be a wild extrapolation to suggest that just as there are differential meanings to these risk variables for the two groups so would there be differential meanings on what such variables might imply for the risks faced by children of these marriages as their young lives develop. Given that there are gender differences in the effects of divorce and remarriage on children (Demo & Acock, 1988; Hetherington, 1989; Orbuch, Thornton, & Cancio, 1997), these marital risks might also have different implications for daughters and sons. In addition, our analyses strongly suggest that the impact of divorce and unhappy marriages on children has to be considered within the contexts of African American and White cultures.

ACKNOWLEDGMENTS

The research in this chapter was supported by NIMH Grant MH41253. The authors would like to thank Libby Douvan, Sandra Eyster, Halimah Hassan, members of the Early Years of Marriage Project Seminar and the Family Studies Seminar at the University of Michigan, and the editor of this volume for their helpful comments and suggestions.

REFERENCES

Acitelli, L. K., Douvan, E., & Veroff, J. (1997). The changing influence of interpersonal perceptions on marital well-being among Black and White couples. *Journal of Social and Personal Relationships, 14,* 291–304.

Ade-Ridder, L., & Brubaker, T. H. (1983). The quality of long-term marriages. In T. H. Brubaker (Ed.), *Family relationships in later life* (pp. 21–30). Beverly Hills: Sage.

Adelmann, P. K., Chadwick, K., & Baerger, D. R. (1996). Marital quality of Black and White adults over the life course. *Journal of Social and Personal Relationships, 13,* 363–385.

Amato, P. R. (1993). Children's adjustment to divorce: Theories, hypotheses, and empirical support. *Journal of Marriage and the Family, 55,* 23–38.

Amato, P. R., & Keith, B. (1991). Separation from a parent during childhood and adult socioeconomic attainment. *Social Forces, 70,* 187–206.

Amato, P. R., & Rodgers, S. T. (1997). A longitudinal study of marital problems and subsequent divorce. *Journal of Marriage and the Family, 59,* 612–624.

Belsky, J., Spanier, G., & Rovine, M. (1983). Stability and change in marriage across the transition to parenthood. *Journal of Marriage and the Family, 47,* 455–462.

Billingsley, A. (1988). *Black families in White America.* New York: Simon & Schuster.

Billingsley, A. (1992). *Climbing Jacob's ladder: The enduring legacy of African-American families.* New York: Simon & Schuster.

Bowman, P. (1988). Research perspectives on Black men: Role strain and adaption across the adult life cycle. In R. L. Jones (Ed.), *Black adult development and aging* (pp. 117–150). Berkeley, CA: Cobb and Henry.

Broman, C. L. (1988). Household work and family life satisfaction of Blacks. *Journal of Marriage and the Family, 50,* 743–748.

Broman, C. L. (1993). Race differences in marital well-being. *Journal of Marriage and the Family, 55,* 724–732.

Carstensen, L. L. (1991). Selectivity theory: Social activity in life-span context. In K. W. Schaie (Ed.), *Annual Review of Gerontology and Geriatrics* (pp. 195–217). New York: Springer.

Carstensen, L. L., Gottman, J. M., & Levenson, R. W. (1995). Emotional behavior in long-term marriage. *Psychology and Aging, 10,* 140–149.

Collins, P. H. (1990). *Black feminist thought.* Boston: Unwin Hyman.

Coon, H. M., & Veroff, J. (1996). *Marital norms and marital stability: Understanding subcultural differences.* Unpublished manuscript, University of Michigan, Ann Arbor.

Cowan, P., & Cowan, C. (1994, September). *Where's the romance? What happens to marriage when partners become parents.* Paper presented at the conference on intimate relationships at Iowa State University, Ames, Iowa.

Crohan, S. E. (1992). Marital happiness and spousal consensus on beliefs about marital conflict: A longitudinal investigation. *Journal of Social and Personal Relationships, 9,* 89–102.

Davis, T. J. (1995). The occupational mobility of Black males revisited: Does race matter. *The Social Science Journal, 32*(2), 121–135.

Demo, D. H., & Acock, A. (1988). The impact of divorce on children. *Journal of Marriage and the Family, 50,* 619–648.

Demo, D. H., & Acock, A. (1996). Family structure, family process, and adolescent well-being. *Journal of Research on Adolescence, 6,* 457–488.

Elder, G., & Caspi, A. (1988). Economic stress in lives: Developmental perspectives. *Journal of Social Issues, 44,* 25–45.

Epps, E. (1985). *Educational and occupational aspirations and early attainment of Black males and females.* Atlanta, GA: Southern Educational Foundation.

Fine, M. A. (1993). Current approaches to understanding family diversity: An overview of the special issue. *Family Relations, 42*(3), 235–237.

Gottman, J. M. (1994). *What predicts divorce?* Hillsdale, NJ: Lawrence Erlbaum Associates.

Hatchett, S., Veroff, J., & Douvan, E. (1995). Marital stability among Black and White couples in early marriage. In M. B. Tucker & C. Mitchell-Kernan (Eds.), *The decline in marriage among African-Americans* (pp. 177–218). New York: Sage.

Henderson-King, D. H., & Veroff, J. (1994). Sexual satisfaction and marital well-being in the first years of marriage. *Journal of Social and Personal Relationships, 11*, 509–534.

Hetherington, E. M. (1989). Coping with family transitions: Winners, losers, and survivors. *Child Development, 60*, 1–24.

Hetherington, E. M. (1993). An overview of the Virginia longitudinal study of divorce and remarriage with a focus on early adolescence. *Journal of Family Psychology, 7*, 39–56.

Hetherington, E. M., & Clingempeel, W. G. (1992). Coping with marital transitions: A family systems perspective. *Monographs of the Society for Research on Child Development, 7*(2–3, Serial No. 227).

Hossain, Z., & Roopnarine, J. L. (1993). Division of household labor and child care in dual-earner African-American families with infants. *Sex Roles, 29*, 571–583.

Hunter, A. G., & Davis, J. E. (1992). Constructing gender: An exploration of Afro-American men's conceptualization of manhood. *Gender and Society, 6*, 464–479.

Hunter, A. G., & Sellers, S. L. (1998). Feminist attitudes among African-American women and men. *Gender and Society, 12*, 81–99.

Huston, T. L., & Chorost, A. F. (in press). Behavioral buffers on the effect of negativity on marital satisfaction: A longitudinal study. *Personal Relationships*.

Johnson, L. B. (1990). The employed Black: The dynamics of work-family tension. In H. E. Cheatham and J. B. Stewart (Eds.), *Black families* (pp. 217–233). New York: Transaction.

Kane, E. W. (1992). Race, gender, and attitudes toward gender stratification. *Social Psychology Quarterly, 55*, 311–320.

Kochman, T. (1981). *Black and White styles in conflict*. Chicago: University of Chicago Press.

Lichter, D. (1988). Racial differences in underemployment in American cities. *American Journal of Sociology, 93*, 771–792.

Lichter, D. T., McLaughlin, D. K., Kephart, G., & Landry D. J. (1992). Race and the retreat from marriages: A shortage of marriageable men? *American Sociological Review, 57*, 781–799.

Littlejohn-Blake, S. M., & Darling, C. (1993). Understanding the strengths of African-American families. *Journal of Black Studies, 23*, 460–471.

Markman, H. J. (1991). Constructive marital conflict is not an oxymoron. *Behavioral Assessment, 13*, 83–96.

Markman, H. J., Renick, M. J., Floyd, F. J., Stanley, S. M., & Clements, M. (1993). Preventing marital distress through communication and conflict management training: A 4- and 5-year follow-up. *Journal of Consulting and Clinical Psychology, 61*(1), 001–008.

McLanahan, S., & Sandefur, G. (1994). *Growing up with a single parent: What hurts, what helps*. Cambridge, MA: Harvard University Press.

Orbuch, T. L., & Custer, L. (1995). The social context of married women's work and its impact on Black husbands and White husbands. *Journal of Marriage and the Family, 57*, 333–345.

Orbuch, T. L., & Eyster, S. L. (1997a). Division of household labor among Black couples and White couples. *Social Forces, 76*, 301–332.

Orbuch, T. L., & Eyster, S. L. (1997b). *Becoming a parent: The social context of story-telling*. Manuscript under review.

Orbuch, T. L., Eyster, S. L., & Veroff, J. (1997). *The early years of marriage for Black couples and White couples*. Paper presented at the annual meeting of the International Network on Personal Relationships, University of Miami, Oxford, OH.

Orbuch, T. L., House, J. S., Mero, R. P., & Webster, P. S. (1996). Marital quality over the life course. *Social Psychology Quarterly, 59*(2), 162–171.

Orbuch, T. L., Thornton, A., & Cancio, J. (1997). *The impact of divorce, remarriage and marital quality on the relationships between parents and their children.* Manuscript under review.

Orbuch, T. L., Veroff, J., & Holmberg D. (1993). Becoming a married couple: The emergence of meaning in the first years of marriage. *Journal of Marriage and the Family, 55,* 815–826.

Seltzer, J. A., & Bianchi, S. M. (1988). Children's contact with absent parents. *Journal of Marriage and the Family, 50,* 663–677.

Smith, A. W. (1991). Personal traits, institutional prestige, racial attitudes, and black students' academic performance in college. In W. Allen, E. Epps, & N. Haniff (Eds.), *College in Black and White: African-American students in predominantly white and in historically black public universities* (pp. 111–126). Albany, NY: SUNY Press.

Stack, C. B. (1974). *All our kin: Strategies for surviving in a black community.* New York: Harper & Row.

Staples, R. (1991). Black male genocide: The final solution. In B. Bowser (Ed.), *Black male adolescents: Parenting and education* (pp. 39–57). Lanham, MD: University Press of America.

Staples, R., & Johnson, L. B. (1993). *Black families at the crossroads.* New York: Jossey-Bass.

Sutherland, L., Went, D., & Douvan, E. (1990). *Traditionalism in gender roles among black and white newlyweds.* Unpublished manuscript, University of Michigan, Ann Arbor.

Taylor, R. J., Chatters, L. M., & Jackson, J. S. (1993). A profile of familial relations among three-generation Black families. *Family Relations, 42,* 332–341.

Taylor, R. J., Chatters, L. M., Tucker, M. B., & Lewis, E. (1991). Developments in research on Black families: A decade in review. *Journal of Marriage and the Family, 52,* 993–1014.

Taylor, R. J., & Zhang, X. (1990). Cultural identity in maritally distressed and non-distressed black couples. *The Western Journal of Black Studies, 14,* 205–213.

Timmer, S. G., & Veroff, J. (1997). *Discontinuity of divorce: Family ties and the marital happiness of newlywed couples form intact and non-intact families.* Manuscript under review.

Timmer, S. G., Veroff, J., & Hatchett, S. (1996). Family ties and marital happiness: The different marital experiences of black and white newlywed couples. *Journal of Social and Personal Relationships, 13,* 335–359.

Tucker, M. B., & Mitchell-Kernan, C. (Eds.). (1995). *The decline of marriage among African-Americans.* New York: Sage.

Veroff, J. (in press). Marital commitment in the early years of marriage. In W. Jones & J. M. Adams (Eds.), *Handbook of interpersonal commitment and relationship stability.* New York: Plenum.

Veroff, J., Douvan, L., & Hatchett, S. (1995). *Marital instability.* Westport, CT: Greenwood.

Veroff, J., Douvan, E., Orbuch, T. L., & Acitelli, L. K. (1998). Happiness in stable marriages: The early years. In T. N. Bradbury (Ed.), *The developmental course of marital dysfunction* (pp. 152–179). New York: Cambridge University Press.

Vinokur, A. D., & Van Ryn, M. (1993). Social support and undermining in close relationships: Their independent effects on the mental health of unemployed persons. *Journal of Personality and Social Psychology, 65,* 350–359.

Walker, H. A. (1988). Black–White differences in marriage and family patterns. In S. M. Dornbusch & M. H. Strober (Eds.), *Feminism, children and the new family* (pp. 87–112). New York: Guilford.

Webster, P., Orbuch, T. L., & House, J. (1995). Effects of childhood family background on adult marital quality and perceived stability. *American Journal of Sociology, 101,* 404–432.

White, L., & Edwards, J. N. (1990). Emptying the nest and parental well-being: Evidence from national panel data. *American Sociological Review, 55,* 235–242.

Williams, D. R., Lavizzo-Mourey, R., & Warren, R. C. (1994). The concept of race and health status in America. *Public Health Reports, 109,* 26–41.

Willie, C. V. (1985). *Black and White families: A study in complementarity.* New York: General Hall.

PART II

Child Adjustment in Different Family Forms

3

Multiple Risks and Adjustment in Young Children Growing up in Different Family Settings

A British Community Study of Stepparent, Single Mother, and Nondivorced Families

Kirby Deater-Deckard
University of Oregon

Judy Dunn
Institute of Psychiatry, London

PARENTAL SEPARATION, divorce, remarriage, and family reconstitution have become common experiences in children's and parents' lives. The idyllic image of the two-parent, multiple-child nuclear family of the 1950s has been replaced with a more complex yet more realistic view of parenting and families in the 1990s. The intricate networks of family relationships that are formed, nurtured, and sometimes broken over the lifecourse of a family that experiences parental separation and remarriage present a complex array of risks as well as protective factors that are, in part, responsible for the wide range of individual differences seen in children's post-divorce and post-remarriage adjustment. There remains no doubt that experiencing such family changes during childhood and adolescence carries some liability for emotional and behavioral problems (Amato & Keith, 1991; Booth & Dunn, 1994; Buchanan, Maccoby, & Dornbusch, 1996). However, the magnitude of this effect and the diversity in children's adjustment forces us to consider the true complexity of individual and family psychological processes that are implicated. This aim—the exploration of multiple pathways of risk for children living in different family contexts following parental separation and family reconstitution—is the impetus for this chapter.

In Britain, changes in family structures and rates of divorce, remarriage, and nonmarital cohabitation mirror the same secular trends in most other Western industrialized nations. Data from the Office for National Statistics (ONS) in the United Kingdom demonstrate that 12.5% of children (1 in 8) in the UK will, at some time during childhood or adolescence, live in a household with a birth parent who has formed a new partnership either through cohabitation or remarriage (Haskey, 1994). For the majority of children whose parents divorce, these changes occur early in life. In the ONS analyses, nearly three quarters of the children who were living in stepfamilies had entered this household structure before the age of 10 years. Furthermore, most children who have parents who divorce live in a single-mother household, at least temporarily. Thus, increasing numbers of children in the UK experience parental separation and remarriage and the recombinations of sibling relationships that are formed. In order to understand more about the impact of these changes on children's adjustment, we explore preschool children's developmental outcomes in different types of families (e.g., divorced, single parent, remarried), taking the opportunity to use information from a large-scale community study of families in England, the Avon Longitudinal Study of Pregnancy and Childhood (ALSPAC; see Golding, 1996).

RISK MODELS: ACCUMULATION AND EQUIFINALITY

Risk and resilience models of psychopathology represent a parsimonious approach to gaining some insight into the distal and proximal processes that operate to produce individual differences in children's post-divorce and post-remarriage adjustment. A number of studies have demonstrated the utility of these multiple and cumulative risk models of psychopathology (for example, Biederman et al., 1995; Jessor, Van Den Bos, Vanderrym, Costa, & Turbin, 1995; Liaw & Brooks-Gunn, 1994; Sameroff, Seifer, Baldwin, & Baldwin, 1993; Shaw & Emery, 1988).

We define *risk factors* as aspects of the individual and his or her external environment that are linked, presumably in a causal way, to poorer social-emotional outcomes (Garmezy & Rutter, 1983). Although there are numerous psychosocial risk factors that have been identified for social-emotional maladjustment in childhood and adolescence, these can be represented in various broad domains (Deater-Deckard, Dodge, Bates, & Pettit, in press), including but certainly not limited to (a) aspects of the child; (b) sociocultural factors, including community and neighborhood contexts; and (c) the home environment, including parent attributes and parenting behavior.

Child risk factors include characteristics of the child, such as adverse temperament (e.g., irritability; see Rothbart & Bates, in press), his or her genetic make-up (Plomin, 1994), and being male (Zahn-Waxler, 1993). These endogenous risk factors are thought to influence the child's behavior, longitudinally and cross-situationally, and to interact with external or exogenous risks found in the other domains. We emphasize here that by endogenous risk, we mean neither intractible nor deterministic characteristics, but rather that aspects of the individual are stable and increase the liability for problems in adjustment. *Sociocultural or demographic risks* can include poverty (Huston, McLoyd, & Coll, 1994), unstable or adverse household characteristics (e.g., living in a single-mother home; Achenbach, Howell, Quay, & Conners, 1991), unsafe neighborhoods (Burton, Price-Sparlen, & Spencer, in press), the number of stressful life events faced by the child (Abidin, Jenkins, & McGaughey, 1992), and parental stress and social isolation (Deater-Deckard, in press). *Home or family factors* include conflict (and in extreme cases, violence) between parents (Abidin et al., 1992; Shaw & Emery, 1988), harsh and negative parenting (Dodge, Pettit, & Bates, 1994), conflicted sibling relationships (Dunn, Slomkowski, Beardsall, & Rende, 1994), and parental psychopathology including depression (Downey & Coyne, 1990).

Of course, these risk factors covary so that on average children who have one or two of these risk factors are likely to have other risk factors as well. It is important to consider multiple risk factors and the effects of these risk processes within the context of other risk factors because it is possible that particular sets of risk factors provide unique or differential predictions of individual differences in children's social-emotional adjustment (Biederman et al., 1995; Liaw & Brooks-Gunn, 1994).

Thus, there are at least three testable and competing hypotheses about the nature and effects of multiple risk factors. The generic multiple-risk hypothesis is that the presence or absence of risk in any of these three domains (i.e., sociocultural, endogenous, parenting) accounts for all of the prediction of children's adjustment problems. If this is the case, then these domain-specific risks are essentially redundant with each other.

In contrast, the *specific* multiple risk hypothesis is that the underlying risk processes indexed by each of these domains of risk provide unique statistical prediction of children's social-emotional adjustment. If the latter hypothesis is true, then each domain of risk should independently increase the prediction of emotional and behavioral problems. Support for the multiple risk hypothesis, however, does not rule out the possibility that these multiple, domain-specific sets of risk factors operate in the same way to produce similar outcomes, a principle called *equifinality* (Cicchetti & Rogosch, 1996). We need then also to explore whether particular multiple risk pathways explain most of the variance in children's social-emotional adjustment, or alternatively, if each multiple risk pathway is associated with similar outcomes.

Individual differences in children's adjustment may be predicted not from particular sets of multiple risks but from the accumulation of risk that is independent of the presence or absence of particular risk factors. The *cumulative risk* hypothesis states that the number of risk factors, and not necessarily the particular domain of risk, is important for understanding the underlying risk process (see Sameroff et al., 1993). Thus, the addition of multiple risk factors (regardless of domain or the specific content of the risk factors) contributes to a general level of stress and adversity for the child, which in turn predicts social-emotional adjustment.

THE ROLE OF FAMILY CONTEXT ON RISK PROCESSES

These multiple and cumulative risk models can be particularly useful in describing the processes that lead to adjustment problems for children following a parental divorce, separation, or remarriage. These risk processes may operate in a very similar way for all children, regardless of the particular family and broader cultural context within which they are embedded. Alternatively, risk processes may be specific to particular contexts. For example, it is possible that differential parental treatment of siblings plays a more important role in the development of emotional and behavioral problems among stepsiblings living in reconstituted families than it does for full siblings in nondivorced families (see Deater-Deckard, Dunn, O'Connor, & Golding, 1997; Mekos, Hetherington, & Reiss, 1996).

AIMS

These multiple risk models to be described here can be used to answer questions about children's and parents' psychosocial adjustment in the different family contexts that arise following parental separation or divorce and parental remarriage and family reconstitution. In this chapter, we attempt to answer four questions about the risk processes that may lead to problems in children's social and emotional development in stepfamilies and single mother families:

1. Multiple risk. How do the known risk factors for problems in children's social-emotional development work together to produce observed individual differences in children's adjustment?
2. Cumulative risk. Do these risk factors operate in a cumulative fashion, so that the number of risk factors, rather than the specific content of these risks, predicts children's adjustment?
3. Equifinality. Are there multiple pathways (i.e., different combinations of risk factors) to similar outcomes, or are there one or two predominant pathways to problems in adjustment?
4. Contextualism. Do these multiple and cumulative risk models operate similarly or differently in nondivorced, single-mother, stepfather, and stepmother families, and if so, what explains this context "effect" on developmental process?

THE AVON LONGITUDINAL STUDY
OF PREGNANCY AND CHILDHOOD

The Avon Longitudinal Study of Pregnancy and Childhood (ALSPAC) is an ongoing epidemiological study of nearly 14,000 women who were pregnant and gave

3. MULTIPLE RISKS AND CHILDREN'S ADJUSTMENT

birth to the target children during a 21-month period (from April 1, 1991, to December 31, 1992) in Avon county, England (see Golding, 1996, for a detailed description). Approximately 85–90% of the eligible population of women participated in the study. This large community sample is representative of Avon county (which includes the city of Bristol), and the sample also resembles the British population generally, with the exception of an underrepresentation of ethnic minority groups (Baker, Morris, & Taylor, 1997). The rates of stepparent, single parent and intact or nonstep families are similar to those found in the UK population, with a slight underrepresentation of single mothers, most likely because the participants were recruited during a pregnancy (O'Connor et al., in press). Attrition has been low—the majority (75%) of the study participants have remained in the study through its first 5 years. The mothers and their partners completed various questionnaires about themselves, the target children, and their older siblings, beginning prior to the target child's birth and continuing throughout the child's first 4 years of life. The sample for the analyses discussed here included just over 6,000 families with complete data pertaining to household structure and various sociodemographic indicators, parenting and the home environment, and child attributes such as gender, temperament and social-emotional adjustment.

Target children and their older siblings were classified into four family types, based on the household composition of biological and step relationships. *Nonstep* families were those families in which all children were biologically related to both parents living in the home. *Stepfather* families were those in which at least one older sibling was the biological child of the mother and a stepchild to her resident partner. These families could also include children who were biologically related to both parents. *Stepmother* or "other" stepfamilies were those families in which at least one of the older siblings was a stepchild of the mother. This category also included complex or blended stepfamilies, where both parents had stepchildren in the home. Finally, *single-mother* families were those in which the target child and older sibling were biologically related to a single mother who had either never married or cohabited or who was currently separated or divorced from the children's father.

We assessed the target children's social-emotional adjustment when they were 4 years old, using the Strengths and Difficulties Questionnaire (SDQ: Goodman, 1997), a 25-item questionnaire that assesses multiple domains of children's positive and negative adjustment (see Goodman, 1997, for details regarding reliability and validity). Because we were interested in exploring general functioning, we focused on the 20-item Total Problems score (scale alpha = .80). This scale includes items pertaining to children's emotional problems, hyperactivity, conduct problems, and peer relationship difficulties.

We estimated children's risk for adjustment problems using four indicators from each of three domains—sociodemographic risks, parenting, and child (endogenous) risks. All risk factors were based on mothers' reports at various time points. All measures had acceptable internal consistency, and composites containing multiple items were computed by summing items or scale scores that were first standardized.

Sociodemographic Risk

Risk factors in this domain were assessed when the children were 21 months old and included socioeconomic status, neighborhood characteristics, children's exposure to violence, and ethnic group membership. *Socioeconomic circumstances* (SES) were estimated by summing standardized scores for three indicators of housing conditions—crowding, home ownership (rented versus mortgaged/owned), and type of home (from low-income housing, apartment, semi-detached or duplex home, to detached home). *Neighborhood risks* were computed by summing four standardized indicators—mothers' concerns about vandalism and property damage, violence (e.g., muggings), burglaries, and disturbances from youths (originally scored: 0 = no opinion or not a problem; 1 = minor problem; 2 = major problem). *Exposure to violence* was indexed by a measure of violence between the mother and her partner, represented by summing two standardized items—hitting or slapping, and throwing or breaking objects (originally scored: 0 = no partner or did not happen; 1 = mother did or partner did; 2 = both mother and partner did). *Ethnicity* was coded as 0 = ethnic majority (Caucasian), and 1 = ethnic minority (e.g., Afro-Caribbean, African, Black British, Asian). For more precise details about these measures, refer to Dunn, Deater-Deckard, Pickering, O'Connor, & Golding (in press).

Parenting Risk

The four risk factors in this domain were assessed at various time points and included maternal negativity toward the target child (48 months), maternal depressive symptoms (21 months), use of spanking (18 months), and parenting stress (21 months). *Maternal negativity* was measured by summing four standardized items from an 8-item positivity/negativity questionnaire designed to tap mothers' negative and aversive feelings toward the target child (alpha = .62; originally scored as yes or no). *Mother's depressive symptoms* were assessed using the 10-item Edinburgh Postnatal Depression Scale (EPDS; Cox, Holden, & Sagovsky, 1987), a valid and reliable instrument that is applicable outside the postnatal period (Thorpe, 1993). These items assess the common symptoms of depression, such as mood, self-blame, and vegetative states (originally scored: 0 = not at all to 3 = as much as I ever did). *Use of spanking or smacking* was measured with the item, "When she/he has temper tantrums how often do you: smack/spank child?" Mothers responded to this item: 1 = never/no tantrums, 2 = sometimes, 3 = often. Finally, *parenting stress* was assessed by summing eight standardized items from a questionnaire designed to measure mothers' feelings about stress and inadequacy in the parenting role (originally scored: 1 = feel never to 4 = feel exactly). Example items included "whining makes parent want to hit child," "having a young child is absolutely exhausting," and "a mother can feel exasperated when she wants to calm her child down and nothing works" (see Deater-Deckard, 1997, for details about this measure).

Child Risks

The four child risk factors included child gender, frequency of temper tantrums (21 months), difficult temperament (6 months), and illness (6 months). *Child gender* was coded: 0 = girl, 1 = boy. *Frequency of temper tantrums* was assessed by a single item and coded: 1 = never, 2 = < once a week, 3 = at least once/week, 4 = most days, 5 = > once/day. *Difficult temperament* was measured using a summed composite of six temperament scales from a modified version of the Carey Infant Temperament Scale (Carey & McDevitt, 1977). Each of 88 items was coded: 1 = almost never, to 6 = almost always. The *difficult temperament* composite was determined from results of a higher order factor analysis of the nine subscales (factor loadings > .4). The *difficult temperament* composite included rhythmicity, approachability, adaptability, mood/emotionality, persistence, and distractibility. Finally, *illness* was assessed by summing two standardized items—the health of the child in the first month of life and the health of the child in the past month (originally coded: 1 = very healthy, 2 = minor problems, 3 = sometimes quite ill, 4 = mostly unwell).

Analysis Method

Hierarchical regression analysis and cluster analysis are useful tools for testing these various competing hypotheses. To test the competing generic and specific multiple risk hypotheses, risk factors within the three specified domains (i.e., sociocultural, endogenous, parenting) can be forced to enter the regression equation as sets of predictors. Through an iterative process using different hierarchical ordering of risk factors, the overlapping and unique prediction from each domain of risk can be estimated. The cumulative risk hypothesis can be tested by adding the number of risk factors for each child to a hierarchical regression model. If the individual risk factors provide unique increments to problems in the children's adjustment beyond the number-of-risks variable, the content of risk rather than solely the accumulated number of risks faced by the children, must be considered as important to the process.

Multiple Risk Factors

The bivariate correlations between the 12 risk factors and children's SDQ Total Problem scores are shown in Table 3.1. We estimated these correlations for the whole sample, as well as separately for each family type, in order to describe patterns in the covariation of multiple risks and child adjustment across family type. The sociodemographic risk factors were modestly correlated with child adjust-

TABLE 3.1

Bivariate Correlations Between Multiple Risk Factors and 4-year-old Children's
Strengths & Difficulties Questionnaire Total Scores, by Family Type

	All Families (n = 6,022)	Nonstep (n = 4,710)	Stepfather (n = 654)	Stepmother (n = 107)	Single (n = 551)
Sociodemographic:					
1. SES	−.15***	−.12***	−.16***	−.14	−.20***
2. neighborhood	.13***	.12***	.17***	.01	.12**
3. violence	.09***	.08***	.13***	.11	.09*
4. ethnicity[a]	.01	.00	.05	—[c]	−.03
Parenting:					
5. negativity	.48***	.48***	.47***	.49***	.52***
6. depression	.26***	.26***	.22***	.13	.23***
7. spanking	.11***	.10***	.13***	.19*	.12**
8. parenting stress	.29***	.29***	.25***	.26**	.30***
Child:					
9. gender[b]	.09***	.09***	.05***	.17	.11**
10. tantrums	.23***	.22***	.25***	.22*	.24***
11. temperament	.21***	.21***	.20***	.26**	.19***
12. illness	.15***	.15***	.10***	.19*	.17***

Note. *p < .05. **p < .01. ***p < .001.

n = minimum sample size based on pairwise deletion of missing data.

[a]0 = ethnic majority, 1 = ethnic minority.

[b]0 = girl, 1 = boy.

[c]No variance in ethnicity for this group.

ment. For the whole sample, children with higher SDQ Total Problems scores were from lower SES families, living in more dangerous neighborhoods, and had higher amounts of exposure to violence in the home. Ethnicity was unrelated to SDQ Total scores. Overall, this pattern of correlations was very similar for children in all four family types.

The parenting and home risk factors were modestly to substantially correlated with child adjustment. For the whole sample, children with higher SDQ scores had more negative relationships with their mothers, had mothers who had more depressive symptoms, were more likely to have been punished physically, and had mothers with higher levels of parenting stress. Again, this pattern of covariation between parenting risk factors and SDQ adjustment scores was very similar for children across all four family types.

The characteristics of the children were also related to the children's SDQ Total Problems scores. Children with more behavior and emotional problems were more likely to be boys and to have had histories of temper tantrums, difficult temperament, and physical illness. As with the sociodemographic and parenting risk domains, the pattern of the correlations between child adjustment and child risk factors was similar for children in nonstep, stepparent, and single-mother families.

We used hierarchical multiple regression analyses to estimate the total explained variance in children's SDQ Total scores and the unique statistical prediction from each of the three domains of multiple risk factors. The unique prediction for each domain was estimated by entering the domain of interest on the last step in the equation. For example, to estimate the unique prediction of the parenting risk factors, predictors were entered into the equation in two steps: (a) sociodemographic and child risk factors; (b) parenting risk factors. We conducted these analyses for the whole sample as well as separately within each of the four family types.

Overall, statistical prediction of children's SDQ Total scores was very good, explaining 29% ($p < .001$) of the variance for the whole sample. The full model predicted SDQ scores equally well in all four family types: nonstep, 29%; stepfather, 28%; stepmother, 29%; single mother, 32%.

The relative predictive weight of each domain varied substantially. For the entire sample, parenting and home risk factors had the largest unique prediction of children's SDQ Total scores, explaining 18% of the variance. Child risk factors explained only 3% of the unique variance and sociodemographic risks only 1% or the unique variance for the whole sample. Thus, 21% of the explained variance was attributable to unique components in these three domains of risk. Subtracting this from the 29% total explained variance, about 7% was attributable to predictive variance that was not unique (e.g., overlapping variance) to any particular domain of risk.

This pattern was quite consistent across the four family types. Parenting and home risk factors accounted for 15% to 20% of the unique variance in children's SDQ scores in the four family types, followed by 2% to 5% for child risks, and less than 1% to 2% for sociodemographic risks. Given that the total explained variance was similar across the four family types, the amounts of overlapping predictive variance between the three domains were also nearly identical across the family types (6 to 7%).

To summarize, each domain of multiple risk factors provided unique statistical prediction of children's SDQ Total scores, although the vast majority of this unique prediction was found in the parenting and home domain. Furthermore, some, but by no means the majority, of the explained variance was overlapping between the three domains of multiple risk factors. Finally, these multiple risk models operated in a very similar way in all four family contexts. This suggests that, on average, the risk processes that are implicated in the development of behavioral and emotional problems in the preschool period are the same in families where parents have divorced and in those where they have not; they are similar too in two-parent and single-parent families.

Cumulative Risk Factors

Next, we developed a cumulative risk model based on the same set of multiple risk factors identified in the previous analyses. In order to construct the cumulative risk

56 DEATER-DECKARD AND DUNN

model, we dichotomized each continuous risk factor by selecting those cases 1 SD
above the whole sample mean as being at risk. This included about 15% of the
whole sample on average, although for any given variable the extreme group could
include as little as 9% of the whole sample or as much as 28% of the whole sample,
depending on the distribution characteristics (i.e., skewness and kurtosis) of the
given variable. Two risk factors were not dichotomized using a threshold score because they were nominal-level variables: child gender (boys being at greater risk)
and ethnicity (ethnic minorities being at greater risk).

Table 3.2 includes the prevalences (i.e., percentages of the sample) of each of the
12 risk factors within the three risk domains for the whole sample as well as within
each of the four family types. With the exception of gender and ethnicity, these risk
percentages are arbitrary, so the comparison of interest is not the actual prevalence
of risk within the whole sample or any subgroup of families but between each of
the four family types. In order to test whether the prevalence of these risk factors
varied as a function of family type, we made all possible comparisons (six in total)
using χ^2 tests. All group comparisons that were significant at $p < .05$ or less are
shown in Table 3.2.

In general, across the sociodemographic and parenting risk domains, nonstep
families had the lowest prevalence rates, stepfather and stepmother families had

TABLE 3.2
Prevalence of Multiple Risk Factors as Percentage of Sample, by Family Type

	All	Nonstep	Stepfather	Stepmother	Single	Tukey tests (p < .05)
Sociodemographic:						
1. low SES	13	9	25	19	35	NS < SM, SF < Single
2. neighborhood	11	10	15	15	20	NS < SF < Single
3. violence	10	9	13	9	10	NS < SF
4. ethnicity[a]	2	1	2	1	4	NS, SF < Single
Parenting:						
5. negativity	18	17	17	16	21	NS, SF < Single
6. depression	9	8	13	13	18	NS < SF < Single
7. spanking	13	14	13	9	12	no differences
8. parenting stress	15	15	15	15	19	NS, SF < Single[b]
Child:						
9. gender[c]	52	52	51	53	51	no differences
10. tantrums	28	26	33	35	34	NS < SF, SM, Single
11. temperament	14	14	15	16	14	no differences
12. illness	25	24	25	24	24	no differences

Note. All risk factors were coded by selecting those individuals with scores more than 1 SD above
the scale mean, unless noted otherwise. NS = nonstep; SF = stepfather; SM = stepmother; Single =
single mother.
[a] Ethnic minority status as risk factor.
[b] Stepmother and single mother groups not significantly different due to small sample size of stepmother group.
[c] Male as risk factor.

higher rates, and single-mother families had the highest rates. The one exception was in the use of physical punishment, where there were no family type differences in the prevalence of this risk factor—9% to 13%. In contrast, for child risk factors, the prevalences were very similar for the whole sample and across the four family types. The one exception was for the presence of temper tantrums at 21 months, where the prevalence for nonstep families (26%) was significantly lower than that in the stepparent and single mother groups (33% to 35%).

Next, we computed three domain-specific cumulative risk variables by summing across the individual risk variables. We also computed a total cumulative risk score by summing across all three domains of risk variables. The mean number of risks across the three domains for the whole sample was 1.98 ($SD = 1.44$). It is not surprising that given the group differences in the prevalences for individual risk factors (see Table 3.2), single-mother families had more risk factors and the greatest variability ($M = 2.34$, $SD = 1.64$), followed by stepfather ($M = 2.18$, $SD = 1.51$) and stepmother families ($M = 2.10$, $SD = 1.53$), then nonstep families ($M = 1.90$, $SD = 1.39$). These domains of cumulative risk were only modestly intercorrelated (rs from .07 to .14, $p < .001$). This pattern of intercorrelations was quite consistent across the four family types.

Next, we estimated bivariate correlations between the three cumulative risk variables and the total cumulative risk variable, and children's SDQ Total scores. These correlations are shown in Table 3.3 for the whole sample and within each family type. For the whole sample, cumulative parenting and home risk showed the strongest correlation with SDQ scores ($r = .27$), followed by cumulative child risk ($r = .22$), then cumulative sociodemographic risk ($r = .14$). The total cumulative risk was the strongest correlate ($r = .34$). This pattern in the magnitudes of these correlations was very similar across the four family types, with the exception of stepmother families, where cumulative child risk was correlated somewhat higher with SDQ scores than was cumulative parenting and home risk. It is noteworthy as well that the total cumulative risk correlation was nearly identical across the four family types.

TABLE 3.3
Bivariate Correlations Between Cumulative Risk Variables and 4-year-old
Children's Strengths & Difficulties Questionnaire Total Scores, by Family Type

	All families (n = 7,172)	Nonstep (n = 5,604)	Stepfather (n = 786)	Stepmother (n = 122)	Single (n = 660)
Sociodemographic	.14***	.11***	.15***	.14	.13***
Parenting	.27***	.27***	.23***	.21*	.32***
Child	.22***	.23***	.17***	.30**	.20***
Total risk	.34***	.34***	.29***	.35***	.34***

Note. *$p < .05$. **$p < .01$. ***$p < .001$.
n = sample size based on listwise deletion of missing data.

As with the analyses of the multiple risk model, we used hierarchical multiple regression analyses to estimate the total explained variance in children's SDQ Total scores from the cumulative risk factors and the unique statistical prediction from each of the three domains of cumulative risk factors. The unique prediction for each domain of cumulative risk was estimated by entering the domain of interest in the last step in the equation. We conducted these analyses for the whole sample and separately by family type.

In general, although the statistical prediction of children's adjustment scores from cumulative risk factors was statistically significant, the effect size was more modest compared to the prediction from the multiple risk factors described earlier. For the whole sample, the three cumulative risk factors (i.e., sociodemographic, parenting, child) accounted for 11% of the variance in children's SDQ Total scores. This prediction was similar across the four family types (nonstep, 11%; stepfather, 9%; stepmother, 12%; single mother, 12%). Compared to the prediction in the multiple risk model (28% to 32%), the cumulative risk model provided relatively poor prediction of children's SDQ scores. This finding suggests that simply knowing the number of risk factors is, at best, only a substitute for the more powerful prediction possible if we know about the variations in the 12 specific risk variables.

Although on the whole the prediction was poorer in the cumulative risk model, it is worth noting that a very similar pattern to the multiple risk model emerged in the unique predictive weights for each of the three domains of cumulative risk. Again, the results were very similar for the entire sample and for each family type. In general, parenting and home cumulative risk explained the most unique variance (3% to 8%), followed by child cumulative risk (2% to 6%), then sociodemographic cumulative risk (less than 1% to 1%). Given that the total explained variance was around 11% to 12%, this means that only about 2% of the explained variance was predicted from overlapping variance among the three cumulative risk factors.

In summary, having more risk factors, particularly in the parenting and child domains, was associated with higher levels of behavioral and emotional problems. The pattern was very similar across the four family types. The cumulative risk model was less robust than the multiple risk model in predicting the SDQ Total scores, suggesting that it is not just the number of risks present that accounts for individual differences in children's behavioral and emotional problems, but their content is key.

Equifinality: Are There Multiple Pathways to Similar Outcomes?

The principle of *equifinality* is that there are multiple pathways to similar outcomes. The development of behavioral or emotional problems among children who have had to adapt to parental conflict, parental separation and divorce, living with a single parent, parental remarriage, and family reconstitution may not be explained by a single predominant process but instead by multiple processes that are quite different in terms of etiology but similar in terms of outcomes.

There is no simple way to demonstrate equifinality in risk processes because risk factors often co-occur (i.e., risk factor correlation) and their effects are conditioned upon the presence of other risk factors (i.e., risk factor interactions). However, we can gain some insight into how these multiple, possibly cumulative risk factors operate by comparing the predictive validity of various clusters or groups of risk factors. These clusters can be determined either empirically (e.g., cluster analysis techniques) or by using theoretically derived groupings of risk factors.

To explore equifinality in this study, we decided to focus on six groups of children determined from the three cumulative risk factors. First, we selected those children who had more risk factors than the sample average (3 or more risk factors; $n = 2,281$), in order to remove from the models those children who were at low levels of risk. We then categorized these at-risk children into six groups based on high levels of risk across the three domains: (1) high sociodemographic risk only, $n = 359$; (2) high parenting risk only, $n = 326$; (3) high child risk only, $n = 1,127$; (4) high sociodemographic and parenting risk, $n = 53$; (5) high sociodemographic and child risk, $n = 106$; (6) high parenting and child risk, $n = 267$. In all, 2,238 children were classified.

Table 3.4 shows the proportion of children from each family type for each of the six groups. The distribution of these groups was not even across the four family types in this study. For instance, the proportion of families with high levels of risk in two domains (groups 4, 5, and 6) was 24% for single-mother families, 21% for stepfather families, 19% for nonstep families, and only 9% for stepmother families.

In order to test for equifinality, we compared the group means on the SDQ Total Problems score for the total selected sample. We were not able to conduct these comparisons separately by family type, due to the small numbers of stepmother and single-mother families in the selected sample.

We conducted two group comparisons, statistically controlling for overall cumulative risk (ANCOVA). First, we compared the three groups that had high levels of risk in only one domain (groups 1, 2, and 3). This group effect was highly signifi-

TABLE 3.4
Percentage of Children Within Each Family Type in Six Cumulative Risk Groups

	Nonstep	Stepfather	Stepmother	Single Mother
Sociodemographic	15	19	20	19
Parenting	15	13	15	15
Child	52	48	56	41
Sociodemographic + parenting	2	4	0	6
Sociodemographic + child	4	7	2	9
Parenting + child	13	10	7	9

Note. The percentage total within each family type may not sum to 100% due to rounding.

cant, $F(2, 1720) = 9.21$, $p < .001$. Post hoc Tukey tests ($\alpha = .05$) revealed that children with high levels of parenting and home environment risk (group 2) had higher SDQ Total scores ($M = 11.37$, $SD = 4.84$) than children with high levels of child risk (group 3, $M = 10.50$, $SD = 4.81$) and high sociodemographic risk (group 1, $M = 9.34$, $SD = 4.67$). Groups 2 and 3 were also significantly different. Thus, among those children who had elevated levels of risk in only one domain, these findings suggest that risky parenting and home environments may be most strongly linked to adjustment problems, a finding that is inconsistent with the equifinality hypothesis. These group effects were not only highly significant but also moderate in magnitude (from about one fifth to nearly one half of a standard deviation). It is interesting to note that the proportions of children with high levels of risk in the parenting and home environment domain were nearly identical across the four family types (13% to 15%).

In the second analysis, we compared the three groups of children who had high levels of risk in two domains (groups 4, 5, and 6). This comparison was much weaker than the previous comparison, although still significant, $F(2, 403) = 3.13$, $p < .05$. However, none of the post hoc Tukey tests were significant. Thus, among those children with elevated levels of risk in two of the three domains, different patterns of risk were associated with similar outcomes. For these highest risk groups of children, the equifinality hypothesis could not be ruled out.

One problem with the equifinality hypothesis is that it is also the null hypothesis—that is, if equifinality is operating, then there will be no group (based on alternative patterns of risk) differences in children's outcomes. However, by incorporating tests for equifinality in other samples using other measures and statistical procedures, researchers will eventually be able to know under which conditions particular patterns of risk or protective factors are associated with particularly good or bad outcomes.

In summary, there was mixed support for the idea of more than one pathway to elevated levels of social-emotional adjustment problems among children in these different family contexts. For those children with moderate levels of risk (i.e., having elevated risk in only one of three domains), the parenting and home environment was particularly salient in the prediction of social-emotional adjustment. In contrast, among the highest risk children (i.e., those with elevated risk in two of the three domains), it appears that all three patterns of risk were associated with similar levels of social-emotional adjustment problems.

CONCLUSIONS

Children react differently to parental separation, remarriage, and family reconstitution. Although there are clearly risks involved in breaking and forming new family structures, the diversity in children's responses to these changes in family structure and functioning is compelling and requires researchers to tackle the difficult questions of how the various risk factors affect children and whether these risks are linked to particular family settings.

In this large, diverse community study of children living in different family situations (e.g., nonstep, stepfather, stepmother, single-mother families), we addressed four questions about multiple risk factors, the accumulation of risk, equifinality in risk processes, and whether these risk processes were specific to particular family types. We found that the three domains of risk we considered (i.e., sociodemographics, parenting and home environments, and child attributes) covaried and were associated with problems in children's behavioral and emotional well-being. Consistent with past research, risk factors such as poverty, neighborhood crime, violence, harsh and negative parenting, maternal depression, child gender, temperament, and illness were all predictive of children's adjustment problems. It is important that each domain of risk provided unique prediction of child adjustment problems, and the number of risk factors present (i.e., cumulative risk) was less important than the risk factors themselves, suggesting that the content of these risk factors is key. Some evidence suggested that problems in parenting and in the home environments (e.g., maternal negativity, depression, parenting stress, and use of physical punishment) were particularly important statistical predictors of children's adjustment. Finally, the predictive links between these various multiple risk factors and adjustment were similar, rather than different, across the four family types considered here. Whether the 4-year-old children we studied were living in single-parent, stepfather, or stepmother families, or in families with both biological parents, the pattern of risk and associated child outcome was similar (see Hetherington & Clingempeel, 1992, for similar findings on the parallel patterns of family process and child adjustment in different family settings).

Several caveats are worth noting. First, as these data are correlational, we cannot draw conclusions regarding causality. Maternal negativity, parenting stress, and maternal depressive symptoms, for instance, could well be in part responses to difficult children. Second, we are relying on mothers' reports of both risk factors and children's outcomes. The associations may reflect the bias of the single reporter. A third caveat concerns the particular sample on which these analyses are based (i.e., a cohort of women recruited in pregnancy) and the age of the children (i.e., 4 years old when their adjustment was assessed). It is not clear how the estimates of risk factors for outcomes of children in this sample of relatively young parents can be compared to the outcomes of either children of older parents or indeed older children. It is likely, for instance, that the number of stepfamilies may be higher and the impact of particular risks may differ among families with older children (Glick, 1989; Hetherington, 1993; Hetherington & Jodl, 1994). For instance, McLanahan (chap. 6, this volume) reports that about half of the prediction of adolescent adjustment problems from father absence is due to reduced or persistently low family income. In contrast, as we have reported previously for this sample of young children (Dunn et al., in press) and in the current chapter, the strongest prediction of preschoolers' and school-age children's behavioral adjustment problems comes from problematic parenting environments and parents' own maladjustment (e.g., depressive symptoms).

We are attempting to address the first two of these shortcomings by conducting an intensive longitudinal study with a subset of families from the ALSPAC study, in which we interview partners and children as well as mothers using a variety of assessment methods (e.g., interviews, questionnaires). We are tackling the third shortcoming with a follow-up of the full sample at a later time point. By doing so, we will be able to gain much needed insight into the nature and course of these notable individual differences in children's post-divorce and post-remarriage adjustment.

ACKNOWLEDGMENTS

We are grateful to the mothers who took part in this study and to the midwives for their cooperation and help in recruitment. The ALSPAC study team comprises interviewers, computer technicians, laboratory technicians, clerical workers, research scientists, volunteers, and managers who continue to make the study possible. This study could not have been undertaken without the financial support of the Medical Research Council, the Wellcome Trust, the Department of Health, the Department of the Environment, British Gas, and other companies. The ALSPAC study is part of the World Health Organization initiated European Longitudinal Study of Pregnancy and Childhood.

REFERENCES

Abidin, R. R., Jenkins, C. L., & McGaughey, M. C. (1992). The relationship of early family variables to children's subsequent behavioral adjustment. *Journal of Clinical Child Psychology, 21*(1), 60–69.

Achenbach, T. M., Howell, C. T., Quay, H. C., & Conners, C. K. (1991). National survey of problems and competencies among four- to-sixteen-year-olds. *Monographs of the Society for Research in Child Development, 56*(3, serial no. 225).

Amato, P. R., & Keith, B. (1991). Parental divorce and the wellbeing of children: A meta-analysis. *Psychological Bulletin, 110*, 26–46.

Baker, D., Morris, S., & Taylor, H. (1997). *A census comparison to assess the representativeness of the ALSPAC sample.* Unpublished manuscript, University of Bristol, Bristol, England.

Biederman, J., Milberger, S., Faraone, S. V., Kiely, K., Guite, J., Mick, E., Ablon, S., Warburton, R., & Reed, E. (1995). Family-environment risk factors for attention-deficit hyperactivity disorder. *Archives of General Psychiatry, 52*, 464–470.

Booth, A., & Dunn, J. (1994). *Stepfamilies: Who benefits? Who does not?* Hillsdale, NJ: Lawrence Erlbaum Associates.

Buchanan, C. M., Maccoby, E. E., & Dornbusch, S. M. (1996). *Adolescents after divorce.* Cambridge, MA: Harvard University Press.

Burton, L. M., Price-Sparlen, T., & Spencer, M. B. (in press). On ways of thinking about measuring neighborhoods: Implications for studying context and developmental outcome for children. In

J. Brooks-Gunn, G. Duncan, & L. Aber (Eds.), *Neighborhood poverty: Context and consequences for children.* New York: Russell Sage.

Carey, W. B., & McDevitt, S. C. (1977). *Infant temperament questionnaire (4–8 months).* Department of Educational Psychology, Temple University, Philadelphia.

Cicchetti, D., & Rogosch, F. A. (1996). Equifinality and multifinality in developmental psychopathology. *Development and Psychopathology, 8,* 597–600.

Cox, J. L., Holden, J. M., & Sagovsky, R. (1987). Development of the Edinburgh Postnatal Depression Scale. *British Journal of Psychiatry, 150,* 782–786.

Deater-Deckard, K. (1997, April). *Parenting stress in different family contexts: A population study of intact, remarried, and single mother families.* Paper presented at the Biennial Meeting of the Society for Research in Child Development, Washington DC.

Deater-Deckard, K. (in press). Parenting stress and child adjustment: Some old hypotheses and some new questions. *Clinical Psychology: Science and Practice.*

Deater-Deckard, K., Dodge, K. A., Bates, J. E., & Pettit, G. S. (in press). Multiple-risk factors in the development of externalizing behavior problems: Group and individual differences. *Development and Psychopathology.*

Deater-Deckard, K., Dunn, J., O'Connor, T. G., & Golding, J. (1997). *Sibling differences in children's adjustment: A community study of nondivorced, stepparent, and single mother families.* Manuscript submitted for publication.

Dodge, K. A., Pettit, G. S., & Bates, J. E. (1994). Socialization mediators of the relation between socioeconomic status and child conduct problems. *Child Development, 65,* 649–665.

Downey, G., & Coyne, J. C. (1990). Children of depressed parents: An integrative review. *Psychological Bulletin, 108,* 50–76.

Dunn, J., Deater-Deckard, K., Pickering, K., O'Connor, T. G., & Golding, J. (in press). Children's adjustment and prosocial behaviour in step-, single-, and nonstep-family settings: Findings from a community study. *Journal of Child Psychology and Psychiatry.*

Dunn, J., Slomkowski, C., Beardsall, L., & Rende, R. (1994). Adjustment in middle childhood and early adolescence: Links with earlier and contemporary sibling relationships. *Journal of Child Psychology and Psychiatry, 35,* 491–504.

Garmezy, N., & Rutter, M. (1983). *Stress, coping, and development in children.* New York: McGraw-Hill.

Glick, P. C. (1989). Remarried families, stepfamilies, and stepchildren: A brief demographic profile. *Family Relations, 38,* 24–27.

Golding, J. (1996). Children of the Nineties: A resource for assessing the magnitude of long-term effects of prenatal and perinatal events. *Contemporary Reviews in Obstetrics and Gynæcology, 8,* 89–92.

Goodman, R. (1997). The Strengths and Difficulties Questionnaire: A research note. *Journal of Child Psychology and Psychiatry, 38,* 581–586.

Haskey, J. (1994). *Stepfamilies and stepchildren in Great Britain.* Population Statistics, OPCS.

Hetherington, E. M. (1993). An overview of the Virginia longitudinal study of divorce and remarriage with a focus on early adolescence. *Journal of Family Psychology, 7,* 39–56.

Hetherington, E. M., & Clingempeel, W. G. (1992). Coping with marital transitions: A family systems perspective. *Monographs of the Society for Research in Child Development, 57* (2–3, Serial No. 227).

Hetherington, E. M., & Jodl, K. M. (1994). Stepfamilies as settings for child development. In A. Booth & J. Dunn (Eds.), *Stepfamilies: Who benefits? Who does not?* (pp. 55–79). Hillsdale, NJ: Lawrence Erlbaum Associates.

Huston, A. C., McLoyd, V. C., & Coll, C. G. (1994). Introduction. Children and poverty: Issues in contemporary research. *Child Development, 65,* 275–282.

Jessor, R., Van Den Bos, J., Vanderrym, J., Costa, F. M., & Turbin, M. S. (1995). Protective factors in adolescent problem behavior: Moderator effects and developmental change. *Developmental Psychology, 31,* 923–933.

Liaw, F., & Brooks-Gunn, J. (1994). Cumulative familial risks and low-birthweight children's cognitive and behavioral development. *Journal of Clinical Child Psychology, 23,* 360–372.

Mekos, D., Hetherington, E. M., & Reiss, D. (1996). Sibling differences in problem behavior and parental treatment in nondivorced and divorced families. *Child Development, 67,* 2148–2165.

O'Connor, T. G., Hawkins, N., Dunn, J., Thorpe, K. J., & Golding, J. (in press). Family type and maternal depression in pregnancy: Factors mediating risk in a community sample. *Journal of Marriage and the Family.*

Plomin, R. (1994). *Genetics and experience.* Thousand Oaks, CA: Sage.

Rothbart, M. K., & Bates, J. E. (in press). Temperament. In N. Eisenberg (Ed.), *Handbook of Child Psychology.*

Sameroff, A. J., Seifer, R., Baldwin, A., & Baldwin, C. (1993). Stability of intelligence from preschool to adolescence: The influence of social and family risk factors. *Child Development, 64,* 80–97.

Shaw, D. S., & Emery, R. E. (1988). Chronic family adversity and school-age children's adjustment. *Journal of the American Academy of Child and Adolescent Psychiatry, 27,* 200–206.

Thorpe, K. (1993). A study of the Edinburgh Postnatal Depression Scale for use with parent groups outside the pospartum period. *Journal of Reproductive and Infant Psychology, 11,* 119–125.

Zahn-Waxler, C. (1993). Warriors and worriers: Gender and psychopathology. Special issue: Toward a developmental perspective on conduct disorder. *Development and Psychopathology, 5*(1–2), 79–89.

4

Family Structure, Parenting Practices, and Adolescent Adjustment: An Ecological Examination

Shelli Avenevoli
Frances M. Sessa
Laurence Steinberg
Temple University

THE SOCIAL ENVIRONMENT in which children develop in contemporary American society has changed dramatically during the last few decades. In particular, the living arrangements and parenting situations of children have been adapted to meet increases in the proportions of children who are born to unmarried mothers, who experience parental divorce, and who experience parental remarriage (Hernandez, 1988). Indeed, nearly half of all American children born during the late 1970s and 1980s will spend part of their lives in a single-parent household (Glick & Lin, 1986). Moreover, the majority of youngsters whose parents divorce will live in step-family homes (Furstenberg, 1990), and because 62% of all remarriages end in divorce, many of these children will experience multiple home environments (Sorrentino, 1990). During recent decades, researchers have recognized these alternative family environments and have examined their effects on child development and adjustment.

Many early studies of family context compared children from different family structures on a variety of outcomes. Findings from these early studies as well as from more recent studies indicated that children from nonintact homes are more likely to do poorly in school, to engage in delinquent behavior, and to be psychologically distressed than are children from intact, two-parent homes (findings often vary depending on gender of child and age at time of divorce; e.g., Dornbusch et al., 1985; Nye, 1957). For example, Dornbusch and colleagues (1985) reported that 12- to 17-year-old adolescents in mother-only homes had higher rates of deviant behavior than adolescents from two-parent homes. Both males and females in the single-parent households displayed higher rates of contact with the law, school disciplinary problems, and smoking behavior. Similarly, Weinmann, Steinberg, and Dornbusch (1990) found that male and female adolescents (ages 14 to 18) from divorced and remarried homes reported more externalizing behaviors (e.g., delinquency, drug use, school misconduct, and susceptibility to antisocial peer pressure) and lower school grades than peers from intact families.

More contemporary studies have gone a step further by attempting to uncover the processes linking divorce, single parenting, or stepfamily environments to poor child adjustment. This research has articulated mechanisms and mediational models that may account for differences in adjustment among children from a variety of family backgrounds (e.g., Aseltine, 1996; Forehand, Long, & Brody, 1988; Forgatch, Patterson, & Skinner, 1988). Studies concentrating on the effects of divorce on child adjustment indicate that economic hardship (Amato & Keith, 1991), family or interparental conflict (Emery, 1982, 1988), inadequate discipline (Forgatch et al., 1988), and other secondary stressors associated with divorce (see Amato & Keith, 1991) augment the negative effects of divorce on children. Furthermore, studies that focus on the effects of single parenting on child adjustment suggest that economic hardship, maternal mental health, and parenting behaviors mediate the relation between single mothering and child maladjustment (e.g., McLanahan & Sandefur, 1994; McLoyd, 1990).

To advance the field further, a logical next step is to examine whether and how a variety of contextual influences (e.g., ethnicity and social class as well as family structure) moderate general family processes. We believe it is necessary to examine whether additional contextual variables such as ethnicity and SES influence the relations between family variables and child outcomes. Although some studies suggest that child outcomes are differentially predicted by family structure depending on the SES and ethnicity of the child (McLanahan & Sandefur, 1994), most previous research has treated additional contextual influences such as ethnicity and social class as nuisance variables (i.e., controlled through selective sampling or controlled statistically). Moreover, studies that have compared ethnic groups, social classes, or family structures on some index of interest have not taken into account all relevant factors simultaneously when making comparisons. For example, African American adolescents from single-parent families may be compared to European American adolescents from single-parent families, but social class is generally ignored or controlled.

Recent statistics on the changing demography of contemporary American society suggest that scientists can no longer ignore the effects of these important ecological factors on child socialization. Ethnic minority families, headed by Asian Americans and Latino Americans, represent the fastest growing segment of the United States population. McAdoo (1993, as cited in Parke & Buriel, 1998) predicted that by the end of this century, the Asian American population will increase by 22%, the Latino population by 21%, and the African American population by 12%. In terms of SES, recent data indicate that the median income of young families with children has dropped 34% in the last two decades, and more children are experiencing poverty than in previous decades (Children's Defense Fund, 1995). Inspired by the theory of Bronfenbrenner (1979, 1986, 1989; Bronfenbrenner & Crouter, 1983) and the changing demography of society, we contend that it is now necessary to determine whether what we know about some general family processes and child adjustment applies differentially across contexts defined by multiple influences.

One area in which it is important to compare family processes across various contexts is the relation between parenting and adolescent adjustment. Although research consistently reports that authoritative parenting—typically characterized by high levels of responsiveness and demandingness—as opposed to authoritarian or indulgent parenting is associated with the development of competence in children and adolescents (Maccoby & Martin, 1983; Steinberg, 1990; Steinberg, Mounts, Lamborn, & Dornbusch, 1991), the generalizability of these findings is limited. Most studies of authoritative parenting are based on White, middle-class adolescents. There is reason to believe, however, that the effects of specific parenting practices on child adjustment may depend on the environment in which the child lives. For example, because authoritative parenting is consistent with mainstream, White, middle-class ideals of democratic discipline and parent–child communication, it may be most beneficial to children from White, middle-class, two-parent homes. On the other hand, authoritarian parenting, with its high level of parental control, may have some benefits among youth living in high-risk environments (see Baldwin, Baldwin, & Cole, 1989; Baumrind, 1972) or in single-parent families.

PARENTING PRACTICES
ACROSS ECOLOGICAL CONTEXTS

Researchers have approached the issue of parenting across ecological contexts in two primary ways. First, they have examined differences in parenting behaviors and styles among families from diverse backgrounds. Second, researchers have examined the associations between parenting practices and child outcomes among families from different backgrounds. Although an abundance of literature examines whether parents from various backgrounds employ different practices, less is known about how parenting is differentially related to adolescent adjustment across ecological contexts.

Research that compares families on their parenting practices suggests differences among families from different ethnic groups and socioeconomic backgrounds. It is generally reported, for instance, that African American parents are more likely to be authoritarian, harsh, and punitive than are European American parents (e.g., Dornbusch, Ritter, Leiderman, Roberts, & Fraleigh, 1987). Also, Asian American parents are typically described as authoritarian (e.g., Dornbusch et al., 1987; Steinberg, Dornbusch, & Brown, 1992; Steinberg et al., 1991) and rejecting (Lin & Fu, 1990). Lower SES parents are reportedly more authoritarian and are generally more punitive, more restrictive, and less supportive than other parents (McLoyd, 1990). Although some theorists have attempted to explain why parents from particular backgrounds adopt nonauthoritative parenting styles (e.g., Chao, 1994; Ogbu, 1981), it is not clear that these parenting practices are beneficial to the adjustment of their children.

Research also suggests that parenting practices vary between parents of intact, biological families and nonintact families (particularly divorced families). During the period surrounding a divorce or separation, parents demonstrate diminished parenting, characterized by decreased affection, communication, control, and monitoring (Hetherington, Cox, & Cox, 1982; Hetherington, Stanley-Hagan, & Anderson, 1989; Wallerstein, 1983). Divorced parents are less likely to employ authoritative parenting styles than other parenting styles (Baumrind, 1991) and more likely to employ an authoritarian parenting style (Guidubaldi, Cleminshaw, Perry, Nastasi, & Lightel, 1986). Similarly, stepfathers tend to be generally disengaged and are also less likely than other parents to display an authoritative parenting style (Hetherington, 1989). However, these findings are often confounded by other ecological factors such as ethnicity and SES (as single parents are disproportionately likely to be ethnic minorities and of lower SES), thereby reiterating the need to examine these factors simultaneously.

To summarize, contemporary research suggests that parenting practices and styles may vary across family structures, ethnicities, and socioeconomic backgrounds. However, it is unknown whether and how parenting practices differ across contexts defined by multiple influences (e.g., family structure, ethnicity, and SES). Although this is an important question, it does not inform research as to how particular practices are related to child adjustment. We believe it is important to move beyond this issue and begin to examine associations between parenting and child adjustment. Specifically, we think it is necessary to determine whether particular parenting styles are differentially related to child adjustment across these various ecological contexts.

Few studies have systematically attempted to examine the relations between parenting and adjustment across different contexts. Nonetheless, there is some evidence to suggest that parenting styles other than authoritativeness may be adaptive in particular contexts. For example, Baldwin, Baldwin, and Cole (1990) found that children of poor minority parents who used more authoritarian child-rearing practices were better adjusted than children of poor minority parents who used more authoritative practices (as cited in Parke & Buriel, 1998). In addition, a study by Deater-Deckard, Dodge, Bates, and Pettit (1996) found that harsh physical discipline was associated with externalizing behavior and aggression in the school setting among European American children but not among African American children.

Two of the most thorough examinations of the moderating effects of family structure, ethnicity, and SES were conducted by Dornbusch et al. (1987) and Steinberg et al. (1991). Dornbusch and colleagues examined adolescent school achievement and three indices of parenting practices—authoritative parenting, authoritarian parenting, and permissive parenting—in a sample of 8,000 high-school students separated into four major ethnic groups. They found that authoritative parenting was significantly predictive of academic achievement only among European American adolescents. Authoritative parenting was marginally predictive of Hispanic American adolescents' achievement but was not at all predictive of achievement for Asian American or African American adolescents. Parental permissiveness was inversely related to achievement among European American adolescents but unrelated to grades in the other groups, and parental authoritarianism was negatively predictive of grades among European Americans, Asian Americans, and Hispanic American girls but not among the other groups. These findings suggest that the benefits of particular parenting practices may not be generalizable across ethnic groups.

As an extension to the work of Dornbusch et al. (1987), Steinberg and colleagues (1991) simultaneously included SES, family structure, and ethnicity as potential moderators of the relation between parenting and adolescent adjustment. In their study of 10,000 high school students, they grouped students into 16 ecological niches defined by ethnicity, SES, and family structure and examined whether adolescents from authoritative homes fared better on multiple indices of adjustment than did adolescents from nonauthoritative homes. They found that, virtually regardless of ethnicity, SES, or parents' marital status, adolescents whose parents are accepting, firm, and democratic earn higher grades in school, are more self-reliant, report less anxiety and depression, and are less likely to engage in delinquent behavior. Yet close inspection of their findings suggests that authoritative parenting is not as important for adolescents from some ecological contexts (e.g., African American adolescents from working-class families).

In this chapter, we extend the work of Steinberg and colleagues further and examine the relations between four types of parenting—authoritative, authoritarian, permissive, and neglectful—and multiple indices of adolescent adjustment within each of the ecological contexts defined by ethnic background, socioeconomic status, and family structure. We chose to include multiple types of parenting and multiple indices of adjustment because such a focus acknowledges that different types of parenting may be beneficial, or at least nonharmful, in certain ecological contexts and with regard to certain outcomes. In addition, for the purposes of this volume, we pay particular attention to differences between intact families and single-parent families.

We begin by examining whether parents from intact and single-parent homes differ in the parenting practices they employ. It is our hypothesis that in the overall sample, parents in intact homes will be more authoritative than parents in single-parent homes. Within ecological niches, however, we do not formulate specific hypotheses because the three variables of family structure, ethnicity, and SES have never been considered simultaneously in such analyses. Next, we examine the associations between parenting and multiple indices of adolescent adjustment in order to determine whether the strength of the relations varies across ecological niches defined by family structure, ethnicity, and SES. We then focus specifically on whether the strength of relations varies between intact and single-parent families both in general and in the various ecological contexts.

METHOD

Sample

Our sample is drawn from nine high schools in Wisconsin and Northern California. The schools were selected to yield a sample of students from different socioeconomic brackets, a variety of ethnic backgrounds, different family structures, and different types of communities (i.e., urban, suburban, and rural). Characteristics of the study sample are presented in Table 4.1. Data for the present analyses were collected during the 1987–1988 school year via self-report surveys filled out by the students on two days of survey administration each school year. Because of its length, the survey was divided into two equal parts and administered on two separate testing days each year.

Procedure

Recent reports suggest that the use of active consent procedures in research on adolescents and their families (i.e., procedures requiring active parental written

TABLE 4.1
Characteristics of the Study Sample

Family structure	
Intact, two-parent families	77.0%
Single-parent families	23.0%
SES	
Working-class families	56.4%
Middle-class families	43.6%
Ethnicity	
African American families	10.5%
European American families	61.3%
Asian American families	13.8%
Hispanic American families	14.4%

consent in order for their adolescents to participate in the research) may result in sampling biases that over represent well-functioning teenagers and families (e.g., Weinberger, Tublin, Ford, & Feldman, 1990). Although groups of participants and nonparticipants generated through such consent procedures may be comparable demographically (i.e., the dimension along which investigators typically look for evidence of selective participation), the procedure screens out a disproportionate number of adolescents who have adjustment problems or family difficulties. Because we were interested in studying adolescents with uninvolved as well as those with involved parents, we were concerned that employing the standard active consent procedure (in which both parents and adolescents are asked to return signed consent forms to their child's school) would bias the sample toward families who were more engaged in school and exclude the substantial number of parents who were not especially involved in their youngsters' educations.

After considering the age of our respondents and their ability to provide informed consent and with the support of the administrators of our participating schools, the school districts' research review committees, representatives of the U.S. Department of Education (our chief funding agent), and our own institutions' human subjects committees, we decided to employ a consent procedure that requested active informed consent from the adolescents but passive informed consent from their parents. All parents in the participating schools were informed, by first-class mail, of the date and nature of our study well in advance of the scheduled questionnaire administration. (We provided schools with letters in stamped, unaddressed envelopes to be mailed by school officials in order to protect the privacy of the families.) Parents were asked to call or write to their child's school or our research office if they did not want their child to participate in the study. Fewer than 1% of the adolescents in each of the target schools had their participation withheld by their parents.

All students in attendance on each day of testing were told the purposes of the study and asked to complete the questionnaires. Informed consent was obtained from all participating students. For each questionnaire administration, of the total school population, approximately 5% of the students chose not to participate or had their participation withheld by parents, approximately 15% were absent from school on the day of the initial questionnaire administration (this figure is comparable to national figures on daily school attendance), and approximately 80% provided completed questionnaires. In the 1987–1988 school year, 11,669 students participated in the study.

Measures

Of interest in the present analyses are the demographic variables used to assign youngsters to the various ecological contexts; the three parenting dimensions used to operationalize authoritative, authoritarian, permissive, and neglectful parenting; and our indices of adolescent adjustment.

Demographic Variables. Students provided information on their parents' educational attainment, their current family structures, and their ethnic background. Socioeconomic status was operationalized in terms of the mean educational level of the adults with whom the adolescent resided and coded into two categories: working class (i.e., less than college completion) and middle class (i.e., college completion or higher). We chose parental education as an index of social class for several reasons. First, research suggests that indices of class based on composite measures of occupation, income, and education fluctuate frequently over the course of an individual child's lifetime because of parental job changes and fluctuations in family finances (e.g., Featherman, Spenner, & Tsunematsu, 1988). Parental education is probably the most stable component of the family's social class. In addition, since 1950 there has been a decline in the significance of parental education for explaining beliefs and values about childrearing (Alwin, cited in Featherman et al., 1988). Similarly, most of the relation between parental income and children's achievements is accounted for by parents' education (Dornbusch, 1982, cited in Weston & Weston, 1987).

Student-provided information on current family structure was used to group individuals into two categories: two-parent biologically intact families and single-parent families. Stepfamilies were excluded from analyses due to small cell sizes in almost all ecological contexts.

Students also provided information on their ethnicity, which was used to categorize individuals into one of four major ethnic groups (i.e., African American, Asian American, Hispanic American, and White). Ecological niches were formed by creating a 2 (SES) × 2 (family structure) × 4 (ethnicity) matrix and assigning students to one of the resulting 16 cells.

Authoritative Parenting. The questionnaires contained many items on parenting practices that were taken or adapted from existing measures (e.g., Dornbusch et al., 1985; Patterson & Stouthamer-Loeber, 1984; Rodgers, 1966) or developed for this program of work. Based on the previous work of Steinberg et al. (1989), a number of items were selected to correspond with the three dimensions of authoritative parenting, and these were subjected to exploratory factor analyses using an oblique rotation. Three factors emerged, corresponding to the dimensions of acceptance/involvement, firm control, and psychological autonomy. These factors are identical to those suggested in the earlier work of Schaefer (1965) and parallel, respectively, to the Supportive Control, Assertive Control, and Directive/Conventional Control scales employed by Baumrind (1991) in her ongoing study of socialization and adolescent competence. Factor analyses were repeated separately for the four ethnic groups, and the basic structure was identical. We have labeled these scales in ways that both capture the item content of each and emphasize parallels between our measures and those used by other researchers.

The *acceptance/involvement* scale measures the extent to which the adolescent perceives his or her parents as loving, responsive, and involved (sample items: " I can count on her to help me out if I have some kind of problem"; "She helps me with my school work if there is something I don't understand"; 15 items, α = .72). The *firm control* scale assesses parental monitoring and limit setting (sample items: "How much do your parents try to know where you go at night?"; "In a typical week, what is the latest you can stay out on school nights [Monday to Thursday]?"; 9 items; α = .76). The *psychological autonomy* scale assesses the extent to which parents employ noncoercive, democratic discipline and encourage the adolescent to express individuality within the family (sample items, reversed scored: "How often do your parents tell you that their ideas are correct and that you should not question them?"; "How often do your parents answer your arguments by saying something like 'You'll know better when you grow up'?"; 12 items, α = .72). Composite scores were calculated on each of these dimensions. For most items, adolescents were asked to describe the parent(s) with whom they lived. On those items for which students in two-parent homes answered separately for their mother and their father, scores were averaged before forming composites.

Correlations among the dimensions suggest that they are related but conceptually distinct aspects of parenting: acceptance with firm control, $r = .34$; acceptance with psychological autonomy, $r = .25$; firm control with psychological autonomy, $r = -.07$. Reliability coefficients for the three dimensions were also calculated within each ecological group; the alpha coefficients were satisfactory across the 16 groups (see Steinberg et al., 1991).

Based on previous work, cluster analyses, and the theoretical models of parenting tested in this study, we constructed ordinal measures of authoritativeness, authoritarianism, permissiveness, and neglect. For the calculation of authoritative parenting scores, families were assigned one point each for scoring above the sample median on the acceptance/involvement, firm control, and psychological autonomy scales. For example, families scoring above the sample median on acceptance/involvement, firm control, and psychological autonomy were assigned an authoritative score of 3. Families scoring below the sample median on all three of the dimensions were assigned an authoritativeness score of 0. Families scoring above the sample median on one or two scales were assigned authoritativeness scores of 1 or 2, respectively.

A similar procedure was used to compute scores for authoritarianism and permissiveness. For the calculation of authoritarian scores, families were given one point for scoring above the sample median on firm control, one point for scoring below the median on acceptance/involvement, and one point for scoring below the median on psychological autonomy. For the calculation of permissiveness scores, families were given one point for scoring below the sample median on firm control, one point for scoring above the median on acceptance/involvement, and one point for scoring above the median on psychological autonomy.

Finally, for the calcuation of neglectful parenting scores, families were given one point for scoring below the median on firm control, one point for scoring below the median on acceptance/involvement, and one point for scoring in the middle tertile on psychological autonomy. The middle tertile was used with the psychological autonomy scale because, in theory and according to the results of a cluster analysis, neglectful parents neither intentionally hamper nor promote their adolescents' autonomy.

Adolescent Adjustment. Five indices were used to assess different aspects of adolescent adjustment: psychological distress, self-esteem, school performance, minor delinquent behavior, and substance use. Our index of psychological distress was taken from a series of items from the Center for Epidemiologic Studies Depression Scale (CES-D; Radloff, 1977); the scale includes items on anxiety, depression, tension, fatigue, insomnia, and others ($\alpha = .88$). The Rosenberg Scale of Self-Esteem was used to index self-esteem (Rosenberg, 1965; 10 items; $\alpha = .87$) and students' self-reported grade point average (GPA; scored on a 4-point scale) was used to index school performance. (Dornbusch et al., 1987, reported that self-reported grades and actual grades taken from official school records are highly correlated, $r = .75$). Two measures were used to index behavior problems. First, respondents reported on their frequency of involvement in such delinquent activities as theft, carrying a weapon, vandalism, and using a phony I.D. These responses were used to form an index of *delinquent activity* ($\alpha = .82$; Gold, 1970). Second, respondents provided information on their frequency of cigarette, alcohol, marijuana, and other drug use, which was used to form an index of *drug and alcohol use* ($\alpha = .86$; Greenberger, Steinberg, & Vaux, 1981).

Means and standard deviations for outcome variables are presented in Table 4.2.

Plan of Analyses

Our analyses proceeded in three stages. First, in order to determine whether parents from intact and single-parent families differ in the parenting practices they employ, we conducted a series of planned t tests on the entire sample and within each ecological niche. According to Rosnow and Rosenthal (1989), when specific two-group contrasts are of interest, the strategy of planned comparisons is preferred over one in which an omnibus analysis of variance is used to examine interaction terms (e.g., between parenting style and SES) because such tests of interaction are vulnerable to Type II error. In each contrast, the parenting practices of parents from intact families were compared to the parenting practices of parents from single-parent families. In addition, because subsample sizes vary considerably across ecological groups (and, consequently, the power to discern differences between parenting practices in the two types of families varies as well), an estimation of the effect size (r) was computed for each contrast.

Second, in order to determine the strength of the relations between parenting practices and adolescent adjustment, we computed correlation coefficients between each of the four indices of parenting and each of the six indices of adolescent adjustment both on the entire subject sample and within ecological niches. Graph-

4. PARENTING AND ADOLESCENT ADJUSTMENT

TABLE 4.2
Means (and Standard Deviations) of Adolescent Adjustment Variables

	Distress	Self-Esteem	GPA	Delinquency	Drug Use
Whole sample	2.51(.83)	2.98(.52)	2.79(.83)	1.20(.39)	1.64(.78)
Ecological niches					
White, working class, intact	2.60(.80)	2.98(.54)	2.80(.75)	1.19(.37)	1.71(.79)
White, working class, single	2.70(.80)	2.99(.54)	2.59(.86)	1.19(.34)	1.86(.84)
White, middle class, intact	2.56(.76)	3.06(.52)	3.18(.69)	1.15(.32)	1.69(.77)
White, middle class, single	2.69(.75)	2.99(.49)	2.87(.81)	1.16(.25)	1.80(.80)
Black, working class, intact	2.31(.84)	3.09(55)	2.58(.71)	1.14(.35)	1.23(.51)
Black, working class, single	2.38(.81)	3.16(.52)	2.44(.73)	1.17(.32)	1.36(.56)
Black, middle class, intact	2.32(.84)	3.11(.56)	2.57(.75)	1.23(.51)	1.43(.68)
Black, middle class, single	2.32(.85)	3.22(.57)	2.52(.69)	1.21(.34)	1.38(.48)
Asian, working class, intact	2.49(.81)	2.84(.53)	3.17(.75)	1.10(.27)	1.19(.44)
Asian, working class, single	2.43(.82)	2.90(.43)	3.01(.70)	1.13(.28)	1.32(.63)
Asian, middle class, intact	2.56(.73)	2.93(.45)	3.41(.66)	1.10(.25)	1.25(.50)
Asian, middle class, single	2.47(.82)	2.94(.51)	3.29(.61)	1.09(.15)	1.30(.58)
Hispanic, working class, intact	2.38(.83)	2.93(.49)	2.50(.82)	1.23(.43)	1.59(.74)
Hispanic, working class, single	2.49(.86)	2.97(.54)	2.36(.71)	1.22(.41)	1.70(.84)
Hispanic, middle class, intact	2.35(.74)	3.01(.47)	2.71(.79)	1.20(.50)	1.49(.75)
Hispanic, middle class, single	2.49(.84)	3.01(.39)	2.58(.83)	1.22(.50)	1.50(.62)

ical inspection of the data indicated linear trends for all associations. In addition, to ascertain whether the strengths of the relations differ across ecological contexts, we computed tests of the heterogeneity of effect sizes within each adjustment variable for each type of parenting.

Third, in order to determine whether the strength of the relations between parenting and adolescent adjustment varies by family structure, we compared the effect sizes of these relations in intact families to those of single-parent families in the entire sample and across the ecological niches. We also compared effect sizes across adjustment variables within each ecological niche in order to examine whether particular types of parenting practices are more beneficial or less harmful to adolescents from intact versus single-parent homes.

RESULTS

Parenting Practices in Intact Versus Single-Parent Homes

Table 4.3 summarizes the results of the contrasts performed. In the overall sample, intact families and single-parent families differ statistically in their levels of authoritative and neglectful parenting. Specifically, intact families appear to be more authoritative and less neglectful than single-parent families, as was expected. The size of these effects ($r = .10$ and $r = .11$) are generally considered to be small in magnitude

TABLE 4.3

Mean Differences (and Standard Deviations) on Four Types of Parenting
Among Parents from Intact and Single-Parent Families

	Authoritative	Authoritarian	Permissive	Neglectful	N
Whole sample					
Intact	1.55(.97)***	1.49(.86)	1.51(.86)	1.30(.91)***	4,471
Single	1.42(.95)	1.49(.85)	1.51(.86)	1.44(.92)	1,210
r	.10	.00	.00	.11	
Ecological niches					
White, working class					
Intact	1.55(.99)**	1.46(.84)	1.54(.84)	1.35(.94)*	1,318
Single	1.38(.97)	1.44(.84)	1.56(.84)	1.47(.89)	328
r	.12	.02	.02	.09	
White, middle class					
Intact	1.77(.97)*	1.27(.84)	1.73(.84)	1.17(.88)*	1,295
Single	1.62(.98)	1.23(.84)	1.77(.84)	1.33(.94)	217
r	.12	.04	.04	.14	
Black, working class					
Intact	1.54(.93)	1.69(.79)	1.31(.79)	1.18(.90)	146
Single	1.47(.98)	1.57(.78)	1.43(.78)	1.38(.99)	191
r	.04	.08	.08	.11	
Black, middle class					
Intact	1.62(.86)	1.46(.85)	1.54(.85)	1.21(.93)	61
Single	1.48(.86)	1.38(.96)	1.63(.96)	1.35(.83)	81
r	.09	.05	.05	.08	
Asian, working class					
Intact	1.18(.92)	1.76(.80)*	1.24(.80)*	1.46(.88)	309
Single	1.28(.97)	1.49(.78)	1.51(.78)	1.55(.88)	47
r	.08	.27	.27	.08	
Asian, middle class					
Intact	1.56(.91)	1.58(.88)	1.42(.88)	1.22(.84)	307
Single	1.35(1.01)	1.68(.82)	1.32(.82)	1.49(.90)	37
r	.18	.09	.09	.25	
Hispanic, working class					
Intact	1.35(.90)	1.72(.83)	1.28(.83)	1.44(.93)	347
Single	1.28(.88)	1.76(.84)	1.24(.84)	1.50(.94)	113
r	.05	.03	.03	.05	
Hispanic, middle class					
Intact	1.63(.99)	1.40(.87)	1.60(.87)	1.31(.94)	52
Single	1.63(1.06)	1.21(.66)	1.79(.66)	1.42(1.14)	54
r	.00	.14	.14	.07	

*p < .05. **p < .01. ***p < .001

(Rosenthal & Rosnow, 1984). Intact families do not appear to differ from single-parent families in terms of authoritarianism or permissiveness in the overall sample: The groups do not differ statistically, and the effect sizes are negligible.

Within ecological niches defined by ethnicity and SES, the contrasts suggest similar findings. In most cases, intact families are more authoritative and less neglectful than single-parent families. Although few of the differences in parenting between intact and single-parent families are statistically significant—statistical significance is found mainly in White families—inspection of effect sizes indicate differences of small or very small magnitude (and in the expected direction) in six of the eight contrasts for authoritative parenting and in all contrasts for neglectful parenting. (An account of the magnitude of effect sizes, as opposed to an examination of statistical significance, is appropriate for the present analysis due to considerable variation in cell sizes across the ecological groups.) In only one of the remaining contrasts for authoritative parenting is the difference in the opposite direction: In Asian, working-class families, parents from intact backgrounds are less authoritative than parents from single-parent homes. Tests of the heterogeneity of effect size indicate that effect sizes do not vary (authoritative: $\chi2(7) = 4.19, p = .76$; neglectful: $\chi2(7) = 2.13, p = .95$), suggesting that differences in parenting between intact and single-parent families do not vary across niches.

Comparing authoritarian and permissive parenting, the findings suggest that parents from intact families are more authoritarian and less permissive than parents from single-parent homes across most ecological niches. Six of eight contrasts for both parenting variables support this finding. However, the magnitude of these differences is very small in half of the contrasts. Although the size of the effects appears larger in Asian, working-class families and Hispanic, middle-class families, comparison of effect sizes across all ecological groups indicate that they are homogeneous, $\chi2(7) = 6.63, p = .47$, suggesting that differences do not vary statistically across niches.

In summary, parents from intact homes from a variety of ethnic and social class backgrounds are generally more authoritative and authoritarian and less permissive and neglectful than parents from single-parent homes, although in most cases the differences in parenting between the two types of families are quite small.

Parenting and Adolescent Adjustment: Ecological Examination

Before turning to an exploration of the differential associations between parenting and adolescent adjustment in intact versus single-parent homes, we first examine the general differences across ecological groups defined by family structure, ethnicity, and SES.

Authoritative Parenting. The results of the correlational analyses between authoritative parenting and adolescent adjustment are presented in Table 4.4. In

TABLE 4.4
Impact of Authoritative Parenting on Adolescent Adjustment

	Adjustment Indices				
	Distress	Self-Esteem	GPA	Delinquency	Substance Use
Whole sample					
Intact (4,037)	−.1401*	.2552*	.2244*	−.2266*	−.1712*
Single (1,037)	−.1464*	.2560*	.1851*	−.2375*	−.2065*
Ecological niches					
White, working class					
Intact (1,192)	−.1574*	**.2121***	.2120*	−.2350*	−.2461*
Single (294)	−.1525*	**.3128***	.2586*	−.2096*	−.2588*
White, middle class					
Intact (1,207)	−.2290*	.2458*	.2878*	−.2885*	−.2680*
Single (195)	−.2263*	.1729*	.2470*	−.3081*	−.2603*
Black, working class					
Intact (120)	−.2599*	.2797*	.2265*	−.2240*	−.2668*
Single (147)	−.1427*	.3180*	.1181	−.1460	−.0993
Black, middle class					
Intact (52)	.1198	.1782	.1595	−.1719	**.0845**
Single (65)	.0004	.1469	−.0252	−.3769*	**−.3778***
Asian, working class					
Intact (289)	−.1701*	.1942*	.1276*	−.1935*	−.1514*
Single (46)	−.2791*	.2849*	.2134	−.1896	−.1473
Asian, middle class					
Intact (291)	**−.0453**	.2271*	.1445*	−.1658*	−.1748*
Single (36)	**−.4377***	−.0475	.0881	−.3007*	−.1530
Hispanic, working class					
Intact (304)	−.1125*	.2723*	.2609*	−.2344*	−.1465*
Single (96)	−.1489	.2499*	.1136	−.2767*	−.1742*
Hispanic, middle class					
Intact (50)	−.3234*	.3720*	.2306	−.1617	−.3193*
Single (21)	−.0337	.3591*	.5764*	−.2802	−.3328

*$p < .05$; Bold type indicates that the effect sizes differ statistically at $p < .05$.

general and as expected, authoritative parenting is significantly related to lower psychological distress, higher self-esteem, higher GPA, and lower levels of minor delinquent behavior and substance use. These findings generally hold for adolescents from both intact and single-parent families in the entire sample and within ecological niches. Although there are a few exceptions to this trend, most of the nonsignificant findings can be attributed to small sample sizes within certain niches. For example, correlations of .10 represent small effects and correlations of .20 represent small-to-moderate effects (Cohen, 1977), but they are not statistically significant due to small sample sizes (and, thus, insufficient power to detect small-to-moderate effects) within particular ecological niches (e.g., Asian, working-class, single-parent families and Hispanic, middle-class families). However, considering that small or moderate effect sizes have practical significance in discussions of adolescent adjustment, authoritative parenting appears to have beneficial effects on development for most adolescents.

In order to determine whether authoritative parenting is differentially related to adolescent adjustment across ecological niches, we tested the heterogeneity of effect sizes within each adjustment variable. Analyses suggest that effect sizes are homogeneous for self-esteem [$\chi2(15) = 10.83$, $p = .76$], delinquency [$\chi2(15) = 10.37$, $p = .80$], and substance use [$\chi2(15) = .17.59$, $p = .28$]. However, effect sizes are heterogeneous for distress [$\chi2(15) = 24.79$, $p = .05$] and GPA [$\chi2(15) = 24.49$, $p = .05$], suggesting differential relations between authoritative parenting and adolescent distress and GPA across ecological contexts. Specifically, authoritativeness is less strongly related to adolescent distress in African American and Hispanic middle-class, single-parent homes and in Asian middle-class, intact homes than in most White, working-class, or intact homes. More notably, authoritativeness is related to greater distress (and greater substance use) in African American middle-class, intact families. No one demographic variable alone—family structure, ethnicity, or SES—appears to moderate the relations between authoritative parenting and distress. In terms of GPA, parental authoritativeness is less strongly related to the GPA of adolescents from most African American families (except working-class, intact), Asian middle-class families, and Hispanic working-class, single-parent families. Overall, authoritative parenting is generally beneficial to all groups; however, in a few cases authoritative parenting is less beneficial in terms of specific outcomes. African American, middle-class adolescents appear to benefit less from authoritative parenting than all other adolescents.

Authoritarian Parenting. In contrast to authoritative parenting, parental authoritarianism is generally related to greater psychological distress, lower self-esteem, lower GPA, and lower substance use (see Table 4.5). Effects are very small in many cases, suggesting that authoritarianism is not strongly related to some aspects of adolescent adjustment within particular contexts and is not as strongly related to different aspects of adolescent adjustment as is authoritativeness.

Authoritarianism appears to be especially detrimental to the self-esteem of adolescents. In 11 of the 16 ecological contexts, parental authoritarianism is significantly related to lower adolescent self-esteem, and in 12 of the 16 contexts, authoritarianism has a small-to-moderate or greater effect on the self-esteem of adolescents. A similar story can be told for the relations between authoritarian parenting and adolescent distress. Authoritarianism is significantly related to psychological distress in 8 of the 16 contexts (see Table 4.5).

As with authoritative parenting, authoritarian parenting is differentially related to certain aspects of adolescent development across ecological niches. Comparison of effect sizes indicate that they are homogeneous for adolescent psychological distress [$\chi2(15) = 14.84$, $p = .46$], self-esteem [$\chi2(15) = 18.56$, $p = .23$], and substance use [$\chi2(15) = 13.77$, $p = .54$] but are heterogeneous for GPA [$\chi2(15) = 27.49$, $p = .02$] and delinquency [$\chi2(15) = 24.66$, $p = .05$].

The relation between authoritarianism and GPA varies greatly across ecological contexts, both in strength and direction. Specifically, parental authoritarianism is related to decreased GPA in 12 of the 16 ecological contexts and is related to increased GPA in the four remaining contexts (e.g., Asian middle-class, intact families, and African American middle-class, single-parent families). However, close inspection of the magnitude of the effects indicates that larger effects are associated with decreased GPA rather than increased GPA. Moreover, the strength of relation between parental authoritarianism and GPA is greater in some ecological contexts than others (e.g., African American middle-class, intact families; Asian working-class, single-parent families; and Hispanic middle-class families), sug-

TABLE 4.5
Impact of Authoritarian Parenting on Adolescent Adjustment

	Adjustment Indices				
	Distress	Self-Esteem	GPA	Delinquency	Substance Use
Whole sample					
Intact (4,037)	.0816*	−.2170*	−.0929*	.0094	−.0895*
Single (1,037)	.0768*	−.2331*	−.1049*	.0594*	−.0606*
Ecological niches					
White, working class					
Intact (1,192)	.0998*	−.1870*	−.0785*	.0203	−.0009
Single (294)	.0755	−.2860*	−.1488*	.0799	−.0012
White, middle class					
Intact (1,207)	.1239*	−.2519*	−.1058*	.0823*	−.0453
Single (195)	.1373*	−.1158	−.1277*	.1126	−.0108
Black, working class					
Intact (120)	.1702*	−.0875	−.0391	−.1278	−.1107
Single (147)	.0507	−.2630*	−.0364	**.0938**	.0118
Black, middle class					
Intact (52)	.0638	−.1080	−.3300*	.0067	−.0967
Single (65)	−.0191	−.1662	**.0737**	.0188	−.0572
Asian, working class					
Intact (289)	.1496*	−.1097*	.0312	.0428	.0285
Single (46)	.0933	−.3196*	−.2349	−.0020	−.0847
Asian, middle class					
Intact (291)	**.1059***	−.1703*	.1247*	−.0064	−.1097*
Single (36)	**.4299***	−.1621	−.0509	.0703	−.1567
Hispanic, working class					
Intact (304)	.1409*	−.2805*	−.0488	−.1219*	−.1693*
Single (96)	.3455*	−.3938*	.0009	−.0338	−.1272
Hispanic, middle class					
Intact (50)	.0741	−.2234	−.1758	−.0590	.0297
Single (21)	−.0496	−.2146	−.1463	.2510	.2107

*$p < .05$; Bold type indicates that the effect sizes differ statistically at $p < .05$.

gesting that authoritarian parenting has a greater impact on adolescents from these family backgrounds.

The relation between authoritarianism and delinquency also varies across ecological contexts. In some cases, authoritarianism is related to increased delinquency (10 of the 16 contexts; e.g., African American working-class, single-parent homes), whereas in other cases, authoritarianism is related to decreased delinquency (6 of 16 contexts; e.g., African American working-class, intact families and Hispanic, working-class intact families). In many cases, however, the relation between authoritarianism and adolescent deviance is quite small.

Permissive Parenting. Permissive parenting is essentially operationalized as the opposite of authoritarian parenting. Thus, the findings and trends for permissive parenting mirror those presented previously. Table 4.6 displays findings for permissive parenting.

Permissive parenting is generally related to lower psychological distress and substance use and higher self-esteem. In terms of GPA and delinquency, parental permissiveness is related to lower GPA and delinquent behavior in some ecological contexts, to higher GPA and delinquent behavior in other contexts, and is unrelated to GPA and delinquency in other contexts. Although permissive parenting appears to be related beneficially to some indices of adolescent adjustment, the relations between authoritativeness and adolescent adjustment are larger for all outcomes except self-esteem. This suggests that authoritativeness is more beneficial than is permissiveness to adolescent adjustment.

Neglectful Parenting. Table 4.7 summarizes the results of the correlational analyses between neglectful parenting and adolescent adjustment. In general, neglectful parenting appears to be related to greater adolescent distress, lower self-esteem, lower GPA, and greater delinquency and drug use in the entire sample as well as across ecological niches. In most cases, findings are statistically significant or represent small or small-to-moderate effects.

The relation between neglectful parenting and psychological distress is small in magnitude across ecological niches, and comparison of effect sizes indicate they are homogeneous [$\chi2(15) = 19.13$, $p = .21$]. Although effect sizes are somewhat larger for self-esteem, GPA, delinquency, and substance use, the relations between neglectful parenting and these outcomes do not vary across ecological niches [$\chi2(15) = 17.67$, $p = .20$; $\chi2(15) = 22.11$, $p = .10$; $\chi2(15) = 11.79$, $p = .69$; and $\chi2(15) = 12.03$, $p = .68$, respectively]. Thus, it appears that neglectful parenting is equally harmful for all adolescents.

Parenting and Adolescent Adjustment: Intact Families Versus Single-Parent Families

Authoritative Parenting. As evidenced by comparisons of effect sizes, the relation between parental authoritativeness and adolescent adjustment does not vary by family structure in the sample for any of the outcome variables (see Table 4.4). However, parental authoritativeness appears to be more beneficial for certain aspects of adolescent adjustment in single-parent families in particular ecological contexts (see Table 4.4). For example, authoritativeness is more strongly related to adolescent psychological well-being in Asian single-parent families than in Asian intact families (the difference is statistically significant in Asian middle-class families but not in Asian working-class families). In addition, authoritativeness is more strongly related to lower delinquency and substance use in African American middle-class, single-parent families than in intact families, and this trend is actually reversed in African American working-class families. There is also a trend for adolescent self-esteem, although the differences are not statistically significant. Specifi-

TABLE 4.6
Impact of Permissive Parenting on Adolescent Adjustment

	Adjustment Indices				
	Distress	Self-Esteem	GPA	Delinquency	Substance Use
Whole sample					
Intact (4,037)	−.0808*	.2179*	.0939*	−.0087	.0903*
Single (1,037)	−.0768*	.2331*	.1049*	−.0594*	.0607*
Ecological niches					
White, working class					
Intact (1,192)	−.0996*	**.1871***	.0788*	−.0229	.0009
Single (294)	−.0755	**.2861***	.1488*	−.0799	.0012
White, middle class					
Intact (1,207)	−.1237*	**.2520***	.1059*	−.0823*	.0453
Single (195)	−.1372*	**.1158**	.1277	−.1126	.0108
Black, working class					
Intact (120)	−.1702*	.0875	.0391	**.1278**	.1107
Single (147)	−.0507	.2630*	.0364	**−.0938**	−.0118
Black, middle class					
Intact (52)	−.0638	.1080	**.3300***	−.0067	.0967
Single (65)	.0191	.1662	**−.0737**	−.0188	.0572
Asian, working class					
Intact (289)	−.1496*	.1097*	−.0312	−.0427	−.0285
Single (46)	−.0933	.3196*	**.2349**	.0020	.0847
Asian, middle class					
Intact (291)	**−.1059***	.1703*	−.1246*	.0064	.1097*
Single (36)	**−.4299***	.1621	.0509	−.0703	.1567
Hispanic, working class					
Intact (304)	−.1409*	.2805*	.0488	.1219*	.1693*
Single (96)	−.3455*	.3938*	−.0009	.0338	.1272
Hispanic, middle class					
Intact (50)	−.0741	.2234	.1758	.0590	−.0297
Single (21)	.0496	.2146	.1463	−.2510	−.2107

*p < .05; Bold type indicates that the effect sizes differ statistically at p < .05.

cally, authoritativeness is more strongly related to adolescent self-esteem in intact than in single-parent, working-class families of all colors, but it is more strongly related to self-esteem in single-parent than in intact, middle-class families of all colors.

In order to determine whether authoritative parenting was more beneficial to overall adolescent adjustment in intact or single-parent homes, we conducted planned comparisons of effect sizes across indices of adolescent adjustment and within each ecological niche. In only one niche, African American working-class homes, did authoritative parenting benefit adolescent adjustment more in one type of family than the other ($z = 1.61, p = .05$). In particular, although beneficial to both, authoritative parenting was more beneficial to adolescents from intact homes than from single-parent homes.

TABLE 4.7
Impact of Neglectful Parenting on Adolescent Adjustment

	Adjustment Indices				
	Distress	Self-Esteem	GPA	Delinquency	Substance Use
Whole sample					
Intact (4,037)	.0751*	−.1568*	−.1549*	.1965*	.1750*
Single (1,037)	.0636*	−.1728*	−.1218*	.1766*	.1761*
Ecological niches					
White, working class					
Intact (1,192)	.0797*	−.1187*	−.1259*	.1714*	.1999*
Single (294)	.0665	−.2141	−.1205*	.1289*	.2303*
White, middle class					
Intact (1,207)	.1539*	−.1995*	−.2077*	.2461*	.2445*
Single (195)	.1203*	−.1903*	−.2724*	.2675*	.2423*
Black, working class					
Intact (120)	.0698	−.1866*	−.1721*	.1329	.2077*
Single (147)	.0693	−.2371*	−.0811	.1455	.0778
Black, middle class					
Intact (52)	−.2375*	−.1137	.0783	.2379	.0549
Single (65)	.0427	−.0998	−.0567	.4233*	.2815*
Asian, working class					
Intact (289)	.0397	−.0784	−.1055*	.1978*	.1145*
Single (46)	.0800	−.1887	−.1487	.1217	.1780
Asian, middle class					
Intact (291)	.0366	−.1415*	−.0909	.1628*	.1687*
Single (36)	.3021*	.2239	−.0026	.1824	.2638
Hispanic, working class					
Intact (304)	.0908	−.1200*	−.2204*	.2051*	.1809*
Single (96)	−.0315	.0314	−.0510	.1975	.1424
Hispanic, middle class					
Intact (50)	.2796*	−.1849	−.1986	.1203	.3905*
Single (21)	−.0213	−.3533	−.4960*	.2542	.3435

*$p < .05$; Bold type indicates that the effect sizes differ statistically at $p < .05$.

Authoritarian Parenting. Table 4.5 displays results of the comparisons of effect sizes between intact and single-parent homes across ecological niches. In a few cases, authoritarian parenting is more harmful in one family type than in the other. First, parental authoritarianism is related to greater psychological distress in Asian middle-class and Hispanic working-class, single-parent families than in intact families. Second, authoritarian parenting is more damaging to the self-esteem of adolescents from single-parent than from two-parent families among White working-class, African American working-class, African American middle-class, and Asian working-class families (not all are statistically different). The opposite is true for White middle-class families: Authoritarianism is more detrimental to the self-esteem of adolescents from intact families than those from single-parent families.

In terms of school grades, authoritarian parenting is significantly more harmful to the grades of adolescents living in intact, African American, middle-class homes than adolescents living in single-parent, middle-class homes. On the other hand, authoritarian parenting is significantly more harmful to the grades of Asian working-class adolescents living in single-parent versus intact homes. In terms of adolescent delinquency, it is especially notable that the relations between authoritarianism and delinquency are in the opposite direction for intact and single-parent African American working-class families.

Only one of the planned comparisons of effect sizes in intact versus single-parent families within ecological niches reached the .05 level of significance. In particular, we found that authoritarianism is more harmful in terms of psychological distress and self-esteem and less beneficial in terms of delinquency and substance use to the overall adjustment of adolescents from Hispanic working-class, single-parent homes ($z = 1.6, p = .05$).

Permissive Parenting. Mirroring the trends of parental authoritarianism, parental permissiveness appears to be more beneficial in one family type over the other only within Hispanic working-class families or only within specific outcomes.

Neglectful Parenting. In only one comparison of effects did the relation between neglectful parenting and adolescent adjustment differ between intact and single-parent homes. In Asian middle-class families, neglectful parenting is related to lower adolescent self-esteem in intact homes but to higher self-esteem in single-parent homes.

Planned comparisons indicated that neglectful parenting is more detrimental to overall adolescent adjustment in intact Hispanic working-class families than in single-parent families ($z = 1.87, p = .03$) and is more detrimental to overall adjustment in African American middle-class, single-parent families versus intact families ($z = 2.00, p = .02$).

DISCUSSION AND CONCLUSIONS

Adolescents in contemporary society experience a broad range of contextual influences that affect their psychosocial adjustment and behavior. In this chapter, we examined how some of these contextual variables (i.e., family structure, ethnicity, and social class) moderate the influence of parenting on adolescents' emotional and psychosocial functioning. The results of this research both validate and expand previous research in three general areas.

First, our findings confirm that adolescents experience different parenting styles in two-parent versus single-parent homes. Regardless of ethnicity and social class, two-parent families tend to be more authoritative, more authoritarian, less permissive, and less neglectful than single-parent families. Although the differences in parenting style between two-parent and single-parent families are generally small, they are consistent with other investigators' observations that single parents exhibit diminished parenting, especially with respect to behavioral control and limit-setting (i.e., more permissive and less involved parenting; Hetherington et al., 1982, 1989; Wallerstein, 1983). Indeed, the multiple demands and stresses (e.g., working and caring for children) placed on single parents may contribute to their decreased capacity to provide sufficient monitoring and structure for their children. In contrast, the combined effort of two parents in intact homes, who often share child-rearing responsibilities, may be additive in terms of how it contributes to an increased capacity for active and involved parenting.

Second, our findings suggest that, with only a few exceptions, the relation between parenting style and adolescent adjustment is more similar than it is different across ecological contexts. Consistent with the results of previous research, two broad generalizations were confirmed in the present study. First, we find that authoritative parenting is related to adaptive adolescent adjustment virtually regardless of family structure, ethnicity, or social class (see Steinberg et al., 1991). Specifically, adolescents from authoritative homes are well-adjusted emotionally, do well in school, have healthy self-esteem, and are less likely to engage in deviant behavior. In contrast, we find that neglectful parenting, characterized by parental disengagement, is associated with emotional distress and deviance, low self-esteem, and poor academic achievement across all ecological niches. Across most ecological contexts, authoritarian parenting is associated with psychological distress, low self-esteem, and poor school performance. Permissive parenting, although associated with more adaptive adolescent development than authoritarian parenting, is still less effective than authoritative parenting.

There are two notable exceptions to the pattern of relations between parenting and adjustment across ecological contexts, however. First, among African American middle-class adolescents, authoritative parenting has a modestly less beneficial influence on their self-esteem and academic performance and is actually associated with diminished psychological well-being and greater involvement in deviant and delinquent behaviors. The interpretation of this finding is unclear, given the general absence of research or theory on parenting in this particular ecological niche. It is possible that African American middle-class parents are attempting to practice a somewhat different, and perhaps less effective, form of authoritative parenting, one that combines two somewhat contradictory orientations to socialization. On the one hand, membership in the middle class may incline these African American parents toward the use of psychologically based discipline techniques such as reasoning and explanation, which are fundamental components of authoritative parenting and widely touted as elements of good parenting by middle-class child-rearing experts (Hoff-Ginsberg & Tardif, 1995). On the other hand, however, the African American heritage condones the use of stricter and harsher approaches to punishment, including physical discipline (Garcia Coll, Meyer, & Brillon, 1995). In the effort to blend these sets of practices within an overall climate of authoritativeness, the effectiveness of this sort of parenting may be diminished.

The second exception to the general pattern of relations between parenting and adjustment is found in the domain of school performance. The relation between parenting, characterized as authoritative, authoritarian, or permissive, and GPA is inconsistent across ecological contexts. For example, although authoritative parenting is associated with good performance in school for almost all adolescents, the benefits of authoritative parenting on school performance are greater among adolescents from particular ethnic and social class backgrounds (i.e., among White, working- and middle-class youth). In addition, authoritarian and permissive parenting are associated with relatively poorer school performance in most niches but with better school performance in other adolescents (e.g., with permissiveness among Hispanic middle-class youth and with authoritarian parenting among Asian middle-class youth).

A final general conclusion is that, although family structure appears to moderate the relation between parenting and adolescent adjustment within some ecological niches (e.g., African American and Hispanic working class), its moderating influence generally holds little practical significance. Specifically, in all cases in which differential effects of parenting on adolescent adjustment were found, the effects varied only in magnitude and not in direction. That is, when differences in the link between parenting and adjustment are found in two-parent versus single-parent homes, these differences do not suggest that one style of parenting is beneficial in one family structure but harmful in another. Rather, the results suggest that a particular parenting style simply may be relatively more beneficial in one group than in another. For example, authoritative parenting buffers against involvement in delinquent behavior among African American middle-class adolescents in both two-parent and single-parent homes. However, there is a relatively stronger relation between authoritative parenting and adolescent delinquent behavior in single-parent homes compared to two-parent homes.

As with all research, the present study has some important limitations. First, due to concerns over having an adequate sample size within particular ecological niches, we combined divorced, widowed, and never married parents in our single-parent family structure category. Previous research indicates that it is important not only to distinguish among types of single-parent families (e.g., Hetherington, 1972) but to quantify the time since separation in cases of divorce (e.g., Wallerstein, Corbin, & Lewis, 1988). Related to this issue, we did not examine parenting and adjustment in families transformed by remarriage. The presence of a step-parent can influence the parenting style experienced by the adolescent and consequently that child's adjustment. Because we partitioned our sample into ethnic and social class ecological niches, however, there was not sufficient sample size to examine variations within the single-parent category or to include remarried families in the study.

Second, our data are limited by the self-report nature of the measures. Because all of the data come from adolescents' self-reports, we can only say that youngsters who characterize their parents in certain ways show particular patterns of behavior and psychological functioning. What this may suggest is that youngsters' subjective experience of parental behavior is an important influence on their own development and well-being. Although it may be informative to investigate whether parents' actual behavior toward their adolescents is associated in similar ways to adolescent adjustment, we do not believe that objective assessments of parental behavior are the only valid indicators of what takes place in the family. In our view, both subjective and objective measures of parenting provide an important window on children's experience in their families.

In conclusion, what can we say about parenting and adolescent adjustment in two-parent and single-parent families? Our results indicate, consistent with previous research, that single parents are less likely than married parents to use the warm, firm, and democratic parenting style that we know is associated with more adaptive adolescent development. However, it is important to bear in mind that this difference in parenting style between single- and two-parent families is relatively small in magnitude and that family structure, per se, exerts a relatively modest effect on parenting style. Furthermore, there is likely considerable variation in authoritativeness within the population of single-parent families; we suspect that less effective or diminished parenting would be most evident during the time when the family is transformed from a two-parent to a single-parent family.

The most important conclusion from this set of analyses, however, is that family structure does not meaningfully moderate the relation between parenting and adjustment across a wide variety of socioeconomic and ethnic groups. Adolescents from one- or two-parent homes who experience authoritative parenting are better adjusted than peers who experience any of the other parenting styles traditionally studied in socialization research. Virtually regardless of ethnic or social class background, across one- and two-parent homes alike, adolescents whose parents are warm and democratic and who provide limits and structure report less psychological distress and more positive self-esteem, perform better in school, and engage in less delinquent behavior than peers.

REFERENCES

Amato, P. R., & Keith, B. (1991). Parental divorce and the well-being of children: A meta-analysis. *Psychological Bulletin, 110,* 26–46.

Aseltine, R. H. (1996). Pathways linking parental divorce with adolescent depression. *Journal of Health and Social Behavior, 37,* 133–148.

Baldwin, A., Baldwin, C., & Cole, R. E. (1990). Stress-resistant families and stress-resistant children. In J. E. Rolf, A. S. Masten, D. Cicchetti, K. N. Wechterlein, & S. Weintraub (Eds.), *Risk and protective factors in the development of psychopathology* (pp. 257–280). New York: Cambridge University Press.

Baumrind, D. (1972). An exploratory study of socialization effects on Black children: Some Black-White comparisons. *Child Development, 43,* 261–267.

Baumrind, D. (1991). Parenting styles and adolescent development. In J. Brooks-Gunn, R. Lerner, & A. C. Petersen (Eds.), *The encyclopedia of adolescence* (pp. 746–758). New York: Garland.

Bronfenbrenner, U. (1979). *The ecology of human development: Experiments by nature and design.* Cambridge, MA: Harvard University Press.

Bronfenbrenner, U. (1986). Ecology of the family as a context for human development. *Developmental Psychology, 22,* 723–742.

Bronfenbrenner, U. (1989). Ecological systems theory. *Annals of Child Development, 6,* 187–249.

Bronfenbrenner, U., & Crouter, A. C. (1983). The evolution of environmental models in developmental research. In W. Kessen & P. H. Mussen (Eds.), *History, theory, and methods: Handbook of child psychology* (Vol. 1, pp. 357–414). New York: Wiley.

Chao, R. K. (1994). Beyond parental control and authoritarian parenting styles: Understanding Chinese parenting through the cultural notion of parenting. *Child Development, 65,* 1111–1119.

Children's Defense Fund. (1995). *The state of America's children yearbook.* Washington, DC: Author.

Cohen, J. (1977). *Statistical power analysis for the behavioral sciences.* New York: Academic.

Deater-Deckard, K., Dodge, K. A., Bates, J. E., & Pettit, G. S. (1996). Physical discipline, among African American and European American Mothers: Links to children's externalizing behaviors. *Developmental Psychology, 32,* 1065–1072.

Dornbusch, S. M., Carlsmith, J. M., Bushwall, S. J., Ritter, P. L., Leiderman, H., Hastorf, A. H., & Gross, R. T. (1985). Single parents, extended households, and the control of adolescents. *Child Development, 56,* 326–341.

Dornbusch, S. M., Ritter, P., Liederman, P., Roberts, D., & Fraleigh, M. (1987). The relation of parenting style to adolescent school performance. *Child Development, 58,* 1244–1257.

Emery, R. E. (1982). Interparental conflict and the children of discord and divorce. *Psychological Bulletin, 92,* 310–330.

Emery, R. E. (1988). *Marriage, divorce, and children's adjustment.* Newbury Park, CA: Sage.

Featherman, D., Spenner, K., & Tsunematsu, N. (1988). Class and the socialization of children: Constancy, change, or irrelevance. In E. M. Hetherington, R. Lerner, & M. Perlmutter (Eds.), *Child development in life-span perspective* (pp. 67–90). Hillsdale, NJ: Lawrence Erlbaum Associates.

Forehand, R., Long, N., & Brody, G. (1988). Divorce and marital conflict: Relationship to adolescent competence and adjustment in early adolescence. In E. M. Hetherington & J. D. Arestah (Eds.), *Impact of divorce, single parenting, and stepparenting on children* (pp. 135–154). Hillsdale, NJ: Lawrence Erlbaum Associates.

Forgatch, M. S., Patterson, G. R., & Skinner, M. L. (1988). A mediational model for the effect of divorce on antisocial behavior in boys. In E. M. Hetherington & J. D. Arestah (Eds.), *Impact of divorce, single parenting, and stepparenting on children* (pp. 135–154). Hillsdale, NJ: Lawrence Erlbaum Associates.

Furstenberg, F. F. (1990). Coming of age in a changing family system. In S. S. Feldman & G. R. Elliot (Eds.), *At the threshold: The developing adolescent* (pp. 147–170). Cambridge, MA: Harvard University Press.

Garcia Coll, C., Meyer, E. C., & Brillon, L. (1995). Ethnic and minority parenting. In M. Bornstein (Ed.), *Handbook of parenting: Vol. 2. Biology and ecology of parenting* (pp. 189–209). Hillsdale, NJ: Lawrence Erlbaum Associates.

Glick, P. C., & Lin, S. (1986). Recent changes in divorce and remarriage. *Journal of Marriage and the Family, 48,* 737–739.

Gold, M. (1970). *Delinquent behavior in an American city.* Belmont, CA: Brooks/Cole.

Greenberger, E., Steinberg, L., & Vaux, A. (1981). Adolescents who work: Health and behavioral consequences of job stress. *Developmental Psychology, 17,* 691–703.

Guidubaldi, J., Cleminshaw, H. K., Perry, J. D., Nastasi, B. K., & Lightel, J. (1986). The role of selected family environment factors in children's post-divorce adjustment. *Family Relations, 35,* 141–151.

Hernandez, D. J. (1988). Demographic trends and the living arrangements of children. In E. M. Hetherington & J. D. Arasteh (Eds.), *Impact of divorce, single parenting, and stepparenting on children* (pp. 3–22). Hillsdale, NJ: Lawrence Erlbaum Associates.

Hetherington, E. M. (1972). Effects of father absence on personality development in adolescent daughters. *Development Psychology, 7,* 313–326.

Hetherington, E. M. (1989). Coping with family transitions: Winners, losers, and survivors. *Child Development, 60,* 1–14.

Hetherington, E. M., Cox, M., & Cox, R. (1982). Effects of divorce on parents and children. In M. Lamb (Ed.), *Nontraditional families* (pp. 233–288). Hillsdale, NJ: Lawrence Erlbaum Associates.

Hetherington, E. M., Stanley-Hagan, M., & Anderson, E. R. (1989). Marital transitions: A child's perspective. *American Psychologist, 44,* 303–312.

Hoff-Ginsberg, E., & Tardif, T. (1995). Socioeconomic status and parenting. In M. Bornstein (Ed.), *Handbook of parenting: Vol. 2. Biology and ecology of parenting* (pp. 161–188). Hillsdale, NJ: Lawrence Erlbaum Associates.

Lin, C. C., & Fu, V. R. (1990). A comparison of child-rearing practices among Chinese, immigrant Chinese, and Caucasian-American parents. *Child Development, 61,* 429–433.

Maccoby, E., & Martin, J. (1983). Socialization in the context of the family: Parent–child interaction. In P. H. Mussen (Series Ed.) & E. M. Hetherington (Vol. Ed.), *Handbook of child psychology: Vol. 4. Socialization, personality, and social development* (4th ed., pp. 1–101). New York: Wiley.

McLanahan, S., & Sandefur, G. (1994). *Growing up with a single parent.* Cambridge, MA: Harvard University Press.

McLoyd, V. (1990). The impact of economic hardship on Black families and children: Psychological distress. Parenting, and socioemotional development. *Child Development, 61,* 311–346.

Nye, F. I. (1957). Child adjustment in broken and in unhappy unbroken homes. *Marriage and Family Living, 19,* 356–361.

Ogbu, J. U. (1981). Origins of human competence: A cultural-ecological perspective. *Child Development, 52,* 413–429.

Parke, R. D., & Buriel, R. (1998). Socialization in the family: Ethnic and ecological perspectives. In W. Damon (Series Ed.) & N. Eisenberg (Vol. Ed.), *Handbook of child psychology: Vol. 3: Social, emotional, and personality development.* New York: Wiley.

Patterson, G., & Stouthamer-Loeber, M. (1984). The correlation of family management practices and delinquency. *Child Development, 55,* 1299–1307.

Radloff, L. S. (1977). The CES-D scale: A self-report depression scale for research in the general population. *Applied Psychological Measurement, 1,* 385–401.

Rodgers, R. R. (1966). *Cornell Parent Behavior Description—An interim report.* Unpublished manuscript, Cornell University, Ithaca, NY.

Rosenberg, M. (1965). *Society and the adolescent self-image.* Princeton: Princeton University Press.

Rosenthal, R., & Rosnow, R. (1984). *Essentials of behavioral research: Methods and data analysis*. New York: McGraw-Hill.

Rosnow, R., & Rosenthal, R. (1989). Statistical procedures and the justification of knowledge in psychological science. *American Psychologist, 44*, 1276–1284.

Schaefer, E. (1965). Children's reports of parental behavior: An inventory. *Child Development, 36*, 413–424.

Sorrentino, C. (1990). The changing family in international perspective. *Monthly Labor Review, 113*, 41–58.

Steinberg, L. (1990). Interdependency in the family: Autonomy, conflict, and harmony. In S. Feldman & G. Elliot (Eds.), *At the threshold: The developing adolescent* (pp. 255–276). Cambridge, MA: Harvard University Press.

Steinberg, L., Dornbusch, S. M., & Brown, B. B. (1992). Ethnic differences in adolescent achievement: An ecological perspective. *American Psychologist, 47*, 723–729.

Steinberg, L., Mounts, N. S., Lamborn, S. D., & Dornbusch, S. M. (1991). Authoritative parenting and adolescent adjustment across varied ecological niches. *Journal of Research on Adolescence, 1*, 19–36.

Wallerstein, J. S. (1983). Children of divorce: Stress and developmental tasks. In N. Garmezy & M. Rutter (Eds.), *Stress, coping, and development in children* (pp. 265–302). New York: McGraw-Hill.

Wallerstein, J. S., Corbin, S. B., & Lewis, J. M. (1988). Children of divorce: A 10-year study. In E. M. Hetherington & J. D. Arasteh (Eds.), *Impact of divorce, single parenting, and stepparenting on children* (pp. 197–214). Hillsdale, NJ: Lawrence Erlbaum Associates.

Weinberger, D., Tublin, S., Ford, M., & Feldman, S. (1990). Preadolescents' social-emotional adjustment and selective attrition in family research. *Child Development, 61*, 1374–1386.

Weinmann, L., Steinberg, L., & Dornbusch, S. M. (1990). *Divorce, remarriage, and adolescent adjustment*. Unpublished manuscript, Temple University.

Weston, S., & Weston, W. (1987, October). *Education and the family*. Mimeo available from the Office of Educational Research and Improvement, U.S. Department of Education, Washington, DC.

PART III

Family Functioning and Child Adjustment
in Divorced and Single-Parent Families

5

Should We Stay Together
for the Sake of the Children?

E. Mavis Hetherington
University of Virginia

ONE OF THE MOST commonly asked questions about divorce is whether it is better to stay in an unhappy conflictual marriage for the sake of the children or to get divorced. In attempting to answer that question researchers have used two main strategies. First, a few investigators have compared the adjustment of children whose parents later divorce to those who do not divorce. The assumption in these studies is that marital conflict and dysfunction will have affected the adjustment of children before divorce and that many of the adverse effects on children's adjustment attributed to divorce are related to earlier marital conflict. Children whose parents later divorce show more problems than those in families that later remain intact; however, even with these predivorce levels of adjustment controlled there are significant differences in the adjustment of children in divorced and nondivorced families (Amato & Booth, 1996; Amato & Keith, 1991a; Block, Block, & Gjerde, 1986; Cherlin et al., 1991).

A second strategy involves examining the adjustment of children in high-conflict nondivorced families and in divorced families. Although there is a substantial literature on the effects of marital conflict and divorce on children's adjustment, there are few studies that directly compare children in nondivorced families with acrimonious marital relations with those in divorced families. Moreover, those that make this comparison often use marital dissatisfaction as a proxy for marital conflict (e.g., Simmons & Associates, 1996), although marital conflict is a better predictor of children's adjustment than is general marital distress or dissatisfaction (Emery & O'Leary, 1984; Johnson & O'Leary, 1987). The few studies that have made direct comparisons between high-conflict nondivorced families and divorced families suggest that the changes and stresses accompanying divorce and life in a single-parent, usually mother-headed, household may contribute more adversely to certain domains of child adjustment than does an unhappy or conflictual marriage (Amato & Booth, 1996; Simmons et al., 1996). However, these studies do not consider the level of marital conflict in divorced families, although conflict between divorced spouses often remains high or escalates following divorce (Maccoby & Mnookin, 1992; Masheter, 1991). It is important to assess the experiences and quality of relationships in the divorced families as well as in nondivorced families, and the changes in risks and resources or protective factors preceding and following divorce.

The response to divorce is influenced by the quality of family relations in the predivorce marriage, the circumstances of marital dissolution, and the experiences and changes that follow divorce. It involves an interplay between individual characteristics of parents and children, family relationships, and extrafamilial factors that serve to support or to undermine the well-being of family members as they negotiate the changes and challenges associated with divorce. Adjustment to divorce is a process that takes place over time. In the first year following divorce, notable disruptions in family roles and relationships, in parenting, and in children's adjustment occur. Restabilization of the family and a new homeostasis in family functioning usually are attained 2 to 3 years following divorce, accompanied by improvement in parent–child relations and in the adjustment of children.

Two of the main challenges confronting parents following divorce are to minimize the amount of conflict to which the child is exposed and to maintain authoritative parenting characterized by high warmth, communication, responsiveness, control and monitoring, and low coerciveness. The effects on child adjustment of other stressors often accompanying divorce are frequently mediated or moderated by the quality of parenting.

THREE STUDIES OF MARITAL TRANSITIONS

In this chapter the effects on children's adjustment of conflict and parenting in nondivorced and divorced families are examined. The data are taken from three longitudinal studies of divorce and remarriage. In the Virginia Longitudinal Study of Divorce and Remarriage (Hetherington, 1993, in press), children whose parents had divorced or who were in nondivorced families were examined in six waves from age 4 to young adulthood. Although the study started with 144 families, it was expanded in subsequent waves and by young adulthood included 450 families equally divided between nondivorced, divorced, and remarried families. The second study, the Hetherington and Clingempeel study of divorce and remarriage (Hetherington & Clingempeel, 1992), examined the effects of marital transitions on early adolescent adjustment and included 202 nondivorced, divorced, or recently remarried families studied three times. Finally, the Nonshared Environment study (Reiss et al., 1994) studied 720 nondivorced families and stepfamilies and two same-sex adolescent sibling pairs in each family twice, 4 years apart.

All studies used multimeasure, multimethod, multi-informant assessments including observations to gather information on family functioning and children's adjustment. Assessment of common constructs and many shared measures were used in all studies, often permitting the combination of data from the three studies. This chapter includes measures of marital conflict; parenting including warmth, negativity/coercion/conflict, monitoring and control, authoritativeness and parentification; and child adjustment including externalizing, internalizing, cognitive agency, social responsibility, social competence, self-esteem, and associations with delinquent peers. Some analyses include families and offspring drawn from all three studies, whereas others include data from only the Virginia Longitudinal Study; therefore, sample sizes vary widely. All of the divorced families are mother-custody families.

This chapter begins with a brief discussion of child adjustment in high-conflict nondivorced and divorced families, followed by an exploration of some family processes associated with the adjustment of children in these families.

THE ADJUSTMENT OF CHILDREN IN HIGH-CONFLICT NONDIVORCED FAMILIES AND IN DIVORCED FAMILIES

On average, children in divorced families in comparison to those in nondivorced families, and children in families with high marital conflict in comparison to those with low marital conflict, show more problems in adjustment (see Amato & Keith, 1991a; Davies & Cummings, 1994; Hetherington & Stanley-Hagan, 1997, in press, for reviews). The type of adjustment problems in children associated with marital conflict and with divorce are similar, with the largest effects obtained with externalizing disorders, lack of self-regulation, low social responsibility, and cognitive agency, and to a lesser extent with internalizing, social agency, and self-esteem. Difficulties in relations with parents, siblings, peers, and teachers also are associated with both marital conflict and divorce. Some of these childhood problems are sustained into adolescence; however, adolescence may trigger behavior problems in children in divorced families who previously have appeared to be functioning reasonably well (Hetherington, 1993).

Recent work suggests that problems in adjustment may remain in young adulthood, long after parental divorce has occurred; these may include problems in relationships in the workplace and with family and spouses, higher rates of marital instability and divorce, more behavior problems, lower socioeconomic attainment, and lower reported well-being (Amato & Keith, 1991b; Amato, Loomis, & Booth, 1995; Booth & Amato, 1994; Hetherington, in press; McLanahan & Sandefur, 1994).

Although on the average there is about a twofold or greater increase in problems such as externalizing disorders, delinquency, teen pregnancy, truancy, school dropout, substance abuse, idleness, and welfare dependency in adolescents from divorced families in comparison to nondivorced families (Hetherington, 1993; Hetherington & Clingempeel, 1992; McLanahan & Sandefur, 1994; Simmons & Associates, 1996), the vast majority of children from divorced families eventually emerge as reasonably competent individuals (Hetherington, 1993; Hetherington & Clingempeel, 1992). The increase in total behavior problems in high-conflict, non-divorced families is somewhat lower than those in divorced families, but the majority of these offspring also are resilient and eventually able to cope with their adverse life situations.

This emphasis on resiliency is not meant to minimize the distress, apprehension, confusion, and anger children experience in response to marital conflict or divorce. Marital conflict and divorce are reported by children and parents to be two of their most stressful life events (Davies & Cummings, 1994; Hetherington, 1993). It is meant to underscore the adaptability and resiliency of children and parents in coping with stressful life transitions.

Factors Contributing to Adjustment

Divorce may offer children and parents an escape from conflict and the opportunity for more fulfilling harmonious personal relationships; however, it also may be associated with an increase in risk factors that make successful parenting and the development of competent children more difficult. Both parents and children report higher rates of negative life events in divorced than in nondivorced families. Among the negative experiences associated with divorce are economic declines leading to multiple changes in residence, loss of friends, moves to poorer neighborhoods with fewer resources, inadequate schools and delinquent peer groups, lack of social supports, family conflict, parental depression, inept nonauthoritative parenting, and loss or diminished contact with the noncustodial parent. All of these variables have been associated with adjustment problems in children following divorce. In this chapter the focus is on family relations and parenting and how they differ in high-conflict nondivorced families and in divorced families because in most of our work we have found that these variables mediate or moderate many of the effects of other stressors on child development.

The effects of conflict, authoritative parenting, and parentification are discussed. Authoritative parenting is parenting that is high on warmth, involvement, responsiveness, communication, control and monitoring, and low on negativity and coercion. Parentification occurs when there is role reversal in supportive caretaking relations and the child takes on instrumental or emotional support of the parent.

Conflict

Repeated exposure to angry, acrimonious, unresolved marital conflict may lead to heightened emotional arousal, sensitization to conflict, an inability to regulate negative affect and behavior, and a lack of emotional security in children (Davies &

Cummings, 1994; Grynch & Fincham, 1993). Conversely, children may learn to regulate their emotions and solve interpersonal problems by observing their parents successfully negotiate marital conflict and solve problems in the conjugal relationship. All children are not equally vulnerable to the effects of marital conflict, and all types of marital conflict are not equally corrosive to children's adjustment. Intelligent, socially mature children with an easy temperament and an internal locus of control are better able to deal both with parental conflict and with divorce (Hetherington, 1989, 1991). In our work we have found that preadolescent boys are more vulnerable to the adverse effects of both conflict and divorce but that gender differences are found less often in adolescence (Hetherington, 1989, 1991, 1993).

Table 5.1 shows the correlations of different types of marital conflict and the child's cognitions or feelings about the conflict with total behavior problems on the Child Behavior Checklist (Achenbach & Edelbrock, 1983) for 100 fifteen-year-olds from nondivorced families and 100 from divorced mother-custody families from the Virginia Longitudinal Study of Divorce and Remarriage. All conflict is not the same in its consequences for child adjustment. Encapsulated conflict to which the child is not directly exposed has no effect on children's well-being.

TABLE 5.1
Correlations Between Different Types of Marital Conflict
and Total Behavior Problems in Adolescents

	Nondivorced (n = 100)	Divorced (n = 100)
Type of marital conflict		
I. Encapsulated		
II. Direct		
Themes		
Economic		
Household tasks		
Personal behavior of spouse	.20*	.33**
Child behavior or discipline	.36**	.52**
Strategies		
Symbolic aggression	.21*	.24*
Physical aggression	.41**	.53**
Reasoning negotiation	−.25**	−.29**
Degree of resolution	−.28**	−.37**
III. Child response		
Guilt		
Shame		
Threat	.27**	.36**
Caught in the middle	.31**	.46**
Disengagement		

Note. Only significant correlations are reported.
*p < .05. **p < .01

Conflict about the child or in which the child feels physically threatened or caught in the middle, which involves physical violence, and/or which is unresolved has the most deleterious effects on children's adjustment.

The largest correlations of marital conflict with child outcomes usually are found for externalizing; however, quarrels about the child or in which the child feels caught in the middle or responsible also are associated with anxiety and depressive symptoms in children (Buchanan, Maccoby, & Dornbusch, 1991; Grynch & Fincham, 1993; Johnston, Gonzalez, & Campbell, 1987; Jouriles et al., 1991). It was unexpected that children who responded to their parents' conflict with shame and guilt did not have elevated scores on total behavior problems: Although they had above average scores on internalizing they had below average scores on externalizing, which diminished their total behavior problems score.

Although age and gender differences are not included in Table 5.1, we have found that older children are more likely than younger children to respond negatively to and attempt to intervene in marital conflicts involving physical aggression. Girls are more likely to blame themselves for their parents' conflicts, and boys are more likely to withdraw from conflict but adolescent boys are most likely to intervene when physical threats are involved. Moderate levels of marital disagreements that may involve negative affect but also involve negotiation, compromise, and resolution are associated with greater later social problem-solving skills in offspring as young adults than either no marital conflict or high levels of hostile marital conflict. A steeling effect may occur with moderate levels of resolved marital conflict. Children learn to deal with disagreements and to solve social problems by observing parents successfully resolving their own differences.

Conflict, Child Adjustment, and Parenting Preceding Divorce.   It often is assumed that conflict diminishes following divorce, and in the long run for most couples it does as disengagement increases. However, all couples with acrimonious marriages do not divorce; fighting is an accepted way of life in some families. Moreover, in about 15% to 20% of divorced couples with children, conflict remains elevated even after the 2-year transition period following divorce. Conflict even may increase following divorce when issues involving child residence, visitation, financial support, division of property, and a variety of parental responsibilities and rights are still being worked through. Maccoby and Mnookin (1992) noted that few couples abide fully by court-ordered decisions and that many of the preceding issues undergo a continuing and dynamic process of renegotiation and change.

In addition, in a substantial group of couples (about 25% in our prospective work on divorce), an emotional divorce may occur long before the legal divorce has occurred, accompanied by avoidance, withdrawal, contemptuous disengagement, and often sadness and diminished overt conflict in the last stage of marital dissolution as the marriage is being evaluated and the decision to separate is being made. In fact, in our prospective work on divorce—involving 108 couples who later divorced, a group of high-conflict (one standard deviation or more above the mean) nondivorcing couples, and a group of moderate- to low-conflict (less than one standard deviation above the mean) nondivorcing couples—marital conflict is significantly lower in the couples who later divorced than in the high-conflict nondivorcing couples but significantly higher than in the low-conflict nondivorcing couples.

It should be noted that, in the analyses to follow, marital conflict is marital conflict to which the child was directly exposed—as reported earlier, encapsulated marital conflict to which the child is not exposed was not correlated with child adjustment. It can be seen in Table 5.2 that the adjustment of children in the families who later divorce usually falls between that of the high- and low-conflict nondivorcing groups, although it also is not usually significantly different from either. The high-conflict nondivorcing group differs from the low-conflict nondivorcing group in all assessed areas of adjustment. Children in the high-conflict nondivorcing group score higher on externalizing and internalizing and lower on cognitive agency, social responsibility, social competence, and self-esteem. Children in families who later divorce also score higher than low-conflict nondivorcing families on externalizing and lower on cognitive agency; however, they are higher than the children in the high-conflict nondivorcing families on cognitive agency. Cognitive agency is the only area where children from divorcing families differ significantly from those in high-conflict nondivorcing families. Unlike the results of other studies that only compared later-divorcing to nondivorcing families (Block et al., 1986), these findings suggest that in comparison to families with harmonious marital relations children are more disadvantaged by being in a highly acrimonious family than in being in one in which parents later divorce. Gender differences also were obtained, with boys scoring higher on externalizing and lower on social responsibility and cognitive agency than girls. However, no gender by family group interactions occurred.

TABLE 5.2

Adjustment of Children Whose Parents Will Later Divorce and
Those in High- and Low-Conflict Nondivorcing Families

	Divorcing (D)		High-Conflict Nondivorcing (HC-ND)		Low-Conflict Nondivorcing (LC-ND)		Significant Contrasts
	Boy	Girl	Boy	Girl	Boy	Girl	
Externalizing	.47	.24	.49	.29	−.18	−.28	D,HC-ND > LC-ND B > G
Internalizing	−.03	.02	.23	.21	−.15	−.13	HC-ND > LC-ND
Cognitive agency	−.20	−.01	−.42	−.23	.04	.28	LC-ND > D > HC-ND G > B
Social responsibility	−.15	−.05	−.40	−.28	.02	.19	LC-ND > HC-ND G > B
Social competence	.01	.06	−.13	−.16	.19	.17	LC-ND > HC-ND
Self-esteem	.04	−.03	−.15	−.19	.20	.16	LC-ND > HC-ND

A similar pattern emerges in parenting with parents in high-conflict nondivorcing families showing more inept parenting than those in low-conflict families. The means for parents in divorcing families were intermediate but often not significantly different from the other two groups.

Mothers in high-conflict nondivorcing families, in comparison to those in low-conflict nondivorcing families, are lower in warmth, monitoring, and control and higher in negative coercive parenting (see Table 5.3). Mothers who later divorce also are higher in negativity and lower in control than those in low-conflict nondivorcing marital relationships, but they have greater control than those in high-conflict nondivorcing families.

Fathers in high-conflict nondivorcing families show lower positivity and control and more negativity than those in low-conflict families (see Table 5.4). Fathers who later divorce also exhibit less warmth than those in low-conflict nondivorcing

TABLE 5.3

Mothers' Parenting in Couples Who Will Later Divorce and
Those in High- and Low-Conflict Nondivorcing Families

	Divorcing (D)		High-Conflict Nondivorcing (HC-ND)		Low-Conflict Nondivorcing (LC-ND)		Significant Contrasts
	Boy	Girl	Boy	Girl	Boy	Girl	
Positivity/Warmth	−.11	−.04	−.28	−.14	.07	.10	LC-ND > HC-ND
Negativity/Conflict	.16	.05	.21	−.01	−.08	−.25	D,HC-ND > LC-ND
							B > G
Monitoring	−.14	.03	−.36	−.15	.06	.14	LC-ND > HC-ND
							G > B
Control	−.13	.05	−.29	−.13	.13	.17	LC-ND > D > HC-ND

TABLE 5.4

Fathers Parenting in Couples Who Will Later Divorce and
Those in High- and Low-Conflict Nondivorcing Families

	Divorcing (D)		High-Conflict Nondivorcing (HC-ND)		Low-Conflict Nondivorcing (LC-ND)		Significant Contrasts
	Boy	Girl	Boy	Girl	Boy	Girl	
Positivity/Warmth	.09	−.04	−.05	−.22	.45	.36	LC-ND > HC-ND
							HC-ND:B > G
Negativity/Conflict	.02	.14	.11	.29	−.13	−.01	HC-ND > LC-ND
							HC-ND:G > B
Monitoring	−.16	.03	−.17	−.04	−.20	.07	G > B
Control	.02	.08	−.15	−.06	.14	.11	LC-ND > D > HC-ND

families. This was the only difference between the divorcing group and either of the other groups found for fathers.

Some gender differences also were obtained. Both mothers and fathers monitor girls' behavior more than boys' behavior, and mothers have more conflictual relations with boys than with girls. In addition, under high marital conflict, fathers are less warm and more negative to girls than to boys. This is a finding we tend to see more often with younger children than with adolescents and concurs with the work of Phil Cowan and his colleagues (Cowan, Cowan, & Schultz, 1996).

In summary, in comparison to low-conflict families, children in high-conflict families are less well adjusted and their parents exhibit less authoritative, more conflictual and coercive parenting. There are some scattered differences in the adjustment of children and in the quality of parenting in harmonious nondivorcing families and those in later divorcing families, but many fewer than those with conflictual nondivorcing families. This finding suggests that before the divorce the family dynamics leading to divorce are less deleterious than those associated with extremely high levels of overt marital conflict.

Conflict and Children's Adjustment After Divorce.   The few studies that have compared conflictual non divorced families with divorced families ignore the level of conflict in the divorced families. We tried to rectify this situation by examining the adjustment of children in high- and low-conflict divorced and nondivorced families. Furthermore, we examined the divorced families in the first 2 years after divorce and 2 or more years after divorce when considerable restabilization in divorced families had occurred.

Figures 5.1 and 5.2 show somewhat different pictures for the adjustment of boys and girls following divorce. In the first 2 years following divorce, a higher percentage of girls in both high- and low-conflict divorced families score above the clinical cutoff on the Child Behavior Checklist than those in high-conflict nondivorced families, and fewer girls in the low-conflict nondivorced families score above the cutoff than in any of the other three groups. In the first 2 years following divorce, a greater percentage of boys from high-conflict divorced families and a lower percentage of boys from low-conflict nondivorced families are above the clinical cutoff than in the other groups. The low-conflict divorced and high-conflict nondivorced groups are not significantly different from each other. The divorce per se, regardless of the level of conflict initially, seems to be affecting the girls, whereas boys are responding differentially both to divorce and to the level of conflict within the divorced families. Two years after divorce, conflict in a divorced family has more adverse effects on both boys and girls than conflict in a nondivorced family. However, the adjustment of girls in low-conflict nondivorced and divorced families is similar, whereas more boys in low-conflict divorced families are still showing serious problems than those in low-conflict nondivorced families.

If conflict is going to continue, it is better for children to remain in an acrimonious two-parent household than to divorce. If there is a shift to a more harmonious

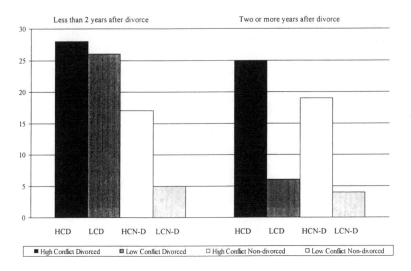

FIG. 5.1.   Percentage of girls scoring above the clinical cutoff on total behavior problems.

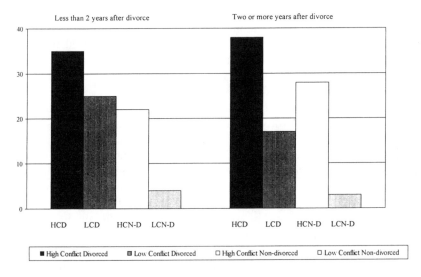

FIG. 5.2.   Percentage of boys scoring above the clinical cutoff on total behavior problems.

household a divorce is advantageous to both boys and girls. However, even with low acrimony between the divorced couple, boys in divorced families are disadvantaged over those in nondivorced families. The gender differences maybe attributable to boys being more sensitive to the relative unavailability of fathers and to the fact that in these mother-custody families divorced mothers and preadolescent boys are more likely to be involved in difficult coercive parent–child relationships.

Conflict and Parenting. The previous discussion of marital conflict and child adjustment is oversimplified. The marital relationship is often viewed as the cornerstone of good family functioning, and certainly a positive marital relationship is associated with authoritative parenting and positive parent–child and sibling relationships (Davies & Cummings, 1994). In contrast, marital conflict is associated with low parental warmth and monitoring, with ineffective, inconsistent control, and with high negativity, coerciveness, and conflict in parent–child and sibling relationships (Cowan et al., 1996; Davies & Cummings, 1994; Simmons & Associates, 1996). The key to the link between marital conflict and child adjustment seems to be parenting. The direct effects of marital conflict on child adjustment are usually found to be small or nonexistent (Davies & Cummings, 1994). They largely are mediated or moderated by the quality of parenting. For younger children the effects of parenting on adjustment are direct and powerful. For adolescents a substantial portion of the effects of parenting are mediated by the peer group, as discussed in a later section on modeling in this chapter.

An ANOVA involving family type (high-conflict divorced, low-conflict divorced, high-conflict nondivorced, low-conflict nondivorced), sex of the child, and mother and father authoritative parenting combination was performed on scores for total behavior problems on the Child Behavior Checklist (Achenbach & Edelbrock, 1983). Significant main effects were obtained for family types, gender, and parenting combination. However, these effects were qualified by complex higher order interactions.

Table 5.5 presents the means and significant contrasts for boys and girls with four different combinations of parenting in high-conflict and low-conflict divorced and nondivorced families. If authoritative parenting, characterized by high warmth, responsiveness, communication, and monitoring can be maintained, the effects of marital conflict are greatly reduced. In nondivorced families there is a protective effect against the adverse effect of marital conflict of even one parent being authoritative but a greater effect of both being authoritative. Moreover, under high conflict, girls in nondivorced families benefit more from authoritative mothers than fathers. In divorced families, however, the parenting of the custodial mother is more salient than that of the noncustodial father for both boys and girls. Under conditions of high conflict between the divorced spouses and a nonauthoritative custodial parent, an authoritative noncustodial parent is an ineffective buffer. Under low conflict, an authoritative father can to some extent protect sons but not daughters from the adverse consequences of the mother's nonauthoritative parenting. This is part of the reason why a significant association between frequency of visitation by the noncustodial parent and child adjustment is rarely found. The effects of visitation depend on the circumstances of visitation and the qualities of the visiting parent. Under conditions of low-conflict visitation by a reasonably well-adjusted (i.e., nondepressed, non-antisocial), authoritative noncustodial parent can have benefits for the adjustment of the child, and these benefits vary with the sex of the child and parent. Under these conditions authoritative

TABLE 5.5

Total Behavior Problems in Adolescents in High- and Low-Conflict Nondivorced
and Divorced Families Under Different Parenting Combinations

Authoritativeness of Parent	Nondivorced (ND)				Divorced Mother Custody (D)			
	M↓F↓	M↓F↑	M↑F↓	M↑F↑	M↓F↓	M↓F↑	M↑F↓	M↑F↑
High conflict								
Boys (B)	62.7	54.2	56.6	42.1	74.2	69.4	58.2	54.6
Girls (G)	59.5	52.4	46.1	40.0	67.9	64.3	54.7	53.9
Low conflict								
Boys (B)	56.1	41.9	44.2	37.4	66.7	56.8	47.3	40.5
Girls (G)	53.2	44.1	42.1	35.3	58.5	57.8	43.9	39.5

Significant contrasts	
B > G	HC-ND-G: M↓F↓ > M↓F↑ > M↑F↓ > M↑F↑
HC > LC	LC-ND: M↓F↓ > M↓F↑, M↑F↓ > M↑F↑
D > ND	HC-D: M↓F↓, M↓F↑ > M↑F↓, M↑F↑
M↓F↓ > M↓F↑, M↑F↓ > M↑F↑	LC-D-B: M↓F↓ > M↓F↑ > M↑F↓ > M↑F↑
HC-D > HC-ND	LC-D-G: M↓F↓, M↓F↑ > M↑F↓, M↑, F↓
HC-ND-B: M↓F↓ > M↓F↑, M↑F↓ > M↑F↑	LC-B: D-M↓F↓, M↓F↑ > ND-M↓F↓, M↓F↑
	LC-G: D-M↓F↑ > ND-M↓F↑

noncustodial fathers are associated with decreased antisocial behavior and higher
social responsibility in sons but have no effect on the adjustment of daughters.

The Relation Among Marital Conflict, Parental Antisocial Behavior, Parenting, Antisocial Peers, and Externalizing in Adolescents

A mediational model of factors that contribute to externalizing in adolescent
boys and girls in divorced and nondivorced families was examined with structural
equation modeling. Figure 5.3 presents the model for fathers and externalizing in
boys ($N = 138$ nondivorced, $N = 123$ divorced families), Fig. 5.4 for fathers and girls
($N = 136$ nondivorced, 121 divorced families), Fig. 5.5 for mothers and boys ($N =$
139 nondivorced, 118 divorced families), and Fig. 5.6 for mothers and girls ($N =$
136 nondivorced, 116 divorced families). Dotted lines indicated nonsignificant
paths, and solid lines significant paths. Ideally mothers and fathers would have
been included in the same model, but this was precluded by sample size. In addition, because of sample size, multiple indicators of a construct were composited,
and all constructs were treated as observed rather than as latent variables. The χ^2
were satisfactory and the goodness of fit for all models were .97 or above.

In all models for both mothers and fathers and boys and girls in divorced and
nondivorced families the effects of marital conflict are indirect and are mediated
by increases in negative coercive relations with children and declines in authoritative parenting. Parental antisocial behavior shows a similar but usually smaller relationship with parenting; however, fathers' antisocial behavior in nondivorced

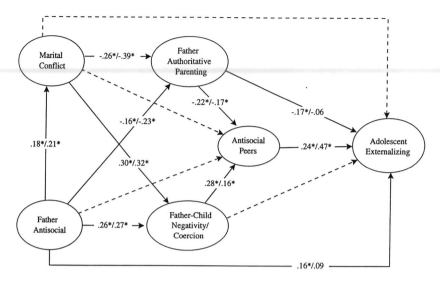

FIG. 5.3. Marital conflict, fathers' antisocial behavior, parenting, antisocial peers, and externalizing in adolescent boys. Nondivorced families are on left; divorced families are on right. Dotted lines are insignificant paths. *p < .05.

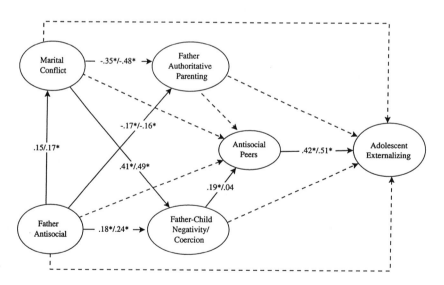

FIG. 5.4. Marital conflict, fathers' antisocial behavior, parenting, antisocial peers, and externalizing in adolescent girls. Nondivorced families are on left; divorced families are on right. Dotted lines are insignificant paths. *p < .05.

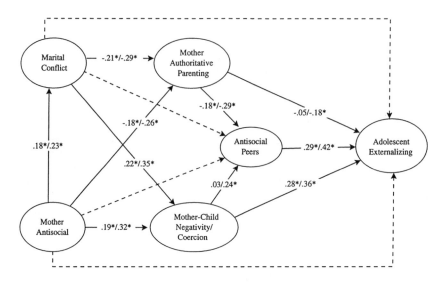

FIG. 5.5.   Marital conflict, mothers' antisocial behavior, parenting, antisocial peers, and externalizing in adolescent boys. Nondivorced families are on left; divorced families are on right. Dotted lines are insignificant paths. *p < .05.

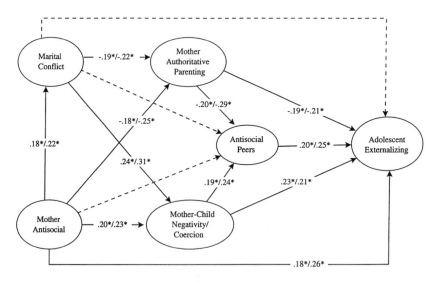

FIG. 5.6.   Marital conflict, mothers' antisocial behavior, parenting, antisocial peers, and externalizing in adolescent girls. Nondivorced families are on left; divorced families are on right. Dotted lines are insignificant paths. *p < .05.

families but not in divorced families is directly linked with externalizing behavior in boys but not girls. Mothers' antisocial behavior is directly associated with externalizing in girls but not in boys in both nondivorced and divorced families. The path is larger for divorced girls. A behavioral genetic theory might predict that the direct links between antisocial behavior in parents and children would be similar across family type and gender. Our results are more congruent with an identification theory where children are prone to identify with and model the behaviors of a same-sex residential parent.

It has been proposed that fathers have a greater influence than mothers on the development of externalizing behavior, especially in sons. Our models in this study suggest that fathers do not contribute more than mothers to the development of externalizing in children but that the paths by which they influence children differ. In addition, past studies also have found noncustodial fathers to be less influential on their children's development than custodial mothers in divorced families or fathers in nondivorced families (see Hetherington & Stanley-Hagan, 1997, in press, for a review). Our models support this position.

The only direct influence of fathers' parenting on externalizing is found in the negative association between authoritative parenting in nondivorced fathers and externalizing in sons. Fathers have a greater influence on the development of externalizing in sons than in daughters, however. The effects of fathers' authoritative parenting and conflict negativity are largely mediated through association with antisocial peers. Moreover, the effects of noncustodial fathers on sons' externalizing is less than that of custodial fathers, and noncustodial fathers have no effect either direct or indirect on the development of externalizing in daughters. Even in nondivorced families, fathers influence daughters only through paternal negativity, with coercion related to greater association with antisocial peers by girls. Thus fathers' inept nonauthoritative or coercive conflictual parenting led children to drift into or seek relationships with antisocial peers and through these peer associations to become more antisocial, disruptive, and noncompliant.

In contrast to fathers, mothers' authoritative parenting and conflict negativity are associated with adolescents' externalizing behavior both directly and indirectly through association with antisocial peers. These associations are somewhat larger and more consistently found with divorced custodial mothers, and the pattern is very similar for sons and daughters. This finding contrasts with that for fathers, where effects are greater and more consistently found with nondivorced fathers and are largely confined to sons.

In all models the largest and most consistently obtained paths are between the association with antisocial peers and adolescent externalizing, and these paths are greater for adolescents with divorced than with nondivorced parents. With younger children we have found that the effects of parenting on adjustment are mainly direct rather than moderated through peer associations.

Past research has found that children in divorced families in comparison to those in nondivorced families spend less time under the supervision of adults, spend more time with peers, and are more influenced by peer behavior (Dorn-busch et al., 1985; Hetherington, 1983). In our work we have found that about one quarter of adolescents in divorced families, in comparison to 10% in nondivorced families, disengage from their families, spending little time in shared family activities and as little time at home as possible. This disengagement is related to family conflict including marital and sibling conflict but is most strongly related to parent–child conflict. High conflict in families is rarely confined only to one family subsystem but tends to pervade the entire family system. Conflict is more strongly associated with adolescent disengagement in divorced than nondivorced families. Disengagement can be a constructive solution to an unhappy acrimonious family situation if the adolescent remains involved with a concerned caring adult such as a parent of a friend, a grandparent, a teacher, a coach, or even an adult sibling living outside the home. Some disengaged adolescents used the parents of friends as surrogate parents and spent most of their time at the friends' homes. However, if the disengaged adolescent lacks the involvement of a caring adult and becomes associated with an antisocial peer group, behavior problems escalate. We have found this risk particularly in early-maturing girls. Especially in divorced mother-headed families, the combination of early physical maturing in daughters, an antisocial or overtly sexually active mother, high conflict, and low authoritative parenting leads to association with an older often antisocial peer group and precocious sexual activity and substance use.

Parentification

It has frequently been remarked that children in divorced single-parent households grow up faster (Weiss, 1979), in part because of their greater number of unsupervised activities and greater power in family decision making. Recent evidence suggests that it also may be attributable to greater parentification, a type of role of reversal where the child assumes roles usually considered to be parental roles (Johnston, 1990; Walper, 1998). Two types of parentification have been identified—instrumental parentification, which involves such things as household tasks and care of siblings, and emotional parentification, which involves emotional support or acting as an advisor or confidant for a needy parent. Increased parentification has been associated not only with divorce but also with maternal depression and marital conflict and with outcomes in offspring such as depression, anxiety, and compulsive caretaking (Hops et al., 1987; Radke-Yarrow et al., 1995; Valleau, Bergner, & Horton, 1995). Almost all research has focused on parentification by mothers, in part because fathers disclose or confide in their children much less often than do mothers, although instrumental parentification may be found with both parents assigning tasks to children. In the analyses that follow, instrumental parentification was a general measure of tasks performed including such things as preparing family meals, doing yard work or dishes, repairing things around the house, and bathing or dressing a younger sibling. Because the parent who assigned the task was not found to be important the measure was not broken down into tasks assigned by the mother and those assigned by the father. However, the emotional parentification measure differentiates between confidences, advice, and support seeking by mothers and fathers because the effects of emotional parentification by mothers and fathers differed.

The Hetherington Parentification Inventory was used to assess parentification. In these analyses instrumental parentification was based on residential parent and child reports. Maternal parentification was based on child and mother reports, and paternal parentification was based on child and father reports.

A MANOVA was run examining the effects of high and low conflict, family type (i.e., divorced, nondivorced), and sex of the child on instrumental parentification and emotional parentification by mothers and fathers. For instrumental parentification, no significant effect was found for conflict and only a marginally significant effect of sex of child ($p < .10$) was found, with girls receiving more instrumental parentification than boys. However, a significant family type effect was obtained. Adolescents in divorced families were assigned more tasks and expected to assume more responsibilities than those in either high- or low-conflict nondivorced families.

In contrast, as can be seen in Table 5.6, family type, conflict, and sex of child were all significant in emotional parentification. Fathers exhibit much less emotional parentification than mothers, but girls encounter more emotional parentification from both mothers and fathers than do boys. High emotional parentification of boys was most likely to occur if the son was an only or eldest child. Emotional parentification of girls by both mothers and fathers was most likely to be seen in high-conflict divorced families, next in high-conflict nondivorced families, then low-conflict divorced families, and least in low-conflict nondivorced families. For boys, a family type but not a conflict effect was obtained, with sons in divorced families more likely than those in nondivorced families to encounter support seeking and self-disclosure from mothers and fathers.

What are the consequences of parentification, and how do they vary for boys and girls in different types of families? Separate multiple regressions were run for social responsibility, internalizing, and externalizing using family process variables in adolescence to predict the adjustment of young adult offspring. In all regressions, gender, family type, and conflict were entered in the first block, instrumental parentification, mothers' emotional parentification, and fathers' emotional parentification in adolescence in a second block, and the interactions among the variables in block 1 and block 2 in a third block. As found in previous analyses, a nondivorced family and a low-conflict family contributed to higher levels of social responsibility and lower levels of externalizing and internalizing. Young adult females were more depressed and responsible and lower in externalizing than were males.

We had expected that emotional parentification might have more adverse consequences in divorced families where only one residential parent was present, but that was not the case. There were no significant family type or conflict interactions with parentification in predicting young adult adjustment.

TABLE 5.6
Emotional Parentification

	Nondivorced (ND)		Divorced (D)		Significant Main Effects and Interactions	Significant Contrasts
	High Conflict (HC)	Low Conflict (LC)	High Conflict (HC)	Low Conflict (LC)		
Mother emotional parentification						
Boys (B)	.11	.06	.27	.24	Gender family type conflict	G > B D > ND HC > LC
Girls (G)	.42	.29	.58	.40	Gender × Family type × Conflict interaction	G:HC-D > HC-ND,LC-D > LC-ND B:D > ND
Father emotional parentification						
Boys (B)	−.41	−.49	−.07	−.14	Gender family type Conflict	G > B D > ND HC > LC
Girls (G)	−.02	−.21	.22	.09	Gender × Family type × Conflict interaction	G:HC-D > HC-ND,LC-D > LC-ND B:D > ND

   High levels of both instrumental and emotional parentification were associated with depressed or anxious internalizing behaviors in daughters but not in sons, with one exception. Young adult sons with fathers who were high in emotional parentification also were depressed. Mothers' emotional parentification also was associated with greater social responsibility in both sons and daughters. Fathers' emotional parentification was not related to the adjustment of daughters, and later analysis revealed that it was not a linear relation for sons. Because a nonlinear relation was found for sons, subsequent MANOVAS were run examining the effects of gender and parentification (divided into low, medium, and high levels of parentification) on internalizing, externalizing, and social responsibility. As can be seen in Fig. 5.7, although moderate levels of emotional parentification by fathers increased social responsibility, very high levels were associated with a decline in social responsibility, an increase in internalizing, and a marginally significant ($p < .10$) in-

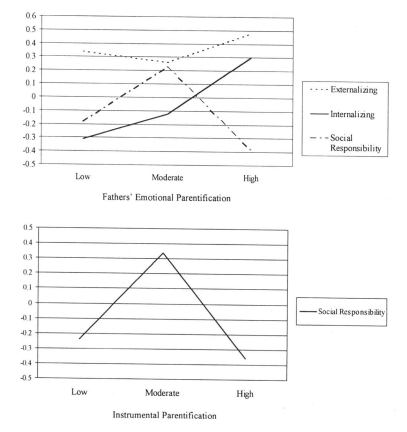

FIG. 5.7. Fathers' emotional parentification and parents' instrumental parentification and the adjustment of young adult sons.

crease in externalizing. This behavior did not involve aggressive acts but subtle resistance and noncompliance to authority, not completing tasks such as homework or household tasks, truancy, breaking curfews, and some substance use. Thus, for sons with extremely high emotionally parentifying fathers a picture emerges of anxiety and depression with unregulated irresponsible behavior. Emotional parentification occurs much less frequently with fathers than with mothers: Rates of emotional parentification average almost a full standard deviation lower in fathers than mothers. Moreover, fathers who scored extremely high on emotional parentification also had higher rates of alcohol consumption, antisocial behavior, and neuroticism than those with low or moderate emotional parentification. These associated father characteristics also may be contributing to problems in the adjustment of boys. Problems in adjustment such as depression and antisocial behavior also were linked to excessively high emotional parentification in mothers, but the association between parental adjustment and emotional parentification was smaller in mothers than fathers. This may be because self-disclosure and help seeking is more atypical, deviant, and less accepted in males.

A similar nonlinear relationship was obtained for instrumental parentification on social responsibility in sons. Sons with moderate levels of household and caretaking tasks show the highest level of social responsibility. Those exposed to very low or to high levels of instrumental parentification in adolescence—especially those who felt overburdened or that their tasks were interfering with social relationships, activities such as sports and extracurricular school programs, and even academic performance—are the least responsible in adulthood. Heavily overloaded sons resent and rebel against responsibility. In contrast, there is a linear association between instrumental parentification and social responsibility in daughters.

Maternal emotional parentification of daughters was greater than of sons especially in high-conflict divorced families. Divorced mothers often talk of their close companionate relationship with their daughters, and they frequently describe daughters as like a friend or a sister and feel they can discuss anything with them. Emotionally parentifying mothers but not fathers report greater feelings of closeness to sons and daughters. Very low confiding and support seeking is associated with distant, often rejecting or conflictual relationships between mothers and daughters. The direction of effects in this association is open to question. Do mothers develop closer feelings to daughters because they have confided in them, or are mothers more likely to self-disclose to daughters with whom they already have a close relationship?

The content of the mothers' self-disclosures is important to the well-being of daughters. Disclosures about intimate and sexual relationships are associated with earlier initiation of sexual relationships and increased externalizing behavior in girls, whereas expressing concerns about economic factors, employment, task overload, and loneliness is associated with increased social responsibility and depression. Moreover, disclosures that involve high levels of caring, complaining, and criticism about the father sometimes leads to a backlash, with both sons and daughters withdrawing and feeling less close to the mother.

Although mothers may find close confiding relationships with daughters gratifying, how do children feel about carrying the emotional burden of a needy parent? Both sons and daughters, but especially daughters, resent and are often angry and irritated by very high maternal emotional parentification but are sympathetic, supportive, and concerned at moderate levels of parentification. However, even supportive children may find the weight of carrying their parents' concerns difficult. One daughter who had been very loyal to an emotionally parentifying mother through an extremely contentious divorce, in trying to explain why she wanted to go away to boarding school, ruefully said, "Mother, I need room to be a fifteen-year-old."

The situation differs with fathers. Low levels of paternal emotional parentification often are associated with feelings of increased warmth, sympathy, and closeness by children, but even moderate levels of paternal emotional parentification are disconcerting, and high levels are sometimes reported to be repugnant. Adolescent children hold sex-stereotyped views of desirable male and female behavior. Vulnerability and emotional neediness are less acceptable in fathers than in mothers, especially to sons.

One 14-year-old boy from a divorced family described an encounter with his father as follows:

Dad picked me up. He had been drinking. He had been passed over for a promotion. He started blubbering about what a failure he was and how lonely he was and how he missed mom and us kids. He always gets maudlin when he drinks. He was crying so hard he had to pull over to the side of the road. He said what can I do? What was I supposed to say? I was totally grossed out and embarrassed. The guy should get a grip.

In summary, children are often less cared for and more overburdened by responsibilities following divorce. Needy, distressed, lonely, or angry parents may force children into the role of servant, caretaker, adviser, confidant, ally, defender, or arbitrator. Some responsibility and nurturing of others may enhance development and lead to more responsible, competent, empathic behavior in adulthood, especially in daughters (Hetherington, 1989). Excessively high demands may lead to competence and responsibility accompanied by feelings of self-doubt, depression, low self-esteem, a lurking sense of failure, and apprehension about performance and personal adequacy in young adult daughters. In our cluster analyses of adjustment, divorced girls were more likely than nondivorced girls to fall into a cluster we labeled "Competent at a cost," characterized by low antisocial behavior, high social and cognitive agency, and high social responsibility but also by elevated depression and low self-worth. Girls with highly emotionally parentifying mothers were overrepresented in this cluster.

Boys are less likely to be leaned on for emotional support by parents, and moderate levels of both instrumental and emotional parentification can increase responsibility in adult sons. However, boys are more sensitive than girls to emotional parentification by fathers and are more likely to resist, rebel, and withdraw from the family when excessive paternal emotional parentification or instrumental parentification occurs, although they too are often anxious and depressed.

Although divorced parents may lean on children, children cannot solve their parents' problems or salvage a lonely, unhappy, angry, or distressed parent. The costs to children may be great in the loss of normal childhood experiences and pleasures and opportunities for individuation and freedom from an enmeshed relationship. Our work suggests that the most effective solution for such difficulties in parents is the formation of an intimate caring relationship with a new partner.

SUMMARY

We return now to the question of whether it is better to stay in an unhappy or conflictual marriage for the sake of the children or to divorce. Both high overt conflict in nondivorced families and divorce put children at greater risk for encountering disruptions in parenting and for developing psychological and behavioral problems. Amato and Keith (1991), in their meta-analysis of divorce and children's adjustment, pointed out that the effect sizes of divorce on adjustment are relatively modest, with the largest occurring for behavior problems. Still, a twofold increase in such things as school dropout, truancy, teenaged pregnancy, teenaged idleness, and the percentage of adolescents scoring above the clinical cutoff on standardized measures such as the Child Behavior Checklist is not trivial. Moreover, the facts that the effects of divorce and parental marital conflict are pervasive and affect so many domains of child development and that the effects of divorce persist into adulthood give reason for concern. The additional stresses that often accompany divorce and the lack of a second residential adult who can play a protective role if the primary caregiver is uninvolved, nonauthoritative, inept, hostile, neglecting, or parentifying may put children at greater risk in divorced than in high-conflict nondivorced families.

It has become fashionable to say that it is family process rather than family structure that is important in children's adjustment, and that is certainly true. However, divorce is associated with an increased probability of experiencing a series of risk factors (such as economic declines, stressful life events, conflict, psychological, behavioral, and health problems in parents, and adverse ecological settings with few resources) that disrupt family processes and undermine parenting and the adjustment of children. Parents and children, although suffering some initial perturbations in adjustment following divorce, can adapt well to their new situation if it is harmonious, if additional or increased stress is not encountered, and most important if the custodial parent is able to sustain authoritative parenting and avoid excessive parentification. The evidence is clear that moving from a conflictual, stressful, unsatisfying two-parent household with destructive parent–child relationships to a nonconflictual, less stressful, more gratifying divorced single-parent household is advantageous to both parents and children. Amato et al. (1995) recently reported that young adults who had perceived their parents' marriages as conflictual were lower in psychological distress and higher in overall life satisfaction, marital happiness, and positive social relationships when they were young adults if their parents had divorced when they were children than if they had not divorced. However, the reverse was true if they had perceived their parents' marriage as not being conflictual. Then divorce was associated with more adverse outcomes as young adults.

The answer to our question about staying together for the sake of the children appears to be that if the stresses and disruptions in family processes, associated with an unhappy conflictual marriage and that erode the well-being of children, are reduced by the move to a divorced single-parent family, divorce may be advantageous. If the diminished resources and increased risks associated with divorce also are accompanied by inept parenting and sustained or increased conflict, not only between the divorced couple but also between parents and children and siblings, it is better for children if parents remain in an unhappy marriage. Unfortunately, these "ifs" are difficult to determine when parents are considering divorce.

REFERENCES

Achenbach, T. M., & Edelbrock, C. S. (1983). *Manual for the Child Behavior Checklist and Revised Child Behavior Profile*. New York: Queen City Printers.

Amato, P. R., & Booth, A. (1996). A prospective study of divorce and parent–child relationships. *Journal of Marriage and the Family, 58,* 356–365.

Amato, P. R., & Keith, B. (1991a). Parental divorce and the well-being of children: A meta-analysis. *Psychological Bulletin, 110,* 26–46.

Amato, P. R., & Keith, B. (1991b). Parental divorce and adult well-being: A meta-analysis. *Journal of Marriage and the Family, 53,* 43–58.

Amato, P. R., Loomis, L. S., & Booth, A. (1995). Parental divorce, marital conflict, and offspring well-being during early adulthood. *Social Forces, 73,* 895–915.

Block, J. H., Block, J., & Gjerde, P. F. (1986). The personality of children prior to divorce: A prospective study. *Child Development, 57,* 827–840.

Booth, A., & Amato, P. R. (1994). Parental marital quality, parental divorce and relations with parents. *Journal of Marriage and the Family, 56,* 21–34.

Buchanan, C. M., Maccoby, E. E., & Dornbusch, S. M. (1991). Caught between parents: Adolescents' experience in divorced homes. *Child Development, 62,* 1008–1029.

Cherlin, A. J., Furstenberg, F. F., Chase-Lansdale, P. L., Kiernan, K. E., Robins, P. K., Morrison, D. R., & Teitler, J. O. (1991). Longitudinal studies of effects of divorce in children in Great Britain and the United States. *Science, 252,* 1386–1389.

Cowan, P. A., Cowan, C., & Schulz, M. S. (1996). Thinking about risk and resilience in families. In E. M. Hetherington & E. Blechman (Eds.), *Stress, coping and resiliency in children and families* (pp. 1–38). Hillsdale, NJ: Lawrence Erlbaum Associates.

Davies, P. T., & Cummings, M. E. (1994). Marital conflict and child adjustment: An emotional security hypothesis. *Psychological Bulletin, 116,* 387–411.

Dornbusch, S. M., Carlsmith, J. M., Bushwall, S. J., Ritter, P. L., Liederman, H., Hsdorf, H., & Gross, R. T.

(1985). Single parents, extended households, and the control of adolescents. *Child Development, 56,* 326–341.

Emery, R. E., & O'Leary, K. D. (1984). Marital discord and child behavior problems in a nonclinic sample. *Journal of Abnormal Child Psychology, 12,* 411–420.

Grynch, J. H., & Fincham, F. D. (1993). Children's appraisals of marital conflict: Initial investigations of the cognitive and contextual framework. *Child Development, 64,* 215–230.

Hetherington, E. M. (1989). Coping with family transitions: Winners, losers, and survivors. *Child Development, 60,* 1–14.

Hetherington, E. M. (1991). The role of individual differences in family relations in coping with divorce and remarriage. In P. Cowan & E. M. Hetherington (Eds.), *Advances in family research: Volume 2. Family transitions* (pp. 323–348). Hillsdale, NJ: Lawrence Erlbaum Associates.

Hetherington, E. M. (1993). An overview of the Virginia Longitudinal Study of divorce and remarriage with a focus on early adolescence. *Journal of Family Psychology, 7,* 39–56.

Hetherington, E. M. (in press). Social capital and the development of youth from nondivorced, divorced and remarried families. In A. Collins (Ed.), *Relationships as developmental contexts: The 29th Minnesota Symposium on Child Psychology.* Mahwah, NJ: Lawrence Erlbaum Associates.

Hetherington, E. M., & Clingempeel, G. (1992). Coping with marital transitions: A family systems perspective. *Monographs of the Society for Research in Child Development, 57,* (2–3, Serial No. 227).

Hetherington, E. M., & Stanley-Hagan, M. S. (1997). The effects of divorce on fathers and their children. In M. Lamb (Ed.), *The role of the father in child development* (pp. 191–211). New York: Wiley.

Hetherington, E. M., & Stanley-Hagan, P. (in press). Divorce and the adjustment of children: A risk and resiliency perspective. *The Journal of Child Psychology and Psychiatry.*

Hops, H., Biglan, A., Sherman, L., Arthur, J., Friedman, L., & Osteem, V. (1987). Home observation of family interactions of depressive women. *Journal of Consulting and Clinical Psychology, 55,* 341–346.

Johnson, P. L., & O'Leary, K. D. (1987). Parental behavior patterns and conduct disorders in girls. *Journal of Abnormal Child Psychology, 15,* 573–581.

Johnston, J. R., Gonzalez, R., & Campbell, L. E. (1987). Ongoing post-divorce conflict and child disturbance. *Journal of Abnormal Child Psychology, 15,* 497–509.

Johnston, J. (1990). Role diffusion and role reversal: Structural variations in divorced families and children's functioning. *Family Relations, 39,* 405–413.

Juriles, E. N., Murphy, C. M., Farres, A. M., Smith, D. A., Richters, J. E., & Waters, E. (1991). Marital adjustment, parental disagreements about childrearing, and behavior problems in boys: Increasing the specificity of the marital assessment. *Child Development, 62,* 1424–1433.

Maccoby, E. E., & Mnookin, R. H. (1992). *Dividing the child: Social and legal dilemmas of custody.* Cambridge, MA: Harvard University Press.

McLanahan, S., & Sandefur, G. (1994). *Growing up with a single parent: What hurts, what helps.* Cambridge, MA: Harvard University Press.

Masheter, C. (1991). Post divorce relationships between ex-spouses: The role of attachment and interpersonal conflict. *Journal of Marriage and the Family, 53,* 101–110.

Reiss, D., Plomin, R., Hetherington, E. M., Howe, G., Rovine, M., Tyron, A., & Stanley-Hagan, M. (1994). The separate worlds of teenaged siblings: An introduction to the study of nonshared environment and adolescent development. In E. M. Hetherington, D. Reiss, & R. Plomin (Eds.), *Nonshared environment* (pp. 64–110). Hillsdale, NJ: Lawrence Erlbaum Associates.

Simmons, R. L., & Associates. (1996). *Understanding differences between divorced and intact families: Stress, interaction and child outcome.* Thousand Oaks, CA: Sage.

Valleau, M. D., Bergner, R. M., & Horton, C. B. (1995). Parentification and caretaker syndrome: An empirical investigation. *Family Therapy, 22,* 157–164.

Walper, S. (1998, February). *Parentification and triangulation in divorced families: Stressful family dynamics and adolescent development.* Paper presented at the meetings of the Society for Research in Adolescence, San Diego, CA.

Weiss, R. S. (1979). Growing up a little faster: The experience of growing up in a single-parent household. *Journal of Social Issues, 35,* 97–111.

6

Father Absence and
the Welfare of Children

Sara S. McLanahan
*Bendheim-Thoman Center for Research on Child Wellbeing,
Princeton University*

INCREASES IN DIVORCE and out-of-wedlock childbearing have dramatically altered the family life of American children. Whereas in the early 1960s, nearly 90% of all children lived with both of their biological parents until they reached adulthood, today less than half of children grow up with both natural parents. Nearly a third are born to unmarried parents, the majority of whom never live together, and another third are born to married parents who divorce before their children reach adulthood. To further complicate matters, a substantial number of children are exposed to multiple marital disruptions and multiple father figures.

These changes have created tremendous uncertainty in children's lives and have led to considerable speculation among policy makers and the public more generally about the consequences of father absence. Some analysts argue that growing up with a single mother is the primary cause of many of the country's most serious social problems, including poverty, high school dropout, teen pregnancy, and delinquency (Blankenhorn, 1995; Popenoe, 1988, 1996; Whitehead, 1993). Others argue that poverty and economic insecurity are the real culprits, causing both father absence and adolescent behavioral problems (Skolnick, 1991; Stacy, 1993). Still others claim that the problems associated with family disruption are rooted in marital discord that begins long before the parents separate or divorce.

To bring empirical evidence to bear on this debate, my colleagues and I have been analyzing several large, nationally representative surveys that contain information on children's family structure while they are growing up as well as their educational attainment and social adjustment in young adulthood. In this chapter, I summarize the major findings from this work as it pertains to the following questions:

- Are children raised apart from their biological fathers worse off than children raised by both parents? How large are the differences, and which groups of children are most affected?
- What factors account for the lower achievement of children in one-parent families? What factors are associated with resilience? Finally,
- Do differences in children's well-being predate family disruption, or are they a consequence of father absence?

Our investigation has been going on for over 10 years now and covers more than 10 data sets. The most important of these are the Panel Study of Income Dynamics (PSID), the National Longitudinal Survey of Youth (NLSY), the High School and Beyond Study (HSB), and the National Survey of Families and Households (NSFH). All these surveys are large enough to allow us to distinguish among different types of single parent families, including families headed by never-married mothers as well as families headed by divorced or separated mothers and remarried mothers. These surveys also allow us to assess differences between boys and girls raised in one- and two-parent families as well as differences between children of different racial and ethnic backgrounds and different social classes.[1]

To summarize briefly, we find that children who grow up apart from their biological fathers do less well, on average, than children who grow up with both natural parents. They are less likely to finish high school and attend college, less likely to find and keep a steady job, and more likely to become teen mothers. The differences are not huge. Indeed, most children who grow up with single parents do quite well. Nor are the differences large enough to support the claim that father absence is the major cause of our country's most serious social problems. However,

---

[1] The PSID is a study of 5,000 families followed since 1968. The primary objective of this survey was to measure family income dynamics, and therefore these data are very useful for addressing questions about the relations between father absence and family income. The PSID follows the children of panel families after they leave home and set up their own households, and therefore these data can be used to examine outcomes in young adulthood, such as graduating from high school and college, getting a steady job, and early marriage and childbearing. The NLSY is a sample of approximately 13,000 young adults who were first interviewed in 1979 when they were between the ages of 14 and 21 years. Like the PSID, the NLSY data contain information on family income during adolescence and on outcomes in young adulthood. They also provide information on children's test scores and attitudes toward school. The High School and Beyond Study contains approximately 50,000 high school sophomores and seniors who were first interviewed in 1980 and followed every other year through 1986. The HSB Study contains fairly detailed information on children's perceptions of parental practices—involvement, supervision, and support—which can be used to study the relations between father absence and parental resources. The HSB data also provide information on educational attainment, early family formation, and early labor force attachment. The final survey is the NSFH, a survey of approximately 13,000 households interviewed in 1987 and again in 1993. These data provide retrospective information on respondents' own family histories while they were growing up as well as extensive information on their current parenting practices and family relationships. The NSFH data also contain information on parental conflict before and after divorce. The NSFH analysis is based on two cohorts of respondents. Cohort 1 includes individuals who were born in a period similar to respondents in the PSID, NLSY, and HSB, and cohort 2 includes individuals who were born during an early period, such as the forties.

the differences between children in one- and two-parent families are not so small as to be inconsequential, and there is fairly good evidence that father absence per se is responsible for at least some of them.[2]

Why would this be so? Why would the loss of a biological father reduce a child's chances of success? We argue that when fathers live apart from their children, they are less likely to share their incomes with the children, and, consequently, mothers and children usually experience a substantial decline in their standards of living when the fathers move out. We estimate that as much as half of the disadvantage associated with father absence is due to economic insecurity and instability. Another quarter is due to the loss of parental time and supervision, and the rest is probably due to a loss of social capital attributable in large measure to the higher incidence of residential mobility among single mothers and remarried mothers. Stated differently, if parents who decide to live apart were able to cushion their children from the economic instability and disruptions in neighborhood ties that often accompany the breakup of a family, and if single mothers were able to establish and maintain regular routines and effective systems of supervision, their children would likely do just as well as children raised in two-parent families. The problem is, these objectives are very difficult to achieve.

In the rest of the chapter, I flesh out these conclusions. I begin by describing some evidence on differences in educational attainment, labor market attachment, and family formation that my colleagues and I have uncovered in our analyses. Next, I discuss the major arguments for why father absence matters and present evidence relative to each of these claims. I end by discussing some of the implications of this research for parents, community leaders, and policy makers.

ASSESSING DIFFERENCES IN ACHIEVEMENT

What constitutes a successful passage from childhood to the adult world? My colleagues and I have focused on three salient factors that largely determine young people's prospects for becoming productive members of society: how far they go in school, whether they avoid early childbearing, and how successful they are gaining a foothold in the work force. In all three instances, children growing up apart from their biological fathers fare significantly worse than children growing up with both parents.

School Achievement

A college education, and at the very least a high school degree, is more crucial than ever in our high-technology, high-skills work environment. The time when a

---

[2]For more detail about the analyses behind these conclusions, see McLanahan and Sandefur (1994), Astone and McLanahan (1991, 1994), Hanson, McLanahan, and Thomson (1996, 1997a, 1997b), Hanson (1996), Thomson, McLanahan, and Braun-Curtin (1992), McLanahan (1985, 1988), McLanahan and Bumpass (1988), and McLanahan and Booth (1989).

young high school dropout could find a reasonably well-paying and secure job is long past. Increasingly, the same could be said for people without a college education. Ominously, the children of single and remarried parents are less likely to graduate from high school, just as they are less likely to earn a college degree.

To be sure, dropping out of high school is a relatively rare occurrence in this country. About 73% of American young people graduate. That proportion combined with the additional 12% who receive a General Equivalency Diploma (GED) means that only about 15% of American young people enter adulthood without a diploma. But although overall rates are low, a substantially higher proportion of children from father-absent households drop out of school than do children from father-present families. After controlling for race, sex, mother's and father's education, number of siblings, and place of residence—all factors that predate father absence and influence educational success—my colleagues and I found that growing up with just one biological parent approximately doubles the risk of dropping out (see Fig. 6.1).

Whether one sees the differences in Fig. 6.1 as large or small is partly a subjective issue. However, a consideration of what the dropout rate would be if all students lived with both biological parents is instructive. Using the NLSY survey, we

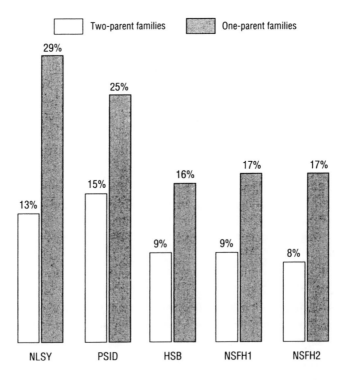

FIG. 6.1.   The risk of dropping out of high school.

found that the overall dropout rate for the country as a whole would fall from 19% to 13% if all children lived with both their biological parents and if all children had the same dropout rates as children currently living with both parents (the latter is a very strong assumption). Thus, father absence appears to account for about six percentage points or a third of the difference in the dropout rates between children from intact and non-intact families.

Most early theories about the effect of growing up without a father held that the consequences were more pronounced for boys, who supposedly were more dependent than girls on a male role model. However, our analysis of dropout rates suggests that father absence affects girls' educational achievement as much as it does boys'. The NLSY reveals an 18 percentage point difference between the dropout rates of girls from intact and non-intact families, as compared with a 15 percentage point difference for boys. The PSID shows an 11 percentage point difference for girls, in contrast with a 7 percentage point difference for boys.

What about race and ethnic differences? Are White children more or less affected by family disruption than Black and Hispanic children? Black and Hispanic children come from less advantaged backgrounds than White children, and their underlying risk of dropping out of school (or experiencing other negative events) is greater than that of Whites to begin with. Thus, we might expect the effect of family disruption to be greater on Blacks and Hispanics than on Whites. On the other hand, because single motherhood is more common and perhaps better institutionalized in the African American and Hispanic communities, we might expect the effect of family disruption on minority children to be smaller than the effect on White children.

In our analyses, the latter hypothesis dominates (see Table 6.1). Proportionally, father absence appears to hurt the educational success of White youth more than other racial and ethnic groups. Living without a father increases the risk of dropping out of school by 150% among Anglo children. In contrast, father absence increases the school failure risk among African Americans and Hispanics by 75% and 96% respectively. Remarkably, growing up without a father in the home appears to nullify the educational advantage of being White. Anglo children from one-parent households are significantly more likely to drop out than Blacks from two-parent homes, and they are nearly as likely to experience school failure as Blacks from similarly disrupted families.

How can we be sure that these differences in school achievement are really due to father absence per se and not to some other variable that is causing both family disruption and school failure? The answer is, short of running an experiment in which children are randomly assigned to intact and non-intact families, we can never be entirely certain. Researchers have used a variety of techniques to try to answer this difficult question, and, to date, their analyses suggests that at least some of the differences between children in one- and two-parent families are due to father absence per se (Haveman & Wolfe, 1994; Manski, Sandefur, McLanahan, & Powers, 1992; Sandefur & Wells, 1997).

Although dropping out of high school represents the extreme of educational failure, a number of other indicators also shed light on the effects of father absence. Our examination of data from the High School and Beyond Study (see Table 6.2) showed that students from two-parent families have higher grade point averages than students from one-parent families. They also have higher test scores, higher college expectations, and better school attendance records. Only in the case of school attitude was no difference apparent. To examine more deeply the effect of

TABLE 6.1

Racial, Ethnic, and Educational Differences
in the Effect of Family Disruption on Children

	High School Dropout Risk		Teen Birth Risk (Women)		Idleness Risk (Men)	
Child Background	Two-Parent Families	One-Parent Families	Two-Parent Families	One-Parent Families	Two-Parent Families	One-Parent Families
Average child						
White	11%	28%	8%	22%	10%	13%
Black	17	30	26	40	21	30
Hispanic	25	49	24	46	20	20
Advantaged child						
White	5	16	1	5	5	6
Black	4	8	6	11	9	14
Hispanic	NA	NA	NA	NA	NA	NA
Disadvantaged child						
White	24	51	19	44	19	24
Black	23	40	29	45	24	33
Hispanic	29	53	24	46	19	19

Source: National Longitudinal Survey of Youth.
Note. One-parent families include steipfamilies. An advantaged child is a child whose two parents have some college education. A disadvantaged child is a child whose two parents have less than a high school degree. All numbers are adjusted for race, mother's education, father's education, number of siblings, and place of residence. NA = sample size too small to estimate.

TABLE 6.2

Differences in High School Performance
of Children Raised in Two-Parent and One-Parent Families

Family Type	Test Score	School Attitude	College Expectations	Grade-Point Average	School Attendance
Two-parent families	2.62	80.4%	37.5%	4.13	9.83
One-parent families	2.51	80.1	32.2	3.92	9.25

Source: High School and Beyond Study.
Note. See text for explanation of categories. One-parent families include stepfamilies. All numbers are adjusted for race, sex, mothers' education, fathers' education, number of siblings, and place of residence.

father absence on grades and attendance, we adjusted for standardized test scores and still found a difference between students from the two types of families. Thus, among equally talented youth, a student from a one-parent household has on average poorer attendance and grades than a student from a two-parent family. Not only does growing up without a father appear to affect aptitude, as captured by the lower test scores, it also seems to hurt motivation as well. (The poorer attendance rates are a red flag; absence from school often accompanies delinquency and other behavior problems.) Once we have ruled out differences in innate intellectual ability as the cause of diminished school performance, we are left to conclude that other factors associated with growing up in a single-parent home—such as parental supervision and emotional issues—are at work.

With respect to college enrollment and graduation (see Fig. 6.2), the pattern is the same; students from one-parent homes again do less well. All five of our data sets show differences, ranging from a few percentage points to 20 points, even after adjusting for family background characteristics that predate divorce and are likely to affect college success. Here, as with the high school dropout rates, the effect of father absence varies by race, sex, and economic circumstances in illuminating ways. Anglo children from advantaged backgrounds have college graduation rates 9 percentage points lower if their parents live apart. The effect appears even stronger

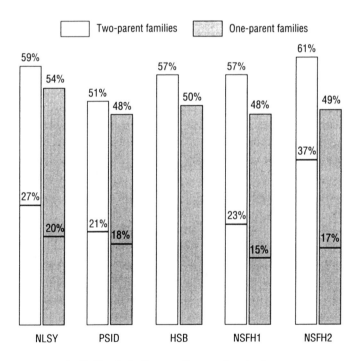

FIG. 6.2. The likelihood of college enrollment and graduation.

with respect to women; young women from advantaged but disrupted families have graduation rates 12 percentage points lower than their peers from intact families. For young men, the equivalent difference is only 4 percentage points. The sex difference in college graduation is in addition to the sex difference in high school graduation reported earlier, because we only examined college graduation for young people who finished high school.[3] The fact that young women from advantaged families are more affected by family disruption could be due to their higher risk of having a teen birth or to their differential access to financial support, from parents, schools, or employers.

Labor Market Detachment

As telling as school achievement is to success, or lack thereof, young people's experiences as they attempt to gain a footing in the working world are also important. A person who forgoes college may nevertheless begin building economic security and skills through steady employment. Most young men—roughly 85%, according to the NLSY—are either working or in school in their late teens and early twenties. Depending on how it is defined, the proportion of young men who are "detached," that is, neither working or not in school, may be as high as 25% according to the other data sets.

   Most important for our purposes is that, regardless of which survey we look at, young men from one-parent families are about 1.5 times as likely to be out of school and out of work as young men from two-parent homes (see Fig. 6.3). Even when we controlled for high school dropout rates, we found the same difference in detachment between young men from one- and two-parent homes. Thus, it appears that growing up apart from one's father hurts not only a young man's hopes for educational success but also his chances of making a permanent attachment to the labor force.

   As we did in our analysis of dropout rates, we controlled for test scores to make sure that the lower success rate of young men from one-parent homes was not due to inferior innate ability. Our analysis indicated that it clearly was not. The variation in test scores accounted for only about 20% of the higher incidence of detachment among males with disrupted families, suggesting that factors other than talent are the more significant cause. Most likely, these are the same factors—parental guidance and encouragement and the emotional strain caused by family dislocation—that we suspect are behind the higher rates of school failure.

   Confirming the belief that growing up in a non-intact family hurts employment prospects, we found that the higher rates of detachment continue deeper into adulthood. By the time they were between 23 and 26 years old, the young men in the NLSY survey with disrupted family backgrounds were still more likely

---

[3]The sex differences in college graduation are limited to one data set, the NLSY, and therefore we are not as confident of this effect as we are of some of the other results.

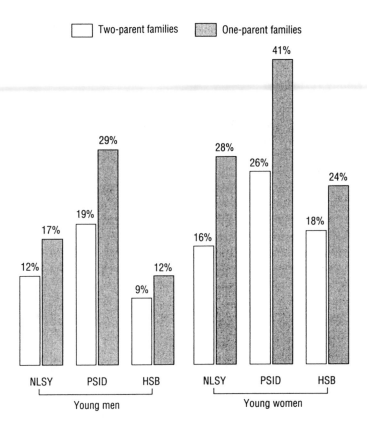

FIG. 6.3.   The risk of being out of school and out of work.

to be out of school and out of work than their peers who grew up in two-parent homes.

The greater incidence of detachment is not exclusive to the men with one-parent backgrounds. The effect of father absence is also apparent in the indicators of young women, in higher proportions among those with disrupted families than those from intact households. Detachment rates overall are higher among young women than men, in large measure because of the different cultural expectations placed on females and the fact that many young women are full-time mothers.

As they do with school failure, race and economic background influence the effect of father absence on labor market success. Whereas Anglo children seem most affected when we examine dropout rates, our analysis of detachment shows that African American children experience the larger effect. According to the NLSY data, being raised in a one-parent home increases the incidence of idleness by about 30% for Anglo children, whereas for Black children, it increases the incidence by about 40%. In the case of Hispanics, however, growing up in a non-intact family appears to have little effect on labor force detachment.

Early Family Formation

Another good predictor of education and economic success is early family forma-tion: The younger the age at which a young woman becomes a mother, the less likely is she to succeed in school and achieve economic security. Adolescent females who become mothers receive less education overall and are more likely to be poor in adulthood (and to be on welfare) than young women who delay their first birth until they are in their 20s.[4] To the extent that the daughters of single or remarried parents become young mothers, we could expect them to face greater odds against their success in school and the job market.

About 20% of the young women in our samples gave birth before age 20. The proportion, however, was much higher among women from non-intact families (see Fig. 6.4). The figures, which include both married and unmarried women, are roughly the same in all four data sets. The exception is the High School and Beyond Study, which had rates of 19% and 14%, respectively. (The HSB does not include young women who dropped out of school before their sophomore years, which may account for its lower percentages of teen mothers.) Notice that Anglo women are not immune from the effect of father absence where early childbearing is con-cerned. Those from disrupted families are about five times as likely as their peers from two-parent homes to become teenage mothers.

Race seems to be a factor in the incidence of early childbearing among offspring of single parents, just as it does with school failure. The effect of father absence is proportionately greater among Anglos, though overall rates of teenage mothering are lower. According to NLSY data, White females from disrupted families have a 14 percentage point greater risk of becoming teen mothers than White females from two-parent families (22% as compared with 8%). For Blacks, the figures are 40% and 26%, respectively; and for Hispanics, they are 46% and 24%. Favorable economic circumstances heighten the odds against early childbearing for both Blacks and Whites, yet being from a non-intact family still increases the risk for both racial groups. For advantaged Whites, the risk is five times greater for those with family disruption; for advantaged Blacks, it is twice as high.

Variation Among Different Types of Nonintact Families

The disadvantage associated with growing up apart from one's biological father cuts across the different forms of disrupted families; it exists for children who live

---

[4]For different perspectives on the consequences of teenage parenthood, see Geronimus and Koren-man (1993), Hoffman, Foster, and Furstenberg (1993), Grogger and Bronars (1993), Klepinger, Lund-berg, and Plotnick (1997), and Maynard (1996).

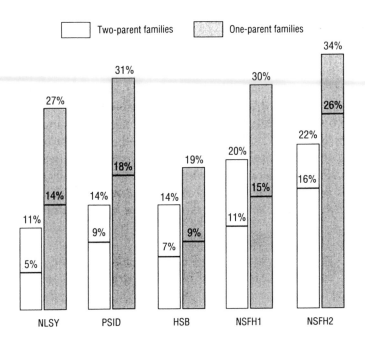

FIG. 6.4.   The risk of teen births for women.

with divorced single mothers, for those whose mothers have never married, and for those in stepfamilies. However, a closer analysis suggests that the offspring of one type of single-parent household fare considerably better. Children who lose a parent to death experience outcomes much closer to those of children from intact families.

Dividing the children of the NSFH into four groups—those with no family disruption, those who lost a parent to death, those whose parents divorced, and those born to never-married mothers—we found significant differences in educational outcomes (see Fig. 6.5). Those whose mothers divorced or never married clearly suffer the most negative effects. Adjusting for the factors that predate father absence and are known to influence school failure, we found that children in these two categories are several times more likely to drop out of school than their peers with intact families are. The dropout risk is 37% for those with never-married mothers and 31% for those with divorced parents, in contrast with the 13% risk of those from families with no disruption. Significantly, the risk for children who lost a parent to death is 15%, virtually the same as that for children from intact homes. Clearly, children of widowed mothers enjoy economic and other advantages over their peers from households headed by divorced or never-married parents.

With early childbearing, as with educational outcomes, the circumstances of family disruption can make a difference. In our analysis of the NSFH data, we found

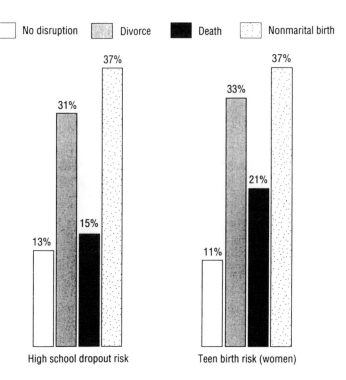

FIG. 6.5.   Is the cause of family disruption related to child well-being?

that young women who lost a parent to death were significantly less likely to become teen mothers than women whose parents divorced—21% for the former, in
contrast with 33% for the latter. However, as we found with educational outcomes,
the difference between young women born out of wedlock and those from divorced families is small and not statistically significant.

Although the nature of a family disruption in some circumstances influences
the effect of father absence, our analysis of the data suggests that the timing of
the disruption does not matter (see Table 6.3). This finding may contradict preva-
lent Freudian-influenced theories that point to early childhood as a critical period
for a child's long-term emotional and mental health, but we believe that adolescence is a period that also calls for a tremendous amount of parental guidance.
Along with the obvious stresses that accompany an adolescent's physical maturation, this period is given to impulsive behavior with serious consequences. A
younger person going through his or her parents' divorce may act out by fighting
with friends or siblings, whereas an adolescent may express negative feelings by becoming sexually active (and perhaps pregnant), taking drugs, or neglecting school,
with possible consequences for college and long-term economic prospects. Older
children, in our view, are no more likely to come out of a family disruption un-

TABLE 6.3
Do the Timing and Duration of Family Disruption
Make a Difference in Child Well-Being?

Condition	High School Dropout Risk	Teen Birth Risk (Women)
Child's age at first disruption		
0–5	33%	35%
6–11	29	30
12+	27	28
Years in a one-parent family		
More than 5	29	30
Fewer than 5	33	33
Number of disruptions		
1 or fewer	31	33
2 or more	32	33
Remarriage		
No	31	30
Yes	30	33

Source: National Survey of Families and Households, Cohort 1.
Note. Sample includes only children from one-parent families. Estimates are based on separate models for each set of predictor variables: age at first disruption, years in a one-parent family, number of disruptions, remarriage. No differences are statistically significant.

scathed than younger ones. Similarly, a child who appears to have adjusted to a divorce in early childhood may exhibit behavioral problems during adolescence.

How long a child lives in a one-parent home does not appear to influence the degree of damage caused by father absence either. Our analysis of the NSFH showed that children who live with a single parent for less than 5 years have the same dropout rate as those who have lived in similar circumstances for more than 5 years. Nearly half of all children with single mothers end up spending at least a portion of their childhoods living with stepfathers, according to research by Bumpass and Sweet (1989). Does being in a stepfamily mitigate the effect of father absence on children? According to our studies, remarriage neither helps nor hurts the child's chances for school success or avoiding a teen birth (we note that in some of our analyses, living with a stepfather increases a boy's chances of finishing high school, especially among African American males). The fact of father absence, in sum, matters much more than the circumstances, except when the single parent is a widow or widower.

Why Father Absence Matters

Father absence clearly diminishes a child's prospects for success in adult life. Why does growing up with a single parent heighten one's risk of school failure, detachment from the labor force, and early childbearing? What is it about a one-parent home that makes it harder for children to make their way in the world?

Economic Instability. The first answer—and the biggest part—is money. It is a simple fact that the one-parent household, which is typically headed by a divorced or never-married mother, has significantly fewer financial resources than an intact family and has reduced access to all the advantages money can buy. Consider poverty statistics: According to the U.S. Census Bureau, approximately half of households headed by single mothers in 1995 were below the poverty line, in contrast with the 10% figure for two-parent households. To be sure, many of these families were poor before divorce, and a significant proportion were headed by mothers who never married. Nevertheless, the lack of a father's income has dire consequences for household finances.

Even in well-off families, income loss exerts a powerful negative force on children's well-being. Non-poor families lose, on average, roughly 50% of their income when parents separate. That may force a mother to enter the labor force prematurely or work more hours, to the detriment of her ability to nurture and supervise her children. It may also force a move to more affordable housing, which, as I explore later, has other negative consequences for children.

Economies of scale are a big part of the reason that family disruption leads almost inevitably to financial disadvantage for children. It is simply more expensive for a once-intact family unit to spread out over two households than it is to stay in one. What's worse, the newly established household—the one typically headed by the principal bread-winner, the father—tends to receive a disproportionate share of the now-divided resources, despite the fact that the original household usually has the lion's share of the people. Not surprisingly, the economic status of the divorced mother usually goes down after the family disruption, whereas that of the nonresident father goes up.

Inadequate child support is perhaps the biggest culprit in this inequitable distribution of funds. Child-support standards and enforcement vary widely across the country, meaning two fathers with similar financial situations may end up paying dramatically different levels of support, depending on where they reside. Because of often-toothless enforcement, some fathers pay nothing at all (Garfinkel, McLanahan, & Robins, 1994; Hanson, Garfinkel, McLanahan, & Miller, 1996).[5]

Another factor is the diminished emotional attachment that often goes with separation from one's children. Fathers who don't see their children on a day-to-day basis can lose touch with their needs and lose interest in their well-being. In this instance, absence clearly does not make the heart grow fonder. With a weaker feeling toward his children—and new commitments, perhaps, to a second wife and stepchildren—a nonresident father may feel less compelled to provide finan-

---

[5]For more information on the current child support system and its effects on parents and children, see Garfinkel, McLanahan, Seltzer, and Meyer (in press).

cial support to his original household. A nonresident father also may balk because the child support must necessarily be funneled through the children's mother, whom he may distrust or dislike. Even the children of never-married mothers lose economically; they grow up without the economic advantages that a father's income would have provided (Seltzer, McLanahan, & Hanson, forthcoming).

The lack of money affects children's well-being, first and foremost, by limiting the quality of education to which they have access. Families with higher incomes can afford to live in neighborhoods with better public schools or send their children to private schools if they wish. Also, nonresident fathers are less likely to support their children's college education than resident fathers. The knowledge that they cannot count on their father's support for college may discourage many children from pursuing higher education, which in turn may affect their high school performance.

Our examination of the four primary data sets indeed bears out these suspected consequences of father absence and its negative effect on children's financial resources. In fact, our analyses suggest that the economic instability accounts for roughly half of the disadvantage associated with growing up in a one-parent home. This finding may be particularly relevant to government policymakers because income is an issue over which public policy has some influence.

Using data from the PSID to compare the incomes of intact families, single-parent families, and stepfamilies, we found, not surprisingly, that two-parent families earn on average more than the other two types of families (see Table 6.4). In 1992 dollars, the median income of two-parent families is more than $60,000, as compared with $54,594 for stepfamilies and $27,065 for single-parent families. (The families surveyed in the PSID have at least one adolescent child, which explains the overall high levels of the incomes; these are families headed by parents who are near the peak of their earning power.) We saw a similar phenomenon when we analyzed the poverty rates of the different types of families. Two-parent families have the lowest rate (5.3%) followed by stepfamilies (8.7%) and single-parent families (26.5%).

TABLE 6.4

Median Income of Two-Parent Families, Single-Parent Families, and Stepfamilies, by Race and by Mother's Education (in 1992 dollars)

Race and Education	Two-Parent Families	Single-Parent Families	Stepfamilies
All families	$61,135	$27,065	$54,594
Whites	$63,270	$31,349	$55,360
Blacks	$39,061	$20,105	$49,692
Less than a high-school degree	$43,693	$22,305	$39,234
High-school degree only	$63,071	$30,297	$57,945
Some college education	$83,748	$37,745	$71,220

Source: Panel Study of Income Dynamics.
Note. Income measured at age 16.

The connection between single parenthood and poverty is particularly strong among Blacks. Nearly half of Black households headed by a single parent are below the poverty line, in contrast with a 19.3% rate for two-parent Black families. Among Whites, the proportions are a less dramatic 13.6% and 3.6%, respectively.

As mentioned before, many of the poor one-parent households were poor even before the family disruption. Is it possible that the economic circumstances are the cause, rather than the result, of the separation or divorce? To explore this, we used the PSID data to look at children who lived with both parents at age 12 (see Table 6.5). We sorted them into two groups: those whose parents separated or divorced by the time the child reached age 17 and those whose parents were still together at that same point.

By this method, we found that family disruption during adolescence leads to a loss of household income, regardless of the racial and educational backgrounds of the families. Over the 5-year period we examined, the median family income of stable families (again in 1992 dollars) rose by roughly $5,000, from $59,741 to $64,789, whereas the unstable families experienced a decline from $55,864 to $33,509.

With respect to Whites, the figures point convincingly toward a conclusion that disruption is a cause, rather than a consequence, of lower income. The unstable

TABLE 6.5
Median Family Income at Ages 12 and 17 for Children in Stable and
Unstable Families, by Race and by Mothers' Education (in 1992 Dollars)

Race, Education, and Family Type	Age 12	Age 17
All		
Stable families	$59,741	$64,789
Unstable families	$55,864	$33,509
Whites		
Stable families	$61,559	$66,696
Unstable families	$62,367	$36,662
Blacks		
Stable families	$39,040	$40,934
Unstable families	$28,197	$18,894
Less than high-school education		
Stable families	$42,659	$45,512
Unstable families	$44,293	$27,821
High-school education		
Stable families	$61,858	$65,798
Unstable families	$60,725	$37,290
Some college education		
Stable families	$80,191	$91,766
Unstable families	$73,833	$38,082

Source: Panel Study of Income Dynamics.
Note. Stable families are those in which the parents did not separate or divorce during the child's adolescence (ages 12–17); unstable families are those in which the parents separated or divorced.

families had slightly higher average incomes than the stable families—$62,367, in contrast with $61,559—when the child was 12. By the time the children in the sample were 17, the unstable families were earning roughly $30,000 less than the stable families. In the case of Blacks, however, the findings are more ambiguous. Stable families were earning nearly $11,000 more ($39,040, as compared with $28,197) when the child was 12, suggesting pre-existing economic difficulty among the families that would later be disrupted. By the time the children were 17, the average income of the intact family had risen to $40,934, whereas the income of the unstable families had dropped to $18,894.

I have demonstrated that father absence is associated with poorer outcomes for children; I next explore the extent to which the income loss associated with family disruption is responsible for phenomena such as school failure and early childbearing. To accomplish this, I compare the well-being of children from disrupted and intact families before and after taking income into account. In Fig. 6.6, I separate single-mother and stepparent families in order to get a clearer picture of the effect of income.

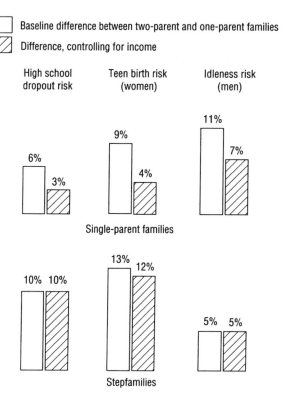

FIG. 6.6.   Does income account for the difference in child well-being?

Before controlling for income, there is a six percentage point difference in the high school dropout risk of children from one- and two-parent homes. After income is taken into account, the difference is just three percentage points. For the teen birth risk, income appears to account for more than half the difference between stable and unstable families. Controlling for income makes little difference in the case of stepfamilies, whose incomes are nearly identical to those of intact families.

To confirm our suspicion that the income effect was a consequence rather than a cause of family disruption, we used the PSID data to examine the effect of income before and after divorce (see Fig. 6.7). Adjusting for differences in family income at age 12 did not "explain" the higher risk of school failure, early childbearing, and detachment faced by children of unstable families. When we took changes in family income when children are between ages 12 and 17 into account, the difference between stable and unstable families was reduced by half. These findings make clear that the income loss caused by family disruption plays a vital role in the diminished outcomes of children from single-parent homes.

This evidence—that income explains many of the problems associated with divorce and single parenthood—is not consistent across different data sets. Income effects, for example, are much larger when we use the PSID data than when we use the NLSY or the NSFH surveys. Moreover, the effects of income often differ according to the particular outcomes that are examined. These inconsistencies are

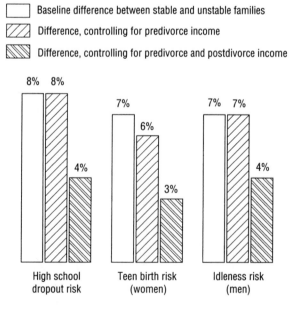

FIG. 6.7.   Does a change in income account for the difference in child well-being?

due to several factors. First, income effects are sensitive to how well income is measured. If the measure is poor, the effect of any variable will be attenuated. Indeed, much of the difference in findings between the large, nationally representative surveys and the smaller, observational studies is probably due to the fact that the former do a better job of measuring variables like income, whereas the latter do a better job of measuring variables such as parenting practices and stress. Second, income effects depend on the amount of variation in the sample. Analyses of families that fall within a narrow income range will always yield smaller income effects than analyses of samples that include the very rich and very poor. Finally, income effects depend on the indicator of child well-being that is being examined. In a recent review of 13 articles comparing the effects of income and family structure on child outcomes, I found that poverty (and economic status) had stronger effects on cognitive and educational outcomes than on emotional and social adjustment (McLanahan, 1997).

Parenting Skills and Resources.   If income is only half the story, what other factors account for the different success rates of children from intact and nonintact families? This question is particularly relevant for understanding stepfamilies, who don't appear to suffer the same income disadvantage as families headed by a single mother.

An important part of the answer is the loss of parental resources that occurs when a child's father lives in a separate household. Children clearly need their parents to read to them, discuss problems, help with homework, and give discipline and supervision. In a father-absent family, there is usually much less parenting to go around. Under such circumstances, the father is certain to see his children less. The effects of the physical separation can be magnified by the bitter feelings of the children, who often blame the father for abandoning the family, even if the mother instigated the split.

The separation can also affect children's relationships with their mothers. Forced to play two roles, that of father and mother, single mothers experience stress and often depression, which can adversely affect their parenting. With their time, energy, and spirits stretched, some single mothers become too lenient; others become too rigid or strict. Lost, too, is the system of checks and balances that helps keep a two-parent household running effectively. Without another parent in the household to consult and to ensure that she "does the right thing," a single mother may exhibit uneven or inconsistent parenting behavior.

The quality of the parenting is often lower still when the mother remarries. For a child who has already suffered through the parents' divorce, the appearance of a new stepparent can amount to yet another disruption. With another change in the personnel can come new rules, new roles, and new confusion. Where a child's well-being is concerned, a stepparent is no substitute for the departed real parent. With a reduced commitment to the child, the stepparent is not likely to be as effective a check on the mother's behavior as the biological father. Nor does the presence of a stepfather ensure that the mother will have more time and energy for parenting; indeed, he may even compete with the children for the mother's time and attention, leaving the mother more stretched than ever. Competition between stepfathers and their new children may be even more stressful for girls than for boys because the former have served as the mothers' confidants after the divorce or separation. There is also evidence that the sexual relationship between stepfathers and mothers may increase daughters' risk of becoming sexually active at an early age.

Conflict between the biological parents is another important factor in the difficulties experienced by children of divorce (Emery, 1982). It is well known that children in high-conflict families have more problems than those in low-conflict homes. As with income, it is important to separate cause from effect. The conflict between the mother and father is often not the result of family instability so much as it is the cause. If alcoholism, addiction, or abuse is at the heart of the conflict, parental resources are lost regardless of a separation or divorce. In that instance, the departure of the addicted or violent parent may be in the best interest of the children.

However, the degree and nature of the conflict bears consideration; not all divorces are caused by something as dramatic as addiction or violence. What if one parent abandons the marriage because he or she feels unfulfilled or falls in love with someone else? Even if the parents' relationship is less than perfect, the presence of both parents in the household may well be better for the children than a divorce or separation. Our analysis of the NSFH data, confirms our suspicion that parental conflict does not account for much of the lower attainment of children in father-absent families (Hanson, 1996). Although high conflict is negatively related to child well-being, the effects of conflict are not especially large. Nor does family disruption appear to resolve the problems of children in high-conflict families. Many of these children continue to experience conflict after divorce (Hanson, McLanahan, & Thomson, 1996). More important, a substantial proportion of parents who divorce do not report high levels of conflict prior to separation. Thus, although predivorce conflict may be an important factor for some children, it is not a major part of the story for the average child who experiences a divorce.

The empirical evidence also bears out our theories about the deficits of parental time and contact available to children whose parents have separated or divorced. Single mothers and remarried mothers, not surprisingly, are less likely to eat with their children than married mothers. On the other hand, single mothers appeared to compensate for the missed dinners by reading to their children more than their married peers.

The group of parents least involved are remarried divorced mothers, who both read less and eat fewer meals with their children. Although this finding appears to support our theory that stepparents diminish, rather than enhance, parental resources, the picture is more complex. When we add in the time children spend with the stepparent, the parental resources available to children of remarried mothers surpasses that of children with single mothers. In a small number of stepfamilies, the children may enjoy access to more parental resources than their counterparts from two-parent homes; this may be so if they maintain significant contact with the departed fathers and have good relationships with the new stepfathers.

Another measure of parents' authority is the degree to which they know their children's whereabouts, whether they leave them home alone, whether they establish a curfew, and whether they set rules for television-watching, bedtime, and household chores. The survey results (see Table 6.6) demonstrate that single mothers exercise less control over their children than do their still-married peers; the difference is particularly great when we compare married mothers, on the one hand, with never-married mothers and mothers with live-in partners, on the other. More than 30% of two-parent families report never leaving a child home alone, in contrast with 20.4% of mothers with partners and 19.3% of never-married mothers. Remarried mothers, interestingly, report about the same level of supervision as mothers in two-parent families.

Although it is clear that parental resources are diminished in disrupted families, we also must explore whether the lower levels of parental involvement and control might pre-date the family disruption. To explore that question, we compared two sets of students from the High School and Beyond Study (see Table 6.7). Both groups lived in intact families in their sophomore years. The families in the first group were still intact by the senior year, whereas those in the second group had experienced parental divorce or separation.

We expected some decrease in involvement in both cases, due simply to the children's maturation, but we found that the decline is substantially greater with disrupted families. Moreover, we found that parental aspirations for their children—an important determinant of their success in achieving a college education and career—increase between the sophomore and senior year in the case of intact families, whereas they decline in disrupted families. These results demonstrate that the

TABLE 6.6
Parental Supervision (Measured by Percentage of Mothers Answering Yes)

Question Put to Mother	Two-Parent Family	Mother and Stepfather	Mother and Partner	Divorced Mother	Never-Married Mother
Child never left alone?	31.1%	28.1%	20.4%	25.5%	19.3%
Know child's whereabouts?	88.3	89.1	86.8	87.3	88.8
Child has curfew?	9.1	9.2	9.0	9.1	9.0
Child has bedtime?	8.8	8.7	8.8	8.7	8.7
Child has TV rules?	35.9	32.2	19.4	31.9	29.6
Child has chores?	50.9	55.1	48.1	51.9	44.4

Source: Thomson, E., McLanahan, S. S., & Curtin, R. B. (1992). "Family structure, gender, and parental socialization." *Journal of Marriage and the Family, 54,* 368–378. Results are based on data from the National Survey of Families and Households, 1987.

Note. All numbers are adjusted for sex, race, mothers' education, fathers' education, number of siblings, and place of residence.

TABLE 6.7
Change in Parental Involvement, Supervision, and Aspirations
Between the Sophomore and Senior Years

Family Type	Mother's Involvement	Father's Involvement	Parental Supervision	Talks With Child	Parental Aspirations
Stable families	−1	−1	−2	−10	4
Unstable families	−10	−19	−13	−20	−2

Source: High School and Beyond Study.
Note. Stable families are those in which the parents did not separate or divorce between the sophomore and senior years; unstable families are those in which the parents separated or divorced.

disruption itself plays a significant role in the loss of parental involvement associated with family disruption.

Finally, can we establish that the changes in parenting that accompany divorce and separation are factors in the children's well-being? As we did with income, we reanalyzed the survey data before and after adjusting for parental involvement, supervision, and aspirations (see Fig. 6.8).

Children in single-parent and two-parent homes have a six percentage point baseline difference before adjustment for the parental resources; after adjustment for resource differences, the gap falls to three percentage points. Thus, these parenting factors appear to account for roughly half the higher dropout rate observed among the children of single-parent homes. With teen birth risk, accounting for parental resources changed the baseline difference by only one percentage point. However, in the case of detachment from the labor force, adjusting for parental resources completely eliminated the gap. When we employed the same statistical technique with stepfamilies, we did not find the same dramatic effect when we adjusted for the parenting factors, suggesting that differences in parental resources do not play as prominent a role for children in stepfamilies as they do for children living with single mothers.

Community Resources. Access to community resources—the web of facilities, programs, people, and care-providers that can supplement and support parents' efforts—is significantly diminished for children in disrupted families. The loss of income that typically accompanies divorce and separation restricts the ability of many families to live in communities with an abundance of this social capital. So too can the absence of one parent reduce a child's chance to connect with the resources that exist.

The longer parents reside in the same community, the more likely they are to know about and take advantage of opportunities for their children. Family disruptions often lead to residential moves, which usually mean adjustments to new communities and the loss of ties with former neighbors. Even if they haven't

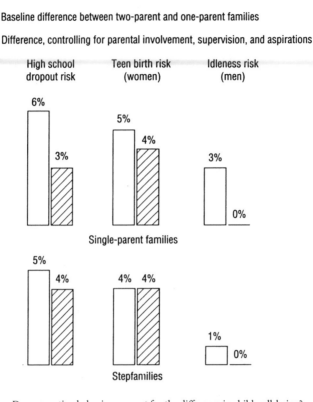

FIG. 6.8. Does parenting behavior account for the difference in child well-being?

moved, children may lose access to people and other resources with whom their noncustodial parent was connected after a divorce. Children can even be cut off from the custodial parent's network; to the extent she is stressed and depressed, the mother may not have the time or energy to maintain those old relationships that she once had (Coleman, 1988).

The loss of social capital can have obvious and deleterious effects on a child's education. An intact family that has been in the same community for a number of years learns about the best educational resources. The parents are more likely to know about after-school programs and the names of the best teachers, and they are more likely to have the connections and influence to access resources for which demand is high and supply limited. The children in such families could be expected to get better educations than those in families that are new to the community.

Social capital can also be an important factor in a child's success at landing a first job. Children in one-parent homes are more likely to live in poorer communities with fewer employment opportunities. In addition, fathers might have valu-

TABLE 6.8

Characteristics of Census Tracts Where Children Live, by Race and by Family Structure

Race and Family Type	Poverty Rate of Census Tract	Percentage of Female-Headed Families in Census Tract	AFDC Rate of Census Tract	Jobless Father Rate of Census Tract	Percentage of Vacant Buildings in Census Tract	High School Dropout Rate of Census Tract
Whites						
Two-parent families	8.7%	12.2%	5.9%	30.0%	5.0%	9.9%
One-parent families	11.0	16.3	7.5	30.4	6.6	12.5
Blacks						
Two-parent families	23.8	30.1	16.8	39.9	8.3	17.4
One-parent families	26.0	36.5	20.6	41.8	9.0	19.5

Source: Panel Study of Income Dynamics, census tract data, characteristics file.
Note. In this table, stepfamilies are combined with two-parent families.

able information about jobs and connections with the people who can give them; children living apart from their fathers may be at a considerable disadvantage.

An examination of the data indicates that race is a more potent factor than family structure in determining the type of community in which a child resides (see Table 6.8). Nevertheless, our examination of census tract data in the PSID shows that, on average, White children from single-parent families live in neighborhoods with higher rates of poverty, welfare use, school failure, and female-headed households than those of White children in two-parent families. According to one of our data sets, the High School and Beyond Study, children in stepfamilies and single-parent families attend schools with higher dropout rates and more student behavior problems than those of their peers from intact families. The NLSY data leads in a slightly different direction; in that data set, children with single parents, but not those in stepfamilies, are found to attend lower quality schools.

The level of resources that exists in a community is only part of the equation; knowing about them and accessing them depends to some degree on the length of time a family has lived in the same community. As discussed previously, disrupted families are often mobile families. The evidence confirms that one-parent families indeed move more frequently than intact families, and stepfamilies move still more. In the PSID data, we found that single-parent families move nearly twice as often as intact families, and stepfamilies move nearly three times as much.

The data also give some idea of the reasons behind the relocation. If a family moves to pursue a better job, the benefits may outweigh the disadvantages. However, if a newly divorced mother moves to less expensive housing because of her reduced means, the negatives are almost certain to outweigh any positives. This latter type of move, which we call "involuntary," is much more common among single-mother households than two-parent families and stepfamilies. Thirty-four percent of single mothers' moves fall into this category, according to the PSID data, more than double the proportion for intact families and stepfamilies. Just 6% of single mothers' moves were for productive reasons—a better job—in contrast with 21% of intact families' moves.

As demonstrated previously, children in disrupted families tend to live in communities with inferior resources, and they are also less likely to have the connections that will give them access to the resources that are available. How significant a factor is this disadvantage in determining their well-being?

Figure 6.9 shows that the effect is particularly important with respect to stepfamilies, accounting for about 40% of the higher school failure rates observed among children in that category. The data from the High School and Beyond Study show a five percentage point difference between the graduation rates of children in stepfamilies and their peers in two-parent homes. However, when we adjusted for school quality and residential mobility, the difference fell to three percentage points. Applying the same technique to the higher school failure rates of children with single parents who have not remarried, we do not find social capital exerting the same effect. For those children, income and parenting resources remain the

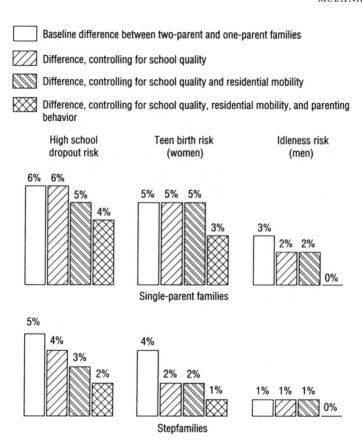

FIG. 6.9.   Do community resources and parental behavior account for the difference in child well-being?

most important factors. We attribute the findings for stepfamilies to the greater residential mobility of these households and to the disruption in parents' and children's social capital associated with a move. Although one data set indicated that children in stepfamilies attended lower quality schools, another did not. In contrast, all the data show much higher residential mobility among children in stepfamilies.

CONCLUSIONS AND IMPLICATIONS

Growing up with a single parent harms children for three primary reasons: A disrupted family usually has fewer financial resources to devote to children's upbringing and education, less time and energy to nurture and supervise children, and reduced access to community resources that can supplement and support parents' efforts. Fortunately, none of these factors is beyond the control of parents and society. Thus, to the extent that parents and government can address these risk factors, the effect of father absence on children's well-being could be significantly softened.

The first and most obvious factor that can and should be addressed is protection of children from the economic insecurity that accompanies father absence. This will require a commitment of both public and private resources. With respect to the latter, we are in the midst of a revolution in child support enforcement policy. During the past two decades, several major pieces of federal legislation have been passed that call for increasing the proportion of children with a child support award, standardizing award levels, and collecting obligations more efficiently. Paternity establishment rates have more than tripled in the last decade, and the proportion of mothers receiving child support payments has gone up substantially.

Stronger child support enforcement may also redress the other two factors that determine children's resilience in the face of family disruption: the loss of parental resources and the loss of community. Fathers who are required to pay child support are likely to demand more time with their children and a greater say in how they are raised. Such demands should lead to more social capital between the father and child. Similarly, greater father involvement is likely to lead to less residential mobility, retarding the loss of social capital in the community. Although at face value these new policies appear to benefit children, they may come with a cost for mothers in terms of their freedom to raise their children as they see fit and to relocate to other cities or states. The new policies may also have costs for fathers and their new families, and in families with a history of abuse, they may even harm some children. The agenda for the next generation of empirical studies is set. How will the new child support policies affect fathers, mothers, and children? Who will benefit, and who will suffer? How large are the different effects and what can be done to mitigate the negative consequences? At this point our ability to answer these questions is limited, yet the answers will have profound effects on the well-being of families and children (see Garfinkel, McLanahan, Seltzer, & Meyer, in press).

With respect to the public responsibility, we are currently in the midst of a giant experiment involving the economic security and stability of single mothers and their children. Welfare reform has removed the federal entitlement to cash benefits and has limited cash assistance to a maximum of 5 years. Currently states have both more money and more discretion over how to use these funds to help single mothers and children. Although it is too soon to judge the outcomes, states appear to be pursuing very different strategies. Some are expanding healthcare coverage, childcare assistance, and job training and placement. Others are imposing strict time limits on mothers' benefits without providing the support needed to achieve independence. Again, researchers who are interested in the consequences of single parenthood will have multiple opportunities to study these natural experiments to see what they can tell us about the role of income, parental resources, and social capital in promoting children's well-being.

ACKNOWLEDGMENTS

The research was supported by grants from NICHD HD29601, HD19375, Office of Population Research, Princeton University Center Grant 5P30HD/AG32030, and the Lowenstein Foundation. I would like to thank Melanie Adams for editorial and technical assistance and Andrea Saville-White for technical assistance and table production. All of the figures and tables in this chapter were previously printed in *Growing Up with a Single Parent: What Hurts, What Helps* by Sara McLanahan and Gary Sandefur. Copyright ©1994 by the President and Fellows of Harvard College. Reprinted by permission of Harvard University Press.

REFERENCES

Astone, N., & McLanahan, S. (1991). Family structure, parental practices, and high school completion. *American Sociological Review, 56,* 309–320.

Astone, N., & McLanahan, S. (1994). Family structure, residential mobility and school dropout: A research note. *Demography, 31,* 575–584.

Blankenhorn, D. (1995). *Fatherless America: Confronting our most urgent social problem.* New York: Basic Books.

Bumpass, L., & Sweet, J. (1989). Children's experience in single parent families: Implications of cohabitation and marital transitions. *Family Planning Perspectives, 21,* 256–260.

Coleman, J. (1988). Social capital in the creation of human capital. *American Journal of Sociology, 94,* 95–120.

Emery, R. (1982). Interparental conflict and the children of discord and divorce. *Psychological Bulletin 92,* 310–330.

Garfinkel, I., McLanahan, S., & Robins, P. (1994). *Child support and child well-being.* Washington, DC: The Urban Institute.

Garfinkel, I., McLanahan, S., Seltzer, J., & Meyer, D. (Eds.). (in press). *Fathers under fire: The revolution in child support enforcement.* New York: Russell Sage Foundation.

Geronimus, A., & Korenman, S. (1993). The socioeconomic consequences of teen childbearing reconsidered. *The Quarterly Journal of Economics, 107,* 1187–1214.

Grogger, J., & Bronars, S. (1993). The socioeconomic consequences of teenage childbearing: Finds from a natural experiment. *Family Planning Perspectives, 25*(4), 156–161.

Hanson, T. (1996). *Does parental conflict explain why divorce is negatively associated with child welfare?* Paper presented at annual ASA meetings, New York.

Hanson, T., Garfinkel, I., McLanahan, S., & Miller, C. (1996). Trends in child support outcomes. *Demography, 33,* 483–496.

Hanson, T., McLanahan, S., & Thomson, E. (1996). Double jeopardy: Parental conflict and stepfamily outcomes for children. *Journal of Marriage and the Family, 58,* 141–154.

Hanson, T., McLanahan, S., & Thomson, E. (1997a). *Divorce family resources and children's welfare.* Paper presented at the Annual PAA Meeting, New Orleans, LA.

Hanson, T., McLanahan, S., & Thomson, E. (1997b). Economic resources, parental practices, and child well-being. In G. Duncan & J. Brooks-Gunn (Eds.), *Consequences of growing up poor* (pp. 190–238). New York: Russell Sage.

Haveman, R., & Wolfe, B. (1994). *Succeeding generations: On the effects of investments in children.* New York: Russell Sage.

Hoffman, S., Foster, M., & Furstenberg, F., Jr. (1993). Reevaluating the costs of teenage childbearing. *Demography, 30,* 1–13.

Klepinger, D., Lundberg, S., & Plotnick, R. (1997). *How does adolescent fertility affect human capital and wages?* University of Wisconsin, IRP Working Paper # 1145–97. Madison, WI.

Manski, C., Sandefur, G. McLanahan, S., & Powers, D. (1992). Alternative estimates of the effects of family structure during childhood on high school graduation. *Journal of the American Statistical Association, 87,* 25–37.

Maynard, R. (Ed.). (1996). *Kids having kids. A special report on the costs of adolescent childbearing.* New York: The Robin Hood Foundation.

McLanahan, S. (1985). Family structure and the reproduction of poverty. *American Journal of Sociology, 90,* 873–901.

McLanahan, S. (1988). Family structure and dependency: Early transitions to female household headship. *Demography, 25,* 1–16.

McLanahan, S. (1997). Parent absence or poverty: Which matters more? In G. Duncan & J. Brooks-Gunn (Eds.), *Consequences of growing up poor* (pp. 35–48). New York: Russell Sage Foundation.

McLanahan, S., & Booth, K. (1989). Mother-only families: Problems, prospects and politics. *Journal of Marriage and the Family, 51,* 557–80.

McLanahan, S., & Bumpass, L. (1988). Intergenerational consequences of family disruption. *American Journal of Sociology, 93,* 130–152.

McLanahan, S., & Sandefur, D. (1994). *Growing up with a single parent: What hurts, what helps.* Cambridge, MA: Harvard University Press.

Popenoe, D. (1988). *Disturbing the nest: Family change and decline in modern societies.* New York: de Gruyter.

Popenoe, D. (1996). *Life without father.* New York: The Free Press.

Sandefur, G., & Wells, T. (1997). *Using siblings to investigate the effects of family structure on educational attainment.* University of Wisconsin, IRP Working Paper #1144–97. Madison, WI.

Seltzer, J., McLanahan, S., & Hanson, T. (forthcoming). Will child support enforcement increase father-child contact and parental conflict after separation? In I. Garfinkel, S. McLanahan, J. Seltzer, & D. Meyer (Eds.), *The effects of child support enforcement on nonresident fathers.* New York: Russell Sage.

Skolnick, A. (1991). *Embattled paradise: The American family in an age of uncertainty.* New York: Basic Books.

Stacy, J. (1993). Good riddance to "the family": A response to David Popenoe. *Journal of Marriage and the Family, 55,* 545–547.

Thomson, E., McLanahan, S., & Braun-Curtin, R. (1992). Family structure, gender, and parental socialization. *Journal of Marriage and the Family, 54,* 25–37.

Whitehead, B. (1993). Dan Quayle was right. *Atlantic Monthly.* 47–84.

7

Children of Divorced Parents
as Young Adults

Paul R. Amato
University of Nebraska–Lincoln

DURING THE LAST three decades, divorce has became normative in American society. As most family scholars know, the divorce rate increased dramatically during the late 1960s and 1970s, then stabilized in the 1980s at a historically high level. According to recent projections, at least one half of recent first marriages will end in divorce (Cherlin, 1992). One might think that people would be more successful the second time around, but the likelihood of divorce is even greater in second or third marriages. The high rate of marital dissolution has touched the lives of a large number of children. Every year in the United States, over one million children experience divorce, and nearly one half of all children will experience divorce prior to reaching the age of 18 (Bumpass, Thompson, & McDonald, 1984). Along with skinned knees, braces, and the first day of school, divorce has become a common event in the lives of America's children.

This trend worries conservatives who assume that a two-parent family is necessary for the successful socialization of children. Because an absent parent is not easily replaced, conservatives believe that children with divorced parents reach maturity with fewer of the skills and resources necessary to enact adult roles successfully. The first generation of children affected by the massive increase in divorce during the 1970s began to enter adulthood in the 1990s. If this generation contains a disproportionate number of poorly functioning individuals, then all our social institutions—government, business, churches, schools, and civic organizations—will suffer. Conservatives see the high rate of divorce as a threat not only to the well-being of individual children but to the well-being of the nation that will one day depend on these children (Blankenhorn, 1995; Popenoe, 1996; Whitehead, 1993).

Most studies show that children of divorced parents are at increased risk for a number of academic, behavioral, psychological, and social problems (Amato &

147

Keith, 1991a; Emery, 1988; Hetherington, 1989). Whether these differences persist
into adulthood, however, is a different question. Many people believe that children
are resilient and adjust successfully, over time, to changes in family structure. Indeed, they argue that children are better off when unhappily married parents divorce. According to this viewpoint, most children enter adulthood with few traces
of earlier divorce-related problems; poverty, neglect, abuse, poorly funded schools,
dangerous neighborhoods, and the lack of government services pose far more serious long-term problems for children than does divorce (Coontz, 1992; Demo,
1992, Edwards, 1987).

In this chapter, I address this issue by reviewing studies of the long-term consequences of parental divorce for children, that is, consequences that are apparent
after children reach adulthood. Focusing on long-term consequences is the most
direct way of assessing the conservative claim that divorce is eroding the success
and well-being of future generations. Although I focus on my own research in this
review, I discuss other studies when appropriate. I supplement this review with a
new analysis that relates parental divorce to multiple dimensions of offspring well-
being in adulthood.

CONCEPTUAL FRAMEWORK

The Life Course

I organize my research around a life course perspective, which has emerged as a key
theoretical orientation in family studies (Elder, 1994; Rossi & Rossi, 1990). This
perspective assumes that circumstances and events in the family of origin affect
children long after they have left the parental home. Congruent with this perspective, some studies have documented the transmission of traits, such as parenting
styles, marital violence, and behavior problems, across generations (Belsky & Pensky, 1988; Caspi & Elder, 1988). The life course perspective also stresses the timing
and sequencing of events over the life course. For example, this perspective predicts that the consequences of divorce depend on events that both precede and follow marital disruption, such as the level of conflict between parents (Amato,
Loomis, & Booth, 1995). In addition, the life course perspective assumes that people do not passively react to events and circumstances; instead, they actively make
decisions based on their perceptions of the opportunities and constraints available
at particular times in their lives.

The circumstances surrounding divorce present many challenges to children.
These circumstances include a degree of family conflict prior to and following divorce, a decline in the quality of interaction between children and custodial parents (usually mothers), a decrease in the frequency of contact with noncustodial
parents (usually fathers), a drop in economic resources, and other stressful events
such as moving (often to neighborhoods with poorer schools and fewer services)

and parental remarriage (which many children resist). Not all children experience all these changes, but most children experience at least a few.

As children from divorced families reach late adolescence and early adulthood, they react to these circumstances, evaluate their opportunities, and make decisions. At this time in the life course, youth decide how much education to obtain, how long to continue living with parents, and, following residential independence, how much contact to maintain with parents. They also make decisions about employment, cohabitation, marriage, and having children.

Parental divorce can affect all these decisions. For example, divorce followed by remarriage might propel some offspring to leave home relatively early. Once they leave home, young adult offspring may maintain relatively weak ties with parents, especially noncustodial fathers. Moreover, loss of access to fathers' financial resources might force some offspring to curtail plans to attend college. Witnessing their parents' divorce might lead some offspring to invest relatively few resources in intimate relationships, assuming that an unhappy marriage can readily be terminated. These interrelated decisions—which are influenced by the circumstances surrounding parental divorce—have consequences for young adults that persist throughout the remainder of the life course.

Risk and Resiliency

The life course perspective is broadly consistent with a focus on risk and resiliency. The stress and coping literature shows that the association between stressful life events and developmental outcomes is not always direct or simple (Garmezy & Rutter, 1983). Exposure to a stressor increases the likelihood of negative psychological and behavioral outcomes, all things being equal, but many factors can intervene in this process, resulting in a considerable degree of diversity in outcomes among children and adults.

People's reactions to stress depend on the resources at their disposal. Resources can reside in the individual (e.g., intelligence, self-efficacy), in interpersonal relationships (e.g., social support), or in the larger physical and social environment (e.g., school quality, neighborhood services, supportive government policies). In general, the quantity and quality of resources in children's lives not only directly improves their well-being but also helps them to cope with everyday strains and major life stressors.

Children from divorced families are exposed to more stressors than are children from continuously intact families, on average. Depending on their access to resources, however, some children are relatively vulnerable to the ill effects of divorce-induced stress, whereas others are relatively resilient. For example, children who must cope with economic hardship are likely to have a more difficult time adjusting to divorce than are children who experience a comfortable postdivorce standard of living. Similarly, strong emotional bonds with parents may buffer children from many of the strains associated with changes in family structure. In general, to understand how divorce affects children, we must look at the larger mix of resources and stressors in their lives (Amato, 1994). (See Hetherington & Blechman, 1996, for examples of a risk and resiliency perspective applied to children and families.)

In summary, both the life course perspective and a risk and resiliency perspective predict that parental divorce has the potential to affect the long-term trajectories of children's lives. However, these perspectives suggest discontinuities as well as continuities between the family of origin and outcomes in adulthood, depending on children's opportunities, resources, and choices. It is not possible in this chapter to discuss all the interconnections between parental divorce, mediating and moderating processes, and long-term consequences. Instead, my objective is to review evidence showing how the life trajectories of children of divorce differ from those of other children. I focus on four types of outcomes: socioeconomic attainment, relationships with spouses, relationships with parents, and subjective well-being.

SOCIOECONOMIC ATTAINMENT

How does divorce affect children's long-term socioeconomic attainment? To answer this question, I carried out a study with Bruce Keith (Amato & Keith, 1991b) using data from the National Survey of Families and Households (NSFH). This is a national, probability sample collected in the United States in 1987–1988. Our analysis involved 4,722 White and 1,419 Black adults. Life history data made it possible to identify respondents who experienced a parental divorce prior to the age of 19.

Figure 7.1 shows the respondents' years of education by whether the respondents' parents were divorced or not divorced. These means were adjusted for the respondent's age and the respondent's parents' years of education and occupational status. Note that for White men, White women, and Black women, parental divorce decreased educational attainment by about one-half year; these differences were statistically significant. The difference was in the same direction (but not statistically significant) for Black men.

Further analyses based on the NSFH revealed additional evidence of how parental divorce affects financial well-being in adulthood. White men whose parents divorced earned about $4,000 less every year than did men whose parents remained married; the corresponding gap for White women was about $2,000 (the differences for African American men and women were not significant). To see if this annual difference in income adds up over time, we also looked at accumulated assets, defined as the worth of a person's home, other real estate, and automobiles, minus what is owed on these items. The typical White man whose parents did not divorce had about $20,000 in equity. The corresponding value for a white man from a divorced family was about half that amount. A similar but slightly smaller

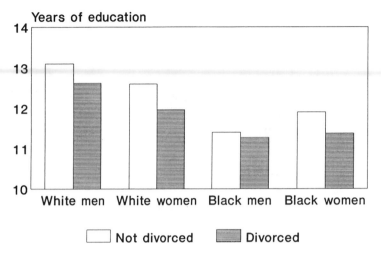

FIG. 7.1.   Adjusted mean years of education for adults from divorced and nondivorced families of origin.

gap was apparent for White women and Black women (once again, the gap for African American men was in the same direction but not significant). Most of the disparity in financial well-being was accounted for by the difference in education, as noted previously.

Other investigators using different national data sets (such as the General Social Survey, the National Longitudinal Survey of Youth, the Panel Study of Income Dynamics, and the Detroit Area Study) have reported comparable results. Compared with offspring from continuously intact families of origin, those who experience parental divorce are more likely to drop out of high school, are less likely to attend college, are more likely to be unemployed, and enter adulthood with fewer financial resources (Keith & Finlay, 1988; Krein, 1986; McLanahan & Sandefur, 1994; McLeod, 1991; Wadsworth & McLean, 1986). These studies consistently show that offspring from divorced families achieve lower levels of socioeconomic attainment in adulthood than do offspring from continuously intact families.

MARITAL QUALITY

In 1991, Alan Booth and I examined marital quality among adult children from divorced families (Amato & Booth, 1991). To accomplish this, we used the Marital Instability Over the Life Course study (MIOLC)—a national probability sample of over 2,000 married adults first interviewed in 1980 and again in 1983, 1988, and 1992 (Booth, Johnson, White, & Edwards, 1991). In this study, people responded to questions about the quality of their own marriages as well as questions about the quality of their parents' marriages.

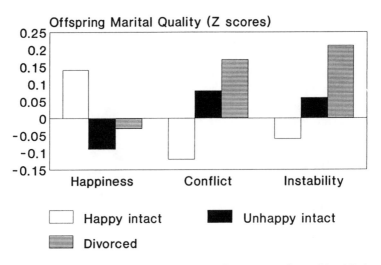

FIG. 7.2. Adjusted mean marital quality *Z* scores (happiness, conflict, and instability) for adults from happy intact, unhappy intact, and divorced families of origin.

Figure 7.2 presents information on adult offsprings' marital quality. It includes measures of marital happiness, marital conflict, and marital instability. Marital happiness refers to how happy people are with various aspects of their marriages, whereas conflict refers to disagreements, serious quarrels, and a history of violence in these relationships. Marital instability refers to the extent to which people think that their marriages are in trouble, consider divorce, talk to others about getting a divorce, and in other ways act as if they are not committed to their relationships. The figure shows the mean levels of these marital outcomes for three groups: those whose parents were happily married, those whose parents were unhappily (but continuously) married, and those whose parents were divorced. The means are adjusted for the respondents' ages, race, and gender, as well as the respondents' parents' education.

The first three bars on the left refer to marital happiness, with higher bars reflecting greater happiness. Adults who grew up in happy intact families reported the highest level of happiness with their own marriages. Those who grew up in unhappy but intact families and those whose parents divorced reported lower levels of marital happiness. A similar pattern appeared for conflict and instability. Those from happy intact families of origin had low levels of conflict and instability in their own marriages, whereas those from unhappy intact and divorced families had high levels of conflict and instability. All these differences across groups were statistically significant.

Studies based on other large data sets yield similar results. For example, McLeod (1991), using the Detroit Area Study, found that married women from divorced families of origin, compared with other women, reported more relationship problems, less trust, and less effective marital problem solving. Similarly, Webster, Orbuch, and House (1995), using the NSFH, showed that individuals from divorced backgrounds were more likely to think their marriages were in trouble and reported a greater likelihood of seeing their own marriages end in divorce. Taken together, these results suggest that marital quality is transmitted across generations.

Is divorce also transmitted across generations? In a recent study, I attempted to answer this question using the MIOLC data (Amato, 1996). In particular, I looked at whether respondents divorced during the period of the study, that is, between 1980 and 1992. In Fig. 7.3, the white bars show the percentage of people in first marriages who divorced. When neither the husband's nor the wife's parents divorced, the percentage of couples who divorced was relatively low—only about 10%. When the husband's parents divorced, or when the wife's parents divorced, the divorce rate was somewhat higher. When both the husband and the wife experienced a parental divorce, the divorce rate was higher yet (nearly 30%).

The grey bars show comparable results for those in second or higher order marriages. The divorce rate for remarried couples is relatively high, regardless of parental divorce. Nevertheless, the overall pattern is the same: The likelihood of divorce was lowest when neither the husband nor the wife came from a divorced family of origin and was highest when both the husband and the wife experienced a parental divorce. These results indicate that divorce, like marital quality, is transmitted across generations. Numerous other studies, based on national data sets, have also documented this phenomenon (Bumpass, Martin, & Sweet, 1991; Glenn & Kramer, 1987; Pope & Mueller, 1976).

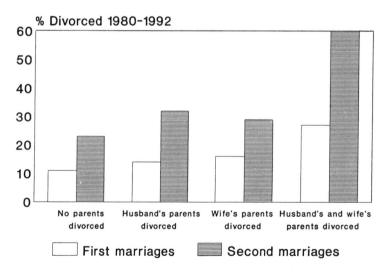

FIG. 7.3. Percentage of respondents divorced between 1980 and 1992 by parental divorce.

In subsequent analyses, I attempted to explain this phenomenon by considering five possible mechanisms. Adult children with divorced parents may be more likely to see their own marriages end in divorce because they, compared with other children, (a) tend to marry at relatively young ages, (b) are more likely to cohabit prior to marriage, (c) have lower socioeconomic attainment, (d) hold more liberal attitudes toward divorce, and (e) are more prone to behave in problematic ways within marriage. To evaluate these explanations, I used event history models, estimated with logistic regression. In particular, I entered the explanatory variables one at a time into equations to see how this affected the original association between parental divorce and offspring divorce; a decline in the magnitude of the original association suggests a mediating role for the explanatory variable.

Although I found some support for each explanation, I found the greatest support for the fifth one. People from divorced families of origin are more likely to exhibit behaviors that undermine relationship quality, such as becoming jealous easily, having difficulty controlling anger, not communicating about problems, and having affairs. These behaviors, in turn, increase the odds of divorce. Controlling for problematic behavior eliminates most of the original association between parental divorce and offspring divorce.

These findings are consistent with the notion that children from divorced families have fewer opportunities to learn interpersonal skills—such as building trust, managing emotions, and communicating effectively—that strengthen intimate relationships. Because they have not been exposed to good parental models while growing up, many of these individuals may enter marriage without adequate repertoires of interpersonal skills to sustain their marriages. These findings are also consistent with the idea that people from unhappy families of origin develop long-lasting feelings of emotional insecurity or other problematic personality characteristics (Caspi & Elder, 1988; Davies & Cummings, 1994). Feelings of insecurity, in turn, can interfere with forming satisfying intimate bonds in later life.

RELATIONS WITH PARENTS

To assess the quality of parent–child relationships, I turn to a study of 471 young adults (between the ages of 19 and 40) and their parents (Amato, Rezac, & Booth, 1995; Booth & Amato, 1994). These data were collected as part of the 1992 follow-up to the MIOLC study, with young adults who were offspring of the original survey respondents. We asked these young adults about their affection for their parents, including questions dealing with trust, respect, understanding, fairness, and feelings of closeness. We then placed these children into three groups: those who grew up in happy intact families, those who grew up in unhappy but intact families, and those who experienced a parental divorce. To determine whether the parental marriage was a happy one, we referred to parents' responses to questions—first asked in 1980—dealing with marital happiness, conflict, and problems.

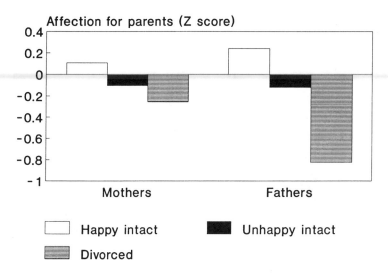

FIG. 7.4. Adjusted mean affection for parents' Z scores for adults from happy intact, unhappy intact, and divorced families of origin.

Figure 7.4 shows adult offsprings' affection for parents (in 1992) by parents' marital happiness (in 1980) or divorce (prior to 1992). These means, as in previously reported analyses, are adjusted for a variety of background characteristics. Offspring had the strongest affection for parents when their parents' marriages were happy and intact. Offspring had less affection for parents when their parents' marriages were unhappy but intact, and offspring had the least affection for parents who divorced. This pattern was statistically significant for both parents, although the differences were greater for fathers than for mothers. This study suggests that marital discord weakens ties of affection between parents and children, and divorce weakens them even more. The father–child relationship is especially vulnerable to parental conflict and divorce—a finding consistent with several prior studies (Aquilino, 1994; Cooney, 1994; White, 1992).

We found one exception to this pattern. Divorce did not appear to weaken the bonds of affection between sons and fathers or between daughters and mothers if it occurred during late adolescence. Presumably, by this point in their development, offspring identified strongly enough with the same-gender parent that divorce was not damaging to the relationship. When children experienced divorce at earlier ages, however, especially if it was followed by remarriage, bonds of affection were weaker, regardless of parents' or children's gender.

Figure 7.5 shows the amount of assistance exchanged between parents and children following divorce. The vertical axis is a summary score that reflects the amount of help exchanged between households, including help with money, transportation, housework, home repairs, and emotional support. In this figure, the white bars reflect help received from parents, whereas the grey bars reflect help

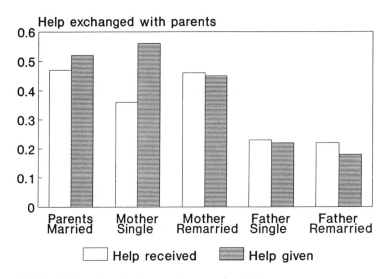

FIG. 7.5. Help exchanged with parents by parents' marital status.

given to parents. The first pair of bars on the left indicates the amount of help exchanged with continuously married parents. Compared with offspring whose parents remained married, those with single mothers gave significantly more assistance but received significantly less assistance. This finding reflects the fact that many single mothers are resource poor. The amount of help given to and received from the households of remarried mothers (as reflected in the middle pair of bars) was not appreciably different from that of continuously married parents.

Help exchanged with fathers was significantly lower in cases of divorce, regardless of whether fathers remained single or remarried. This finding is shown in the two pairs of bars on the right-hand side of the figure. These results indicate that many fathers cease to be part of their children's support networks following divorce. We found, for example, that most divorced fathers contributed little or no money to their children's college educations. It seems likely that when these fathers reach old age, they will receive relatively little assistance from their adult offspring in return. Once again, our findings are congruent with those of other researchers using different national data sets (Furstenberg, Hoffman, & Shreshta, 1995; White, 1992).

SUBJECTIVE WELL-BEING

Information on subjective well-being appears in Fig. 7.6. These data come from the sample of 471 young adults described previously. This figure shows adjusted means for two outcomes: a single-item indicator of self-reported happiness and a summary measure of satisfaction with multiple areas of life, such as job, home, neighborhood, and leisure activities. Young adults who grew up in happy intact families had the highest levels of happiness and satisfaction, whereas those from divorced families had the lowest (these differences across groups are statistically significant). Similar to some of the findings discussed previously, these results suggest that interparental conflict lowers children's well-being, and divorce lowers it even more.

These findings are congruent with those of other studies (Glenn & Kramer, 1985; McLeod, 1991). One study, by Chase-Lansdale, Cherlin, and Kiernan (1995), is particularly noteworthy. The researchers found, using a large, longitudinal sample of children in England, that parental divorce is associated with an increased risk of psychological problems in young adulthood. Furthermore, this increase persisted even after controlling for children's behavioral and academic problems, measured prior to divorce. This finding suggests that the estimated effects of divorce are not due to predivorce factors, such as marital conflict or economic stress. Taken together, these studies indicate that young adults' subjective sense of well-being can be affected by parents' decisions about divorce many years earlier.

CAUSAL MODEL

Although parental divorce is associated with multiple dimensions of offspring well-being, it is likely that these different dimensions also are associated with one another. In Fig. 7.7, I present a structural equation model that relates subjective

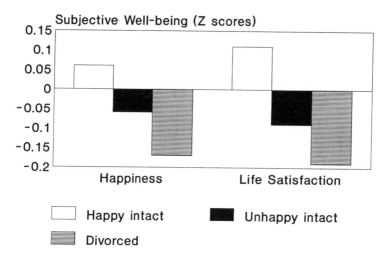

FIG. 7.6. Adjusted mean subjective well-being Z scores for adults from happy intact, unhappy intact, and divorced families of origin.

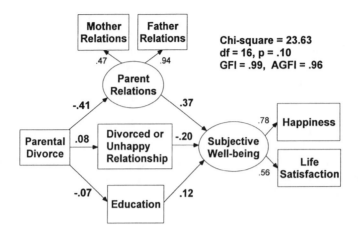

FIG. 7.7. Structural equation model relating parental divorce to parent–child relations, relationship status, education, and subjective well-being.

well-being to parental divorce as well as to the other outcomes described in this chapter.

The model assumes that three variables mediate the impact of parental divorce on offsprings' subjective well-being. First, it is likely that a high level of educational attainment promotes subjective well-being. Education not only makes it possible for people to attain a comfortable standard of living but also provides people with self-confidence and cognitive skills that are useful in dealing with the vicissitudes of life (Ross & Wu, 1995). Second, being happily married is associated with good mental health, whereas being divorced or in an unhappy marital relationship is associated with poor psychological health (Waite, 1995). Presumably, a strong marriage provides people with companionship, social support, and a readily available confidant in times of emotional need. Third, close ties with parents appear to facilitate psychological well-being in early adulthood (Barnett, Kibria, Baruch, & Pleck, 1991; Barnett, Marshall, & Pleck, 1992). Although it is often assumed that the parent–child bond becomes weaker when offspring achieve residential independence, most young adults continue to maintain close ties with their parents and rely on them in times of emotional or material need (Rossi & Rossi, 1990). As noted previously, parental divorce lowers educational attainment, lowers the likelihood of being happily married, and weakens ties with parents, especially fathers. For these reasons, these three variables may be responsible for the relatively low level of subjective well-being among adults from divorced families of origin.

To test this model, I used the AMOS (Analysis of Moment Structures) program with maximum likelihood estimation (Arbuckle, 1995). The results in Fig. 7.7 are based on the sample of 471 young adults described previously. All coefficients in the model are standardized and are statistically significant ($p < .05$).

The results suggest that parental divorce lowers offspring education, which is indicated by the coefficient of −.07. The middle variable is dichotomous and identifies individuals who are either divorced or in unhappy marriages (1 = divorced or unhappily married, 0 = other). Parental divorce increases the likelihood that people are divorced or unhappily married; this is indicated by the positive coefficient of .08. Finally, parent relations is a latent variable based on people's reports of affection for their mothers and fathers. The model suggest that parental divorce lowers the quality of ties with parents, as reflected in the coefficient of −.41.

In this model, subjective well-being is a latent variable based on people's reports of happiness and life satisfaction. Education increases well-being, as indicated by the coefficient of .12. Being divorced or in an unhappy marriage lowers well-being, as indicated by the coefficient of −.20. Affection for parents increases well-being, as reflected in the coefficient of .37. The original significant association between parental divorce and subjective well-being, shown in Fig. 7.6, is no longer significant with these three mediating variables in the equation.

These results suggest that parental divorce affects people's sense of well-being in adulthood by lowering educational attainment, increasing the likelihood of marital relationship failure, and weakening ties of affection with parents. Of course, because all the data are from a single source, it is possible that people's psychological states are coloring their evaluations of their marital happiness and affection for parents. For this reason, in future research (based on data currently being obtained), I will use independent sources of information to test the same model. Nevertheless, the current results are congruent with theory as well as previous research.

CONCLUSIONS

Consistent with a life course perspective, research suggests that the consequences of parental divorce persist well into adulthood. Adult offspring from divorced families of origin, compared with those from two-parent families of origin, enter adulthood with less education, earn less money, have fewer financial assets, have poorer quality marriages, are more likely to divorce, have less affection for their parents (especially fathers), exchange less assistance with their fathers, and have lower levels of subjective well-being. Given these findings, perhaps the warnings of conservatives are correct. Perhaps we should be alarmed about the well-being of the next generation and the future of our society.

Before reaching this conclusion, however, it is necessary to put these results into perspective. The risk and resiliency paradigm suggests that children react in a variety of ways to the stress of parental divorce, with some children being vulnerable and others being resilient. Consistent with this notion, the mean differences between children from divorced and nondivorced families, although statistically significant, are modest in magnitude. This finding indicates that there is considerable variability in outcomes, not only among offspring with divorced parents but also among offspring with continuously married parents.

For example, the mean difference in subjective well-being between those from divorced and nondivorced families of origin (described previously) represents about one fifth of a standard deviation. This indicates a substantial overlap in the two distributions. If we assume that subjective well-being is normally distributed in the populations from which the samples were drawn, then 42% of children with divorced parents reach adulthood with a level of personal well-being higher than that of the average child from a two-parent family. In comparison, 42% of children with nondivorced parents reach adulthood with a level of subjective well-being lower than that of the average child from a divorced family. Growing up in a stable, two-parent family does not guarantee a happy future, and growing up in a divorced family does not preclude the possibility of future happiness.

The same principle applies to other outcomes. Many children from divorced families graduate from college, have successful careers, are happily married, and have close ties with mothers and fathers. In contrast, many children from two-parent families fail to achieve these goals. Although divorce increases the risk of a variety of negative outcomes, most children from divorced families develop into reasonably competent citizens. These considerations suggest that the current high divorce rate is not placing future generations of youth, and society itself, in serious danger.

Nevertheless, we should not be complacent about the relatively small differences between children from divorced and nondivorced families. Although the estimated effects of divorce are modest, divorce affects a very large number of children every year. Consequently, divorce may be responsible for a mean decline in the well-being of future generations that is equivalent to that of more damaging but less commonly encountered stressors (such as neglect or abuse).

This conclusion suggests that decreasing the number of children exposed to divorce would be an appropriate policy goal. However, decreasing the incidence of divorce would not be beneficial if it means increasing the number of children living in unhappy two-parent households. As noted previously, children in high-conflict families exhibit many of the same problems as do children in divorced families. Indeed, research is consistent in showing that children develop best when their parents are happily married to one another. Therefore, the fundamental policy goal should not be to decrease the frequency of divorce but to increase the number of happy two-parent families.

This goal is difficult but not impossible to attain. Governments and private organizations could make premarital education, marriage enrichment programs, and marital counseling more widely available. In addition, programs that improve the economic well-being of two-parent families, especially those that are close to or below the poverty line, would help. Studies show that economic stress undermines marital quality (Conger et al., 1990) and increases the likelihood of divorce (Hernandez, 1993). It seems likely, therefore, that some marriages at high risk for divorce could be salvaged if parents' economic burdens were eased. The Earned Income Tax Credit is a good example of a program that benefits many working poor families with children and could be expanded further (McLanahan & Sandefur, 1994). Similarly, workplace policies that reduce work–family conflict, such as paid parental leave, would strengthen marriages. Most two-parent families are dual-earner families these days, and tensions caused by the conflicting demands of families and jobs are stressing too many couples (Spain & Bianchi, 1996).

What about changing the legal system to make divorce more difficult to obtain? Currently, several state legislatures are considering returning to an exclusively fault-based system of divorce. The assumption underlying this movement is that if divorces are harder to get, then fewer people will divorce and fewer children will be harmed. This strategy, however, is problematic for two reasons. First, restricting divorce is likely to increase the number of couples who separate permanently, and from a child's perspective, separation is no better from divorce. Second, restricting divorce will trap more children in high-conflict marriages; this is not a positive alternative to divorce. Indeed, some research indicates that some children in families marked by chronic conflict are better off if their parents divorce (Amato, Loomis, & Booth, 1995). Given that the legal system cannot make parents live together happily, it makes little sense to force parents to remain in marriages against their will. Although a return to a fault-based system of divorce may satisfy ideological goals—and may be desirable to some people for that reason—it is unlikely to benefit children.

In conclusion, research indicates that the long-term consequences of divorce for children are complex. On the one hand, divorce does not doom most children to unproductive and unhappy lives as adults. On the other hand, divorce is not a trivial event to which most children readily adjust with few enduring negative consequences. Although the effects of divorce are modest, they are widespread (affecting large numbers of children) and pervasive (affecting many areas of life). The decline of the stable, two-parent family as the primary institution for raising children, therefore, is reason for concern. Finding ways to make marriage a more satisfying arrangement—an arrangement that parents will work hard to maintain—is a current policy challenge.

REFERENCES

Amato, P. R. (1996). Explaining the intergenerational transmission of divorce. *Journal of Marriage and the Family, 58,* 628–640.
Amato, P. R. (1994). Life-span adjustment of children to their parents' divorces. *Future of Children, 25,* 1031–1042.
Amato, P. R., & Booth, A. (1991). Consequences of parental divorce and maritalunhappiness for adult well-being. *Social Forces, 69,* 895–914.
Amato, P. R., Loomis, L. S., & Booth, A. (1995). Parental divorce, marital conflict, and offspring well-being in early adulthood. *Social Forces, 73,* 895–916.

Amato, P. R., Rezac, S., & Booth, A. (1995). Helping between parents and young adult offspring: The role of parental marital quality, divorce, and remarriage. *Journal of Marriage and the Family, 57*, 363–374.

Amato, P. R., & Keith, B. (1991a). Consequences of parental divorce for children's well-being: A meta-analysis. *Psychological Bulletin, 110*, 26–46.

Amato, P. R., & Keith, B. (1991b). Separation from a parent during childhood and adult socioeconomic attainment. *Social Forces, 70*, 187–206.

Aquilino, W. S. (1994). Impact of childhood family disruption on young adults' relationships with parents. *Journal of Marriage and the Family, 56*, 295–313.

Arbuckle, J. L. (1995). *AMOS 3.5 for Windows.* Chicago: Smallwaters.

Barnett, R. C., Kibria, N., Baruch, G. K., & Pleck, J. (1991). Adult daughter–parent relationships and their associations with daughters' subjective well-being and psychological distress. *Journal of Marriage and the Family, 53*, 29–42.

Barnett, R. C., Marshall, N. L., & Pleck, J. H. (1992). Adult son–parent relationships and their associations with sons' psychological stress. *Journal of Family Issues, 13*, 505–525.

Belsky, J., & Pensky, E. (1988). Developmental history, personality, and family relationships: Toward an emergent family system. In R. A. Hinde and J. Stevenson-Hinde (Eds.), *Relationships within families: Mutual influences* (pp. 193–217). Oxford: Clarendon.

Blankenhorn, D. (1995). *Fatherless America: Confronting our most urgent social problem.* New York: Basic Books.

Booth, A., & Amato, P. R. (1994). Parental marital quality, parental divorce, and relations with parents. *Journal of Marriage and the Family, 56*, 21–34.

Booth, A., Johnson, D. R., White, L. K., & Edwards, J. N. (1991). *Marital instability over the life course: Methodology report and code book for a three wave panel study.* Department of Sociology, University of Nebraska–Lincoln.

Bumpass, L. L., Martin, T. C., & Sweet, J. A. (1991). The impact of family background and early marital factors on marital disruption. *Journal of Family Issues, 12*, 22–42.

Bumpass, L. L., Thompson, E., & McDonald E. (1984). Children and marital disruption: A replication and update. *Demography, 21*, 71–82.

Caspi, A., & Elder, G. H., Jr. (1988). Emergent family patterns: The intergenerational construction of problem behaviors and relationships. In Robert Hinde and Joan Stevenson-Hinde (Eds.), *Relationships within families: Mutual influences* (pp. 218–240). Oxford: Clarendon.

Chase-Lansdale, P. L., Cherlin, A. J., & Kiernan, K. E. (1995). The long-term effects of parental divorce on the mental health of young adults: A developmental perspective. *Child Development, 66*, 1614–1634.

Cherlin, A. (1992). *Marriage, divorce, remarriage.* Cambridge, MA: Harvard University Press.

Conger, R., Elder, G. H., Lorenz, F. O., Conger, K. J., Simons, R. L., Whitbeck, L., Huck, S., & Melby, J. N. (1990). Linking economic hardship to marital quality and instability. *Journal of Marriage and the Family, 52*, 643–656.

Cooney, T. M. (1994). Young adults' relations with parents: the influence of recent parental divorce. *Journal of Marriage and the Family, 56*, 45–56.

Coontz, S. (1992). *The way we never were: American families and the nostalgia trap.* New York: Basic Books.

Davies, P. T., & Cummings, E. M. (1994). Marital conflict and child adjustment: An emotional insecurity hypothesis. *Psychological Bulletin, 116*, 387–411.

Demo, D. H. (1992). Parent–child relations: Assessing recent change. *Journal of Marriage and the Family, 54*, 104–114.

Edwards, J. N. (1987). Changing family structure and youthful well-being: Assessing the future. *Journal of Family Issues, 8*, 355–372.

Elder, G. H., Jr. (1994). Time, agency, and change: Perspectives on the life course. *Social Psychology Quarterly, 57*, 5–15.

Emery, R. (1988). *Marriage, divorce, and children's adjustment.* Newbury Park, CA: Sage.

Furstenberg, F. F., Hoffman, S., & Shreshta, S. (1995). The effect of divorce on intergenerational transfers: New evidence. *Demography, 32,* 319–333.

Garmezy, N., & Rutter, M. (Eds.). (1983). *Stress, coping, and development in children.* New York: McGraw-Hill.

Glenn, N. D., & Kramer, K. B. (1985). The psychological well-being of adult children of divorce. *Journal of Marriage and the Family, 47,* 905–912.

Glenn, N. D., & Kramer, K. B. (1987). The marriages and divorces of the children of divorce. *Journal of Marriage and the Family, 49,* 811–825.

Hernandez, D. (1993). *America's children: Resources from family, government, and the economy.* New York: Russell Sage Foundation.

Hetherington, E. M. (1989). Marital transitions: A child's perspective. *American Psychologist, 44,* 303–310.

Hetherington, E. M., & Blechman, E. A. (Eds.). (1996). *Stress, coping, and resiliency in children and families.* Mahwah, NJ: Lawrence Erlbaum Associates.

Keith, V. M., & Finlay, B. (1988). The impact of parental divorce on children's educational attainment, marital timing, and likelihood of divorce. *Journal of Marriage and the Family, 50,* 797–809.

Krein, S. F. (1986). Growing up in a single parent family: The effect on education and earnings of young men. *Family Relations, 35,* 161–168.

McLanahan, S., & Sandefur, G. (1994). *Growing up with a single parent.* Cambridge, MA: Harvard University Press.

McLeod, J. D. (1991). Childhood parental loss and adult depression. *Journal of Health and Social Behavior, 32,* 205–220.

Pope, H., & Mueller, C. W. (1976). The intergenerational transmission of divorce: Comparisons by race and sex. *Journal of Social Issues, 32,* 49–66.

Popenoe, D. (1996). *Life without father.* New York: The Free Press.

Ross, C. E., & Wu, C. (1995). The link between education and health. *American Sociological Review, 60,* 719–745.

Rossi, A., & Rossi, P. (1990). *Of human bonding: Parent-child relations across the life course.* New York: Aldine de Gruyter.

Spain, D., & Bianchi, S. (1996). *Balancing act: Motherhood, marriage and employment among American women.* New York: Russell Sage Foundation.

Waite, L. J. (1995). Does marriage matter? *Demography, 32,* 483–507.

Wadsworth, M. E. J., & Maclean, M. (1986). Parents' divorce and children's life chances. *Children and Youth Services Review, 8,* 145–159.

Webster, P. S., Orbuch, T. L., & House, J. S. (1995). Effects of childhood family structure on adult marital quality and perceived stability. *American Journal of Sociology, 101,* 404–432.

White, L. (1992). The effect of parental divorce and remarriage on parental support of adult children. *Journal of Family Issues, 13,* 234–250.

Whitehead, B. D. (1993). Dan Quayle was right. *Atlantic Monthly* (April), 47–84.

8

Young African American Multigenerational Families in Poverty
The Contexts, Exchanges, and Processes of Their Lives

P. Lindsay Chase-Lansdale
Rachel A. Gordon
Rebekah Levine Coley
Lauren S. Wakschlag
University of Chicago

Jeanne Brooks-Gunn
Columbia University

YOUNG, African American multigenerational families are composed of young mothers, grandmothers, and children. These multigenerational families exist both within and outside of shared living arrangements. Grandmothers, or grandmother figures, living in close proximity to young mothers can provide advice, emotional support, and practical assistance, as can grandmothers who share homes with young mothers and children. Indeed, some grandmothers and young mothers live in quite immediate residences—on different floors of the same apartment building or at different addresses on the same block—providing privacy from but still ready access to each other.

The grandmother in these families has long been a hidden member, often ignored by researchers, journalists, and policymakers who view families with a "single-parent versus two-parent" lens. However, grandmothers have recently received increased interest, in part because of the important role they play as potential coparents to teenage mothers and as primary parents when their grandchildren face parental incapacitation due to drug abuse, mental illness, or incarceration (see

Creighton, 1991, and Little, 1995, for media portrayals and Burton, 1992, 1995; Jendrek, 1993; LaPoint, Pickett, & Harris, 1985; and Minkler, Roe, & Robertson-Beckley, 1994, for recent research), and in part due to the growing general recognition of the diversity of family structures in social science research (see Bumpass & Raley, 1995; Furakawa, 1994; Hernandez, 1993). Indeed, the Personal Responsibility and Work Opportunity Reconciliation Act of 1996, which revamped the nation's social welfare system, has mandated a multigenerational household structure for unmarried, minor parents and charged the U.S. Bureau of the Census with expanding data collection efforts "concerning the growing trend of grandparents who are the primary caregivers of grandchildren" (Section 105, paragraph a; see also Gordon, Chase-Lansdale, Matjasko, & Brooks-Gunn, 1997).

In contrast, African American scholars have long recognized the multiplicity of structures within African American households and families (see Wilson, 1986, and Gordon, 1993, for reviews). For example, in the 1960s, Billingsley (1968) called for terminology that moved beyond the two parent–single parent dichotomy, and Hill (1977) later examined the diversity of household configurations that support the developing African American child. In the 1970s, ethnographic research portrayed the vital nature of multigenerational African American families in rich detail (see Ladner, 1971; Martin & Martin, 1978; Shimkin, Shimkin, & Frate, 1978; Stack, 1974). Although strong multigenerational families persist today, recent research has cautioned against a view of grandmothers as a panacea for the problems associated with young motherhood, highlighting the multitude of demands that can be placed on young African American grandmothers (see Burton, 1995; George & Dickerson, 1995).

The two parent–single parent dichotomy also excludes those men who are part of children's lives but not connected by the traditional marital bond. Indeed, as demographic changes in marital patterns occurred over recent decades, researchers were slow to recognize the increasing importance of partnerships formed outside of marriage. Yet for about 14% of the time African American children spend in so-called single-parent households, they actually share a household with a cohabiting father figure (Bumpass & Raley, 1995). Moreover, even the absence of a husband or male partner from the household does not signify a total loss of men from family life. Rather, many men maintain a continued presence in the lives of their children through regular visits and through relationships fostered between the young mother's family and the father's family of origin (Coley & Chase-Lansdale, 1997; Furstenberg, 1995).

Multigenerational families often live in poverty, so much so that some researchers suggest that this family configuration may be a general adaptive response to harsh economic conditions, with impoverished families forming complex kin networks that pool resources and share childrearing across generational lines. Others link multigenerational families more closely to young motherhood, suggesting that these families are a byproduct of early transitions to parenthood, especially across generations, and high rates of single motherhood, both of which are associated with poverty. Still others suggest that African American extended kin networks reflect family structures consonant with African heritage that have endured in the West Indies as well as the United States and that persist when African American families move out of poverty. Elements of each of these explanatory frameworks may work together to sustain the multigenerational families that are evident today.

A risk and resilience model might guide the study of African American multigenerational families in poverty; such families need not be seen as uniformly at risk or uniformly adapting to extremely difficult social contexts (McLoyd, 1990; Slaughter, 1988; Spencer, 1990). The purpose of this chapter is to examine the diversity of experiences within these families when they form around a young mother and her child, emphasizing both coping and difficulty, answering questions such as: Who are young multigenerational African American families? What are the challenges that they face? Multigenerational African American families are best understood by considering three major features: context, exchange, and process. We describe and develop each of these aspects of young multigenerational families, with illustrations from the Baltimore Multigenerational Family Study (BMFS).

THE BALTIMORE MULTIGENERATIONAL FAMILY STUDY

The Study Design

The Baltimore Multigenerational Family Study (BMFS) was conceived from a family systems perspective to reflect the complex family networks in which young African American mothers are embedded (see Chase-Lansdale, Brooks-Gunn, & Zamsky, 1994, for additional details and demographic characteristics of the sample). Consistent with Furstenberg's original Baltimore Study begun in the late 1960s and other pathbreaking studies of the structure of teenage mothers' households (Furstenberg, Brooks-Gunn, & Morgan, 1987; Furstenberg & Crawford, 1978; Hardy, Astone, Brooks-Gunn, Shapiro, & Miller, in press; Kellam, Adams, Brown, & Ensminger, 1982), information about the presence and role of the grandmother was elicited. However, the BMFS was unique in also developing new observational measures of each component of the multigenerational family system (e.g., child–mother dyad, child–grandmother dyad, mother–grandmother dyad, and child–mother–grandmother triad). Although not with the same observational detail as the grandmother–mother–child system, information was also collected from mothers about the children's fathers' role in their own and their children's lives. The study was not designed to compare multigenerational families to other family structures but rather to address the following individual difference question: What aspects of multigenerational family life promote healthy functioning in the face of multiple risks?

Who is "young" in these multigenerational families? First, the mothers were young at first birth. Approximately two thirds were teenage mothers at first birth (ages 13–18), and the remaining third were young adult mothers at first birth (ages

19–25). This design allowed teenage mothers to be contrasted with mothers who had a first birth as they were negotiating the transition to adulthood. The grandmothers in these multigenerational families were also young at their first birth, as the BMFS was designed to be a sample of multiple generations of early parenthood. Nearly half of the sample mothers (45%) were the children, or partners of the children, of the teenage mothers from follow-ups of the Baltimore Study of adolescent parenthood (Furstenberg et al., 1987). The remaining mothers were drawn from a prenatal clinic (35%) or the networks of the Baltimore Study and clinic-sample families (20%). As was the case for the sample of mothers, about two thirds of the grandmothers had been teenagers (age 13–18) and one third had been young adults (19–25) at first birth.[1] Finally, the children in these multigenerational families were also young. The vast majority (83%) were the targeted age of 3 years at the time of the study. The BMFS collected detailed psychometric, mother-reported, grandmother-reported, and observational information about how these children were doing at toddlerhood, as well as retrospective and concurrent demographic information about the families since the mothers' pregnancies. For example, current and retrospective life history data were collected about marriage and cohabitation, jobs, school, fertility, child care arrangements, and coresidence among the multigenerational family members.

Some Notes on the Data and Procedures

Data collection for the BMFS was performed by teams of primarily older African American women skilled in developing rapport with families. First, the mother participated in a 2½-hour home visit, filling out a structured interview and standardized psychometric tests (e.g., the Peabody Picture Vocabulary Test, PPVT). With the mother's permission, the grandmother or grandmother figure was then approached. A similar home visit procedure was then conducted with the grandmother, usually about 3 to 6 weeks later. During the second visit, family members also participated in several videotaped interaction sequences.

Three important issues must be kept in mind as we present various results from the BMFS. First, not all family members participated in all assessments, resulting in different sample sizes across measures. The full sample includes 136 African American families. In 135 of these families, the mother completed a structured interview, and in 107 families, the grandmother completed a structured interview. In addition, 103 families participated in videotaped interactions of the mother–child and the grandmother–child dyads, 96 families participated in a mother–grandmother interaction sequence, and 101 families participated in triadic mother–grandmother–child free play. Consequently, substantive analyses of different top-

---

[1] Of the remaining grandmothers and grandmother figures, one each was age 28, 29, and 30 at first birth, and four surrogate grandmothers (two maternal great aunts of the child, one paternal aunt of the child, and one friend of the mother) had not given birth to children of their own.

ics, requiring different measures of the family, have different amounts of available data. We found no differences between the families that did and did not agree to videotaping or to the grandmother interview on a range of background variables available from mother interview data (e.g., participation in AFDC, mother's age at first birth, mother's marital status).

Second, the term *grandmother* has a broader meaning than a strict biological relationship. If the maternal grandmother was unavailable, the mother was asked to designate "the person most like a grandmother to your child." In the majority of cases, the grandmother who participated in the study was the child's maternal grandmother (79 of 107 cases). However, in the remainder (29 cases), the grandmother role was filled by the child's maternal great-grandmother, maternal great aunts and aunts, paternal grandmothers or aunts, or women who were not related to the child.

This distribution of grandmother figures reflects the predominance of the maternal grandmother as identified in past research (see George & Dickerson, 1995; Gonzalez, 1969; Kellam et al., 1982; McAdoo, 1983; Shimkin et al., 1978), but is also consistent with recent ethnographic research that highlights the range of family members providing intergenerational support to young mothers and their children (see Burton, 1995). Analyses that draw on the BMFS observational measures or utilize information reported by grandmothers in structured interviews include this pool of grandmothers and grandmother figures, and we use the general term *grandmother* to refer to this set of women. However, information that the young mothers reported in their structured interviews about their own biological mothers, the children's fathers, and the children's paternal grandmothers provides an alternative approach to depicting the variety of persons who make up these young families. In that case, we use the specific terms *maternal grandmother* and *paternal grandmother* to identify particular family members.

Finally, although the sample includes families experiencing young motherhood across generations, the sample does not exclusively comprise currently young grandmothers. Each mother was not necessarily the grandmother's first child, the study child was not necessarily the grandmother's first grandchild, and, as just noted, some grandmothers were not the child's maternal grandmothers. Indeed, the grandmothers ranged in age from 21 to 69 at the study child's birth. Whereas the full sample and maternal grandmothers are predominately concentrated in their thirties and forties, the grandmother figures are more evenly distributed over the age range, likely due to the younger sisters and friends and older great-grandmothers who took on surrogate grandmother roles (see Table 8.1).

THE CONTEXTS OF MULTIGENERATIONAL FAMILIES

We now describe the context of the BMFS participants (i.e., household structure and poverty) and then consider variation in family interactions that underlies

TABLE 8.1
Distribution of Grandmothers' Age at the Study Child's Birth:
Maternal Grandmothers and Grandmother Figures

	Relationship to Child		
Age at Child's Birth	All Grandmothers (n = 107)	Maternal Grandmother (n = 79)	Not Maternal Grandmother (n = 28)
Twenties	5.6%	1.3%	17.9%
Thirties	51.4%	57.0%	35.7%
Forties	28.0%	30.4%	21.4%
Fifties	8.4%	7.6%	10.7%
Sixties	6.5%	3.8%	14.3%

Note. Columns sum to 100%.

these structural factors. Specifically, how do family members negotiate the day-to-day needs of caring for children? To what extent do family members exchange support, even when not sharing a household? What is the quality and the quantity of parenting provided by mothers and grandmothers?

Socioeconomic Contexts

Poverty is a common condition that shapes the lives of young African American multigenerational families, both in terms of the economic resources available within their family networks and in terms of the financial capital found in their local communities. In the BMFS, many have turned to government transfer income as a source of support. Nearly 90% of mothers had relied on Aid to Families with Dependent Children (AFDC) at some time in their children's lives, and close to 60% were drawing on AFDC for income at the time of the study. Although considerably less extensive, grandmothers also showed recent use of government transfer income, with just over 20% currently receiving AFDC. On average, both mothers and grandmothers had achieved less than a high school education (about 11½ years on average). At the neighborhood level, comparisons with the 1990 statistics in the Baltimore metropolitan area reveal the relative disadvantage of the BMFS sample. Compared to the average neighborhood in Baltimore, the study families lived in neighborhoods that had 40% or more lower average family income, about one grade level lower average schooling, and an occupational composition that was on average predominately blue and pink collar in contrast to the typical Baltimore area neighborhood, which was predominately white collar. On average, about twice as many males in the study neighborhoods than in the Baltimore area as a whole were out of the labor force, were unemployed, and were underemployed (i.e., working 26 weeks or less in the last year). In terms of racial composition, about one fourth of the residents in the average Baltimore neighborhood were African American, as compared to 80 to 90% of residents in the typical study neighborhood.

Residential Arrangements of BMFS Families

To what extent do the study families share households or reside apart? We examined these issues extensively in a recent paper (Gordon et al., 1997) and summarize those results here along with additional evidence about times the children spend in other living arrangements (e.g., mother–father–child, mother–father–grandmother–child, child–grandmother). The BMFS provides unique data regarding the residential arrangements of young mothers. At the time of the study, a little more than half the families shared households, whereas in the remaining families the grandmothers lived in separate residences apart from the mothers and children. Because both mothers and grandmothers were interviewed, and we know where both women lived if not coresident, we have rich information about the household and neighborhood contexts of those multigenerational families who share residences and those in which the mother and grandmother live apart. We thus could ask, "What family and neighborhood characteristics relate to families' coresidence status?" (Gordon et al., 1997).

Very few main effect differences are evident between the multigenerational families that coreside and those that live in separate residences in terms of their demographic characteristics and their household and neighborhood contexts.[2] For example, coresiding mothers and grandmothers did not differ from mothers and grandmothers living independently in terms of age at first birth, level of education, marital status, intellectual ability, or mother's reliance on AFDC. Many more differences are revealed when interactions between coresidence and the young mother's age at first birth are examined. In particular, we found that young adult mothers (ages 19–25 at first birth) appeared to react to resources and competition in the neighborhood and household context when choosing living arrangements. These mothers were less likely to coreside when the grandmothers lived in extremely impoverished settings and tended to move into better surroundings than those where the grandmothers lived. Contextual factors did not relate to coresidence status for teenage mothers (ages 13–18 at first birth). Instead, we found that the absence of support provided by the grandmother early in the child's life (i.e., the mother reported that the grandmother was not supportive during her pregnancy and did not help care for her child during his or her first 6 months of life) was related to living apart for teenage mothers. We expect that these moderated

---

[2]A few exceptions are evident. Young mothers who reside with grandmothers are more likely to live in owned versus rental housing than young mothers who reside apart; non-coresiding grandmothers live in neighborhoods that contain significantly fewer adults per children than the neighborhoods of coresiding grandmothers; and grandmothers in non-coresiding families have more young children of their own (below the age of 13) than do grandmothers in coresiding families (see Gordon, Chase-Lansdale, Matjasko, & Brooks-Gunn, 1997, for details).

effects may reflect teenage mothers' greater need for a grandmother's coresidential support during the transition to parenthood (Gordon et al., 1997).

The Fathers

A small proportion of biological fathers were consistent, residential family members in the years immediately following the birth, either through marriage to or cohabitation with the mothers. Within the entire sample of 135 families, 11% of the parents married, although these marriages showed fairly high rates of instability. By the time the families were interviewed, about 3 years after the child's birth, approximately one third of the marriages had ended in divorce or separation. An additional 5% of fathers resided with mothers and children in nonmarital partnerships at the time of the interview. Finally, the advent of new partnerships is also seen in this sample; by the child's toddlerhood, 9% of the mothers had husbands or residential partners who were not the biological fathers of the children. Although these young couples more often live apart from the grandmother than not, some share multigenerational households.

Two-Parent and Multigenerational Households

Does the tendency to live with the child's father or the child's grandmother change over the child's life? Table 8.2 provides a descriptive portrait of children's living arrangements through their third birthdays. The first panel lists the average fraction of time spent in various living arrangements, and two patterns stand out.

TABLE 8.2
A Descriptive Portrait of Children's Living Arrangements Before Age Three

		Coresident Caregivers					
Child's Age	M	GM	M-F	M-H/P	M-GM	M-F-GM	M-H/P-GM
Average fraction of time spent with various caregivers at each year of age[a]							
Pregnancy	20.4	0.0	8.6	0.0	60.6	10.3	0.0
Birth through age 1	13.9	1.3	9.4	0.0	64.8	8.8	1.5
Age 1 to age 2	16.8	2.6	13.5	2.1	56.6	7.2	1.1
Age 2 to age 3	20.7	2.0	14.2	4.1	51.0	7.2	0.8
Fraction of children who had ever and had always lived with various caregivers							
Ever: Birth through age 3	40.0	5.7	23.8	5.7	78.1	19.0	4.8
Always: Birth through age 3	5.7	2.0	4.8	0.0	32.4	2.9	0.0

Note. The categories are mutually exclusive (caregivers not listed are not present in the household). M = child's mother; F = child's father; GM = child's grandmother or grandmother-figure; H/P = mother's husband or cohabiting male partner (other than the child's father). $n = 105$.

[a]Row percentages do not always sum to 100, due to rounding error and a small fraction of time children spend in other living arrangements.

First, across the period of time from pregnancy through toddlerhood, mother–grandmother coresidence appears to be at a peak when the child is an infant, likely reflecting the intense demands faced by young mothers in the transition to parenthood. When their children are age two, mothers are more likely to spend time living apart from the grandmothers, either on their own (20.7%), with the child's father (14.2%), or with husbands or male partners other than the child's father (4.1%). Second, in our sample children had spent little time living apart from the mothers with the grandmothers only prior to their third birthday. Additional analyses of these data indicate that less than 15% of children had ever lived apart from the mother for an extended period of time, and these spells spent away from the mother from infancy through toddlerhood tended to be of short duration. The second panel of Table 8.2 presents the fraction of children who had ever and had always lived in each of the living arrangements from birth through their third birthdays. These statistics highlight the prevalence of mother–grandmother coresidential household structures in our young multigenerational families: Over three fourths of children had ever lived in such a living arrangement and nearly one third had lived in such a setting continuously until toddlerhood.

EXCHANGES WITHIN MULTIGENERATIONAL FAMILY SYSTEMS: THE MEANING OF STRUCTURE

Multigenerational families use a variety of strategies to address the day-to-day needs of family members, including frequent contact and exchange of assistance. We find that these types of exchanges often supersede household boundaries, although sharing a home sometimes facilitates them.

Contact and Exchange With Grandmothers

The multigenerational family members in our study who did not share households were in regular contact with one another. All grandmothers who were not currently living with the young mothers reported talking with them on the phone at least once a week, with two thirds talking with them almost daily. In addition, these women reported seeing the young mother and her child at least once or twice a month, with two thirds getting together at least two or three times a week. We emphasize, however, that all noncoresidential study grandmothers and grandmother figures lived close enough to the young mothers that seeing one another regularly was not precluded by distance (i.e., noncoresidential grandmothers lived on average within 4 miles of young mothers; the range is 0 to 57 miles, with 90% living within 10 miles of each other). When young mothers live far from their own mothers, they may draw on other kin and friend networks or face greater social isolation than young mothers with large local kin networks (see Jayakody, Chatters, & Taylor, 1993; Parish, Hao, & Hogan, 1991; Taylor, 1986). Indeed, in the current study, many of the grandmother figures had reportedly taken on the grandmother role because the maternal grandmother lived far away from the young mother.

Grandmothers also told us more specifically about the time they spend providing regular care for their grandchildren. Such grandparental care is an important component of the child care choices made by young mothers (Presser, 1989) and has been found to be a protective factor for the development of preschoolers (Baydar & Brooks-Gunn, 1991). In the BMFS, both mothers and grandmothers report that the young mothers are most often primarily responsible for the care of the children on weekdays and weekends, and a relatively small fraction of grandmothers told us that they take on this primary caregiver role (i.e., about 11% of non-coresidential grandmothers and 18% of coresidential grandmothers). However, a substantial fraction provide backup child care for at least 4 hours a day on either the weekend or the weekday: Over 60% of coresiding grandmothers report providing backup child care on the weekend and during the week. Grandmothers living apart provide less support during the week (40%) but more during the weekends (75%).

Other types of exchange between a young mother and grandmother, and activities shared by grandmother and grandchild are also frequent, with some differences and similarities for multigenerational families that share a household and those that live apart. It is not surprising that grandmothers who live with a young mother and child report more exchange of help with errands, household chores, and home repairs than do noncoresiding grandmothers (over 80% of coresiding grandmothers versus about one third of noncoresiding grandmothers report giving and receiving such assistance). However, whereas most grandmothers report loaning or giving money to a young mother regardless of residence (i.e., 86% of coresiding and 79% of noncoresiding grandmothers), grandmothers who share a household with a young mother are significantly more likely to report receiving such cash transfers from the young mother (i.e., 79% of coresiding and 60% of noncoresiding grandmothers). Finally, grandmothers are equally likely to spend time with their grandchildren in activities such as visiting the doctor, going to church, and going shopping, regardless of current coresident living arrangements: In the full sample, 25%, 50%, and 85% report sharing each of these respective activities with their grandchildren in the past year).

Contact and Exchange With Fathers

The BMFS also points to a need to go beyond simple rates of marriage, cohabitation, and divorce in understanding young African American multigenerational families. Although married and cohabiting men tend to be consistently present and involved with their children, many nonresidential fathers also strive to be active and involved parents. These fathers work to build relationships with their children and to continue relationships with their children's mothers, even outside a romantic involvement.

This process appears to start during the mother's pregnancy and at the birth of the child, when fathers are faced with decisions of whether or not to be active players in the lives of their children. Early presence appears to have long-term payoffs in relation to fathers' involvement with their children over time. Of the three fourths of fathers who visited their babies in the hospital, 60% went on to be involved with their children during the preschool years, whereas only 30% of the fathers who did not visit their babies were involved 3 years later. This bridge from early to later involvement continues during the child's infancy. When the children were 1 year old, 48% of fathers were actively involved in providing care for their children on a regular basis. Of these fathers, 80% remained highly involved 2 years later, whereas only 28% of their peers who did not provide infant care were highly involved during the preschool years.

These associations could be due to numerous factors. For example, men who desire to play active fathering roles are likely to be involved both at the time of birth and continuously during the children's lives. However, it is also possible that the early experience of playing a part in the birth of one's child and being involved from the beginning can both help to build a sense of connection between the father and child, recognized by the entire family, and encourage fathers to feel competent and active in their new role as parent.

What Does Father Involvement Look Like?   This question reverberates through much of the current research on fathers, especially research focused on nonresidential fathers. Much of this research, conducted with national samples of children from large longitudinal studies, has very narrow choices among variables measuring fathers' involvement with their children (e.g., King, 1994; Seltzer, 1991) and tends to use only measures such as the number of times per year fathers see their children and the amount of child support they pay. However, new research with more detailed and qualitative data, as well as theoretical work, is delineating the numerous areas of parenting that are not covered by such narrow measures, such as a father's commitment to his children, his level of responsibility and decision-making role in parenting decisions, the closeness of the father–child relationship, the father's availability as a role model and confidant, and the types and frequency of activities that fathers and children engage in together (e.g., Coley, in press; Furstenberg & Harris, 1993; Marsiglio, 1995; McAdoo, 1993; Zimmerman, Salem, & Maton, 1995).

In the BMFS, we measured many of these more detailed areas of fathers' involvement with their children. For example, at the time of the interview, mothers reported on five different constructs of father involvement: the quantitative areas of financial contributions and the frequency of fathers' visits with children; the more exchange-oriented concepts of fathers' provision of child care and the level of parental responsibility undertaken; and finally the process-oriented area of the closeness of the father–child relationship. These measures capture a unified construct of fathers' presence in the lives of their children, as reflected in both factor and cluster analyses (see Coley & Chase-Lansdale, 1997). Mothers report that half (53%) of the fathers in this study were consistently involved with their preschool-age children: They contributed financially, provided regular care, and were responsible for, available to, and emotionally close with their children. In contrast, the other fathers (47%) were reportedly not involved in a significant way in any of these aspects of parenting, instead fitting the description of a truly absent father.

Why are Some Fathers Involved With Their Children and Others Not?

What other characteristics of families and fathers predict who will stay active in the family system and who will not? We used OLS regression models to address this question (see Coley & Chase-Lansdale, 1997, for details). In these models, we considered the relative importance of four sets of variables: maternal characteristics, such as age at child's birth, education, and employment; paternal characteristics, similar to those of mothers; the mothers' ratings of intrafamilial relationships, including relations between mothers and fathers, mothers and maternal grandmothers, maternal grandmothers and children, and paternal grandmothers and children; and the mothers' reports of the fathers' involvement with the children at one year of age. From this analysis we found that paternal characteristics, family relationships, and previous father involvement are the strongest correlates of fathers' emotional and behavioral ties to their preschool children in multigenerational families. More specifically, fathers who are employed tend to be more involved with their preschool children. In addition, when mothers and fathers remain close, when mothers and grandmothers have a strong relationship, and when paternal grandmothers are involved with the children, fathers are significantly more likely to be highly involved in parenting their children in both emotional and practical ways.

These findings indicate several patterns in the family systems of these young multigenerational families. Although grandmothers are very important parental figures in the lives of their grandchildren, this does not preclude the additional involvement of fathers. Fathers are not kept away by actively involved grandmothers, either their partners' mothers or their own mothers. In addition, when mothers have strong relationships with other family members, then fathers are likely to also have strong relationships with their children. This finding could indicate an intergenerational transmission of emotional attachment and relationship building or a modeling experience. A mother who has a strong relationship with her own mother, or a father who sees his own mother involved with his children, may work diligently to keep the mother–father relationship close and civil and to support the father's parental involvement with his child, even outside of a coresidential situation. However, these findings are based on the mothers' reports about multiple familial relationships, and extending this research by interviewing fathers and children or by directly observing their relationships will help clarify these potential explanations.

OBSERVED PROCESSES
WITHIN MULTIGENERATIONAL FAMILIES

To extend this look at the varied relationships in young multigenerational families, we used observational measures of the ways in which family members relate to one another and to the children. A recent theoretical approach—family systems theory—offers a valuable framework of the family as an organized system, composed of a number of interrelated relationships or subsystems (Chase-Lansdale, Brooks-Gunn, & Paikoff, 1991; Gordon & Chase-Lansdale, 1998; Hinde & Stevenson-Hinde, 1988). Family systems theory has been applied primarily to mother–father–child families (e.g., Belsky, 1984). This line of work has shown that the marital relationship between the mother and the father, the mother–child relationship, and the father–child relationship are all interdependent. We applied family systems theory in the design of the BMFS, but we focused on the two women—the child's mother and grandmother—who are parent figures for the child. This focus leads to a conceptualization of family functioning that is exemplified in Fig. 8.1.

Clearly, our model moves beyond structural aspects of whether the grandmother is present or absent and to what extent she exchanges money and time with her daughter and addresses the quality of relationships. As with the marital relationship in the nuclear family, the quality of the mother–grandmother relationship is a significant aspect of healthy family functioning in multigenerational families. This relationship is posed as reciprocally influencing a child's functioning and

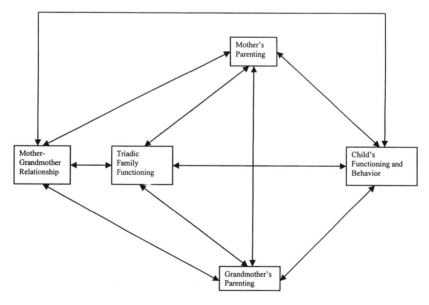

FIG. 8.1.   A family systems approach to the impact of young motherhood on children.

behavior, the quality of the mother–child relationship, the quality of the grand-mother–child relationship, and the emotional quality of the family as a whole. We now turn to a discussion of our measures and models of various components of this system.

Childrearing Provided by Mothers and Grandmothers

Measurement of Mothering and Grandmothering.   It was our conviction that grandmothers in young, African American multigenerational families were often operating as coparents along with young mothers. This hypothesis repre-sented a departure from the literature that has focused on grandparenthood as a stage of later life, highlighting such domains as distal emotional support to par-ents, short-term help during crises, and interactions with children that are usually playful and not so constrained by issues of discipline and control (Cherlin & Furstenberg, 1986; Tinsley & Parke, 1984). We measured the quality of mothers' and grandmothers' parenting using the Puzzle Task, which is an assessment that challenges and engages a child in fun, interesting, yet frustrating ways and provides an opportunity to observe and evaluate a parent's capacity to foster autonomy, to guide a child who is tackling a difficult task, and to provide emotional support. The child is presented with four puzzles of increasing difficulty, and the mother is in-structed to let the child work on the puzzles as independently as possible but to give any help needed (Chase-Lansdale et al., 1994). Mothers and grandmothers were observed and videotaped separately with the child (with different but equally challenging sets of puzzles), often in living or dining rooms, while the other parent was in the kitchen or elsewhere filling out questionnaires.

Parental problem-solving styles, disciplinary styles, and affect were rated using a coding system (see Chase-Lansdale, Zamsky, & Brooks-Gunn, in press) adapted from Hetherington and Clingempeel (1988), Owen and Henderson (1988), and Sroufe, Matas, and Rosenberg (1980). Problem-solving styles focused on the care-givers' capacity to foster autonomy in task completion (e.g., grading of hints, fos-tering exploration) and to provide emotional support (e.g., involvement, encour-agement). Disciplinary styles focused on the balance of warmth and appropriate control and included ratings of authoritative parenting (i.e., high warmth, high con-trol), authoritarian parenting (i.e., low warmth, high control), permissiveness (i.e., high warmth, low control), and disengagement (i.e., low warmth, low control).

Parenting by Young Mothers.   A major social concern regarding adolescent motherhood is that teenage mothers' parenting may be inadequate and pose risks to children (Maynard, 1997). Many studies of teenage parenthood have contrasted adolescent mothers with older mothers whose age at first birth extends into their late 20s and 30s, thereby confounding maternal age with poverty status. For exam-ple, poor parenting by teens is related to the difficult contexts in which they live, factors that also lead to teenage pregnancy in the first place—family and neighborhood poverty, families headed by single mothers, low educational attainment across generations, and restricted access to health care and other services (cf. Brooks-Gunn & Chase-Lansdale, 1995; Chase-Lansdale & Brooks-Gunn, 1994). In addition, for teenage mothers, emotional problems that bring on early sexual activity and childbirth, the transition to parenthood itself, and entering the motherhood role at such a young age may heighten psychological distress, which may in turn diminish parenting quality (Wakschlag et al., 1997).

However, the BMFS provides a more refined test of differences in parenting by age at first birth, contrasting adolescent mothers to mothers in their young 20s. It is highly likely, given similarities in economics, education, ability, and family structure between the two groups of mothers in the BMFS, that risks to parenting might be just as great for the young 20s mothers as for the adolescent mothers. Indeed, this proved to be the case. We compared the means and standard deviations of the parenting variables for the two age groups of mothers and found them to be highly similar. In addition, we examined the effects of maternal age at first birth on parenting using OLS multiple regression analyses that controlled for all the other background variables. This more stringent test of the impact of teenage parenthood on parenting also showed that for these multigenerational families, mothers' age at first birth was not a significant predictor of the quality of mothering (see Chase-Lansdale et al., 1994, for details).

Parenting of Grandmothers Versus That of Mothers.   Prior to the BMFS, only one other study had included observations of both mothers and grandmothers interacting with children, a small pilot study of 24 families and their infants (Stevens, 1984). Grandmothers were found to be more responsive toward infants than were mothers. No other study has included observations of both mothers and grandmothers interacting directly with preschoolers. Instead, the emphasis has been on how much and what kind of emotional and practical support grandmothers provide to mothers (e.g., Crockenberg, 1987). We developed the hypothesis that grandmothers would likely demonstrate superior parenting because of their maturity and prior experience with childrearing.

We compared the average difference in the quality of parenting provided by mothers to that of grandmothers, using multiple analysis of covariance with a paired design (see Chase-Lansdale et al., 1994, for details). There were no differences between mothers and grandmothers in the levels of positive and negative affect, quality of assistance, supportive presence, or for authoritative, authoritarian, permissive, and disengaged parenting. In fact, these scores, derived from largely independent raters, were virtually identical for mothers and grandmothers. Even when we compared the ratings of adolescent mothers' parenting (excluding women who became mothers in their 20s), grandmothers' parenting was not superior. These findings did not confirm our hypothesis and instead suggest that the parenting of grandmothers, despite age and experience, may not be of higher quality than their daughters' due to factors such as economic hardship, the compilation of too many other adult responsibilities, the additional demands of their own young children and multiple grandchildren, or from having been young mothers themselves.

Coresidence and Mothers' and Grandmothers' Parenting. Earlier work on multigenerational families showed that the presence of grandmothers in the homes of young mothers and children was a positive factor, both for the mothers themselves (i.e., higher educational attainment) and the children (i.e., better socioemotional adjustment; Furstenberg, 1976; Furstenberg et al., 1987; Horwitz, Klerman, Kuo, & Jekel, 1991; Kellam, Ensminger, & Turner, 1977). Furstenberg and colleagues noted that coresidence was particularly protective during a young mother's pregnancy and the early years of a child's life. Negative effects of coresidence on educational and occupational attainment were apparent when young mothers lived with the grandmothers for 5 or more years. More recent studies have found negative effects of coresidence on mothers' parenting (Black & Nitz, 1995; Speiker & Bensley, 1994; Unger & Cooley, 1992; Wasserman, Brunelli, & Raub, 1990; but see Pope et al., 1993). When we designed the BMFS in the mid-1980s, we viewed grandmother coresidence as a supportive environment and expected it to be beneficial to young mothers' parenting quality. However, we also expected that grandmothers' parenting would be negatively influenced by coresidence because of the strain of having such additional responsibilities all the time at home (Burton, 1990). To explore this question, we employed OLS regression models, testing the effects of coresidence on each of the eight types of parenting for mothers and grandmothers separately. In these analyses, we controlled for mothers' and grandmothers' ages, education levels, intellectual abilities, marital status, and participation in the welfare system (see Chase-Lansdale et al., 1994, for statistical details).

As expected, these analyses revealed that coresidence had negative consequences for many domains of grandmothers' parenting. However, interactions with the mother's age at first birth qualified this main effect. The group of women who became mothers in their early 20s showed the negative relationship seen in the main effect: Grandmothers' parenting was of higher quality when these young adult women lived independently compared to when mothers and grandmothers were in the same household. It may be that prolonged coresidence with young adult mothers is particularly stressful for grandmothers, who may feel that their older daughters should be more independent. In contrast, grandmothers showed higher levels of parenting when the teenage mothers (i.e., motherhood between ages 13 and 18) were coresiding than when they were living independently, consistent with our finding that teenage mothers who live apart report a lack of support from grandmothers.

Unexpectedly, coresidence also had negative consequences for mothers' parenting. As we discussed in our section on context, for the BMFS sample as a whole, mothers and grandmothers who lived together did not differ from those who lived apart in terms of economic hardship, household composition, educational attainment, intellectual ability, or marital status. Thus, there is not an obvious structural explanation, such as lower economic resources in coresident households, for why mothering is negatively affected by coresidence. Rather, we believe that psychological processes may be at work. A coresident young mother may feel that sharing her child with her mother is stressful and difficult, perhaps exacerbating competition and conflict with the grandmother. Another possible explanation involves increased role diffusion between coresident mothers and grandmothers. It may be that when mother and grandmother share a household, it is less clear who is really the primary, responsible parent, making the quality of mothering poorer. We present some evidence regarding possible explanations later in the chapter.

Quality of the Mother–Grandmother Relationship

Key Emotional Dimensions of the Mother–Grandmother Relationship. The mother–grandmother relationship is complicated for young mothers, who must negotiate the developmental tasks of adolescence (i.e., becoming emotionally and behaviorally autonomous) at the same time that their need for help and support from their own mothers has increased (Wakschlag, Chase-Lansdale, & Brooks-Gunn, 1996). In other words, the daughters are experiencing the transformation from dependency to young adulthood at the same time that they are making the transition to parenthood. The developmental task for these young women is to become autonomous from the grandmothers while redefining connectedness and closeness in a new, more adult way. Moreover, for the children in the BMFS, the preschool period involves a similar change in the mother–child relationship. Mothers of preschoolers are challenged by the children's emerging independence and must find the appropriate combination of closeness and warmth with increased discipline and control (see Wakschlag, Pittman, Chase-Lansdale, & Brooks-Gunn, in press, for a discussion of parallels between individuation and optimal parenting during the preschool years).

We anticipated links between the mother–grandmother relationship and the mother–child relationship across multiple domains. First, we expected that mothers who were more individuated from grandmothers would be more adept at balancing autonomy and connectedness with their preschoolers as well. Second, we expected that connectedness or closeness between mothers and grandmothers would be related to competent parenting of the next generation, due to mothers' feelings of emotional support from the grandmothers. Third, as in the marital literature, we expected that conflict between mothers and grandmothers would be related to poorer parenting (Emery, 1982). Finally, we explored the grandmothers' perspective, especially their ability to be authoritative and direct with their daughters, expecting that this style would relate to grandmothers' competent parenting toward the grandchildren and also to mothers' provision of authoritative parenting to their own children.

To assess these qualities of the mother–grandmother relationship, we developed a 10- to 15-minute disagreement paradigm, asking both grandmother and mother to select disagreement topics of their own choosing without consulting one another, then decide whose issue would be discussed first, then talk about each topic in turn for about 5 minutes each and try to come to some resolution about each disagreement. These interactions were videotaped and coded on the basis of the Scale of Intergenerational Relationship Quality (SIRQ), developed for the study (see Wakschlag, Chase-Lansdale, & Brooks-Gunn, in press, for details). We used exploratory factor analysis to derive meaningful dimensions of the mother–grandmother relationship (see Wakschlag et al., 1996, and Wakschlag, Pittman, Chase-Lansdale, & Brooks-Gunn, in press, for more technical and statistical details), including three of the four constructs just discussed: Individuation, Emotional Closeness and Positive Affect, and Grandmother Directness. We were not able to isolate a conflict factor; low scores or the absence of conflict and anger loaded highly on the emotional closeness factor. To test for possible connections between the mother–grandmother relationship and mothers' parenting, we conducted OLS regressions with the four SIRQ factor scores as independent variables and the previously discussed parenting variables as dependent variables. In these analyses, we combined the positive aspects of parenting into a single linear dimension (Competent Parenting) and the negative aspects of parenting into a single linear dimension (Problematic Parenting) using multifacet Rasch analyses (see Wakschlag et al., 1996). We also controlled for background variables of mothers and grandmothers, similar to the regressions described previously.

We found that the individuation dimension of the mother–grandmother relationship was significantly positively related to mothers' competent parenting and negatively related to mothers' problematic parenting. These findings suggest parallels in maternal behavior across contexts. Mothers whose relationships with their own mothers were mature and flexible were likely to offer similarly flexible and authoritative parenting toward their own preschoolers. Surprisingly, none of the other three dimensions of the mother–grandmother relationship were linked significantly to mothers' parenting. Thus, our prediction that a supportive mother–grandmother relationship would bolster mothers' parenting was not borne out. Grandmothers' directness did not relate to mothers' authoritative parenting.

One could argue that what we have found is that mothers with high psychological resources in general will be competent in their relationships both with the grandmothers and with their children. Although this is a possibility, a number of indicators suggest that individuation is an explanatory variable above and beyond mothers' personal characteristics. First, the individuation factor was not related to mothers' age or age at first birth; in other words, it is not a proxy for maturation. Second, the individuation factor was not related to mothers' intellectual ability, as measured by the Peabody Picture Vocabulary Test, suggesting that individuation was not a proxy for mothers' verbal fluency.

We also tested a person × process × context model, as outlined by Bronfenbrenner (1989), hypothesizing that the mother–grandmother relationship (i.e., "process") would influence mothers' parenting quality in different ways, depending upon living with or apart from grandmother (i.e., "context") and mothers' age at first birth (i.e., "person"). We added interaction terms to the regression models and found them to be significant (see full statistical details in Wakschlag et al., 1996). The moderated relationships fit a risk and resiliency model. Specifically, a higher quality mother–grandmother relationship appears to be a buffering factor for the most risky scenarios. In our multigenerational families, risks appear to be highest for young mothers (i.e., adolescents at time of first birth) living on their own and for older mothers (i.e., first birth in their early 20s) who coreside with the grandmother during their mid to late twenties. Specifically, under noncoresiding conditions, younger mothers who were high on individuation with the grandmothers showed significantly higher levels of competent parenting and lower levels of problematic parenting. Similar associations between individuation and parenting are seen for older mothers when they are coresident rather than noncoresiding.

It may be the case that selection factors are operating here. Earlier, we presented findings that teenage mothers living apart report distance and noninvolvement from the grandmothers during pregnancy and the early years of their children's lives. A well-individuated relationship between mother and grandmother appears to protect against negative effects of living on one's own as a young, parenting teenager. Among older mothers, those who share residences with a grandmother when their children are preschoolers are at risk for becoming generally dependent, unable to strike out on their own, and less skilled in parenting. A more adultlike, autonomous relationship with the grandmother may be a buffering factor for these older mothers.

Finally, we examined the influence of the quality of the mother–grandmother relationship on grandmothers' parenting (Wakschlag, 1992). To our surprise, there were virtually no significant relationships between the four SIRQ factors and grandmothers' quality of parenting. It may be that other adult relationships in the grandmothers' lives are more influential to the quality of their parenting, such as relationships with husbands or boyfriends or their general social support network. In addition, life stress and the psychological reaction to early grandparenthood could be related to their parenting as well. All these latter aspects were not measured in our study and would be promising lines of future research.

Triadic Family Functioning

A final observational measure, the Multigenerational Family Q-Sort (MFQ) was developed to assess functioning within the full, triadic multigenerational family system (Chase-Lansdale, Van Widenfelt, & Gordon, in press). The Georgia Family Q-Sort (Wampler, Halverson, Moore, & Walters, 1989), a measure of mother–father–child families grounded in family systems theory, was adapted, extended, and supplemented to reflect the young African American multigenerational family system, also drawing upon the work of Owen and Henderson (1989). To implement the MFQ, the three family members were videotaped as they engaged in free play together with a variety of toys. Trained coders assessed the family's interactions during this free play, including aspects of the full triadic system (e.g., positive affect, conflict) and its various subsystems (e.g., emotional support and engagement in the grandmother–mother, child–mother, and child–grandmother subsystems; child's compliance with mother and grandmother; see Gordon & Chase-Lansdale, 1995, 1998).

A portion of the MFQ characterizes how the grandmother and mother negotiate their shared parenting of the child. With this information, we have defined four parenting strategies adopted by multigenerational families: (a) neither adult is in charge of parenting, (b) mother is in charge of parenting, (c) grandmother is in charge of parenting, or (d) mother and grandmother share parenting of the child. In the BMFS sample, only a small fraction of families show neither parent in charge (7.9%), whereas nearly a third display a style of shared parenting (31.7%). When only one of the two women takes primary responsibility for parenting, it is more often the grandmother than the mother (37.6% versus 22.8% of families).

To describe the styles of interaction among the three family members further, we considered variation by these four parenting strategies in other aspects of the family system that are tapped by the MFQ and the puzzle task measures of parenting. Families with neither mother nor grandmother in charge of parenting show problematic interactional styles, with high levels of conflict, low levels of child compliance, and low levels of emotional support and engagement in the various components of the family system. Families in which mother and grandmother coparent the child tend to show the highest level of functioning. However, families with the mother in charge of parenting are generally more similar to families with shared parenting, whereas the families in which the grandmother is the primary parent show more conflict and less emotional support and engagement in the triadic and mother–grandmother systems than do families in which mother and grandmother coparent the child. Finally, as might be expected, the emotional support and engagement in the dyadic system of child–grandmother or child–mother reflect the parenting style in the family. For example, when the mother takes primary parenting responsibility in the family, the child–mother relationship is particularly strong (e.g., more competent and less problematic parenting by mothers) and the child–grandmother relationship is weaker (e.g., less competent parenting by grandmothers).

How Do Children Fare?

A final important question we have considered regarding multigenerational families concerns the functioning of children. In the BMFS we have only one snapshot of the children, and this is at age 3 years. Our measures of cognitive development include the McCarthy Scales of Intellectual Abilities (McCarthy, 1972) and the Peabody Picture Vocabulary Test–Revised (Dunn & Dunn, 1981). Our measures of socioemotional development include a shortened form of the Achenbach Child Behavior Checklist for 2- and 3-year-olds (CBCL/2-3; Achenbach, Edelbrock, & Howell, 1987) and assessments of children's enthusiasm, persistence, positive affect, anger, and negativity during the puzzle task observation with mother–child and grandmother–child dyads.

The first important finding regarding children from the BMFS is that they seem to be faring relatively well. For the sample as a whole, children had scores on the PPVT, McCarthy, and the behavior problems checklist more similar to national norms than had been anticipated. Indeed, although mothers and grandmothers had similar PPVT standardized scores (of about 75), children's verbal ability was on average higher than that of the mothers and grandmothers (mean of 91.35; Pittman, McHale, Chase-Lansdale, & Brooks-Gunn, 1997). These PPVT scores of the BMFS children are similar to those of a national sample of 3- and 4-year-old children born to young mothers, the children of the NLSY (91.35 versus 90.68). In addition, between 14 and 21% of the children fell above the 90th percentile clinical cutoff on the three CBCL/2-3 dimensions for which our short form provided full information (i.e., social withdrawal, depression, and destruction). Other studies reveal that children of teenage mothers do not exhibit problems until they commence the transition to school (Brooks-Gunn & Furstenberg, 1986; Coley & Chase-Lansdale, 1998; Furstenberg et al., 1987; Furstenberg, Hughes, & Brooks-Gunn, 1992; Horwitz et al., 1991; Moore, Morrison, & Greene, 1997), and the timing of the BMFS in the lives of these children may be capturing the period before typical problems emerge. The children's development may also have benefited from preschool educational enrichment, programs that were less available to earlier generations in their families and whose effects typically fall off somewhat during later childhood and adolescence. Unfortunately, we have not followed the complete BMFS sample to see if increased problems in development occur as the children in these multigenerational families grow older.

A second key finding regarding child outcomes has to do with the influence of mothers' age at first birth. As previously discussed, the sample was carefully chosen to compare two groups of young women: those who became mothers during adolescence and those who became mothers in their early 20s. A theme throughout this chapter has been how similar the social ecologies of these two groups are. Comparing child outcomes for younger versus older mothers, we found no differences in either cognitive or social development (Pittman et al., 1997).

What, then, explains individual differences in children's outcomes? Coresidence and quality of mothering, but not grandmothering, appear to be important parts of the answer to this question, with coresidence being a risk for some outcomes but not others and mothers' parenting quality a buffer. Degree of father involvement, at least as we have measured it in the BMFS, does not seem to be a significant predictor of better child outcomes. Analyses detailing the complexity of influences on children in multigenerational families are ongoing (Pittman et al., 1997). What we were not able to measure—and thus we recommend for future research on multi-generational families—is a consideration of children's capacities to understand the complexity of their family lives. How and when does the child learn who is a part of the family, whom to count on, and how to interpret fluidity and change in parent figures and living arrangements?

CONCLUSION

This chapter has focused on young African American multigenerational families in poverty. We have shown that such a family form is an important, complex structure. The families in our study were characterized by high rates of single mother-hood and an early transition into that role across generations, practical exchanges with and economic involvement of grandmothers, the sharing of childrearing across generations, and, although a substantial fraction of absent fathers, a sizable fraction of highly involved fathers as well.

A central conclusion from the Baltimore Multigenerational Family Study is that the full family context must be taken into account in order to draw accurate con-clusions regarding the strengths and difficulties in these families. A focus only on the young mothers themselves, for example, would fail to capture the complexity of family life, parent figures, and socialization of children. Grandmothers are key members of these families, and the structure of households with grandmother coresidence is an important context to be considered. Although father absence from the household is high, father involvement with children is more extensive than coresidence, and future studies should consider constructs across multiple domains (e.g., household structure, degree of contact, quality of interactions).

Like studies of other types of family structure, we have shown that a focus on multigenerational structure per se can be misleading. Grandmother coresidence is neither uniformly beneficial nor uniformly negative. Here we have highlighted the complexity of this living arrangement, documenting how its impact often depends on mothers' age at first birth and is related to the quality of the mother–grand-mother relationship, the quality of mothering, and the quality of grandmother-ing—all significant dimensions in healthy family functioning. The BMFS also sug-gests that preschoolers in these multigenerational families can develop adequately. Future research is needed to examine the trajectories over time of children in this family form, especially with an eye toward further delineating those aspects of con-text, exchange, and process that facilitate healthy development.

ACKNOWLEDGMENTS

The Baltimore Multigenerational Family Study was supported by the Office of Adolescent Pregnancy Programs, the National Institute of Child Health and Human Development, the Chapin Hall Center for Children, NORC, and the Educational Testing Service. Portions of this work are an outgrowth of the Working Group on Communities, Neighborhoods, Family Processes, and Individual Development of the Social Science Research Council. We are grateful for our interactions with this group and especially the members of the Phenomenon Based Cluster on Young Multigenerational Family Processes (Linda Burton, Greg Duncan, and Robin Jarrett) for their insights regarding our cluster activities. These collaborations were made possible through funding by the William T. Grant Foundation, the Smith-Richardson Foundation, and the Russell Sage Foundation. We are also appreciative of the support of the NIMH Family Research Consortium to Chase-Lansdale and Brooks-Gunn during the course of this research. In addition, we also thank the John D. and Catherine T. MacArthur Foundation for its support of the Network on the Family and the Economy. We are deeply appreciative of the commitment of the study staff to careful data collection and of the generous contribution of time and insights from the family members who joined us in the study. The skillful geocoding of addresses by Telemap (Chicago, IL) and consultation with Fay Booker, Data Librarian, Social Sciences and Public Policy Computing Center, regarding Census data made the contextual bases of this study possible.

REFERENCES

Achenbach, T. M., Edelbrock, C. S., & Howell, C. T. (1987). Empirically-based assessment of the behavioral/emotional problems of 2- and 3-year old children. *Journal of Abnormal Psychology, 15*, 629–650.

Baydar, N., & Brooks-Gunn, J. (1991). Effects of maternal employment and child-care arrangements on preschoolers' cognitive and behavioral outcomes: Evidence from the Children of the National Longitudinal Survey of Youth. *Developmental Psychology, 27*, 932–945.

Belsky, J. (1984). The determinants of parenting: A process model. *Child Development, 55*, 83–96.

Billingsley, A. (1968). *Black families in white America.* Englewood Cliffs, NJ: Prentice Hall.

Black, M. M., & Nitz, K. (1995). Grandmother co-residence, parenting, and child development among low income, urban teen mothers. *Journal of Adolescent Health, 16*, 1–9.

Bronfenbrenner, U. (1989). Ecological systems theory. In R. Vasta (Ed.), *Annals of child development: A research annual* (pp. 188–249). Greenwich, CT: JAI Press.

Brooks-Gunn, J., & Chase-Lansdale, P. L. (1995). Adolescent parenthood. In M. H. Bornstein (Ed.), *Handbook of parenting, Volume 3: Status and social conditions of parenting* (pp. 113–150). Hillsdale, NJ: Lawrence Erlbaum Associates.

Brooks-Gunn, J., & Furstenberg, F. F., Jr. (1986). The children of adolescent mothers: Physical, academic, and psychological outcomes. *Developmental Review, 6*, 224–251.

Bumpass, L., & Raley, R. K. (1995). Redefining single parent families: Cohabitation and changing family reality. *Demography, 32*, 97–110.

Burton, L. M. (1995). Intergenerational patterns of providing care in African-American families with teenage childbearers: Emergent patterns in an ethnographic study. In V. L. Bengtson, K. W. Schaie, & L. M. Burton (Eds.), *Adult intergenerational relations: Effects of societal change* (pp. 79–96). New York: Springer.

Burton, L. M. (1992). Black grandparents rearing children of drug-addicted parents: Stressors, outcomes, and social service needs. *The Gerontologist, 32*, 744–751.

Burton, L. M. (1990). Teenage childbearing as an alternative life-course strategy in multi-generational Black families. *Human Nature, 1,* 123–143.

Chase-Lansdale, P. L., & Brooks-Gunn, J. (1994). Correlates of adolescent pregnancy and parenthood. In C. B. Fisher & R. M. Lerner (Eds.), *Applied developmental psychology* (pp. 207–236). New York: McGraw-Hill.

Chase-Lansdale, P. L., Brooks-Gunn, J., & Paikoff, R. (1991). Research and programs for adolescent mothers: Missing links and future promises. *Family Relations, 40,* 396–404.

Chase-Lansdale, P. L., Brooks-Gunn, J., & Zamsky, E. S. (1994). Young African-American multigenerational families in poverty: Quality of mothering and grandmothering. *Child Development, 65,* 373–393.

Chase-Lansdale, P. L., Van Widenfelt, B., & Gordon, R. A. (in press). *The Multigenerational Family Q-Sort.* In J. Touliatos, B. F. Perlmutter, & G. W. Holden (Eds.), *Handbook of family measurement techniques, second edition.* Thousand Oaks, CA: Sage.

Chase-Lansdale, P. L., Zamsky, E. S., & Brooks-Gunn, J. (in press). *Puzzle Task coding manual: Parent–child interactions in young African-American multigenerational families.* In J. Touliatos, B. F. Perlmutter, & G. W. Holden (Eds.), *Handbook of family measurement techniques, second edition.* Thousand Oaks, CA: Sage.

Cherlin, A. J., & Furstenberg, Jr., F. F. (1986). *The new American grandparent: A place in the family, a life apart.* New York: Basic.

Coley, R. L. (in press). Children's socialization experiences and functioning in single- mother households: The importance of fathers and other men. *Child Development.*

Coley, R. L., & Chase-Lansdale, P. L. (1997). *Young African American fathers' involvement in the birth and early years of their children.* Manuscript under review.

Coley, R. L., & Chase-Lansdale, P. L. (1998). Adolescent pregnancy and parenthood: Recent evidence and future directions. *American Psychologist, 53,* 152–166.

Creighton, L. L. (1991, December 16). Silent saviors. *U.S. News & World Report,* 80–89.

Crockenberg. S. (1987). Support for adolescent mothers during the postnatal period: Theory and research. In C. F. Z. Boukydis (Ed.), *Research on support for parents and infants in the postnatal period* (pp. 3–24). Hillsdale, NJ: Lawrence Erlbaum Associates.

Dunn, L. M., & Dunn, L. M. (1981). *Peabody Picture Vocabulary Test–Revised.* Circle Pines, MN: American Guidance Service.

Emery, R. E. (1982). Interparental conflict and the children of discord and divorce. *Psychological Bulletin, 91,* 310–330.

Furakawa, S. (1994). *The diverse living arrangements of children: Summer 1991* (CPR P70–38). Washington, DC: U.S. Bureau of the Census.

Furstenberg, F. F., Jr. (1976). *Unplanned parenthood: The social consequences of teenage childbearing.* New York: Free Press.

Furstenberg, F. F. Jr., (1995). Fathering in the inner city: Paternal participation and public policy. In W. Marsiglio (Ed.), *Fatherhood: Contemporary theory, research, and social policy* (pp. 119–147). Thousand Oaks, CA: Sage.

Furstenberg, F. F., Jr., Brooks-Gunn, J., & Morgan, P. S. (1987). *Adolescent mothers in later life.* New York: Cambridge University Press.

Furstenberg, F. F., & Crawford, A. G. (1978). Family support: Helping teenage mothers to cope. *Family Planning Perspectives, 10,* 322–333.

Furstenberg, F. F., Jr., & Harris, K. M. (1993). When and why fathers matter: Impacts of father involvement on the children of adolescent mothers. In R. I. Lerman & T. J. Ooms (Eds.), *Young unwed fathers: Changing roles and emerging policies* (pp. 117–138). Philadelphia: Temple University Press.

Furstenberg, F. F., Jr., Hughes, M. E., & Brooks-Gunn, J. (1992). The next generation: Children of teenage mothers grow up. In M. K. Rosenheim & M. F. Testa (Eds.), *Early parenthood* (pp. 3–135). New Brunswick, NJ: Rutgers University Press.

George, S. M., & Dickerson, B. J. (1995). The role of the grandmother in poor single-mother families and households. In B. J. Dickerson (Ed.), *African American single mothers: Understanding their lives and families* (Sage Series on Race and Ethnic Relations, Volume 10). Thousand Oaks, CA: Sage.

Gonzalez, N. S. (1969). Black carib household structure. *American Ethnological Society Monographs, 48.*

Gordon, R. A. (1993). *Young-African American family functioning: Theoretical dimensions and psychometric properties of the multigenerational family Q-sort.* Unpubished manuscript, University of Chicago.

Gordon, R. A., & Chase-Lansdale, P. L. (1995). *Observational measures of diverse family forms: Conceptual issues and an application with young, multigenerational African American families* (PRC Discussion Paper 95-12). NORC and the University of Chicago: Population Research Center.

Gordon, R. A., & Chase-Lansdale, P. L. (1998). *The Multigenerational Family Q-Sort: An observational measure of full family functioning in young African American families.* Unpublished manuscript, University of Chicago.

Gordon, R. A., Chase-Lansdale, P. L., Matjasko, J. L., & Brooks-Gunn, J. (1997). Young mothers living with grandmothers and living apart: How neighborhood and household contexts related to multigenerational coresidence in African-American families. *Applied Developmental Science, 1,* 89–106.

Hardy, J., Astone, N., Brooks-Gunn, J., Shapiro, S., & Miller, T. (in press). Like mother, like child: Intergenerational transmission of patterns of age at first birth across the reproductive age span: A report from the Pathways to Adulthood Study. *Developmental Psychology.*

Hernandez, D. J. (1993). *America's children: Resources from family, government, and the economy* (Census Monograph Series: The Population of the United States in the 1980s). New York: Russell Sage Foundation.

Hetherington, E. M., & Clingempeel, G. (1988). *Longitudinal study of adjustment to remarriage: family interaction global coding manual.* Unpublished manuscript, University of Virginia, Charlottesville.

Hill, R. B. (1977). *Informal adoption among Black families.* Washington, DC: National Urban League.

Hinde, R., & Stevenson-Hinde, J. (1988). *Relationships within families: Mutual influences.* Oxford: Clarendon Press.

Horwitz, S. M., Klerman, L. V., Kuo, H. S., & Jekel, J. F. (1991). Intergenerational transmission of school-age parenthood. *Family Planning Perspectives, 23,* 168–172, 177.

Jayakody, R., Chatters, L. M., & Taylor, R. J. (1993). Family support to single and married African American mothers: The provision of financial, emotional, and child care assistance. *Journal of Marriage and the Family, 55,* 261–276.

Jendrek, M. P. (1993). Grandparents who parent their grandchildren: Effects on lifestyle. *Journal of Marriage and the Family, 55,* 609–621.

Kellam, S. G., Ensminger, M. E., & Turner, R. J. (1977). Family structure and the mental health of young children. *Archives of General Psychiatry, 34,* 1012–1022.

Kellam, S. G., Adams, R. G., Brown, C. H., & Ensminger, M. E. (1982). The long-term evolution of the family structure of teenage and older mothers. *Journal of Marriage and the Family, 44,* 539–554.

King, V. (1994). Nonresident father involvement and child well-being: Can Dads make a difference? *Journal of Family Issues, 15,* 78–96.

Ladner, J. A. (1971). *Tomorrow's tomorrow: The Black woman.* New York: Doubleday.

LaPoint, V., Pickett, M. O., & Harris, B. F. (1985). Enforced family separation: A descriptive analysis of some experiences of children of Black imprisoned mothers. In M. B. Spencer, G. K. Brookins, & W. R. Allen (Eds.), *Beginnings: The social and affective development of Black children* (pp. 239–255). Hillsdale, NJ: Lawrence Erlbaum Associates.

Little, H. M. (1995, September 10). Out of retirement: Parenting the second time around isn't always so grand. *Chicago Tribune.* NW1, NW6.

Marsiglio, W. (1995). Fatherhood scholarship: An overview and agenda for the future. In W. Marsiglio (Ed.), *Fatherhood: Contemporary theory, research, and social policy* (pp. 1–20). Thousand Oaks, CA: Sage.

Martin, E. P., & Martin, J. M. (1978). *The Black extended family.* Chicago: University of Chicago Press.

Maynard, R. A. (Ed.). (1997). *Kids having kids: Economic costs and social consequences of teen pregnancy.* Washington, DC: Urban Institute Press.

McAdoo, H. P. (1983, March). *Extended family support of single Black mothers* (Final Rep. 5-R01-MH32159). Washington, DC: National Institutes of Mental Health.

McAdoo, J. (1993). The roles of African American fathers: An ecological perspective. *Families in Society, 74*, 28–35.

McCarthy, D. (1972). *Manual for the McCarthy Scales of Children's Abilities.* Cleveland, OH: The Psychological Corporation.

McLoyd, V. C. (1990). The impact of economic hardship on Black families and children: Psychological distress, parenting, socioemotional development. *Child Development, 61*, 311–346.

Minkler, M., Roe, K. M., & Robertson-Beckley, R. J. (1994). Raising grandchildren from crack-cocaine households: Effects on family and friendship ties of African-American women. *American Journal of Orthopsychiatry, 64*, 20–29.

Moore, K. A., Morrison, D. R., & Greene, A. D. (1997). Effects on the children born to adolescent mothers. In R. A. Maynard (Ed.), *Kids having kids: Economic costs and social consequences of teen pregnancy* (pp. 145–180). Washington, DC: The Urban Institute Press.

Owen, M. T., & Henderson, V. K. (1988). *Manual for scoring mother and child behavior in the Puzzle Task.* Unpublished manuscript, Timberlawn Research Foundation, Dallas, TX.

Owen, M. T., & Henderson, V. K. (1989). *The Georgia Family Q-Sort: Revised manual.* Unpublished manuscript, Timberlawn Psychiatric Research Foundation, Dallas, TX.

Parish, W. L., Hao, L., & Hogan, D. P. (1991). Family support networks, welfare, and work among young mothers. *Journal of Marriage and the Family, 53*, 203–215.

Personal Responsibility and Work Opportunity Reconciliation Act of 1996, Pub. L. No. 104–193, 110 Stat. 2105 (1996).

Pittman, L., McHale, J., Chase-Lansdale, P. L., & Brooks-Gunn, J. (1997). *Child development in young African-American multigenerational families.* Manuscript in preparation.

Pope, S. K., Whiteside, L., Brooks-Gunn, J., Kelleher, K. J., Rickert, V. I., Bradley, R. H., & Casey, P. H. (1993). Low-birth-weight infants born to adolescent mothers. *Journal of the American Medical Association, 269*, 1396–1400.

Presser, H. B. (1989). Some economic complexities of child care provided by grandmothers. *Journal of Marriage and the Family, 51*, 581–591.

Seltzer, J. A. (1991). Relationships between fathers and children who live apart: The father's role after separation. *Journal of Marriage and the Family, 53*, 79–101.

Shimkin, D. B., Shimkin, E. M., and Frate, D. A. (1978). (Eds.). *The extended family in Black societies.* Paris: Mouton.

Slaughter, D. T. (Ed.). (1988). Black children and poverty: A developmental perspective. *New directions in child development* (No. 42). San Francisco: Jossey-Bass.

Speiker, S., & Bensley, L. (1994). Roles of living arrangements and grandmother social support in adolescent mothering and infant attachment. *Developmental Psychology, 30*, 102–111.

Spencer, M. B. (1990). Development in minority children: An introduction. *Child Development, 61*, 267–269.

Sroufe, L. A., Matas, L., & Rosenberg, D. M. (1980). *Manual for scoring mother variables in Tool-Use Task applicable for two-year-old children.* Unpublished manuscript, Institute of Child Development, University of Minnesota, Minneapolis.

Stack, C. B. (1974). *All our kin: Strategies for survival in a Black community.* New York: Harper & Row.

Stevens, J. H. (1984). Black grandmothers' and Black adolescent mothers' knowledge about parenting. *Developmental Psychology, 20*, 1017–1025.

Taylor, R. J. (1986). Receipt of support from family among Black Americans: Demographic and familial differences. *Journal of Marriage and the Family, 48*, 67–77.

Tinsley, B. J., & Parke, R. D (1984). Grandparents as support and socialization agents. In M. Lewis & L. Rosenblum (Eds.), *Social connection: Beyond the dyad* (pp. 161–194). New York: Plenum.

Unger, D., & Cooley, M. (1992). Partner and grandmother contact in Black and White teen parent families. *Journal of Adolescent Health Care, 13*, 546–552.

Wakschlag, L. S. (1992). *Intergenerational continuities: The influence of the mother–grandmother relationships on parenting in African-American young-mother families.* Unpublished doctoral dissertation, University of Chicago.

Wakschlag, L. S., Chase-Lansdale, P. L., & Brooks-Gunn, J. (in press). *Scale of Intergenerational Relationship Quality.* In J. Touliatos, B. F. Perlmutter, & G. W. Holden (Eds.), *Handbook of family measurement techniques, second edition.* Thousand Oaks, CA: Sage.

Wakschlag, L. S., Chase-Lansdale, P. L., & Brooks-Gunn, J. (1996). Not just "ghosts in the nursery": Contemporaneous intergenerational relationships and parenting in young African-American families. *Child Development, 67,* 2131–2147.

Wakschlag, L. S., Gordon, R. A., Lahey, B., Loeber, R., Green, S., & Leventhal, B. (1997). *Maternal age at first birth and sons' risk of conduct disorder.* Manuscript under review.

Wakschlag, L. S., Pittman, L., Chase-Lansdale, P. L., & Brooks-Gunn, J. (in press). "Mama, I'm a person too!": Individuation and young mothers' parenting competence. In A. M. Cauce & S. T. Hauser (Eds.), *Adolescence and beyond: Family processes and development.* Mahwah, NJ: Lawrence Erlbaum Associates.

Wasserman, G., Brunelli, S. A., & Raub, V. A. (1990). Social supports and living arrangements of adolescent and adult mothers. *Journal of Adolescent Research, 5,* 54–66.

Wampler, K. S., Halverson, C. F., Moore, J. J. & Walters, L. H. (1989). The Georgia Family Q-Sort: An observational measure of family functioning. *Family Process, 28,* 223–237.

Wilson, M. N. (1986). The Black extended family: An analytical consideration. *Developmental Psychology, 22,* 246–258.

Zimmerman, M., Salem, D. A., & Maton, K. I. (1995). Family structure and psychological correlates among urban African American adolescent males. *Child Development, 66,* 1598–1613.

9

Protective Factors in the Development of Preschool-Age Children of Young Mothers Receiving Welfare

Martha J. Zaslow
M. Robin Dion
Child Trends, Inc.

Donna Ruane Morrison
Georgetown University

Nancy Weinfield
John Ogawa
University of Minnesota

Patton Tabors
Harvard Graduate School of Education

IN THIS CHAPTER we focus on the development of children in a sample of families headed by young mothers receiving welfare. It is clear from available evidence that both birth to an adolescent mother and growing up in poverty represent risks to positive child development. Yet not all children of young mothers in poverty show difficulties in behavioral adjustment or cognitive development. Indeed, the evidence points to substantial variation among children in these circumstances. Part of the difference in outcomes may be due to the presence for some children of protective factors that mitigate against these otherwise stressful circumstances. During an era of diminishing tolerance for welfare dependency, it is critically important to identify the factors that support more positive development in this doubly at-risk group of children.

To address this question empirically, we examine children in a highly disadvantaged sample: those born to families headed by young mothers, all of whom had

had their first children as teenagers, who were receiving public assistance, and who had already dropped out of school. The data come from the New Chance Observational Study, a substudy embedded in a larger evaluation of the New Chance Demonstration, a comprehensive program for young welfare mothers and their children (Quint, Bos, & Polit, 1997; Quint, Fink, & Rowser, 1991; Quint, Polit, Bos, & Cave, 1994). The study affords us a unique opportunity, within a longitudinal data set, to examine child outcome measures in light of observational as well as survey data on the mother–child relationship and data on a range of other family and contextual factors that may be important to the children's development.

For the sample of 290 families in the New Chance Observational Study, we investigate the importance of child, maternal, and family characteristics, as well as characteristics of the larger social context surrounding the families, in buffering the effects of teenage motherhood and poverty for preschool-age children. Among the protective factors considered, we pay particular attention to the role of positive parenting behavior in enhancing the well-being of this high-risk group of children.

FAMILIES HEADED BY YOUNG UNMARRIED MOTHERS AS A PARTICULAR FORM OF SINGLE-PARENT FAMILY

The present volume considers children's development in the context of different types of single-parent families, noting the prevalence as well as characteristics of such differing family forms as those headed by divorced and never-married parents. Within this framework, we note that children born to unmarried adolescent mothers constitute a sizeable group. In 1995, 5,862,000 children in the United States were living with never-married mothers. Of those, 480,000 resided with mothers ranging from 15 to 19 years old (Saluter, 1996).

Furthermore, although children born to unmarried women under the age of 20 represent about one third of all nonmarital births (Ventura, Peters, Martin, & Maurer, 1997), and only about 8% of all children living in never-married families have mothers who are currently in their teens (Saluter, 1996), families started by teenage mothers contribute disproportionately to the caseload receiving public assistance. In 1995, for example, 29% of mothers receiving Aid to Families with Dependent Children (AFDC) had had their first children as teenagers, compared to only 15% of non-AFDC mothers (Bureau of the Census, 1995). Moreover, young unmarried mothers tend to go on welfare shortly after the births of their first children and remain for relatively long periods (Klerman, 1991; Moore et al., 1992). One third of AFDC recipients who began receiving benefits when they were under age 22 have welfare spells of 10 years or more, compared to roughly one fourth of those who first receive welfare between ages 22 and 30 (U.S. House of Representatives, Ways and Means Committee, 1996 Green Book). Maynard (1997) has estimated that the annual net cost to taxpayers of adolescent childbearing is $6.8 billion.

Awareness of such estimates brought young unmarried mothers to the center of the recent debate on welfare reform. The new law (the Personal Responsibility and Work Opportunity Reconciliation Act of 1996) requires unmarried adolescent mothers to stay in school and live at home or in adult-supervised settings in order to receive assistance.

DOUBLE RISK FACTORS OF POVERTY AND BIRTH TO AN ADOLESCENT MOTHER

It is clear from previous research that children reared in poverty and children born to adolescent mothers are at risk in terms of developmental outcomes. Family income is strongly associated with children's cognitive development, academic progress and behavioral adjustment (Duncan, Brooks-Gunn, & Klebanov, 1994). Zill, Moore, Smith, Stief, and Coiro (1995), contrasting the health and development of children in families receiving AFDC with children in non-poor families in two national surveys (i.e., the National Health Interview Survey on Child Health and the National Longitudinal Survey of Youth–Child Supplement), found that children from families receiving AFDC were more often reported by their mothers to be in only fair or poor health, to have repeated a grade in school, to be in the bottom half of their classes academically, to show behavior problems at home, and to have behavior problems at school that resulted in a request that the parent come to school for a conference. Zill and colleagues also asked whether findings on children's development differed substantially for those children in poverty who were and were not receiving public assistance. Their findings indicate that "poor children from families that do not receive AFDC show similar levels of health and behavior problems, and nearly as many learning problems, as children from AFDC families" (Zill et al., 1995, p. 47).

Yet at the same time, evidence points to substantial variation in the development of children in poverty. Recent research suggests that the timing and duration of poverty are both important to development, with poverty during the early years of development and poverty that is enduring rather than episodic associated with particularly detrimental effects on child outcomes (Duncan & Brooks-Gunn, 1997). Even within a sample of welfare families, Moore, Zaslow, Coiro, Miller, and Magenheim (1995) found heterogeneity in the development of preschool-age children, with measures of school readiness, receptive vocabulary, and social maturity differing significantly for families differing in terms of such background characteristics as duration of time receiving public assistance, number of children in the household, maternal education, and the mother's sense of efficacy or control over events in her life.

This basic pattern of findings, that there are differences between the development of children in poverty and non-poor children (i.e., between-group differences) but also substantial heterogeneity within the group of children in poverty

(i.e., within-group differences), is closely echoed in the research on the development of children born to adolescent mothers versus older mothers. For example,
more than a decade ago, a pattern of findings had begun to emerge indicating that
beginning in their preschool years, children of adolescent mothers were at greater
risk of poor developmental outcomes (Baldwin & Cain, 1980; Brooks-Gunn &
Furstenberg, 1986; Furstenberg, Brooks-Gunn, & Chase-Lansdale, 1989). The evidence pointed to small differences on measures of cognitive development (e.g., direct assessments of IQ) but more substantial differences on measures of academic
progress and achievement. Furstenberg and colleagues (1989, p. 315), summarized
findings indicating that by their own teenage years, the children of adolescent
mothers showed "markedly lower" achievement in school. Findings also pointed to
problems with self-control and aggression, particularly among sons of adolescent
mothers.

Yet this earlier set of studies also noted that group differences were smaller
when such factors as maternal education and family size were taken into account
in analyses. Some of the group-difference findings appear to be attributable to the
factors that are associated with and predictive of adolescent childbearing, rather
than with having a very young mother per se. In addition, some of the early studies
did not use appropriate comparison groups, failing, for example, to account for
marital status.

An important refinement in more recent studies is that researchers increasingly
recognize the importance of accounting both for background characteristics of the
families and for more subtle variables (i.e., unobservables such as maternal motivation and perception of life chances) that are correlated with the likelihood of becoming a teenage mother and with the kind of environment a young mother may
provide for her child. Recent work has also used greater care in defining comparison groups. For example, it is more realistic from a policy perspective to understand the implications for children of a year or two delay in their mothers' age at
first birth than to compare the outcomes for children of teenage and subtantially
older mothers. In one such examination of the issue, Moore, Morrison, and Greene
(1997) found that children born to teenage mothers were provided with less stimulating and emotionally supportive home environments and performed less well
on a variety of cognitive tests than those whose mothers were in their early twenties at the time of their births. Moreover, the older the comparison group's age at
first birth, the greater the comparative deficit of having been born to a teenage
mother.

Although group differences persist even in the more rigorous recent studies,
much as in the research on child poverty, researchers caution that there is substantial heterogeneity in the development of children born to adolescent mothers.
Dubow and Luster (1990), for example, observed that although the children of
adolescent mothers may be at risk on average, many of these children show good
performance on measures of cognitive development and are progressing well in
school. In their examination of behavioral adjustment among children of teenage

mothers in the National Longitudinal Survey of Youth–Child Supplement, many children had scores comparable to the national average on the measure used, the Behavior Problems Index.

THE IMPORTANCE OF
A PROTECTIVE FACTORS APPROACH

These studies urge us to shift our attention from the issue of group differences to a focus on the factors that contribute to variation in development (Moore, 1986). We are challenged especially to ask what factors predict more positive developmental outcomes among children born to young mothers in poverty. The research on protective factors and resilience in children's development provides a framework to guide us in asking this question within the present sample.

Studies within the research tradition on protective factors and resilience focus on "the manifestation of competence in children despite exposure to stressful events" (Garmezy, Masten, & Tellegen, 1984, p. 98). Garmezy (1985) identified three broad sets of variables that have been found to operate as protective factors, ameliorating the effects of stress on children: child characteristics, family characteristics, and external supports. The research on child resilience implicitly affirms the ecological model (Bronfenbrenner, 1986), which argues that children's development is shaped by multiple spheres of influence, beginning with child characteristics and then moving outward to progressively broader settings, including the family and social contexts surrounding the family.

Previous research helps to identify more specifically the child characteristics, family characteristics, and external supports that can function as protective factors (the evidence has been reviewed by Garmezy, 1985; and Luthar & Zigler, 1991). Characteristics in the child that appear to protect against the effects of stress include positive responsiveness to others, reflectiveness, easy-going temperament, and history of good health; the evidence is somewhat contradictory as to whether higher IQ serves as a protective factor (e.g., Alexander & Entwisle, 1988; Dubow & Luster, 1990; Garmezy, 1991; Rutter, 1979; Werner, 1989). Within the family, protective factors include parental competence in individual functioning, a reciprocally warm and positive parent–child relationship, and low conflict among family members (e.g., Egeland, Carlson, & Sroufe, 1993; Luster & McAdoo, 1994; Rutter, 1979). Beyond the family, findings point to the importance of positive school environments, the child having a positive role model, and social support available to the family (e.g., Werner, 1993; Werner & Smith, 1982).

Studies suggest that it is not only the presence of particular protective factors that is important to children's development but also the total number of protective factors. Protective factors can function cumulatively. Thus, for example, Luster and McAdoo (1994) found that the presence of a greater number of protective factors (including completion of high school by the mother, greater maternal self-esteem and cognitive attainment, family economic status above poverty, two or fewer children in the family, and higher scores on a measure of support and stimulation in the home environment) predicted more favorable cognitive and behavioral development in a sample of African American children. Similarly, Bradley and Caldwell (1984) found that for premature low-birthweight children living in poverty, the presence of a greater number of protective factors increased the probability that children's scores on measures of health and developmental outcomes were in a positive range.

An important pattern that can be seen in the research on resilience to date is that findings differ according to the particular child outcome studied. That is, rather than a single pattern underlying response to stressful circumstances, there may be multiple patterns. Thus, in a study of urban third to sixth graders, Masten et al. (1988) found that the number of protective factors that a child had was important to each of three school-related outcomes: classroom disruptiveness, classroom engagement, and academic achievement. Yet when a greater number of protective factors was combined with a high level of stress for the children, findings for the three outcomes differed. For example, at high levels of stress, children with multiple protective factors tended to show lower scores on the classroom engagement measure but not in achievement.

We can glean from the research to date that if we are seeking to examine factors that serve protective or buffering roles for children's development within the present sample, we should be careful to define the set of stressors that the children in the sample are facing, identify potential protective factors from all three levels of variables that have been noted as important (i.e., child characteristics, family characteristics, and external supports), consider not only whether particular protective factors predict more favorable development but also whether protective factors function cumulatively, and examine child outcomes in more than one aspect of development.

OPERATIONALIZING PROTECTIVE FACTORS
WITHIN THE PRESENT STUDY

Our selection and operationalization (that is, definition and construction of particular measures) of potential protective factors is informed by the literature briefly reviewed above, but also by the previous research on children of adolescent mothers and children in poverty. It is also governed by the information available to us in terms of particular measures included in the New Chance Observational Study.

Child Characteristics

Regarding child characteristics, we evaluate the role of two particular candidates as protective factors: *child sociability* and *child attentiveness*. The rationale for considering child sociability has been well developed in previous work on protective factors. Children who can be characterized as more sociable may be able to engage with social partners more easily and thus to find stimulation and support through interaction more readily.

Regarding child attentiveness, we are guided especially by research that suggests that a combination of such factors as poor prenatal care, preterm birth, low birthweight, undernutrition, and environmental hazards may place children in poverty at higher risk for attentional disorders (Dion, 1997). In addition, Dion (1997), studying a different sample of preschool-age children from welfare families, found that a summary rating of children's behavior in terms of restlessness, overactivity, and inattentiveness significantly predicted both school readiness and social maturity in the children, even after the home environment was taken into account. Ratings available in the present study permit characterizations of such child behaviors as persisting and staying on task when engaging in interesting but challenging mother–child teaching tasks. The ability to attend in such circumstances could be an important marker of the extent to which the child can make use of cognitive stimulation through materials and interactions.

Family Characteristics: Maternal Well-Being and Functioning

We chose to differentiate between two categories of family characteristics: measures of mothers' psychological well-being and functioning and measures of parent–child relations. We focus on two specific measures within each of these categories, again selecting particular measures based on previous research.

Two measures of maternal well-being and functioning that have emerged as particularly important within research on welfare families are maternal depression and maternal sense of efficacy. Symptoms of depression are higher among mothers in poverty, and specifically mothers receiving public assistance, than in broad community samples (Moore et al., 1995). On the Center for Epidemiological Studies Depression Scale (CES-D), scores of greater than 15 indicate a high level of depressive symptoms (Comstock & Helsing, 1976). Whereas about 20% of respondents in community samples score 16 or above, 42% of a sample of welfare mothers with preschool-age children were found to score within this range (Moore et al., 1995). Furthermore, there is evidence that depressed mothers are more critical of, and less responsive to, their preschool children (e.g., McLoyd & Wilson, 1991).

In the study of welfare families with young children conducted by Moore and colleagues (1995), maternal sense of efficacy, or locus of control, was found to be significantly related to multiple measures of children's development. Moore and colleagues reported that mothers' internal locus of control, or greater sense of efficacy, was associated with more favorable descriptions of their children's social behavior but also more positive ratings of the children's health and higher scores on direct assessments of the children's receptive vocabulary and school readiness. Efficacy has been found to be important in other studies involving low-income families as well. For example, Stevens (1988) found maternal locus of control to be significantly associated with the extent to which mothers provide stimulating environments for their young children. In keeping with these findings, we hypothesized that low levels of depressive symptoms and a greater sense of efficacy might serve as protective factors for children's development in the New Chance Observational Study.

Family Characteristics: Parent–Child Relations

As measures of relationships within the family pertaining to parent–child interactions, we again chose two measures, one focusing on the mother–child relationship and one on the extent of father involvement. Our focus on the mother–child relationship derives directly from the research on protective factors summarized above, in which it has been found that a reciprocally warm and positive mother–child relationship can buffer children from stress. From the component of the New Chance Observational Study that involved direct observation of mother–child interaction, we used a global rating, Quality of Relationship, that captured this dyadic quality of mother–child relations well.

Evidence indicates that within welfare families, fathers who are not married to the children's mothers or living with the children may nevertheless maintain contact with their children and provide support to the family in both formal (e.g., child support) and informal (e.g., providing food, clothes, and toys) ways. Greene and Moore (1996) noted the importance of distinguishing between such informal forms of support and more formalized arrangements such as child support agreements for families in poverty. Analyses that they conducted point to small but positive associations with children's developmental outcomes when fathers in welfare families provide both forms of support. However, these analyses also indicate that associations with child outcomes are stronger for informal forms of support.

In the present study we wished to explore continued father involvement as a possible protective factor rather than to restrict our focus only to the mother–child relationship. We considered the number of different forms of contact and support that the father engaged in, including such modalities as visiting, babysitting, providing food or toys, and providing child support.

External Supports

In the category of protective factors pertaining to the family's external supports, previous findings on adolescent mothers underscore the importance of social support. Findings indicate, for example, that mothers with more support from a male partner are less rejecting and punitive with their children (Unger & Wandersman, 1988) and that mothers of infants with more support from family members are more accessible and sensitive in responding to their babies (Crockenberg, 1987). Our measure of social support combines maternal ratings of the number of sources of social support available and mothers' satisfaction with the social support available to her.

The research on low-income families indicates that social networks can be a source of further stress rather than support (e.g., Lindblad-Goldberg & Dukes, 1985). Accordingly, we sought to include a measure that captured events in the broader social context that could be depleting rather than replenishing, such as having conflicts with partners or relatives. We hypothesized that a smaller number of such difficult familial circumstances in the broader social context might function in a protective manner for the children's development.

SPECIAL CONSIDERATION OF MATERNAL PARENTING BEHAVIOR AS PROTECTIVE

There are important reasons to focus in greater detail on parenting behavior as a possible protective factor for children's development. As we have noted, protective factors come from multiple levels of the ecological model, ranging from child characteristics to the larger social context. From the point of view of the child, the mother–child relationship is a key integrator of these levels of influence. Indeed, there is good evidence that mothers respond, in their parenting behavior and in the way they organize the home environment, to child characteristics and their own psychological well-being on the one hand and to social support and stressful external circumstances on the other.

McLoyd (1990) hypothesized, along these lines, that parenting is a key mediator between economic hardship and child outcomes. In particular, she noted a sequence in which mothers and fathers facing more severe economic stress themselves feel greater psychological distress. This distress is manifested especially in terms of greater harshness and less accessibility in interactions with children, which in turn are predictive of more problems in child behavioral adjustment. Dodge, Pettit, and Bates (1994) explicitly examined the possibility that parenting behavior acted as a conduit for the relation between poverty and child outcomes. These researchers found at least half of the variance in child behavior problems associated with income level to be mediated by a set of parental socialization variables.

In accord with this special integrative role that parenting behavior may play, we follow up on our analyses in which a single measure of the dyadic quality of the mother–child relationship is examined as one possible protective factor in a longer list. In particular, we go beyond the global rating of the dyadic quality of the relationship, "unpackaging" it to examine three specific dimensions of parenting behavior: warmth in interaction, low levels of harsh punitive interaction, and cognitive stimulation.

Previous research underscores the importance of these particular aspects of parenting. Theory and research on the dimensions of parenting have suggested that high parental warmth is an important contributor to healthy development, particularly when it is combined with high expectations for maturity. Baumrind's (1971, 1989) research on parents and their preschool-age children demonstrates that parents who were affectively warm and placed high demands on their children for appropriate behavior had children who were more content, self-reliant, self-controlled, and open to exploration in the school context.

Research suggests that both the quantity and the quality of cognitive stimulation provided to a preschool-age child will influence the child's language development and school achievement and may also influence behavioral competencies. Empirical evidence has demonstrated that children who live in safe, organized, and stimulating home environments have higher school achievement than children who live in less stimulating homes (Bradley & Caldwell, 1981; Elardo & Bradley, 1981). Molar measures of the quantity of stimulation, such as number of books available to the child in the home, have been shown to predict child behavioral adaptation in school (Dodge et al., 1994). The quality of stimulation also appears to be vital to children's development. This can be captured, for example, in studies of book reading interactions between parents and children. Observational research has demonstrated that when parents use a reading style that challenges and engages their children, the children show increases in expressive language abilities over children whose parents use less stimulating reading techniques (Bus, Van Ijzendoorn, & Pellegrini, 1995; DeTemple, 1994, 1997; Whitehurst, Galco, Lonigan, & Fischel, 1988).

In addition to focusing on those parenting interactions that foster good developmental outcomes, research and theory have explored the role of physically punitive, coercive, and otherwise harsh parenting interactions in putting preschool-age children at risk for poor developmental outcomes. In research with preschoolers and their parents, Dodge and his colleagues (Dodge et al., 1994; Weiss, Dodge, Bates, & Pettit, 1992) have found that both maternal report and interviewer report of harsh parental discipline predict later problems with aggressive behavior in school settings. Research on maltreatment has demonstrated that severely punitive parent–child interactions lead young children to be less compliant, more negative, more impulsive, and more dependent on adults than nonmaltreated children (Erickson, Egeland, & Pianta, 1989).

SUMMARY OF KEY QUESTIONS

To summarize, in the present chapter, we ask the following questions: Within this sample of families who are highly disadvantaged and quite similar in terms of maternal education, depth of poverty, and marital status, is it nevertheless the case that there is variation in terms of the number of protective factors present from among the list we have chosen? Furthermore, is it the case that the number of protective factors matters to the children's development? From the list of protective factors, which ones are significant predictors of development? Do we see a different pattern of prediction when we look at different developmental outcomes? Focusing on parenting behavior as an integrator of the different levels of the environment for children, what more specifically can we say about dimensions of parenting? Are the specific dimensions of warmth, low levels of harsh punitive interaction, and cognitive stimulation important to the developmental outcomes examined here?

SAMPLE FOR THE PRESENT ANALYSES

We examine these questions within a sample of 290 families who participated in the New Chance Observational Study. The New Chance Observational Study was a study of mother–child interaction embedded within the New Chance Demonstration, an evaluation of an intensive and comprehensive program for young welfare mothers. Each family in the sample was headed by a young woman who had had a child by age 19. In addition, each mother in the sample had dropped out of high school, marking this as an especially disadvantaged sample. Each family had a preschool-age child at the time of enrollment in the study.

The sample was predominantly African American (84.1%), with the remainder of the sample White. The mothers in the sample averaged 18.7 years of age at the time they enrolled in the study but averaged 16.6 years of age at the birth of their first children. Very few mothers in the sample had ever been married (5.2%), and few were living with a partner at the time they enrolled in the evaluation (10.6%). Mothers in the sample had, on average, completed tenth grade. A majority of the mothers in the sample (71.0%) had grown up in families that had received public assistance.

There are numerous indications that the mothers participating in the New Chance Demonstration were facing multiple serious stressors in their lives. New Chance staff reported the occurrence of such problems among the young mothers as being evicted or being asked to leave a residence, substance abuse, the experience of physical or emotional abuse, and discouragement by parents and partners from participating in the program. "Strikingly, almost three-quarters had experienced at least one of these unquestionably serious situations. . . . The personal problems faced by the large majority of New Chance clients makes them an indisputably hard-to-serve group" (Quint & Egeland, 1995, p. 107).

The New Chance Demonstration was one of very few interventions targeted specifically to this extremely disadvantaged group (i.e., young welfare mothers who had already dropped out of school). In recognition of the multiple needs of the mothers in this group, the New Chance Demonstration focused not only on mothers' education and employment skills (through basic education and preparation for the General Equivalency Degree examination, job skills training, employability development, and apprenticeships) but also on their life skills and health (through parenting education classes, life skills education, family planning, individual and group counseling, and access to health services for the mothers). In addition, New Chance also provided services to the young children of participating mothers. Children received child care, often on-site, while their mothers participated in the program, as well as access to health care services. Young mothers, most of whom volunteered to participate in the program, were randomly assigned to a program group (with access to New Chance Program services) or a control group (without access to New Chance services but given a listing of services available in the community). The New Chance Demonstration was carried out in 16 sites in 10 states throughout the United States.

Of the families who participated in the full New Chance Demonstration, 290 from seven of the study sites participated in the observational study. These families were chosen on the grounds that they had a child in the age range appropriate for the special procedures for the observational study (i.e., approximately 30 to 60 months) and they had completed the in-home interview carried out 18 months after enrollment (which was considered important because this interview provided detailed information on many aspects of the children's experiences). The decision was made to limit the sample to African American and White families rather than to include Hispanic families as in the full sample because the sample size for the observational study did not permit examination of subgroups differing in language and country of origin. In the sites chosen for the observational study, families considered eligible for participation were asked to participate in the special study in their order of enrollment in the larger study until the desired sample of about 300 families had been enrolled (297 observational sessions were actually completed, but in 7 cases technical problems with the observational sessions yielded unusable data, yielding a final sample size for the study of 290). Seventy-nine percent of those considered eligible for the observational study went on to participate in it. No systematic differences were found between those eligible families who did and did not participate in the observational study.

The children in the observational study sample ranged in age from 27 to 63 months at the time the observational component of the study was carried out. Of the sample of 290, 148 of the children were boys and 142 were girls. When a family had more than one preschool-age child, one was randomly selected to be the focal child, or child focused upon in developmental assessments and in interview questions about family and child care experiences.

Elsewhere we have presented findings on the impacts of the New Chance Program on parenting behavior and on children's developmental outcomes within the observational study sample (De Temple, 1997; Weinfield, Ogawa, Hennighausen, & Egeland, 1997; Zaslow & Eldred, 1998). However, our focus in the present chapter is on longitudinal predictors of children's development in the sample as a whole. Accordingly, our analyses control for research group (i.e., experimental and control), and report on findings for the full sample of 290 families in the New Chance Observational Study sample.

PROCEDURES OF THE
NEW CHANCE OBSERVATIONAL STUDY

Families in the New Chance Observational Study participated in the procedures of the full evaluation study as well as in an additional visit to their homes to complete the procedures specific to the observational study.

As part of the full evaluation, at the time they volunteered to be in the New Chance Program, all mothers completed a baseline enrollment form providing background information. At baseline mothers completed a test of literacy, the Test of Adult Basic Education. As part of the full evaluation, interviews were conducted in the families' homes about 18 and 42 months after enrollment (Quint et al., 1997; Quint, Musick, & Ladner, 1994). The 18- and 42-month follow-up interviews addressed a range of topics, including program participation, educational attainment, employment and earnings, family receipt of public assistance and other benefits, maternal psychological well-being, family living circumstances, parenting behavior and the home environment (as reported on by the mother and rated by the interviewer), social support, and child care participation. The 42-month interview also included measures of the children's development (selected measures are described later in the chapter).

For the observational study, a visit was arranged to the families' homes soon after the 18-month follow-up visit (on average 21 months after baseline). During this visit, mothers completed a brief interview, and mothers and children were videotaped engaging in a series of structured mother–child interaction tasks. These tasks were originally designed by Block and Block for their longitudinal study of personality development (Harrington, Block, & Block, 1978), modified by Egeland and colleagues for use in the Mother–Child Project (Rahe, 1984), and then further adapted for use in the present study (Eldred, 1998). The tasks were designed to be challenging but interesting and to require the mother to provide some guidance or instruction to the child. The tasks included the mother reading a picture book to her child and discussing the book with her child, the mother helping her child to match a block model by using a variety of smaller blocks, a word game involving the mother trying to get her child to name things with wheels, the mother helping her child to complete a sorting board, and the mother assisting the child in drawing a line through a maze drawn on an Etch-a-Sketch board. The videotapes of mother–child interaction were coded at two research laboratories using different coding schemes. A team led by Egeland and colleagues at the University of Minnesota coded the videotapes from the point of view of the affective quality of interactions (see Weinfield, Egeland, & Ogawa, 1998) and a team led by Snow and colleagues at Harvard University coded the tapes from the point of view of literacy-related interactions (see De Temple & Snow, 1998).

STRATEGY OF ANALYSIS

Our analyses seek to examine the relationships between sets of predictor variables and measures of children's development. Our predictor variables come from two time periods: baseline and about 1½ years after enrollment (i.e., the 18-month follow-up interview and the special home visit carried out for the observational study about 21 months after baseline). The outcomes measures are all measures of the children's development taken from a later time period, the 42-month follow-up. Thus, our analyses examine whether variables from an earlier period predict later development.

Our first step was to examine the incidence of the individual protective factors and the extent of variation in the total number of protective factors present within families. We then used multiple regression to examine whether a summary score indicating the number of protective factors present acts as a significant predictor of developmental outcomes above and beyond the background characteristics of the families. We followed up on this set of analyses by looking at which individual protective factors predict each of the outcomes significantly. For these analyses we examined each of the protective factors separately as a predictor of each of the outcomes, controlling in each instance for background characteristics.

We then focused more specifically on parenting behavior as a key protective factor. We distinguished between the particular aspects of parenting behavior of cognitive stimulation, warmth in mother–child interaction, and harsh/punitive interaction, asking which of these is important to developmental outcomes. Again we used multiple regression, entering the three parenting variables into the regression equation at the same time, controlling statistically for background characteristics. Finally, we asked whether these specific measures of parenting continue to predict to the child outcomes once the number of other protective factors (withdrawing from the summary score the measures of parent–child relationships) are taken into account.

MEASURES

Table 9.1 provides details about the source of specific variables (e.g., maternal report measures, interviewer ratings, or coded observational variables), describes how the discrete measures used in our analyses were defined, and provides psychometric information where composite variables have been created. As can be seen in Table 9.1, our measures fall into four broad categories: background characteristics of the families, protective factors, specific dimensions of parenting behavior, and child outcomes. Here we summarize the measures in each category, building on the earlier discussion of particular protective factors and dimensions of parenting behavior.

TABLE 9.1

Measures Used in Analyses

Category	Measures	Description of Measures
I. Background Characteristics		
These background characteristics of the families are used as covariates in all analyses.		
	Child's age	Children's ages ranged from 27 to 63 months at the time of the observational study.
	Child's gender	
	Number of children in family	
	Maternal literacy score	The maternal literacy score was derived from the Test of Basic Education (TABE).
	Philadelphia site	This site variable was included because it was associated with a number of parenting variables in a way that differed from other sites.
	Portland site	This site variable was included because it was associated with a number of parenting variables in a way that differed from other sites.
	Experimental/control group status	Research group status is also used as a covariate because we are not seeking here to examine the role of the New Chance Program in predicting children's outcomes.

II. Parenting Measures

The parenting measures are composites relying on data from at least 2 of 3 sources from the time of the 18-month interview or the observational session: (1) ratings derived from direct observation of mother–child interaction; (2) scales from the abbreviated version of the HOME inventory (Home Observation for Measurement of the Environment; Caldwell & Bradley, 1984), which relies on a combination of interviewer ratings and maternal report; and (3) scales based entirely on maternal report. The three parenting composite variables were significantly though not highly correlated (correlations ranged from .27 to .36).

| | Maternal Warmth | The composite for Maternal Warmth is an average of three standardized scores: (1) Mother's supportive presence, an observational measure that involved rating the degree to which the mother expresses positive regard and emotional support for her child; (2) the Emotional Support subscale of the HOME–Short Form, which describes the support available to the young child in the home; and (3) a brief (three item) maternal report scale of Warmth/Responsiveness. The Maternal Warmth composite variable has a mean of zero and a standard deviation of .69. |

Continued

TABLE 9.1 (Continued)

Category	Measures	Description of Measures
	Harsh Discipline	The composite for Harsh Discipline is an average of three standardized scores: (1) an observational measure of Harsh Treatment (a summary score including a rating of Mother's Hostility during the teaching tasks and the occurrence or nonoccurrence of six items from a checklist of such behaviors as threatening or punishing the child during the teaching tasks); (2) the Harsh Discipline subscale of the HOME–Short Form, which documents the mother's use of physical punishment; and (3) a six-item maternal report scale of Control/Restrictiveness, a measure of the mother's degree of authoritarian control over the child. The Harsh Discipline composite variable has a mean of zero and standard deviation of .70.
	Cognitive Stimulation	The composite for Cognitive Stimulation averages two standardized measures: (1) the Cognitive Stimulation subscale of the HOME–Short Form, which documents the availability of cognitively stimulating materials in the home and the frequency of cognitively stimulating interactions (such as book reading) and outings (such as trips to the museum); and (2) a summary variable comprising four coded observational measures: Mother's Non-Immediate Talk in the book reading context, or talk that relates the book to outside objects, events and experiences; Book Reading Quality, or mother's comfort level, intonation, and fluency in reading to the child; Ease of Ideas in providing clues in the word guessing game task; and a rating of overall Quality of Instruction across the teaching tasks. The four coded observational measures were significantly but not highly intercorrelated (correlations ranging from .12 to .35). Scores for the four observational measures were standardized and averaged into a single summary score that was then included in the overall composite. The composite variable for Cognitive Stimulation had a mean of zero and a standard deviation of .85.

III. Protective Factors Index

Two specific variables were identified for each of four types of protective factors. All variables were drawn from the 18-month follow-up interview or the visit for the observational study around 21 months after baseline. A score above the median on each variable was considered presence of a protective factor and thus received a code of 1, whereas scores at or below the median received a score of zero. The eight variables were then summed, resulting in a total number of protective factors for each respondent. The summary variable had a range of 0 to 8, with a median of 3 and mean of 3.2. In analyses that examine the simultaneous contribution of the protective factors and parenting composites, the component for positive parent–child relationships was excluded from the Protective Factors Index.

A. Child characteristics	Positive Sociability	The Child Characteristics category includes a summary variable for Positive Sociability. The measure of sociability is a composite of four maternal report ratings of such characteristics as the child's helpfulness and cheerfulness. The items were summed and resulted in a scale with an internal consistency reliability of .63.

TABLE 9.1 (*Continued*)

Category	Measures	Description of Measures
	Attentiveness	The Child Characteristics category also includes a measure of Attentiveness based on observational variables and interviewer ratings of the child's attention and persistence during the mother–child tasks. The items were standardized and summed to form the composite variable. The Attentiveness scale is highly reliable, with an internal consistency reliability of .84.
B. Maternal psychological well-being	Efficacy	The Maternal Psychological Well-Being category includes a measure of the mother's Efficacy. This scale is an abbreviated version of the scale developed by Pearlin et al. (1981). The measure of efficacy had an internal consistency reliability of .70 in the full New Chance Evaluation sample (see Quint et al., 1994).
	Low Risk of Depression	The Maternal Psychological Well-Being category also includes a measure of the mother's risk for depression. Risk for depression was measured using the full 20-item Center for Epidemiological Studies-Depression scale, a widely used and valid measure (Radloff, 1977). The CES-D was found to have an internal consistency reliability of .88 in the full New Chance Evaluation sample (see Quint et al., 1994).
C. Positive parent–child relationships	Quality of Mother–Child Relationship	The category for positive parent–child relationships includes an observational rating of Quality of Mother–Child Relationship. This global rating focuses on the dyadic affective aspects of the mother–child relationship.
	Father Involvement	The category for positive parent–child relationships includes a summary rating of Father Involvement to consider the father–child relationship. As the sample is composed nearly entirely of single-parent families, the Father Involvement measure measures participation of the child's father in the child's life in a variety of ways that do not require co-residence, including visiting, babysitting, providing food or toys, and providing child support. The total number of occurrences of father involvement was summed to create the composite measure. These are maternal report measures of Father Involvement.
D. Larger social context	Social Support	The larger social context component includes a summary measure that asks the mother to report on the number of sources of social support available to her, as well as her satisfaction with the available support. The composite was formed by first dividing each score at the median and then summing the two items.
	Few Difficult Life Circumstances	The larger social context component also includes a summary index of Difficult Life Circumstances facing the mother. This scale measures major life changes as well as habitual or ongoing stress due to events such as having a boyfriend or someone close to the mother die or be jailed or having many conflicts with partners or relatives. The summary measure was created by totaling the number of occurrences out of a list of 10 items. The measure was adapted from a scale by Booth et al. (1989).

Continued

TABLE 9.1 (*Continued*)

Category	Measures	Description of Measures
IV. Child Development Outcomes		
A. Domain of cognitive development	Bracken Basic Concept Scale, School Readiness Component	The Bracken Basic Concept Scale is a direct assessment of child receptive vocabulary. The subtests that make up the School Readiness Component focus on the concepts of color, letter identification, numbers and counting, comparisons, and shapes. Polit (1996) reported internal consistency reliability of .98 for this measure within the full New Chance Evaluation sample and further noted that teacher ratings of the children's academic performance within the evaluation sample varied significantly with the children's scores on the Bracken Basic Concept Scale School Readiness Component. The raw scores in this sample ranged from 1 to 19, with a mean of 7.3 and standard deviation of 3.25.
B. Domain of social/behavioral development	Behavior Problems Index	For the Behavior Problems Index (Zill, 1985), a parent or teacher reports on the frequency with which a child shows behavior problems in six areas: antisocial, anxious/depressed, headstrong, hyperactive, dependent, and peer conflict/withdrawn behavior. In the present analyses we use maternal report of the child's behavior problems, and we use the total score rather than subscale scores. Previous work has shown the Behavior Problems Index to have strong reliability as well as validity. In the full New Chance Evaluation sample, the total score on the Behavior Problems Index was significantly related to interviewer ratings of the child's behavior during the 42-month follow-up interview as well as to the mother's report that there had been a communication from the child's school regarding a discipline problem (Polit, 1996). Scores in this sample ranged from 24.7 to 75.9, with a mean of 50 and a standard deviation of 10.

Background Variables

Background variables that we controlled for in these analyses include child's age, child's gender, number of children in the family, mother's literacy score on the Test of Basic Education and family race/ethnicity. Because we were not seeking here to examine the role of the New Chance Program in predicting children's developmental outcomes, we controlled for group (i.e., experimental or control). We also controlled for two site variables that we found to be associated with parenting variables in a way that was different from the others sites.

Protective Factors Summary

We examined protective factors under four headings: characteristics of the child, maternal functioning and well-being, positive relationships within the family, and social support beyond the family. For each type of protective factor, we identified two specific variables. All variables were drawn from the follow-up period around 1½ years after baseline (i.e., the 18-month follow-up interview or the visit for the observational study around 21 months after baseline).

In the category of child characteristics, we created summary variables of Positive Sociability and Attentiveness. In the category of maternal psychological well-being, we used measures of the mother's Efficacy (Pearlin, Menaghan, Lieberman, & Mullan, 1981), and Depression (using the 20 item CES-D scale). In the category of positive parent–child relationships, we used the observational rating of Quality of Mother–Child Relationship to consider the mother–child relationship and a summary rating of Father Involvement to consider the father–child relationship. Finally, in the category of the larger social context, we created a summary measure of Social Support that taps the number of sources of social support available to the mother and her satisfaction with the support available to her. We also computed an index of Difficult Life Circumstances facing the mother and considered it protective if the mother was facing few such circumstances. Table 9.1 provides the details about variable definitions and about the range viewed as protective for each variable. Intercorrelations of the eight protective factors generally fell in the low to moderate range, with most not exceeding .20.

Specific Dimensions of Parenting

As can be seen in Table 9.1, we created three composite parenting variables from among the multiple discrete parenting measures available in this study: composite measures of Maternal Warmth, Harsh Discipline, and Cognitive Stimulation. The composite measures rely on data from three sources: ratings derived from direct observation of mother–child interaction; scales from the abbreviated version of the HOME Inventory (Home Observational for Measurement of the Environment; Caldwell & Bradley, 1984) completed as part of the 18-month follow-up interview, which rely on a combination of interviewer ratings and maternal report; and scales based entirely on maternal report from the 18-month follow-up interview and the brief interview at the time of the observational session. In order to assure that each composite was built on information from multiple informants, each composite draws upon at least two of these three data sources. The three parenting composite variables were significantly though not highly correlated (the absolute value of the correlations ranged from .27 to .36).

Outcome Variables

In keeping with the findings of previous research on protective factors, we examined children's development in multiple domains of development. In particular, we focused on the Bracken Basic Concept Scale School Readiness Component and the total score of the Behavior Problems Index. Thus, we have one outcome in the domain of cognitive development and one in the domain of social development and adjustment.

The Bracken Basic Concept Scale is a direct assessment of child receptive vocabulary. The subtests that make up the School Readiness Component focus on the concepts of color, letter identification, numbers and counting, comparisons, and shapes. Polit (1996) reported internal consistency reliability of .98 for this measure within the full New Chance Evaluation sample and further noted that teacher ratings of the children's academic performance within the evaluation sample were significantly associated with the children's scores on this subscale of the Bracken.

For the Behavior Problems Index (Zill, 1985), a parent or teacher reports on the frequency with which a child shows behavior problems in six areas: antisocial, anxious or depressed, headstrong, hyperactive, dependent, and peer conflict or withdrawn behavior. In our analyses we used maternal report of the children's behavior problems, and we used the total score rather than subscale scores. Previous work has shown the Behavior Problems Index to have strong reliability as well as validity. In the full New Chance Evaluation sample, the total score on the Behavior Problems Index was significantly related to interviewer ratings of the child's behavior during the 42-month follow-up interview as well as to the mother's report that there had been a communication from the child's school regarding a discipline problem (Polit, 1996).

RESULTS

Within this sample of disadvantaged families, who are homogeneous in terms of key markers of socioeconomic status, do we nevertheless see variation in the number of protective factors present? There was a substantial range in the number of protective factors present for children in this sample, from none to all eight of the possible protective factors. Families averaged 3.2 protective factors. Interestingly, even though this is a uniformly disadvantaged sample in terms of economic resources, about one fifth of the sample had 5 or more protective factors.

Does a greater number of protective factors in a child's life predict more positive development? As can be seen in Table 9.2, the number of protective factors in a child's life significantly predicted scores on both the Behavior Problems Index and the Bracken assessment in analyses controlling for background variables. Children with more protective factors had significantly lower behavior problem scores and higher Bracken scores.

Which particular protective factors were associated with more favorable developmental outcomes? Table 9.3 presents results regarding the role of the individual variables that comprised the protective factors summary in predicting the child outcomes. As can be seen, nearly all of the individual protective factors were predictive of scores on the Behavior Problems Index. Only the Father Involvement measure failed to predict the outcome. By contrast, for the measure of school readiness a smaller set of protective factors appeared to be of importance, net of background control variables. The child characteristics (both Sociability and Attentiveness) remained significant predictors. However, of the remaining variables,

TABLE 9.2
Regression Coefficients for Effect of Protective Factors Index
on Child Development Outcomes, Controlling for Baseline Characteristics

Predictor Variable	Behavior Problems Index	Bracken
Covariates		
Experimental/Control group status	2.01	−.14
Child age	.02	.03*
Philadelphia site	−.13	−.40
Portland site	−.65	−1.63*
Number of children	.11	−1.22**
Child gender	−1.01	.61
Race/ethnicity	4.44*	.14
Protective Factors		
Protective Factors Index	−1.62***	.30**
Total R^2	.12***	.11***

Source: New Chance data from baseline enrollment form, 18-month follow-up survey, coded observational study variables from 21-month visit, variables from brief interview accompanying observational study session, and 42-month follow-up survey.

Note. Sample size = 235. Coefficients are unstandardized. All variables were entered simultaneously in this model. Statistical significance indicated as: $*p \leq .05$; $**p \leq .01$; $***p \leq .001$. Race/ethnicity was coded so that 0 = Black and 1 = Not Black.

TABLE 9.3

Standardized Regression Coefficients for Effect of Individual Components
of the Protective Factors Index on Child Development Outcomes,
Controlling for Baseline Characteristics

Component of Protective Factors Index	Behavior Problems Index	Bracken
Positive sociability	−.14*	.13*
Attentiveness	−.15*	.29***
Efficacy	−.22***	.06
Low depression	−.24***	.05
Quality of M–C relationship	−.18**	.18**
High father involvement	−.03	−.00
High social support	−.23***	.12⁺
Few DLC	−.11⁺	.02

Source: New Chance 18-month follow-up survey, coded observational
study variables, brief interview accompanying observational session, and
42-month follow-up survey.

Note. Each line in the table corresponds to a separate analysis where the
protective factor component is entered after the block of seven covariates
(experimental/control group status, child age, Philadelphia site, Portland site,
number of children, child gender, and race/ethnicity). That is, the eight protective factors are not entered simultaneously in this model because we are
interested in the contribution of each individual category. Due to missing
data from some respondents' questionnaires or videotape problems, sample
size varies for particular measures, ranging from 213 to 248. All coefficients
are standardized to facilitate comparison. Statistical significance is indicated
as: $^+p \le .10, ^*p \le .05, ^{**}p \le .01, ^{***}p \le .001$.

only quality of the mother–child relationship was a significant predictor, with social support approaching significance.

Which specific aspects of parenting are important to the outcomes? In the analyses
just presented, it appears that the quality of the mother–child relationship was important in predicting both the behavioral and cognitive outcomes considered here.
The next set of analyses provides a more differentiated view of mother–child relations. In these analyses we again controlled for background characteristics and
asked whether three specific dimensions of parenting predict the child outcomes.
In particular, we examined the parenting dimensions of Warmth, Harsh Discipline, and Cognitive Stimulation.

These analyses suggest that each of the three dimensions of parenting is of importance. Yet in a manner consistent with the literature we have summarized in
this chapter, different aspects of parenting appear to be of importance to the two
domains of child development examined. As Table 9.4 shows, children who experienced Harsh Discipline infrequently had fewer subsequent behavior problems. Although greater Cognitive Stimulation and Warmth did not predict better behavioral adjustment, these dimensions of parenting were important to a child's school

TABLE 9.4
Regression Coefficients for Effect of Parenting Measures
on Child Development Outcomes, Controlling for Baseline Characteristics

Predictor Variable	Behavior Problems Index	Bracken
Covariates		
Experimental/Control group status	2.50$^+$	−.44
Child age	−.02	.02
Philadelphia site	−.80	−.04
Portland site	−.38	1.50*
Number of children	−.16	−1.12**
Child gender	−1.34	.73$^+$
Race/ethnicity	6.17**	−.13
Parenting Composites		
Harsh Discipline	2.83**	.15
Warmth	.26	.60$^+$
Cognitive Stimulation	−.90	.55*
Total R^2	.09**	.12**

Source: New Chance data from baseline enrollment form, 18-month follow-up survey, coded observational study data from 21-month visit, and 42-month follow-up survey.

Note. Sample size = 235. All variables were entered simultaneously in this model. Coefficients are unstandardized. Race/ethnicity was coded so that 0 = Black and 1 = Non-Black. Statistical significance indicated as: $^+p \le .10$; $^*p \le .05$; $^{**}p \le .01$; $^{***}p \le .001$.

readiness: Cognitive Stimulation was significantly, and Warmth marginally significantly, predictive of higher school readiness scores.

Are the specific dimensions of parenting important regardless of the number of other protective factors? Does the number of protective factors continue to be of importance above and beyond specific parenting behaviors? In a final set of analyses, we asked whether the specific dimensions of parenting behavior continue to be important even controlling for the number of other protective factors present. In the same way, we asked whether the number of protective factors continues to predict development even controlling for the influence of specific dimensions of parenting. For these analyses, we deleted from the protective factors summary the variables related to relationships within the family (i.e., the Quality of Relationship and Father Involvement variables).

Findings presented in Table 9.5 show that when all the variables of interest are considered simultaneously, Harsh Discipline and the protective factors summary continue to be uniquely predictive of children's behavior problems. For the Bracken school readiness assessment, the coefficients for Cognitive Stimulation and the protective factors summary approach but do not reach statistical significance.

TABLE 9.5
Regression Coefficients for Unique Effect of Parenting and Protective Factors
on Child Development Outcomes, Controlling for Baseline Characteristics

Predictor Variable	Behavior Problems Index	Bracken
Covariates		
Experimental/Control group status	1.77	−.64
Child age	.01	.03
Philadelphia site	−.47	−.16
Portland site	.23	−1.50*
Number of children	−.09	−1.32**
Child gender	−1.20	.50
Race/ethnicity	5.03**	−.12
Parenting Composites		
Harsh Discipline	2.60**	.14
Warmth	.78	.50
Cognitive Stimulation	.12	.43
Protective Factors Index[a]		
Protective Factors Summary	−1.96***	.23
Total R^2	.16***	.13***

Source: New Chance data from baseline enrollment form, 18-month follow-up survey, coded observational study data from 21-month visit, and 42-month follow-up survey.

Note. Sample size = 247. All variables were entered simultaneously in this model; thus coefficients represent the unique effect of each factor. Statistical significance is indicated as: *$p \le .05$, **$p \le .01$, ***$p \le .001$. Coefficients are unstandardized. Race/ethnicity was coded so that 0 = Black and 1 = Non-Black.

[a]The Protective Factors Index used in this analysis excludes the category for positive parent–child relationships.

DISCUSSION

This study provides a particularly stringent examination of the protective factors perspective for the development of children in stressful circumstances due to the nature of the present sample. In many studies of risk and resilience, although families can all be characterized as facing stress, there is variation in terms of such key characteristics as extent of poverty, marital status, and maternal education. In the present study, all mothers had dropped out of school, all were receiving Aid to Families with Dependent Children at the start of the study, all were teenagers upon the birth of their first children, and nearly all were unmarried.

Our findings indicate that even in this extremely disadvantaged sample, families nevertheless have important resources that can buffer their children from stress. Despite the relative homogeneity in their economic circumstances, these families varied substantially in terms of the number of protective factors that were present. Furthermore, protective factors functioned cumulatively, such that children's development in both the behavioral and cognitive domains was more positive among children whose families had more protective factors.

We also see clear affirmation for the view that children draw upon resources at multiple levels of the ecological model. In our analyses, protective factors from each of the four levels or categories that we considered (i.e., child characteristics, maternal functioning, parent–child relationships, and external supports) emerged as significant individual predictors of development. Indeed, only a single variable from among the eight we considered in the protective factors summary failed to serve as a significant predictor: The measure of father involvement predicted neither children's behavior problems nor school readiness.

Why might it be the case, in the present analyses, that father involvement was unrelated to the child outcomes, particularly given previous research (Greene & Moore, 1996) pointing to the importance of father involvement in welfare families? The present study focused on adolescent mothers, whereas the previous research focused on a sample of mothers who were all 20 years of age or older. In addition, the associations shown previously between father involvement and child outcomes were documented in analyses within a single time period (i.e., associations were contemporaneous), whereas the present analyses are longitudinal. It is possible that for the young mothers in the present sample, who were themselves undergoing important developmental transitions (Quint & Egeland, 1995), the relationships with the children's fathers are also changing over time. Perhaps concurrent but not longitudinal predictions would have shown associations with the child outcomes under these circumstances. The work of Greene and Moore (1996) also suggests that rather than summing across all forms of father involvement, as we have done here, it may be important to look separately at the components of visitation, informal financial support, and the provision of child support. Finally, it may be that we need to examine measures of the quality of father involvement in combination with measures of the extent of father involvement, and we may require father report data in addition to or instead of mother report data.

In our analyses, we see that child characteristics and the quality of the mother–child relationship were important to development in both the cognitive and behavioral domains, whereas measures of the mothers' functioning and of the broader social context emerged as important only to the children's behavioral adjustment. As suggested by previous research, within this sample, protective factors appear to function somewhat differentially for differing outcomes of interest.

Dion (1997) noted that research on the development of children in poverty tends to bypass the possible influence of child characteristics, despite the fact that poverty may increase the prevalence of such problems as chronic health conditions and conditions that indicate risk for attentional disorders. The present analyses, working within the protective factors framework, affirm the importance of taking child characteristics into account. It is especially interesting that positive sociability predicted school readiness and not just behavioral adjustment, and similarly that attentiveness predicted both outcomes.

We have noted that parenting behavior may serve a pivotal role among the different protective factors, integrating the influences of such variables as child characteristics and social support. In the present analyses, we see multiple indications of the importance of parenting behavior, or rather more specifically, maternal behavior with the child. Like the child characteristics, the variable describing the dyadic quality of the mother–child relationship predicted both developmental outcomes. Further, we saw that all three specific dimensions of parenting we considered, Cognitive Stimulation, Warmth, and Harsh Discipline, were significant predictors of development. Finally, even in analyses that controlled for background characteristics and the presence of other protective factors, parenting behavior emerged as a significant predictor.

Among the specific dimensions, the absence of harsh interactions emerged as particularly robust in these analyses controlling for other protective factors. This is in agreement with the conceptual perspective and research of McLoyd (McLoyd, 1990; McLoyd, Jayaratne, Ceballo, & Borquez, 1994), in which harsh treatment is viewed as a key means by which parental distress in response to economic deprivation is conveyed to the child. This finding has emerged in work ranging from consideration of the implications of the Great Depression for children, to work on poverty among rural families, and as McLoyd has noted, specifically in research on African American families in poverty.

These descriptive findings may be used as a resource for considering how to enhance the development of children facing the double stressors of poverty and birth to a teenage mother. They raise the possibility that it may be important to address multiple levels in the ecological model in order to enhance children's development. Although previous interventions for adolescent mothers in poverty have been clear as to the importance of enhancing parenting behavior and providing broader social support to the young mothers, interventions have not routinely screened the children for early indications of attention deficit or other learning disorders for which early intervention could be extremely important. Similarly, few interventions have provided mental health components that are in keeping with the pervasiveness of depression documented in samples of welfare families or the evidence of the severity of symptoms in some mothers. Our findings may also be used to target those aspects of interventions focusing on parenting behavior. A critical first step may be to work with young mothers on reducing harsh and punitive interactions. Indeed, this may be a prerequisite to increasing the supportiveness and stimulation in interactions (Egeland & Zaslow, 1995).

Finally, although the findings of this study can be seen as a source of optimism in that they reveal important sources of strength for children in extremely disadvantaged families, we must conclude with a sobering caveat. The children in the New Chance sample were at high risk for problems in development. For example, the mean score on the Bracken measure of school readiness for the children in this sample corresponds to the 16th percentile nationally (with only 12.4% of the children scoring above the national average). Although the presence of multiple protective factors was clearly and strongly predictive of higher scores on the measure of school readiness, for the children in the present analyses, it did not assure development at the level of national norms. The 31 children in our sample with six to eight protective factors, on average, still scored only at the 32nd percentile on the measure of school readiness. This is double the average percentile score for children in the observational study sample, but it does not nearly meet the average percentile (50%) for the national standardization sample. Thus, it is critical to think not only of the resources already available within these families that can buffer the children's development but also of how to strengthen and broaden the set of protective factors.

ACKNOWLEDGMENTS

This chapter was written with funding from the Family and Child Well-Being Research Network of the National Institute of Child Health and Human Development (NICHD Grant 1 U01 HD3093 0-01). The New Chance Observational Study was carried out with funding from the Foundation for Child Development, the William T. Grant Foundation, and an anonymous funder. The interdisciplinary team for the New Chance Observational Study was assembled by the Manpower Demonstration Research Corporation (MDRC). We gratefully acknowledge the work of Robert Granger in coordinating the overall work of the team. Hans Bos and Janet Quint of MDRC also helped assure coordination of the research with the larger New Chance Evaluation. Independent research and evaluation consultant Carolyn Eldred was instrumental in adapting the observational procedures of the New Chance Observational Study for fielding in a survey research context. This chapter reflects many helpful suggestions from a careful review by Kristin Moore. We thank Jennifer Sargent of Child Trends for her work in helping to bring this manuscript to closure.

REFERENCES

Alexander, K. L., & Entwistle, D. R. (1988). Achievement in the first 2 years of school: Patterns and processes. *Monographs of the Society for Research in Child Development, 53* (2, Serial No. 218).
Baldwin, W., & Cain, V. (1980). The children of teenage parents. *Family Planning Perspectives, 12,* 34–43.
Baumrind, D. (1971). Harmonious parents and their preschool children. *Developmental Psychology, 4,* 99–102.
Baumrind, D. (1989). Rearing competent children. In W. Damon (Ed.), *Child development today and tommorrow* (pp. 349–378). San Francisco: Jossey-Bass.
Booth, C. L., Mitchell, S. K., Barnard, K. E., & Spieker, S. J. (1989). Development of maternal social skills in multiproblem families: Effects on the mother–child relationship. *Developmental Psychology, 25,* 403–412.
Bradley, R. H., & Caldwell, B. M. (1981). The HOME inventory: A validation of the preschool scale for black children. *Child Development, 52,* 708–710.

Bradley, R. H., & Caldwell, B. M. (1984). The relation of infants' home environment to achievement test performance in first grade: A follow-up study. *Child Development, 55,* 803–809.

Bronfenbrenner, U. (1986). Ecology of the family as a context for human development: Research perspectives. *Developmental Psychology, 22,* 723–742.

Brooks-Gunn, J., & Furstenberg, F. F., Jr. (1986). The children of adolescent mothers: Physical, academic and psychological outcomes. *Developmental Review, 6,* 224–251.

Bureau of the Census. (1995). *Statistical brief. Mothers who receive AFDC payments: Fertility and socioeconomic characteristics* (SB/95-2). Washington, DC: U.S. Government Printing Office.

Bus, A. G., Van Ijzendoorn, M. H., & Pellegrini, A. D. (1995). Joint book reading makes for success in learning to read. A metaanalysis on intergenerational transmission of literaccy. *Review of Educational Research, 65,* 1–21.

Caldwell, B. M., & Bradley, R. H. (1984). *Home Observation for Measurement of the Environment.* Little Rock, AR: University of Arkansas.

Comstock, G. W., & Helsing, K. J. (1976). Symptoms of depression in two communities. *Psychological Medicine, 6,* 551–563.

Crockenberg, S. (1987). Predictors and correlates of anger toward and punitive control of toddlers by adolescent mothers. *Child Development 58,* 964–975.

De Temple, J. (1994). *Book reading styles of low-income mothers with preschoolers and children's later literacy skills.* Unpublished doctoral dissertation, Harvard University, Cambridge, MA.

De Temple, J. (1997, April). Mothers' book reading with young children: An observational study within the New Chance Demonstration Project. In L. Sherrod (Chair), *Mother-child relations in the context of contrasting programs for welfare families.* Symposium conducted at the biennial meeting of the Society for Research in Child Development, Washington, DC.

De Temple, J., & Snow, C. (1998). Mother-child interactions related to the emergence of literacy. In M. J. Zaslow & C. A. Eldred (Eds.), *Parenting behavior in a sample of young single mothers in poverty: Results of the New Chance Observational Study.* New York: Manpower Demonstration Research Corporation.

Dion, M. R. (1997, April). Implications of child characteristics for children's developmental outcomes in a welfare sample. In K. Moore (Chair), *Factors in the development of children in welfare families: An ecological perspective.* Symposium conducted at the biennial meeting of the Society for Research in Child Development, Washington, DC.

Dodge, K. A., Pettit, G. S., & Bates, J. E. (1994). Socialization mediators of the relation between socioeconomic status and child conduct problems. *Child Development, 65,* 649–665.

Dubow, E., & Luster, T. (1990). Adjustment of children born to teenage mothers: The contribution of risk and protective factors. *Journal of Marriage and the Family, 52,* 393–404.

Duncan, G. J., & Brooks-Gunn, J. (1997). Income effects across the life span: Integration and interpretation. In G. Duncan & J. Brooks-Gunn (Eds.), *Consequences of growing up poor* (pp. 596–610). New York: Russell Sage Foundation.

Duncan, G., Brooks-Gunn, J., & Klebanov, P. K. (1994). Economic deprivation and early childhood development. *Child Development, 65,* 296–318.

Egeland, B., Carlson, E., & Sroufe, L. A. (1993). Resilience as process. *Development and Psychopathology, 5,* 517–528.

Egeland, B., & Zaslow, M. (1995, March). The effects of the New Chance program on mother–child interaction. In A. Huston (Chair), *Effects of welfare on children and parenting processes.* Symposium conducted at the biennial meeting of the Society for Research in Child Development, Indianapolis, IN.

Elardo, R. D., & Bradley, R. H. (1981). The Home Observation for Measurement of the Environment (HOME) scale: A review of research. *Developmental Review, 1,* 113–145.

Eldred, C. A. (1998). Implementing observational research within a survey context. In M. J. Zaslow & C. A. Eldred (Eds.), *Parenting behavior in a sample of young single mothers in poverty: Results of the New Chance Observational Study.* New York: Manpower Demonstration Research Corporation.

Erickson, M. F., Egeland, B., & Pianta, R. (1989). The effects of maltreatment on the development of young children. In D. Cicchetti & V. Carlson (Eds.), *Research and theory: Child maltreatment* (pp. 647–684). London: Cambridge University Press.

Furstenberg, F. F., Brooks-Gunn, J., & Chase-Lansdale, L. (1989). Teenage pregnancy and childbearing. *American Psychologist, 44,* 313–320.

Garmezy, N. (1985). Stress-resistant children: The search for protective factors. In J. E. Stevenson (Ed.), *Recent research in developmental psychology* (pp. 213–233). Oxford: Pergamon.

Garmezy, N. (1991). Resiliency and vulnerability to adverse developmental outcomes associated with poverty. *American Behavioral Scientist, 34,* 416–430.

Garmezy, N., Masten, A. S., & Tellegen, A. (1984). The study of stress and competence in children: A building block for developmental psychopathology. *Child Development, 55,* 97–111.

Greene, A. D., & Moore, K. A. (1996). *Nonresident father involvement and child outcomes among young children in families on welfare.* Paper presented at the Conference on Father Involvement, sponsored by the National Institute of Child Health and Human Development's Family and Child Well-Being Network, Bethesda, MD.

Harrington, G., Block, J. H., & Block, J. (1978). Intolerance of ambiguity in preschool children: Psychometric considerations, behavioral manifestations, and parental correlates. *Developmental Psychology, 14,* 242–256.

Klerman, L. V. (1991). The association between adolescent parenting and childhood poverty. In A. C. Huston (Ed.), *Children in poverty.* Cambridge, England: Cambridge University Press.

Lindblad-Goldberg, M., & Dukes, L. J. (1985). Social support in Black, low-income, single-parent families: Normative and dysfunctional patterns. *American Journal of Orthopsychiatry, 55,* 42–58.

Luster, T., & McAdoo, H. P. (1994). Factors related to the achievement and adjustment of young African-American children. *Child Development, 65,* 1080–1094.

Luthar, S. S., & Zigler, E. (1991). Vulnerability and competence: A review of research on resilience in childhood. *American Journal of Orthopsychiatry, 61,* 6–22.

Masten, A. S., Garmezy, N., Tellingen, A., Pellegrine, D. S., Larkin, K., & Larsen, A. (1988). Competence and stress in school children: The moderating effects of individual and family qualities. *Journal of Child Psychology and Psychiatry, 29,* 745–764.

Maynard, R. A. (1997). The costs of adolescent childbearing. In R. Maynard (Ed.), *Kids having kids: Economic costs and social consequences of teen pregnancy* (pp. 285–337). Washington, DC: The Urban Institute.

McLoyd, V. C. (1990). The impact of economic hardship on black families and children: Psychological distress, parenting, and socioemotional development. *Child Development, 61,* 311–346.

McLoyd, V. C., Jayaratne, T. E., Ceballo, R., & Borquez, J. (1994). Unemployment and work interruption among African-American single mothers: Effects on parenting and adolescent socioemotional functioning. *Child Development, 65,* 562–590.

McLoyd, V., & Wilson, L. (1991). The strain of living poor: Parenting, social support, and child mental health. In A. C. Huston (Ed.), *Children in poverty: Child development and public policy* (pp. 105–135). New York: Cambridge University Press.

Moore, K. A. (1986). *Children of teen parents: Heterogeneity of outcomes.* Final Report to the Center for Population Research, National Institute for Child Health and Human Development, Grant No. HD-184262.

Moore, K. A., Morrison, D. R., & Greene, A. D. (1997). Effects on the children born to adolescent mothers. In R. A. Maynard (Ed.), *Kids having kids: Economic costs and social consequences of teen pregnancy* (pp. 145–180). Washington, DC: The Urban Institute.

Moore, K. A., Myers, D., Morrison, D. R., Nord, C. W., Brown, B., & Edmonston, B. (1992). *Age at first birth and later poverty.* Paper presented at the National Institute for Child Health and Human Development Conference on outcomes of early childbearing: An appraisal of recent evidence, Bethesda, MD.

Moore, K. A., Zaslow, M. J., Coiro, M. J., Miller, S. M., & Magenheim, E. B. (1995). *How well are they far-*

ing? AFDC families with preschool-age children in Atlanta at the outset of the JOBS Evaluation. Washington, DC: U.S. Department of Health and Human Services, Office of the Assistant Secretary for Planning and Evaluation.

Pearlin, L. I., Menaghan, E. G., Lieberman, M. A., & Mullan, J. T. (1981). The stress process. *Journal of Health and Social Behavior, 22,* 337–356.

Polit, D. F. (1996). *Parenting and child outcome measures in the New Chance 42-month survey.* New York: Manpower Demonstration Research Corporation.

Quint, J. C., Bos, J. M., & Polit, D. F. (1997). *New Chance: Final report on a comprehensive program for young mothers in poverty and their children.* New York: Manpower Demonstration Research Corporation.

Quint, J. C., & Egeland, B. (1995). Two generation programs for families in poverty: A new intervention strategy. In S. Smith (Ed.), *Two-generation programs for families in poverty* (pp. 199–225), Norwood, NJ: Ablex.

Quint, J. C., Fink, B. L., & Rowser, S. L. (1991). *New Chance: Implementing a comprehensive program for disadvantaged young mothers and their children.* New York: Manpower Demonstration Research Corporation.

Quint, J. C., Musick, J. S. & Ladner, J. A. (1994). *Lives of promise, lives of pain: Young mothers after New Chance.* New York: Manpower Demonstration Research Corporation.

Quint, J. C., Polit, D. F., Bos, H., & Cave, G. (1994). *New Chance: Interim findings on a comprehensive program for disadvantaged young mothers and their children.* New York: Manpower Demonstration Research Corporation.

Radloff, L. S. (1977). The CES-D Scale: A self-report depression scale for research in the general population. *Applied Psychological Measurement, 1,* 385–401.

Rahe, D. F. (1984). *Interaction patterns between children and mothers on teaching tasks at age 42-months: Antecedents in attachment history, intellectual correlates, and consequences on children's socioemotional functioning.* Unpublished doctoral dissertation, University of Minnesota.

Rutter, M. (1979). Protective factors in children's responses to stress and disadvantage. In M. W. Kent & J. Rolf (Eds.), *Primary prevention of psychopathology, Vol. III: Social competence in children* (pp. 49–74). Hanover, NH: University Press of New England.

Saluter, A. (1996). *Marital status and living arrangements March 1995* (Update). Current Population Reports, P20-494. Washington, DC: U.S. Bureau of the Census, U.S. Department of Commerce.

Stevens, J. H. (1988). Social support, locus of control, and parenting in three low-income groups of mothers. Black teenagers, black adults, and white adults. *Child Development, 59,* 635–642.

Unger, D. G., & Wandersman, L. P. (1988). The relation of family and partner support to the adjustment of adolescent mothers. *Child Development, 59,* 1056–1060.

U.S. House of Representatives, Ways and Means Committee. (1996). *Green Book, 1996.* Print WMCP: 104-14. Washington, DC: U.S. Government Printing Office.

Ventura, S. J., Peters, K. D., Martin, J. A., & Maurer, J. D. (1997). Births and deaths: United States, 1996. *Monthly Vital Statistics Report* (Vol. 46, No. 1, Supp 2). Hyattsville, MD: National Center for Health Statistics.

Weinfield, N. S., Egeland, B., & Ogawa, J. R. (1998). Affective quality of mother–child interaction. In M. Zaslow & C. Eldred (Eds.), *Parenting behavior in a sample of young single mothers in poverty: Results of the New Chance Observational Study* (pp. 71–113). New York: Manpower Demonstration Research Corporation.

Weinfield, N. S., Ogawa, J. R., Hennighausen, K. H., & Egeland, B. (1997). Helping mothers, helping children? Predicting child outcomes from mother–child interaction in the New Chance Demonstration. In L. Sherrod (Chair), *Mother–child relations in the context of contrasting programs for welfare families.* Symposium conducted at the biennial meeting of the Society for Research in Child Development, Washington, DC.

Weiss, B., Dodge, K., Bates J., & Pettit, G. (1992). Some consequences of early harsh discipline: Child aggression and a maladaptive social information processing style. *Child Development, 63,* 1321–1335.

Werner, E. (1989). High-risk children in young adulthood: A longitudinal study from birth to 32 years. *American Journal of Orthopsychiatry, 59,* 72–81.

Werner, E. (1993). Risk, resilience and recovery: Perspectives from the Kauai Longitudinal Study, *Development and Psychopathology, 5,* 503–515.

Werner, E., & Smith, R. (1982). *Vulnerable but invincible: A longitudinal study of resilient children and youth.* New York: McGraw-Hill.

Whitehurst, G. J., Galco, F. L., Lonigan C. J., Fischel, J. E. (1988). Accelerating language development through picture book reading. *Developmental Psychology, 24,* 552–559.

Zaslow, M. J., & Eldred, C. A. (Eds.). (1998). *Parenting behavior in a sample of young single mothers in poverty: Results of the New Chance Observational Study.* New York: Manpower Demonstration Research Corporation.

Zill, N. (1985). *Behavior problem scales developed from the 1981 Child Health Supplement to the National Health Interview Survey.* Washington, DC: Child Trends.

Zill, N., Moore, K. A., Smith, E. W, Stief, T., & Coiro, M. J. (1995). The life circumstances and development of children in welfare families: A profile based on national survey data. In L. P. Chase-Lansdale & J. Brooks-Gunn (Eds.), *Escape from poverty: What makes a difference for children?* (pp. 38–59). New York: Cambridge University Press.

Family Functioning and Child Adjustment in Repartnered Relationships and in Stepfamilies

10

Contexts as Predictors of Changing Maternal Parenting Practices in Diverse Family Structures

A Social Interactional Perspective of Risk and Resilience

David S. DeGarmo
Marion S. Forgatch
Oregon Social Learning Center

STUDIES COMPARING the social and academic adjustment of youngsters living in diverse family structures provide convincing evidence that divorce and repartnering are transitions that place youngsters at risk. Such family structure transitions are associated with increased risk for conduct problems, school problems, and peer rejection (Brody, Neubaum, & Forehand, 1988; Capaldi & Patterson, 1991; Chase-Landsdale, Cherlin, & Keirnan, 1995; Forgatch, Patterson, & Ray, 1996; Furstenberg & Seltzer, 1986; Hetherington & Clingempeel, 1992; Zill, Morrison, & Coiro, 1993). Why do most youngsters weather these family transitions relatively unscathed while a substantial subset suffers? One answer appears to lie within the parent–child context. Effective parenting practices contribute significantly to differential adjustment for the children who live in divorced and repartnered families (Anderson, Lindner, & Bennion, 1992; Bray & Berger, 1993; Capaldi & Patterson, 1991; Forgatch & DeGarmo, 1997; Hetherington, 1993; Hetherington & Clingempeel, 1992; Vuchinich, Vuchinich, & Wood, 1993). Some mothers are able to maintain effective parenting practices even while gaining or losing an intimate partner. This ability to remain constant in parenting may reflect a balance in protective and risk factors within the mother's social environment.

From a social interactional perspective, the contexts surrounding interpersonal interactions affect the microsocial behaviors that are exchanged between individu-

FIG 10.1.   Maintaining balance on the parenting path.

als (Patterson, in press; Patterson & Forgatch, 1990). As these exchanges become patterned and habitual, they can generalize to other social settings. Patterned behaviors are assumed to form within influential social settings. For most children, the family is the primary socializing setting (Patterson, 1982). Parents teach their children how to interact with others through their use of parenting practices, such as discipline and interpersonal problem solving. For example, coercive discipline practices may teach youngsters to employ coercive tactics with peers and teachers (Patterson, 1986; Snyder, Peterson, & St. Peter, 1997). Effective problem solving, on the other hand, may teach children how to resolve conflict and get along with others (Forgatch, 1989; Forgatch et al., 1996; Forgatch & DeGarmo, 1997).

Family structure transitions generate profound changes in social context for parents and children. If these potentially disruptive changes take place with few protective factors, the quality of parenting practices may decline. Throughout this chapter, we examine how changes in the mother's social environment are related to the quality of her discipline strategies and interpersonal problem solving practices. Within a social interactional framework, we summarize recent findings that suggest how certain contexts may protect or interfere with parenting practices. Figure 10.1 illustrates the dynamics of weathering stormy transitions for divorced and repartnered mothers. Transitions generate a multitude of risk factors, making it difficult for a parent to maintain balance on the path of parenting during transitions. Protective factors can provide the balance necessary to stay on course.

A SOCIAL INTERACTIONAL VIEW OF RISK

Family structure transitions are embedded within the environment in which the family lives (Capaldi & Patterson, 1991). Several studies show that divorce and repartnering are transitions associated with background factors that interfere with effective parenting (Bank, Forgatch, Patterson, & Fetrow, 1993; Conger, Patterson, & Ge, 1995; Forgatch et al., 1996; Hetherington, Stanley-Hagan, & Anderson, 1989; Patterson & Forgatch, 1990; Simons, Beaman, Conger, & Chao, 1993). These background factors include stress, maternal depression, socioeconomic disadvantage, and antisocial parents. The social interactional model argues that the association between such contextual risk factors and negative child outcomes is mediated by parenting practices in all family structure types (Forgatch et al., 1996; Patterson, 1986). Some parents maintain effective child-rearing practices even while transitioning in and out of intimate relationships. What contexts contribute to this sort of parenting stability?

In the first part of this chapter, we conceptualize family structure transitions as a dynamic contextual factor that has a profound impact on the family social environment. In an at-risk population-based sample, we evaluate parenting practices across four family structure types (i.e., nuclear, first-time single mother, first-time stepfamily, multiple transitions). We then show how the process of coupling and uncoupling for these families affects their parenting across time. In the second part of the chapter we examine social support as a protective factor enhancing the quality of parenting during divorce and repartnering.

The LIFT Study

Data for this part of the chapter are from the LIFT study (Linking Interests of Families and Teachers). LIFT was part of a population-based randomized intervention trial sponsored by the National Institute of Mental Health center for the prevention of conduct disorders (Reid, 1993). Details on the design, sample characteristics, and intervention outcomes are described elsewhere (Reid, Eddy, & Fetrow, in press). The preventative intervention was designed for all first and fifth grade elementary school boys and girls and their families living in at-risk neighborhoods characterized by high rates of delinquency.

The LIFT sample was drawn from 12 eligible schools. Of the 762 families contacted in these schools, 12% declined to participate, resulting in 671 first and fifth graders (51% were girls). Participants tended to be White (89%), to be in the middle to lower socioeconomic classes, and to have completed high school or some college education. Approximately 25% received some type of financial assistance. Of those 671 participating families, our sample for this report was drawn from 621 families, excluding single fathers and stepmother families because our focus was on the relation between transitions and maternal parenting. The data for the current analyses were collected across 2 years with four assessments (i.e., Baseline-Time 1, a 6-month follow-up—Time 2, a 1-year follow-up—Time 3, and a 2-year follow-up—Time 4). The final longitudinal sample consisted of 444 families with complete data on contextual predictors and observed parenting variables. The family structures were distributed evenly across grade and gender with no differential rates of missing longitudinal data, χ^2 (3) = 2.98, p = .26.

Transitions

We defined family structure types as a combination of family configuration and the cumulative number of transitions at baseline. *Nuclear* families consisted of two biological parents living together with the focal child. No prior separations or divorces had occurred for either parent. *Single-mother* families included a focal child living with a biological mother who had no cohabiting intimate partner (i.e., never-married single mothers and once separated or divorced mothers). *First stepfamilies* included a single mother who cohabited with a spouse or intimate partner and the mother's biological child. *Multiple-transition* families included a focal child with a biological mother who had experienced several separations or reunions with the same or different partners. In our analysis there were 344 nuclear families (55%), 84 single-mother families (14%), 91 first-time stepfamilies (15%), and 102 multiple-transition families (16%).

Parenting Practices

Two aspects of parenting practices were measured using direct observations of mother–child interactions in the laboratory, conflict bouts initiated by the mother and family problem-solving outcome. For the first graders, there were four mother–child interaction tasks: a 5-minute communication task, a 5-minute social teaching task, a 5-minute problem-solving task, and a 10-minute clean-up task, for a total of 25 minutes. For the fifth graders, there were three interaction tasks: a 5-minute family warm-up task (mother–child, or mother–father–child for two-parent families), a 10-minute problem-solving task with mother and child only, and a 10-minute family problem-solving task, for a total of 25 minutes.

Conflict Bouts. This microsocial measure reflected a form of coercive discipline in which a mother initiated a conflict bout. A bout was an exchange of aversive behaviors in which the child had to respond with an aversive behavior within 12 seconds. The bout ended when there was a period of 12 or more seconds without aversive behavior. The frequency of bouts was scored with the negative content and affect codes from the Interpersonal Process Code (IPC; Rusby, Estes, & Dishion, 1991). Ten percent of the interactions were randomly selected and coded by independent observers for interobserver reliability. Average percent agreement was 85% for content and 86% for affect. Kappa was .70 for content and .60 for affect.

Problem-Solving Outcome. Mothers and children chose topics from the Issues Checklist (adapted from Prinz, Foster, Kent, & O'Leary, 1979) listing common conflicts. Dyads were asked to attempt to resolve issues rated as "hottest." A six-item scale (e.g., quality of solutions, likelihood of follow through, and family seemed satisfied with resolution) was based on IPC coder ratings after scoring discussion of each issue during the problem solving tasks (alphas ranged from .85 to .89).

Contextual Predictor Variables

The contextual variables were mother's age, maternal depression using the Center for Epidemiological Study Depression scale (CES-D; Radloff, 1977), number of parental arrests based on court records, and socioeconomic status (SES) using the Hollingshead Index of Social Status (Hollingshead, 1975).

The Relation Between Family Transitions and Parenting Practices

We first examined the mean scores for parenting practices across time by family structure using repeated-measures ANOVA. Mean trends in the data for mother-initiated conflict bouts are illustrated in Fig. 10.2 in the form of bar graphs. First, there was a significant decrease for the sample as a whole, $F(3, 444) = 4.33$, $p =$

.005, illustrated by the general decrease in bars for each family structure going from left to right. Second, nuclear families had fewer mother-initiated conflict bouts over the 2-year period compared to other family types on the average, F (3, 446) = 8.78, $p < .001$. All of the bars for nuclear families fell below 1.5 bouts, whereas the other families were higher on the average. The ANOVA revealed no differences in the rate of decrease comparing each family structure type.

The mean trends for family problem-solving outcome are illustrated in Fig. 10.3. Nuclear families again fared better on the average over time compared to non-nuclear families, F (3, 458) = 4.31, $p = .005$. The levels for nuclear families were rather stable, with a mean score of approximately 2.9. In general, single-mother families and the multiple-transition families showed a linear increase in problem solving; however, the ANOVA revealed no mean trend for the sample or significant differences over time by family structure type. In summary, both Figs. 10.2 and 10.3 showed that nuclear families exhibited better parenting over time than other family types.

The graphs illustrate mean trends; however, they do not show the influence of other contextual factors related to parenting, nor, more important, the impact of any change in family structure that occurred during the study. To show these particular effects we employed growth models that included predictors of the rates of change using hierarchical linear modeling (HLM; Bryk & Raudenbush, 1992; Raudenbush, 1995). HLM growth models combine individual and group levels of analysis, thus allowing for the assessment of both intra-individual change and inter-individual differences in change. In general, least-squares regression curves are fit to the repeated measures of each family. The individual growth curves then become the outcome focus of analysis. Estimates in the model for each individual are derived from both the information on each family's growth curve and information from the covariates. The final estimates are weighted combinations of each family's growth curve parameters and the predictors of change.

The first step in the analysis tests an unconditional model or the estimated mean levels before entering predictor variables. Controlling for error, the estimated average number of conflict bouts was 1.61 for the sample, and the average score for problem solving was 2.78. The sample significantly declined in conflict bouts with a mean slope of $-.132$ ($p < .05$) and significantly improved in problem solving with a mean slope of .034 ($p < .05$). The estimated HLM mean levels produced a slightly different result than the repeated-measures ANOVA that showed no mean trend for problem solving.

We then modeled covariates of growth by entering the contextual predictors of baseline levels and change in parenting practices. Results of the parenting growth models are presented in Table 10.1 in the form of unstandardized beta coefficients. At baseline, Table 10.1 shows that family structure, maternal depression, and parental arrests were all significant risk factors associated with more conflict bouts. Higher SES and maternal age were marginally associated with fewer conflict bouts. For problem solving, SES was significantly associated with higher scores at baseline

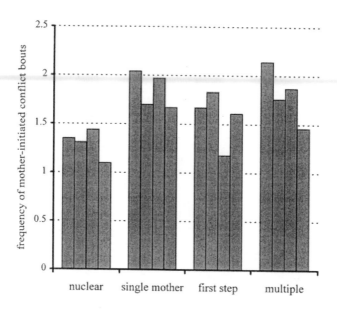

FIG 10.2.   Mean trends for mother-initiated conflict bouts from Time 1 to Time 4 by family structure type in LIFT ($n = 444$).

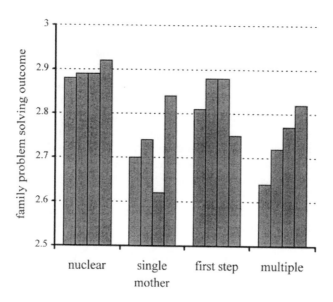

FIG 10.3.   Mean trends for family problem solving outcome from Time 1 to Time 4 by family structure type in LIFT ($n = 444$).

TABLE 10.1
Contexts as Predictors of Growth in Parenting Practices
Controlling for Grade and Gender of Child

	Mother-Initiated Conflicts	Problem Solving Outcome
Baseline status as DV		
Intercept	2.045***	2.360***
Family structure	.131*	−.034
Mother's age	−.023^t	.009^t
SES	−.010^t	.006*
Maternal depression	.016*	−.007*
Parent arrests	.066*	−.012
Rate of change as DV		
Intercept	−.177	.095
Family structure	−.010	.023
Mother's age	.009	−.003
SES	.000	.001
Maternal depression	−.014*	−.000
Parent arrests	.022	−.007

Note. DV = dependent variable; $n = 444$; ***$p < .001$; **$p < .01$; *$p < .05$; $^t p < .10$.

and maternal depression with lower scores at baseline. Older mothers also scored marginally better on problem-solving outcome.

For change in parenting over the 2-year interval, higher levels of maternal depression at baseline were associated with decreases in conflict bouts, whereas none of the predictors was associated with growth in problem-solving outcome. In summary, the contextual variables explained more of the initial status differences in parenting for the LIFT sample than change over time.

We next wanted to address the question of family structure transitions that occurred during the 2-year study period. We modeled additional transitions as a time-varying covariate, meaning this variable could change with time. In other words, the model shows the effect of change in family structure as it covaries with change in parenting practices. The time varying model produced a significant effect for additional transitions on conflict bouts ($\beta = .090$, $p < .01$) and a significant effect for problem solving outcome ($\beta = -.034$, $p < .05$). These coefficients mean that although parenting improved over time for the sample, family transitions that occurred had a negative impact on the quality of discipline strategies and problem solving. The risk of having transitions is illustrated in Figs. 10.4 and 10.5.

Taking into account the effect of improvement over time and the detrimental effect of transitions during the study, the final slopes indicated that transitions had a negative impact on parenting by slowing down the rate of improvement. For example, Fig. 10.4 shows the rate of decrease for mother-initiated conflict bouts was steeper than for families that transitioned. Similarly, Fig. 10.5 shows that the rate of

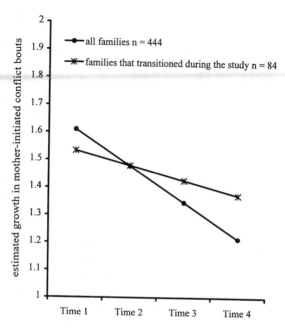

FIG 10.4. Estimated growth curves for mother-initiated conflict bouts for the LIFT sample and families that transitioned during study.

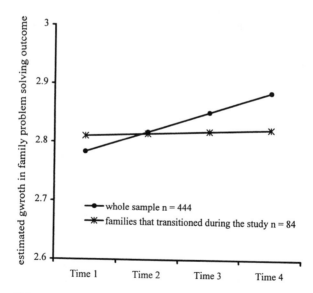

FIG 10.5. Estimated growth curves for family problem solving outcomes for the LIFT sample and families that transitioned during study.

change for families that transitioned was flat compared to the improvement for the whole sample.

The Relation Between Contexts and Transitions

In a final model, we wanted to investigate contextual factors that were related to the risk family structure transition. The results are displayed in Table 10.2. Significant risk factors associated with the number of transitions at the study's baseline were maternal depression, parental arrests, younger maternal age, and lower SES. For change over the 2-year period, younger mothers as well as those who were depressed were at risk for additional transitions. We also examined transitions during the study by family structure at baseline. Nuclear families experienced fewer transitions during the study compared to non-nuclear families, $F(3, 617) = 8.06$, $p < .001$. In total, 11% of the nuclear families experienced a transition, 33% of the single-mother families, 20% of the stepfamilies, and 37% of the multiple-transition families. These data indicated that a prior history of transition was a risk factor for further family disruption. Indeed, entering family structure as a predictor of growth (not shown) was the greatest risk factor.

In summary, data from the LIFT sample showed that family structure accounted for differences in effective parenting practices. Nuclear families and more stable families over time had better parenting compared to families with transitions. Baseline family structure type did not predict growth in conflict or problem solving. One might conclude there was little risk for parenting over time. However, this interpretation would only be part of the picture. We found an informative ap-

TABLE 10.2
Contexts as Predictors of Family Transitions
Controlling for Grade and Gender

	Family Transitions During Study
Baseline status as DV	
Intercept	2.811***
Mother's age	−.056***
SES	−.014*
Maternal depression	.030***
Parent arrests	.092**
Rate of change as DV	
Intercept	.215*
Mother's age	−.005*
SES	.001
Maternal depression	.004*
Parent arrests	.010

Note. DV = dependent variable; $n = 444$; ***$p < .001$; **$p < .01$; *$p < .05$; $^{t}p < .10$.

proach was to conceptualize and model transitions as a process. The longitudinal model of transitions indicated that any disruption in the organization of family life had a detrimental impact on parenting practices.

Our analyses reflect an attempt to move beyond a static view of family structure based on comparisons of family typologies. The field of family research has provided convincing evidence of the linear and cumulative risks for parenting that are associated with family structure. However, family structure typologies may mask the dynamic nature and heterogeneity within transitional families that may account for variation of individual differences. For example, detailed family structure histories for the LIFT families indicated that for families who had experienced any transition (45%), there were 89 different pathways to their baseline family structure (e.g., going from nuclear family, to single-mother family, to stepfamily, and then back to single-mother family before baseline). Conceptualizing transitions as a process may be a more informative way to predict microsocial aspects related to child outcomes. For example, we considered single mothers with multiple transitions as different than once-divorced mothers. By using methods and typologies that capture process we can better understand adjustment outcomes. This first section of the chapter has examined how transitions and contexts were risk factors for parenting practices. We turn now to the study of social contexts that enhance parenting quality.

A SOCIAL INTERACTIONAL VIEW
OF PARENTING RESILIENCE

Social support has long been studied as a protective factor that contributes to a person's well-being in the face of stress (Barrera, 1986; Cohen & Wills, 1985; Coyne & Downey, 1991; Rook, 1987) and as a source of resiliency for adolescents (Wills, Blechman, & McNamara, 1996; Wills, Vaccaro, & McNamara, 1992). The concept of resiliency is often discussed as strengths within individuals that help them overcome adversity. The social interactional perspective looks for these strengths within the social environment, for example, contingent and supportive behavioral exchanges between adults or between parents and children. We have been particularly interested in how adult support functions to help mothers maintain quality parenting practices as they make family structure transitions.

Divorce research shows that support and companionship from close relationships buffer stress for single women and single mothers (Aseltine & Kessler, 1993; Hughes, Good, & Candell, 1993; Kitson, 1992; Simons et al., 1993). Changing parental demands are a major source of stress for divorced mothers, who are likely to be custodial caretakers. Effective social support can benefit the quality of parenting for these mothers (Belsky & Vondra, 1989; Holloway & Machida, 1991; Simons & Johnson, 1996). However, the relation between social support and parenting is not well understood for a number of reasons.

A social interactional view of the role of support in parenting must take into account several factors. These include the personal characteristics of the interactants, how these characteristics interrelate and contribute to support as an outcome, how support functions as a predictor of relevant outcomes (in this case parenting quality), and how larger contexts (e.g., SES) influence support processes. Personal characteristics can lead to the loss of support or to the availability of support givers who have little of use to offer. A stress maintenance framework suggests how an individual can become entrapped in a stress-generating process (Patterson & Forgatch, 1990). For example, in an analysis of mothers studied shortly after separation, maternal stress, irritability, and depressed mood were associated with irritable interactions observed between the mothers and their confidants. These negative exchanges resulted in poor problem-solving outcomes for the discussions, and poor problem-solving outcomes contributed to future stress and reductions in future support contacts (Patterson & Forgatch, 1990). A similar perspective, the support erosion model (Kaniasty & Norris, 1993), states that a person's heightened distress can be aversive and promote increased stress for support providers, resulting in loss in the amount or the quality of support given. Longitudinal studies have shown that emotional distress and negativity erodes a partner's support for patients with physical health impairments (Bolger, Foster, Vinokur, & Ng, 1996; Lane & Hobfoll, 1992).

A fascinating turn in support research was taken with the position that not all support is helpful. Costs can be incurred when the support is given in the context of poor quality relationships (Burleson, 1990; La Gaipa, 1990). Support providers who are themselves distressed or socially unskilled can increase stress levels for the recipient (Belle, 1982; Patterson & Forgatch, 1990; Sarason, Sarason, Hacker, & Basham, 1985). Bad timing in provision of support and support that is incongruent with the needs of the situation are not useful (Cutrona, 1990). Too little emphasis on the study of characteristics of support providers has limited our understanding of factors that promote or that erode quality support (DeGarmo & Forgatch, 1997b; Duffy, 1993; Hobfoll, 1990).

There has been some disagreement about whether the relation between support and parenting is direct or indirect. In the most comprehensive review to date on social support and quality of parenting, Simons and Johnson (1996) specified both direct and indirect effects of social support on parenting, depending on who provides the support. Direct effects of support on parenting tend to be hypothesized for spousal support, whereas social support from nonspousal relationships is assumed to be indirect (Belsky, 1984). Cox, Owen, Lewis, and Henderson (1989), for example, using observational measures found a direct relation between spousal support and quality parenting for nuclear families. Simons et al. (1993) found indirect effects of nonspousal support on parenting through psychological well-being using self-reports of single mothers.

The marital partner in nuclear families is seen as the primary support person. Because couples share responsibility for socializing children, partners are each other's primary source of parental support. Belsky and Vondra (1989) suggested that when marital support is absent, the social networks become more important for single mothers and are the principal source of parental support. Simons and Johnson (1996), however, argued that nonspousal support is likely not direct because it is unlikely to substitute for or function as parenting support from spouses, and therefore its impact on parenting is indirect through the mother's well-being. Our position is in keeping with that of Belsky and Vondra (1989) that divorced mothers maintain quality parenting by drawing on the support of their confidants.

Reliance on self-report has also limited the study of support process (Coyne & Downey, 1991; Cutrona, 1989; Schwarzer & Leppin, 1991). Within the field of divorce, this is particularly relevant, because divorced women tend to be stressed or depressed. The well-known cognitive distortions associated with depression make such individuals poor reporters of the quality of support they receive as well as the quality of their own parenting practices. We have addressed these measurement issues in our studies. Most of our models are based on observations of what transpired between mothers and their support confidants. Characteristics of both participants in the support relationship (i.e., mother and confidant) were assessed using multiple methods and in some cases multiple agents. We defined social support as both quality and amount of supportive behaviors provided by a confidant during attempts to solve the mother's own parenting and personal problems.

The social interactional view specifies a direct effect of social support on parenting when considering the characteristics of the support provider and the measurement of support and parenting. We argue that a proximal measure of social support in relation to parenting will have a direct effect. For example, support provided in the context of discussing and trying to resolve parenting and personal problems is more proximal to parenting practices than are global assessments of support networks or perceived availability. Self-reported measures of available support may be more likely to be associated with self-reported measures of well-being. In fact, on this issue, Dunkel-Schetter and Bennett (1990) argued

> (1) that the context of support receipt is extremely important to consider, and (2) that the level of specificity of measurement for stressors, receipt of support, and well-being should be comparable. . . . In addition, it is likely that the effects of received support will be more apparent in a sample that shares a common negative life event than in community and student samples experiencing diverse stresses. Before these problems can be properly addressed, the conceptualization and measurement of received support must be further developed. (p. 288)

Raising children in divorced and reconstituted families is an extraordinarily complex problem. We are convinced that much of the variability in parenting quality in such families is explained by mothers' abilities to find helpmates and to engage them in the struggle. For this reason, we have conducted a series of studies to understand how this process operates. In this effort we have focused on three main questions: How do personal characteristics of divorced mothers and their confidants relate to the support process? How does confidant support relate to maternal parenting practices? and How do contextual factors, confidant support, and problem solving relate to parenting and child outcomes? To address these questions, data from the Oregon Divorce Study were employed.

The Oregon Divorce Study

The Oregon Divorce Study (ODS) was conducted in two phases with independent samples of recently separated single mothers and their sons. The first phase (ODS-I) began in 1984 and was a passive longitudinal study designed to develop and test models relevant to children's adjustment following marital separation. Phase two (ODS-II) began in 1992 and was a randomized experimental longitudinal study. An intervention based on social learning and social interactional perspectives was carried out. The program focused on improving child outcomes and preventing children's adjustment problems by strengthening maternal parenting practices. Participants in both samples were recruited within the same medium-sized Pacific Northwest metropolitan area.

Assessment procedures were similar and used extensive multiple-agent and multiple-method measurement. In both studies, each mother selected a confidant who was either a friend, family member, or intimate partner to participate in the study. Data in this chapter were obtained from laboratory interviews and questionnaires with mothers, telephone interviews with the mothers and their confidants, observations of problem-solving interactions between mothers and confidants in the laboratory, observations of several structured laboratory tasks between the mothers and focal children, and questionnaires filled out by teachers.

ODS-I Participants

Participants were 196 recently separated single mothers and their sons. Families were recruited through divorce application records, media advertisements, and flyers distributed throughout the community. In eligible families, mothers had been separated from their partners within the prior 3 to 15 months, resided with their sons, who were in Grades K–7, and did not cohabit with new partners. The racial/ethnic composition of the boys was representative of the local community: 89% White, 1% African American, 3% Latino, 3.6% Native American, and 3.6% other. Demographics are provided in Table 10.3.

Generally, families were living in poverty, having experienced a dramatic drop in median annual income from $15,000 before separation to $7,200 afterward. The mean annual income for ODS-I mothers was somewhat lower than that reported for female-headed households with children in the county where the study was conducted, according to 1980 census data ($6,600 and $9,400, respectively). Although most of the women were employed and quite well educated, 55% of the families were receiving public assistance.

Confidant data in ODS-I were gathered in Year 4 (referred to here as T3). At T3, 40% of the mothers were cohabiting with a new partner and one half of the part-

TABLE 10.3
Demographic Characteristics of the Oregon Divorce Study

	ODS-I Began 1984 (n = 196)	ODS-II Began 1992 (n = 238)
Education		
Some high school	8%	4%
High school graduate	20%	20%
High school plus	55%	58%
College graduate and beyond	17%	18%
Occupation		
Unskilled	3%	30%
Semiskilled	20%	22%
Clerical/skilled	32%	23%
Medium business/minor professional	39%	23%
Major business/major professional	6%	2%
Employed outside the home	60%	67%
Receiving public assistance	55%	76%
Median annual income	$7,200	$12,500
Mean mother age	33.1	34.8
Mean boy age	8.7	7.8
Average months separated	6.4	9.2
Average number of children	2.2	2.1

nered mothers were remarried. Forty-seven percent of the confidants were friends, 24% were family members, and 29% were partners. Sixty-six percent were female. Detailed demographic characteristics of the support confidants in T3 of ODS-I are provided by DeGarmo and Forgatch (1997b).

ODS-II Participants

Participants were 238 recently separated single mothers and their sons recruited using the same methods as ODS-I. To be eligible in phase two, mothers had to be separated from their partners within the prior 3 to 24 months, reside with their sons, who were in Grades 1–3, and not cohabit with new partners. The racial/ethnic composition of the boys was representative of the local community: 86% White, 1% African American, 2% Latino, 2% Native American, and 9% other minority groups.

Similar to the ODS-I sample, families experienced a sharp decline in median annual income after separation, from $25,000 to $12,500, and 76% of the families were receiving public assistance. The mean annual income for ODS-II mothers was similar to that reported for female-headed households with children in the county, according to 1990 census ($14,900 and $15,300, respectively). ODS-II mothers were similar to their ODS-I counterparts in their education but not in their occupation. Women in ODS-II tended to work more in lower status jobs compared to women in ODS-I (respectively, 29% and 3% for unskilled jobs, and 45% and 25% for professional-level jobs).

Measures

Multiple methods were used to build constructs from both samples of ODS for maternal distress, confidant negativity, social support (observed and perceived), adult problem-solving outcome, parenting (aversive discipline and problem solving), and antisocial behavior of the focal boy. Unless specifically noted, the measurement for both samples was the same.

Maternal Distress. This construct was measured with three self-report indicators scaled to the same metric. *Family stress* was assessed with the Family Events Checklist (Patterson, 1982). *Life events stress* summed negative events rated on the Life Experience Survey (Sarason, Johnson, & Siegel, 1978). *Depressed mood* was measured by the CES-D (Radloff, 1977). For chronic distress, the indicators were averaged to compute a distress score at baseline, 1 year later, and 4 years after baseline.

Confidant Negativity. This construct evaluated negative emotional qualities and personality traits of the confidant with three indicators. *Interviewer report of irritability* rated how angry or irritable the confidant appeared during telephone interviews made once a week over 6 weeks. *Irritability self-report* was a self-reported telephone interview item describing the confidant's mood in the last day. Each telephone indicator was aggregated from the mean of the six calls. *Depressed mood* was measured by the CES-D, filled out on the day of the mother–confidant problem-solving task prior to the interaction.

Observed Confidant Support. This construct was measured by three indicators obtained from observations of the mother–confidant problem-solving task at T3 of the ODS-I study using a set of microsocial coders and a set of global raters. Mothers selected two topics to discuss from an issues checklist of common concerns for single mothers regarding parenting issues and personal problems. Mothers selected one topic from each area and were videotaped discussing them with the confidants for 10 minutes. *Interpersonal support* evaluated the amount and quality of support as rated with the Problem Solving System (PSS; Forgatch & Lathrop, 1988). A mean score was computed from five items following each topic (e.g., how supportive the confidant was to the mother, how often the confidant offered emotional support). *Confidant likeability* was one item rated by PSS coders, "How would you like this person for your support person?" *Emotional support* was the rate per minute of supportive behaviors scored with the microsocial coding system, Specific Affects (SPAFF; Gottman, 1989). The indicator score was computed by dividing the frequency of support behaviors by the total time.

Perceived Support. This construct had three indicators measuring the mothers' evaluations of the confidants and their help with problems. *Relationship sup-*

port was assessed with six items obtained from the mothers in face-to-face interviews about the confidants (e.g., understands and sympathizes when you are upset, would go out of their way to do you a favor). *Supportive affect* was measured by two items from the repeated telephone calls (i.e., how happy–enthusiastic and how calm is the confidant). *Help with problems* was measured by an item asked during the repeated telephone interviews (i.e., how helpful were discussions with the confidant for solving problems).

Adult Problem-Solving Outcome. This construct was a score from the two mother–confidant problem-solving interactions rated by coders using the PSS rating system. The scale used the same six items as mother–child problem-solving outcome.

Parenting Practices. This construct was measured with indicators of *problem solving outcome* and *aversive discipline* using similar measures described for the LIFT analysis. For ODS-I, problem solving used the same scale score as LIFT and included one mother issue and one child issue. The discipline measure was the mean of the conflict bout score described previously for LIFT plus a global rating of how often the mother withdrew from interaction in a negative or avoidant way. For ODS-II, problem-solving outcome was scored with three mother-picked issues, and discipline used conflict bouts and a scale score for global ratings of discipline (e.g., nagging, inconsistent, inappropriate).

Boy Antisocial Behavior. This construct reflected a variety of antisocial behaviors rated by parents, teachers, and the boys. Teacher and parent reports were collected using the Child Behavior Checklist (Achenbach & Edelbrock, 1983). Separate child and parent reports were collected from six telephone interviews regarding the boys' misbehavior at home.

Personal Characteristics as Predictors of Support

The first model addressed the first question of how maternal and confidant characteristics affect the support that transpires during discussions about a mother's parenting and personal problems. Results of the social interactional model including chronic maternal distress (i.e., average levels over 4 years) and confidant negativity at T3 are displayed in Fig. 10.6 with standardized paths. This model, which is adapted from DeGarmo and Forgatch (1997b), controlled for relationship intimacy. New partner was a variable coded 1 for those mothers who were repartnered at T3 and 0 for those who were single at T3.

Chronic maternal distress was associated with higher levels of confidant negativity (β = .28). This path supports the notion of stress contagion or spillover within the erosion model. Another explanation for this path is the homophily hypothesis that suggests persistently distressed mothers select or are selected by con-

ODS-I Time-1 to Time-3

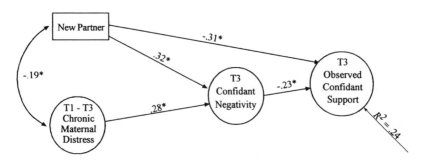

FIG 10.6.   ODS-I process model predicting supportive confidant behaviors, controlling for relationship intimacy. χ^2 (67, N = 138) = 84.82, p = .07; comparative fit index = .96; *p < .05. Adapted from DeGarmo and Forgatch (1997b) with permission.

fidants who are themselves negativistic. Chronic levels of maternal distress were correlated negatively with having a partner at T3, reflecting previous findings in this ODS-I sample in which depressed mothers were less likely to repartner by 1 year after baseline (Forgatch et al., 1996). Negative characteristics of a confidant were associated with less support ($\beta = -.23$) as predicted by the social interactional model of stress maintenance. Thus a mother's chronic distress may have contributed to her having a distressed confidant, which resulted in her receiving less support.

The model also showed that repartnering can be a risk factor for single mothers in terms of supportive behaviors observed during problem solving. Compared to confidants who were friends or relatives, confidants who were intimate partners provided less support ($\beta = -.31$) and had higher levels of negativity ($\beta = .32$). Partners had lower mean scores for all three indicators of observed support (DeGarmo & Forgatch, 1997b). Less support scored for intimate partners was puzzling. It is possible that gender may have contributed to mean differences for partners because all coders were female and the majority of partners were male with the exception of one lesbian couple.

The Relation Between Support and
Maternal Parenting Practices

In this section we examine a set of models testing the direct effect of confidant support on parenting practices, controlling for maternal distress and confidant negativity. We employed measures of support that are proximal to the parenting outcome, rather than global measures of social support. The first model was a cross-sectional analysis from ODS-I at T3 using the same measure of observed support and a similar measure of maternal distress as shown in Fig. 10.6. The difference was that it was current distress that was not chronic. Because the sample had both spousal and nonspousal relationships at T3, we controlled for type of confidant relationship. The results are shown in Fig. 10.7.

The findings supported the hypothesis that support provided during discussions of parenting problems directly predicts parenting practices, regardless of confidant relationship type ($\beta = .55$). The model including observed confidant support explained 36% of the variance in the measure of observed parenting. The observations of support and of parenting were scored from different settings with variant coding systems. Without the temporal specification present in the prior model, we modeled a correlational association between maternal distress and confidant negativity and found them to be related as expected ($r = .39$).

We next wanted to answer the question of whether perceived measures of social support also had a direct effect on parenting using a more proximal and comparable level of specificity for measurement. This model employed data from ODS-II at baseline. Although the prior model controlled for confidant relationship, this model (displayed in Fig. 10.8) was a more robust test of the direct nonspousal support hypothesis because none of the ODS-II mothers was repartnered at baseline.

The ODS-II baseline model replicated the direct effect from social support to parenting practices ($\beta = .36$). The model also replicated the path from confidant negativity to perceived support ($\beta = -.32$). Consistent with models using self-reported support, distressed mothers in ODS-II at baseline were less likely to report that they had supportive confidants ($\beta = -.29$). One could also argue that perceived support had an additive buffering effect reducing maternal distress. Therefore, we ran an alternative model with a path from perceived support to maternal distress. We specified a model with identical fit, except for one key difference. The alternative model had a test of a direct and an indirect effect of support on parenting. If support were indirect through parental well-being, then the direct effect would become nonsignificant. However, this was not the case. Perceived confidant support had a direct effect on observed parenting practices.

In both ODS samples, measures of support were specified as behaviors that were related to some degree to parenting. Both studies indicated that nonspousal support directly enhanced parenting practices. We argue that it is reasonable to assume a direct effect when support is more proximal to the outcome. Global perceptions of availability of a broad network may incorporate a mixture and combination of effective and ineffective support providers.

The Relation of Confidant Support and Contextual Factors to Child Adjustment

Confidants may contribute to reducing the stress of divorced mothers if they are helpful collaborators in the problem-solving process (Patterson & Forgatch, 1990). In the next step in our study of how support contributes to parenting, we expanded the model and conceptualized it as a progression. Given the social interactional perspective that small behaviors have an impact on interpersonal processes

ODS-I Time-3

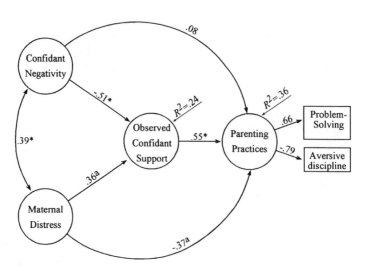

FIG 10.7. ODS-I process model of observed confidant support predicting parenting practices controlling for son's age. χ^2 (44, N = 138) = 52.18, p = .19; comparative fit index = .97; $^*p < .05$, $^a p < .10$. Reprinted from DeGarmo and Forgatch (1997a), with permission of Cambridge University Press.

ODS-II Time-1

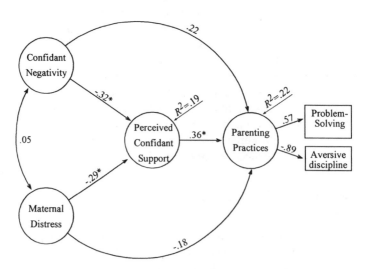

FIG 10.8. ODS-II replication process model of perceived confidant support predicting parenting practices controlling for son's age. χ^2 (45, N = 144) = 58.62, p = .08; comparative fit index = .98; $^*p < .05$.

and outcomes, we hypothesized that confidant support observed during problem solving enriches the quality of the problem-solving outcomes and that positive outcomes contribute to effective parenting practices. In this manner, the effect of confidant support on parenting practices is mediated by problem-solving outcome in the mother–confidant domain. We also hypothesized that the effect of confidant support and problem solving outcome on children's antisocial behavior is mediated by parenting practices. To extend the model further yet, we added measures of mothers' socioeconomic status (Hollingshead, 1975) and antisocial qualities. We employed ODS-I data at T3 for this model with a multiple agent construct of antisocial behavior (Forgatch & DeGarmo, 1997). The findings are summarized in Fig. 10.9.

The data supported the hypotheses. Confidant support enhanced the problem-solving outcomes. Those outcomes, in turn, contributed to effective parenting practices, which predicted lower levels of child antisocial behavior. Thus, the supportive behaviors provided by the confidant during the interaction contributed to parenting practices by helping to reduce the mother's parenting and personal problems. Parenting practices contributed to the child's adjustment. The model followed the progression we had hypothesized.

ODS-I Time-3

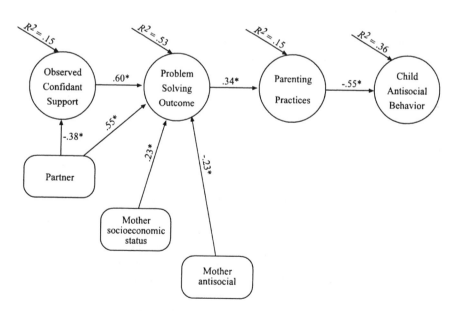

FIG 10.9. ODS-I progression model linking confidant support and contextual factors to child adjustment. χ^2 (63, N = 144) = 82.44, p = .05; comparative fit index = .92; *p < .05. Reprinted from Forgatch and DeGarmo (1997), with permission.

An interesting note within this model was that interactions between mothers and their cohabiting partner resulted in better problem-solving outcomes, even though they provided less support during the discussion. Perhaps partners have more at stake in resolution of the parenting and personal issues, and so their efforts are more solution focused. Their intimate familiarity with the problems may be another factor that contributed to the better outcomes. Certainly, effective problem solving is relevant to support for parenting.

Socioeconomic status was associated with better problem-solving outcome, which is consistent with a similar association found in the LIFT sample for SES and parent–child problem-solving outcome. The negative impact of maternal antisocial qualities on problem solving was expected. What was surprising in this model was that adult problem-solving outcome mediated the effect of maternal antisocial qualities on parenting practices.

SUMMARY AND CONCLUSIONS

We have expanded the concept of risk and resiliency by using a social interactional model as a theoretical framework for the study of parenting practices during separation, divorce, and repartnering. Conceptualizing family transitions as both structure and process proved useful in each of the three samples studied. The use of flexible methodology and typologies that capture process are strategies that are likely to lead to better understanding of family diversity.

In the first part of the chapter, we found trends that showed family structure transitions were detrimental to average levels of parenting practices over time with nuclear families faring the best. For the sample as a whole, parenting practices improved over time; however, any family transition occurring in the population-based sample was detrimental to parenting practices over time. Families who had at least one transition by baseline were most likely to have another within the next 2 years. Contexts contributed differentially to initial levels of parenting and to change in parenting over time. Maternal depression and parental arrests contributed to higher levels of conflict bouts at baseline. SES was related to higher baseline levels of problem solving, and maternal depression was related to lower levels. Maternal depression at baseline was related to decreases in conflict bouts over time, and no contextual variables predicted change in problem-solving outcomes.

In the second part of the chapter we examined the adult social environment of divorced and repartnered mothers as a protective factor for the quality of maternal parenting practices. The data showed that positive confidant traits and supportive behaviors directed to divorced mothers during problem-solving interactions were directly related to parenting. This was true for marital and nonmarital support relationships for two samples. Problem-solving outcomes achieved by the mothers and their partners accounted for the association between support and parenting. Drawing on skillful support confidants, a divorced mother can maintain quality parenting and buffer family stress. The social interactional view of social support provided a comparable level of specificity between the measures of observed and self-report social support and observed parenting practices.

Families who have experienced divorce are projected to be the predominant family form in the next century (Ahrons, 1994). Children from these families are increasingly likely to be involved with their mothers and fathers in two or more different households, a reality that may or may not include stepparents, stepsiblings, and half siblings. Because family structures are becoming so complex, we must understand the factors that contribute to quality parenting during the process of transition.

ACKNOWLEDGMENTS

The writers gratefully acknowledge the support provided by the following NIMH grants from the Prevention and Behavioral Medicine Research Branch, Division of Epidemiology and Services Research: MH 54703 and MH 38318, Marion S. Forgatch, Principal Investigator, and grants P50 46690 and MH 54248, John B. Reid, Principal Investigator. The authors would also like to acknowledge Will Mayer for providing figures, Charles Martinez and Kelly Shook for their comments and feedback, and Linda Mason for assistance with data. We thank Gerald Patterson and Mike Stoolmiller for their instructive conversations on the analysis of change and family process.

REFERENCES

Achenbach, T. M., & Edelbrock, C. S. (1983). *Manual for the Child Behavior Checklist and the Revised Child Behavior Profile*. Burlington, VT: University of Vermont, Department of Psychiatry.

Ahrons, C. (1994). *The good divorce: Keeping your family together when your marriage comes apart*. New York: Harper Perennial.

Anderson, E. R., Lindner, M. S., & Bennion, L. D. (1992). The effect of family relationships on adolescent development during family reorganization. In E. M. Hetherington & W. G. Clingempeel (Eds.), *Coping with marital transitions: Monographs of the Society for Research in Child Development, 57* (2–3, Serial No. 227, pp. 178–200).

Aseltine, R. H., & Kessler, R. C. (1993). Marital disruption and depression in a community sample. *Journal of Health and Social Behavior, 34*, 237–251.

Bank, L., Forgatch, M. S., Patterson, G. R., & Fetrow, R. A. (1993). Parenting practices of single mothers: Mediators of negative contextual factors. *Journal of Marriage and the Family, 55*, 371–384.

Barrera, M. J. (1986). Distinctions between social support concepts, measures, and models. *American Journal of Community Psychology, 14*, 413–445.

Belle, D. H. (1982). Social ties and social support. In D. Belle (Ed.), *Lives in stress: Women and depression* (pp. 133–144). Beverly Hills, CA: Sage.

Belsky, J. (1984). The determinants of parenting: A process model. *Child Development, 55*, 83–96.

Belsky, J., & Vondra, J. (1989). Lessons from child abuse: The determinants of parenting. In D. Cicchetti & V. Carlson (Eds.), *Child maltreatment: Theory and research on the causes and consequences of child abuse and neglect* (pp. 153–202). New York: Cambridge University Press.

Bolger, N., Foster, M., Vinokur, A. D., & Ng, R. (1996). Close relationships and adjustment to a life crisis: The case of breast cancer. *Journal of Personality and Social Psychology, 70,* 283–294.

Bray, J. H., & Berger, S. H. (1993). Developmental issues in StepFamilies Research Project: Family relationships and parent-child interactions. *Journal of Family Psychology, 7,* 76–90.

Brody, G. H., Neubaum, E., & Forehand, R. (1988). Serial marriage: A heuristic analysis of an emerging family form. *Psychological Bulletin, 103,* 211–222.

Bryk, A. S., & Raudenbush, S. W. (1992). Applications in the study of individual change. In A. S. Bryk & S. W. Raudenbush (Eds.), *Hierarchical linear models* (pp. 130–154). Newbury Park, CA: Sage.

Burleson, B. R. (1990). Comforting as social support: Relational consequences of supportive behaviors. In S. W. Duck & R. C. Silver (Eds.), *Personal relationships as social support* (pp. 66–82). Newbury Park, CA: Sage.

Capaldi, D. M., & Patterson, G. R. (1991). Relation of parental transitions to boys' adjustment problems: Mothers at risk for transitions and unskilled parenting. *Developmental Psychology, 27,* 489–504.

Chase-Lansdale, P., Cherlin, A. J., & Kiernan, K. E. (1995). The long-term effects of parental divorce on the mental health of young adults: A developmental perspective. *Child Development, 66,* 1614–1634.

Cohen, S., & Wills, T. A. (1985). Stress, social support, and the buffering hypothesis. *Psychological Bulletin, 98,* 310–357.

Conger, R. D., Patterson, G. R., & Ge, X. (1995). It takes two to replicate: A mediational model for the impact of parents' stress on adolescent adjustment. *Developmental Psychology, 66,* 80–97.

Cox, M. J., Owen, M. T., Lewis, J. M., & Henderson, V. K. (1989). Marriage, adult adjustment, and early parenting. *Child Development, 60,* 1015–1024.

Coyne, J. C., & Downey, G. (1991). Social factors and psychopathology: Stress, social support, and coping processes. *Annual Review of Psychology, 42,* 401–425.

Cutrona, C. E. (1989). Ratings of social support by adolescents and adult informants: Degree of correspondence and prediction of depressive symptoms. *Journal of Personality and Social Psychology, 57,* 723–730.

Cutrona, C. E. (1990). Stress and social support: In search of optimal matching. *Journal of Social and Clinical Psychology, 9,* 3–14.

DeGarmo, D. S., & Forgatch, M. S. (1997a). Confidant support and maternal distress: Predictors of parenting practices for divorced mothers. *Personal Relationships, 4,* 305–317.

DeGarmo, D. S., & Forgatch, M. S. (1997b). Determinants of observed confidant support. *Journal of Personality and Social Psychology, 72,* 336–345.

Duffy, M. E. (1993). Social support: The provider's perspective. *Journal of Divorce and Remarriage, 19,* 57–73.

Dunkel-Schetter, C., & Bennett, T. L. (1990). Differentiating the cognitive and behavioral aspects of social support. In B. R. Sarason, I. G. Sarason, & G. R. Pierce (Eds.), *Social support an interactional view* (pp. 267–296). New York: Wiley.

Forgatch, M. S. (1989). Patterns and outcome in family problem solving: The disrupting effect of negative emotion. *Journal of Marriage and the Family, 51,* 115–124.

Forgatch, M. S., & DeGarmo, D. S. (1997). Confidant contributions to parenting and child outcomes. *Social Development, 6,* 237–253.

Forgatch, M. S., & Lathrop, M. (1988). *Problem solving system* (Unpublished instrument). Eugene, OR: Oregon Social Learning Center.

Forgatch, M. S., Patterson, G. R., & Ray, J. A. (1996). Divorce and boys' adjustment problems: Two paths with a single model. In E. M. Hetherington & E. A. Blechman (Eds.), *Stress, coping, and resiliency in children and the family* (pp. 67–105). Mahwah, NJ: Lawrence Erlbaum Associates.

Furstenberg, F. F., Jr., & Seltzer, J. A. (1986). Divorce and child development. *Sociological Studies of Child Development, 1,* 137–160.

Gottman, J. M. (1989). *The specific affect coding system* (unpublished manual). Seattle, WA: University of Washington.

Hetherington, E. M. (1993). An overview of the Virginia longitudinal study of divorce and remarriage with a focus on early adolescence. *Journal of Family Psychology, 7,* 39–56.

Hetherington, E. M., & Clingempeel, W. G. (1992). Coping with marital transitions. *Monographs of the Society for Research in Child Development, 57* (2–3, Serial No. 227).

Hetherington, E. M., Stanley-Hagan, M., & Anderson, E. R. (1989). Marital transitions: A child's perspective. *American Psychologist, 44,* 303–312.

Hobfoll, S. E. (1990). The importance of predicting, activating, and facilitating social support. *Journal of Personal and Social Relationships, 7,* 435–436.

Hollingshead, A. B. (1975). *Four factor index of social status.* Unpublished manuscript, Yale University.

Holloway, S. D., & Machida, S. (1991). Child-rearing effectiveness of divorced mothers: Relationship to coping strategies and social support. *Journal of Divorce and Remarriage, 14,* 179–201.

Hughes, R., Good, E. S., & Candell, K. (1993). A longitudinal study of the effects of social support on the psychological adjustment of divorced mothers. *Journal of Divorce and Remarriage, 19,* 37–57.

Kaniasty, K., & Norris, F. H. (1993). A test of the social suport deterioration model in the context of natural disaster. *Journal of Personality and Social Psychology, 64,* 395–408.

Kitson, G. C. (1992). *Portrait of divorce: Adjustment to marital breakdown.* New York: Guilford.

La Gaipa, J. L. (1990). The negative effects of informal support systems. In S. W. Duck & R. C. Silver (Eds.), *Personal relationships and social suport* (pp. 122–139). Newbury Park, CA: Sage.

Lane, C., & Hobfoll, S. E. (1992). How loss affects anger and alienates potential supporters. *Journal of Consulting and Clinical Psychology, 60,* 935–942.

Patterson, G. R. (1982). *A social learning center: Coercive family process.* Eugene, OR: Castalia.

Patterson, G. R. (1986). Performance models for antisocial boys. *American Psychologist, 41,* 432–444.

Patterson, G. R. (in press). Performance models for parenting: A social interactional perspective. In J. Grusec & L. Kuczynski (Eds.), *Parenting and the socialization of values: A handbook of contemporary theory.* New York: Wiley.

Patterson, G. R., & Forgatch, M. S. (1990). Initiation and maintenance of process disrupting single-mother families. In G. R. Patterson (Ed.), *Depression and aggression in family interaction* (pp. 209–245). Hillsdale, NJ: Lawrence Erlbaum Associates.

Prinz, R. J., Foster, S., Kent, R. N., & O'Leary, D. K. (1979). Multivariate assessment of conflict in distressed and nondistressed mother–adolescent dyads. *Journal of Applied Behavior Analysis, 12,* 691–700.

Radloff, L. S. (1977). The CES-D scale: A self-report depression scale for research in the general population. *Applied Psychological Measurement, 1,* 385–401.

Raudenbush, S. W. (1995). Hierarchical linear models to study the effects of social context on development. In J. M. Gottman (Ed.), *The analysis of change* (pp. 165–201). Hillsdale, NJ: Lawrence Erlbaum Associates.

Reid, J. B. (1993). Prevention of conduct disorder before and after school entry: Relating interventions to developmental findings. *Journal of Development and Psychopathology, 5,* 243–262.

Reid, J. B., Eddy, M. J., & Fetrow, R. A. (in press). Description and immediate impacts of a preventive intervention for conduct problems. *American Journal of Community Psychology.*

Rook, K. S. (1987). Social support versus companionship: Effects on life stress, loneliness, and evaluations by others. *Journal of Personality and Social Psychology, 25,* 1132–1147.

Rusby, J. C., Estes, A., & Dishion, T. (1991). *The interpersonal process code (IPC).* Unpublished report, Oregon Social Learning Center.

Sarason, B. R., Sarason, I. G., Hacker, T. A., & Basham, R. B. (1985). Concomitants of social support: Social skills, physical attractiveness and gender. *Journal of Personality and Social Psychology, 49,* 469–480.

Sarason, I. G., Johnson, J. H., & Siegel, J. M. (1978). Assessing the impact of life changes: Development of the life experiences survey. *Journal of Consulting and Clinical Psychology, 46,* 932–946.

Schwarzer, R., & Leppin, A. (1991). Social support and health: A theoretical and empirical overview. *Journal of Social and Personal Relationships, 8,* 99–127.

Simons, R. L., Beaman, J., Conger, R. D., & Chao, W. (1993). Stress, support, and antisocial behavior trait as determinants of emotional well-being and parenting practices among single mothers. *Journal of Marriage and the Family, 55,* 385–398.

Simons, R. L., & Johnson, C. (1996). The impact of marital and social network support on quality of parenting. In G. R. Pierce, B. R. Sarason, & I. G. Sarason (Eds.), *Handbook of social support and the family* (pp. 269–287). New York: Plenum.

Snyder, J., Peterson, L., & St. Peter, C. (1997). Origins of antisocial behavior: Negative reinforcement and affect dysregulation of behavior as socialization mechanisms in family interaction. *Behavior Modification, 21,* 187–215.

Vuchinich, S., Vuchinich, R., & Wood, B. (1993). The interparental relationship and family problem solving with preadolescent males. *Child Development, 64,* 1389–1400.

Wills, T. A., Blechman, E. A., & McNamara, G. (1996). Family support, coping, and competence. In E. M. Hetherington & E. A. Blechman (Eds.), *Stress, coping, and resiliency in children and families* (pp. 107–133). Mahwah, NJ: Lawrence Erlbaum Associates.

Wills, T. A., Vaccaro, D., & McNamara, G. (1992). The role of life events, family support, and competence in adolescent substance use: A test of vulnerability and protective factors. *American Journal of Community Psychology, 20,* 349–374.

Zill, N., Morrison, D. R., & Coiro, M. J. (1993). Long-term effects of parental divorce on parent–child relationships, adjustment, and achievement in young adulthood. *Journal of Family Psychology, 7,* 91–103.

II

From Marriage
to Remarriage and Beyond
Findings From the Developmental Issues
in StepFamilies Research Project

James H. Bray
Baylor College of Medicine

THE PAST 20 years have seen a rapid increase in the number of stepfamilies due to the increase in the divorce rate in the United States. Although the divorce rate is high, people appear to value the institution of marriage, but with a series of partners. The divorce rate for second and subsequent marriages is higher than for first marriages and has been partially attributed to the presence of children from previous relationships (Bumpass, Sweet, & Castro-Martin, 1990; Glick, 1989). This chapter presents results from the Developmental Issues in StepFamilies (DIS) Research Project, which investigated the longitudinal impact of divorce and remarriage on children's social, emotional, and cognitive development (Bray, 1988b; Bray & Berger, 1993a).

STEPFAMILIES

The stepfamily is a common family structure that has been present since ancient times and will certainly continue in the future. The term *stepfamily* originated from the Anglo-Saxon word *Steop* meaning to bereave or to make orphan (Bray & Berger, 1992). The term was applied to children whose parents had died. Although stepfamilies are still formed after the death of a parent, it is far more common today that a stepfamily is established because of another type of loss, the termination or end of a marriage.

There are many names for stepfamilies. Stepfamilies are referred to as *remarried families, reconstituted families, REM families, blended families, bi-nuclear families, second families,* and *two-fams.* These seem to be the most common names in the literature.

Stepfamilies are more complicated than first-marriage families because of the multiple relationships and families that make up a remarried family system. They come in a variety of different family structures. There are stepfather families, stepmother families, and blended families, in which both parents have custody of children from previous marriages.

Despite the increase in numbers of stepfamilies, the term *stepchild* or *stepparent* still has a negative or pejorative connotation to it (Bray, Berger, & Boethel, 1994; Ganong, Coleman, & Mapes, 1990). There are many fairy tales and folk stories of the "wicked stepparent." Family members, and especially children, may enter a stepfamily with fears and anxieties that are unconsciously reinforced by descriptions and names for stepfamilies as a result of the prevailing myths and stories about stepfamilies. These factors set a social context that needs to be considered in evaluating research and clinical writings about stepfamilies.

DEVELOPMENTAL ISSUES IN STEPFAMILIES RESEARCH PROJECT

The DIS Research Project was initially a cross-sectional study of stepfamilies during the first 7 years after remarriage and first-marriage nuclear families. The stepfamilies were selected at 6 months, 2½ years, and 5 to 7 years after remarriage and compared to nuclear families with comparably aged and demographically similar children. These families were reinterviewed 3 to 4 years later to examine longitudinal changes and predictors of children's adjustment. Throughout this chapter the cross-sectional findings are discussed when we refer to the DIS project, and the longitudinal findings are discussed when we refer to the Longitudinal Followup.

We studied stepfamilies after 6 months of remarriage to investigate the transitional issues and process of early remarriage. Previous divorce research indicated that it takes about 2 years for a family to adjust after a marital transition (Hetherington, Cox, & Cox, 1982). To understand how stepfamilies function after the initial stabilization, we studied a second group of stepfamilies after 2½ years of remarriage. The literature on stepfamilies indicates that it may take between 2 and 4 years for a stepfamily to stabilize and adjust to the remarriage transition. Furthermore, divorce statistics suggest that the average length of second marriages was approximately 5 years. Thus, we studied a third group of stepfamilies 5 to 7 years after their marriages to examine the long-term issues in forming a successful stepfamily and the impact on family members. In addition, we were interested in the impact of children who were entering adolescence on the functioning of the stepfamily. In each of these groups we also interviewed first-marriage, nuclear families with comparably aged children to differentiate the unique issues for stepfamilies from the process of development and adjustment in families who have not experienced multiple marital transitions.

A total of 200 children and their families participated in the DIS project (see Table 11.1). There were 100 nuclear families and 100 stepfamilies. Ninety-eight families had males as target children, and 102 families had females as target children. In the DIS study the ages of the children in the stepfamilies were staggered to control for the length of time in a stepfamily. Thus, all children entered a stepfamily when they were between the ages of 6 and 8 years.

In the longitudinal study, 180 families were reinterviewed. All families were evaluated between 3 and 4 years after their first interview. This chapter discusses only families that had no changes in parents' marital status or parental custody since the original DIS interview. Nine nuclear families separated, divorced, or remarried, and 20 stepfamilies separated, divorced, or remarried at the time of the follow-up interviews. In addition, eight children in stepfamilies had changed custody from mother to father at the time of the follow-up interviews.

The study was a multi-method, multi-perspective study of the parents, children, and extended family members and included extensive interviews, psychological assessments, family assessments, and videotapes of families interacting. The videotapes were rated using standard behavioral coding systems (Hetherington et al., 1986). The data provide a rich source of information about divorce and remarriage and their impact on children and adults.

The first aim of the DIS Project was to study the impact of stepfamily development and process on the psychosocial and cognitive adjustment of children in these families. The second goal of the DIS Project was to investigate differences in family process and organization during a 7-year period in stepfather families. The third aim was to study the differences in intrafamily relationships (e.g., [step]parent–child, husband–wife) and the relation between family organization and process and subsystems within stepfamilies and nuclear families. The fourth goal was to explore the impact of extended family relationships on intrafamily relationships and adjustment of family members.

TABLE 11.1
Developmental Issues in StepFamilies Research Project Design: Sample Sizes

| | Time Since Remarriage | | |
	6-Month Groups	2.5-Year Groups	5–7-Year Groups
	Age of Target Child		
Family Structure/Gender of Child	6–9	8.5–11.5	11–14
Stepfamily boys	18	17	16
Stepfamily girls	16	16	17
Nuclear family boys	16	15	16
Nuclear family girls	18	17	18

We used a developmental family systems model as a theoretical basis for understanding and describing family process and change in divorce and remarriage (Bray & Berger, 1993a; Bray, Berger, Silverblatt, & Hollier, 1987; McGoldrick & Carter, 1988; Whiteside, 1982). A systems approach to families in which family members are viewed as part of an interdependent emotional and relational system that mutually influences other aspects of the family system is the basis of this model. Change within one component of the system is believed to produce change in other parts of the system, concurrently and over time. Stepfamily systems include not only the residential family but also nonresidential family members. The lack of attention to these complex relations in previous research limits our understanding of stepfamilies.

In addition to the interactional aspects of family relationships, developmental factors for both the families and individual members are considered important for understanding remarried families. Families undergo predictable and unpredictable life cycle changes that mutually influence individual family members' developmental courses (Carter & McGoldrick, 1988). However, the normative family life cycle progression is disrupted by divorce and remarriage, and these transitions interact with the normal developmental trajectories of children and adolescents. Therefore, factors such as length of time since the divorce, time since remarriage, and ages of adults and children are important factors to consider in delineating the family life cycle progression of remarried families. Unfortunately, much of the research on divorce and remarriage has implicitly or explicitly viewed these transitions as discrete events by examining families at one point following the marital transition, ignoring time as a factor, or combining stepfamilies with vastly different individual and family life cycle periods. As a result, the developmental progression of stepfamilies is not thoroughly documented.

RISK AND RESILIENCY FACTORS FOR STEPFAMILIES

A number of risk factors have an impact on adults and children in stepfamilies. The risk factors include family conflict, parenting conflict, stress, difficulties in the stepparent–child relationship, problems with the nonresidential parent, and role ambiguity. In addition, having adolescents in stepfamilies is a risk for increased family problems. Stepfamilies may thrive and be resilient because of previous experiences in which they learned to cope more effectively with stress, social maturity and responsibility of parents, effective parenting practices, and marital and family support and satisfaction.

Figure 11.1 presents a developmental family systems model of child adjustment in stepfamilies. The model is based on the previous research that has shown that stress, marital adjustment, parenting, parent/stepparent–child relations, family process (especially family conflict), and nonresidential parent relations are key predictors of children's adjustment in stepfamilies. The factors in boxes with solid

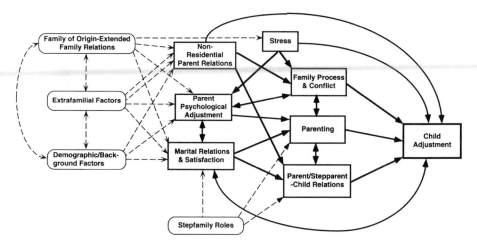

FIG 11.1.   Developmental family systems model of child adjustment in stepfamilies.

arrows in the model represent the central, direct effects hypothesized to have an impact on children's adjustment. The factors with dashed lines are hypothesized as contextual, indirect effects that mainly work through the direct effects. Findings from the DIS Research Project related to these direct factors are discussed later in this chapter.

Although the model is illustrated as a static one, stepfamilies are developing, interactional family systems that evolve over time. Research and clinical observation suggest that unique normative issues and tasks occur during the stepfamily life cycle (Bray & Berger, 1992, 1993b; McGoldrick & Carter, 1988; Whiteside, 1982). Relationships in stepfamilies change over time and are affected by previous individual and family experiences, developmental issues within the stepfamilies, and developmental issues for individual family members. Marital and family experiences during the first marriage, separation, and divorce may have a great impact on the functioning of a stepfamily (Bray & Hetherington, 1993). Thus, the multiple developmental trajectories of family members and the stepfamily life cycle are important to consider in the discussion of risk and resilience factors.

Children's Adjustment in Stepfamilies

Differences between the psychosocial functioning of children in stepfamilies and children in nuclear families vary according to the duration of the remarriage (Bray, 1988b; Bray & Berger, 1997; Bray, Berger, Boethel, Maymi, Touch, 1992). Children in the 6-month stepfamily group and the 5- to 7-year stepfamily group had more behavior problems, more stress, and lower social competence than comparable-age children in nuclear families. Few differences were found in children's adjustment in the two family types for the 2½-year groups: The only significant difference was that children in stepfamilies had lower social competence than comparably aged children in nuclear families. The children in the 6-month stepfamily group had more externalizing problems than children in the 2½-year and 5- to 7-year stepfamily groups. At the Longitudinal Followup, children in stepfamilies had more stress, less social competence, and more externalizing problems than children in nuclear families. These findings are similar to those found in the cross-sectional 5-year groups and thus replicate the previous findings. In the Longitudinal Followup children in both family types had increases in behavior problems over time. However, adolescents in stepfamilies had more difficulty dealing with the developmental issues of adolescence than children in nuclear families.

We were surprised by these findings. We expected children in stepfamilies to have more behavior problems than children in nuclear families during the early transitional phase after stepfamily formation. However, children suddenly erupted after several years of seemingly healthy adjustment to stepfamily life. The increased behavior problems for young adolescents was initially unanticipated until we examined the previous divorce literature and the unstructured interviews.

From the follow-up interviews with the families and adolescents, it appears that the adolescents were again struggling with their parents' divorces. These findings may be similar to what has been termed the sleeper effect of divorce (Hetherington et al., 1982), in which children who experience a parental divorce between the ages of 4 and 6 years come to terms with it when they reach adolescence.

Why would this disruption occur now and not before? The hypotheses about the reemergence of behavior problems for adolescents in stepfamilies relates to the struggle to individuate and develop autonomy during this period. Part of the individuation process is to interact with parents as a means of finding out who one is and who one is not. However, in stepfamilies, an important person is often not present—the nonresidential parent, who is usually the father. Thus, the individuation process is transferred onto the stepfather and may become problematic because adolescents need their other parents to complete this process. As part of this process, it is common for children in stepfamilies to develop an increased interest in their nonresidential parents. We found that about 20% of adolescents temporarily or permanently changed residents from their mothers to their fathers during this period.

In addition, a stepparent may respond to the increased behavior problems by disengaging, which further contributes to externalizing behavior by adolescents. Stepfathers made statements such as, "I don't understand why he is suddenly sullen and rude with me. It seems like he is angry about something, but he won't talk with me about it." Whereas we found that stepfather disengagement occurred in long-term stepfamilies, Hetherington and Clingempeel (1992) reported that it was more frequent and difficult for new stepfamilies with adolescents. Comparison of the two studies suggests that it is particularly difficult to form a new stepfamily with young adolescents.

There were few gender differences in children's adjustment in the DIS study. We found gender differences in family relationships, which are discussed later. However, at the longitudinal follow-up girls in stepfamilies reported more stress than other children. All children experienced an increase in life stress over time.

Previous research on divorced families indicates that family conflict may mediate the relation between family structure and children's behavior problems (Borrine, Handal, Brown, & Searight, 1991; Hetherington et al., 1982; Kurdek & Sinclair, 1988). In addition, given the increased levels of stress and potential conflict between ex-spouses in stepfamilies, we hypothesized that these processes may also be mediators. In the DIS project parents' life stress and family conflict mediated family structure differences in children's stress and internalizing problems, but not for children's externalizing problems and social competence. However, stress and conflict explained a significant amount of the variance in externalizing problems and children's adjustment in both family types (Bray & Berger, 1997). Thus, factors in addition to conflict and stress account for the higher level of behavior problems and lower social competence for children in stepfamilies.

These findings indicate that children who experience a parental divorce and remarriage are at risk for developing psychological problems and adjustment difficulties during the transition to remarriage and later as they enter adolescence. However, on the Child Behavior Checklist (Achenbach & Edelbrock, 1983), a standardized measure of children's adjustment, 80% of children in stepfamilies were functioning within a normal range. Thus, 20% had clinically significant levels of behavioral problems, whereas only 10% of children in nuclear families had significant behavioral problems. This conclusion is further supported by the lack of differences in self-esteem for children in stepfamilies and children in nuclear families. These results are consistent with meta-analysis of the literature on the effects of divorce on children (Amato & Keith, 1991).

A comparison with national data shows that children's responses to marital transitions vary considerably depending on their ages, family structure, race, and socioeconomic status (Amato & Keith, 1991; Demo & Acock, 1996; Hetherington & Clingempeel, 1992; Hetherington, Bridges, & Insabella, 1998). Zill and Schoenborn (1990), using a national probability sample, found that children from divorced, single-parent, and remarried homes are at risk for greater morbidity and behavioral disturbances (see Table 11.2). These data indicate that children in single-parent and stepfamily homes are about twice as likely to have developmental, learning, or emotional problems than children in nondivorced, intact families.

It is clear that not all children from divorced and remarried homes have emotional and behavioral problems, but they are at greater risk for developing these kinds of problems (Amato & Keith, 1991; Demo & Acock, 1996; Hetherington & Clingempeel, 1992; Hetherington & Jodl, 1994), and the problem behaviors may be present even prior to the divorce (Amato & Booth, 1996; Block, Block, & Gjerde, 1986; Cherlin et al., 1991). The difficulty is that much of the research in this area has focused on problems and deficiencies rather than success and adaptation.

TABLE 11.2

Percent of Children Ages 3–17 Who Have Had a Delay in Growth or Development,
a Learning Disability, or an Emotional Problem

Family Structure	Delay in Growth or Development	Learning Disability	Emotional or Behavioral Problem	Any Type of Problem
Intact family	3.8	5.5	8.3	14.6
Stepfather family	3.7	9.1	23.6	29.6
Mother custody	4.5	7.5	19.1	24.8
All others	4.8	8.3	22.2	28.2

Source: Zill, N., & Schoenborn, C. A. (1990). Advanced data from Vital Health Statistics: No. 190. National Centers for Health Statistics.

Marital Relationships in Stepfamilies

Since remarriage creates an instant family with children from the beginning, marital relations are reasonably different in stepfamilies than in first marriages or remarriages without children. The expected honeymoon period following a second marriage is either brief or nonexistent. The lack of a honeymoon period is most likely due to the presence of children from the beginning of the relationship (Bray & Berger, 1993a; Bray et al., 1987; Hetherington, 1993; Hetherington & Clingempeel, 1992). Hence, the period after the marriage, when a newlywed couple normally spends time alone and creates a marital bond, is compromised by the demands of caring for children.

The remarriage may create for children a sense of abandonment by their parents and competition with the new stepparents as their parents devote time and energy with their new spouses. Remarried parents may feel guilty about their children's reactions and therefore may ignore their marriages in response to their children's demands. Over time children's behavioral adjustment and their relationships with the stepparents have a significant impact on stepfamily marital adjustment and satisfaction. This is different than in nuclear families, in which the marriage typically affects child adjustment. The influence of adolescent behavior on the marital functioning occurs particularly in stepfamilies and appears to be stronger in newly formed stepfamilies with adolescents (Hetherington & Clingempeel, 1992).

There were few differences in marital adjustment and interactions between first-marriage and remarried couples in the DIS project for each period after remarriage (Bray & Berger, 1993a; Bray et al., 1987). After 5 years of remarriage stepfathers reported higher marital satisfaction than first marriage husbands; however, first-marriage couples were rated in behavioral observations as more positive in their interactions than remarried couples at this same period. There were also no differences between groups in marital satisfaction at the Longitudinal Followup. As Vemer, Coleman, Ganong, and Cooper (1989) reported in their review of the remarriage literature, marital relations and satisfaction with marriages in first and second marriages are usually quite similar. Overall, research shows that having children is associated with lower marital satisfaction. Thus, these findings are consistent with the view that residential children may affect marital satisfaction, and their presence may further explain the lack of a honeymoon effect for newly remarried couples.

However, in contrast to the self-report findings of marital satisfaction, observations of couples interacting indicated that remarried couples were more negative and less positive to each other than first-marriage couples. This occurred in the 6-month stepfamilies and in the 5- to 7-year stepfamilies. In the follow-up interviews remarried couples were more negative to each other, and stepfathers were less positive to their wives than were couples in nuclear families.

The reasons for the increased negative interactions in remarried couples probably differs for the two groups. In the 6-month stepfamilies, the more negative and less positive interactions are probably due to the stress and change with the new marriage and forming the stepfamily. However, this effect could also reflect a skills deficit for divorced persons (Bray et al., 1987). In the 5- to 7-year stepfamilies the more negative interactions are probably due to the increased stress and behavior problems of the young adolescents. It is quite common when couples are under increased stress to engage in more negative communications and interactions (Bray & Jouriles, 1995).

The marital subsystem appears to affect other family subsystems differently in stepfamilies than in first-marriage families (Bray, 1988a; Bray & Berger, 1993a), yet marital conflict is a crucial factor in both first marriages and remarriages (Bray & Jouriles, 1995). During early remarriage marital adjustment and satisfaction have little impact on children's behavior (Bray, 1988a; Hetherington & Clingempeel, 1992), in contrast to first-marriage families in which marital relationships are usually predictive of more adjustment difficulties for children (Emery, 1988). After several years in a stepfamily, marital relationships have more impact on children's adjustment and parent–child interactions, similar to first-marriage families (Bray & Berger, 1993a; Hetherington & Clingempeel, 1992).

Parent–Child and Stepparent–Child Relationships

Family relationships in stepfamilies, and particularly stepparent–child relationships, typically are more distant and have more conflict and other negative interactions than those in nuclear families (Bray, 1988b; Bray & Berger, 1993a; Hetherington & Clingempeel, 1992; Perkins & Kahan, 1979; Santrock Warshak, Lindberg, & Meadows, 1982). In addition, the relationships have more coalitions and triangles than do those in nuclear families (Anderson & White, 1986; Bray, 1992). Thus, parent–child relationship problems are a greater risk in stepfamilies, especially with adolescents, and individual behavioral and emotional problems are more likely in response to these difficulties (Bray & Harvey, 1995; Garbarino, Sebes, & Schellenbach, 1984).

Younger children seem to accept stepparents more quickly than young adolescents do. Boys appear to accept stepfathers faster than girls do. Thus, the development of a good relationship between stepparent and child is related not only to the stepparent's desire and attempts in forming a close relationship but also to the child's readiness and developmental status. When stepparents attempt to be involved with their stepchildren too quickly, even when they behave in positive and otherwise reasonable ways, the children may withdraw or be hostile toward the stepparents. This behavior may result in the stepparents disengaging from the children (Bray & Berger, 1992; Hetherington, 1987; Hetherington & Clingempeel, 1992). Over time, this disengagement is related to poorer behavioral adjustment for children.

In addition, in new stepfamilies children may view affection and bonding differently than adults. For example, in the DIS Research Project stepfathers' reports of expression of affection toward their stepchildren, especially girls, were related to more adjustment problems for the children, whereas the children's reports of the stepfathers' expression of affection were related to fewer adjustment problems for the children. To understand this apparently contradictory finding we re-interviewed the children and stepparents and found that they defined affection in very different ways. Stepfathers indicated that they attempted to show affection through physical contact, such as embraces or hugs. The children, and especially the girls, were uncomfortable with these types of affection. Children in stepfamilies stated that they liked verbal affection, such as praises or compliments, and this type of behavior was related to better adjustment.

No differences were found between mother–child relationships in stepfamilies and nuclear families in the follow-up interviews (Bray et al., 1992). All families, both first-marriage and stepfamilies, had more negative and less positive mother–child relationships across time, as the children entered adolescence. At the follow-up interviews, stepfathers were more negative and less positive in their interactions with their stepchildren than nuclear fathers were with their children. In addition, children in stepfamilies were less positive toward their stepfathers than were children in nuclear families toward their fathers. Stepfathers were less positive to their stepchildren over time than were nuclear fathers to their children. Stepfathers and sons had the largest decreases in positive interactions over time. These findings are in essential agreement with Anderson and White's (1986) and Hetherington and Clingempeel's (1992) findings that stepfathers have more distant and less positive relationships with their stepchildren than do biological fathers and children.

These findings highlight the ongoing changes in stepfamily relationships and suggest the continuing difficulties for stepparents, particularly with adolescents. These findings may reflect the difficulty that arises as the boys deal with their identity formation during adolescence. The struggle to develop identity and to individuate from the family may interfere with and take its toll on this relationship. However, although these relationships are more negative in stepfamilies than in nuclear families, they are not necessarily pathological or problematic.

Parenting in Stepfamilies

Parenting and stepparenting are the most difficult and stressful aspects of stepfamily life, during early remarriage as well as in longer term stepfamilies (Bray, 1988a, 1988b; Bray & Berger, 1997). Forgatch, Patterson, and Ray (1995) found that parenting mediates the impact of divorce and other family changes on children's adjustment. Our data indicate that the role of parenting on children's adjustment depends on the developmental status of the stepfamily and child.

During the early months of remarriage a stepparent may have difficulty playing a parental role, even when he or she uses authoritative parenting. A stepparent who acts as a friend or like a camp counselor, rather than a parent, may be more readily accepted (Bray, 1988a; Visher & Visher, 1988). Children are more likely to accept a stepparent who first attempts to form a relationship with the children instead of actively trying to discipline or control the children. In new stepfamilies, even when stepparents used effective parenting skills, they were often rebuffed, and the children responded with more behavior problems. This finding was quite surprising because the videotaped interactions demonstrated that stepparents used authoritative parenting skills that are usually associated with positive child outcomes in nuclear families. However, after 2½ years in a stepfamily, the stepparent played an important parental role, and the use of authoritative parenting was related to positive outcomes for children.

In new stepfamilies, strong marital bonds with minimal parental conflict facilitates parenting coalitions. A biological parent may unconsciously respond to a stepparent's attempt to discipline by undermining the stepparent out of loyalty to the children, even when he or she has overtly invited the stepparent to play an active parental role. It appears that having the custodial parent remain primarily responsible for control and discipline of the children during early remarriage is a useful approach to parenting in stepfamily. This approach creates time for a positive relationship to develop between the stepparent and children.

Active monitoring by the stepparent of the children's behavior and activities is a beneficial parental activity that facilitates children's adjustment during both early and later remarriage (Bray, 1988b; Hetherington, 1987; Hetherington & Clingempeel, 1992). After a relationship is formed, which may take many several months to more than a year, more active authoritative parenting by a stepparent can be beneficial to children in a stepfamily. Boys seem to respond more quickly to this process than do girls in stepfather families (Bray, 1988b; Hetherington & Clingempeel, 1992). This developmental flow is important for the near-term adjustment of children and is also predictive of better adjustment during later remarriage (Bray & Hetherington, 1993).

Older adolescents relay on peer relationships and extrafamilial sources of support as they become more independent from their families (Baumrind, 1991; Bray & Berger, 1992). However, effective parenting and stepparenting are still important for adolescents as seen from our longitudinal findings. A consistent relation between more paternal monitoring and better adjustment in stepchildren highlights the importance of this parenting practice for stepfathers across time. Mothers in both family types reported warmer and more involved relationships with their children over time (Bray et al., 1992). However, stepfathers' warmth decreased over time toward both genders of stepchildren. Stepfathers' reduced warmth appears to be contraindicated, as less warmth and involvement is related to poorer adjustment for stepchildren.

In contrast to Hetherington's (1987) findings, fathers and stepfathers in our study reported more warmth toward girls than toward boys. Warmth and involvement, as more indirect ways of sharing positive affect with stepchildren, appear to be generally more acceptable to stepchildren than direct expressions of affection. Furthermore, parents in both family types reported more parental monitoring over girls than over boys. More awareness by stepfathers of stepsons' activities and interests related to better behavioral adjustment in stepchildren. A consistent relation between more paternal monitoring and better adjustment in stepchildren highlights the importance of this parenting practice for stepfathers across time.

Over time, increases in authoritarian parenting by mothers and stepfathers were the most consistent correlates of behavior problems and lower social competence for adolescents in stepfamilies and girls in first-marriage families (Bray, 1994). Parenting in long-term stepfamilies was similar to parenting in first-marriage families. Authoritative parenting related to fewer behavior problems and higher social competence, whereas authoritarian parenting was associated with poorer adjustment. Disengaged parenting was also related to poorer adjustment for boys in stepfamilies and girls in first-marriage families.

Overall, early parenting styles were not strong longitudinal predictors of later adolescent adjustment, particularly for stepfathers. This finding is not surprising given the changes in parenting styles in stepfamilies and the rapid changes that frequently occur during the early years of remarriage. There were many similarities between parenting in long-term stepfamilies and first-marriage families. This finding suggests that after a period of years these two family types converge in their parenting toward what is best for adolescents' adjustment.

Conflict in Stepfamilies

Within families there are multiple types and degrees of conflict, and these various kinds of conflict may have different effects on children. In nuclear families, there is the potential for marital conflict, interparental conflict, parent–child conflict, sibling conflict, parent–grandparent conflict, and other general forms of family disharmony. In stepfamilies the potential sources of conflict include those already mentioned and the possibility of stepparent–parent conflict, stepparent–child conflict, and conflict between former spouses. Family conflict and interparental conflict that involves the children are key predictors of children's adjustment, especially in divorced or remarried families (Borrine et al., 1991; Hetherington &

Clingempeel, 1992; Johnston, Kline, & Tschann, 1989; Kline, Johnston, & Tschann, 1991; Kurdek & Sinclair, 1988).

In the DIS Project children's adjustment was significantly predicted both concurrently and longitudinally by various types of family conflict. Although both stepfamilies and first-marriage families shared some types of conflict that predicted children's adjustment—such as conflict between parents over childrearing issues and parenting and physical conflict—there were also notable differences that are lost in studies that fail to distinguish various types of conflict within families (Borrine et al., 1991). In stepfamilies, stepfather–child conflict was an important predictor, whereas mother–child conflict was an important predictor in nuclear families. Overall, conflict was more predictive of children's adjustment in stepfamilies than in first-marriage families. Furthermore, conflict has a stronger contemporaneous and longitudinal effect on children's externalizing problems than on other indices of adjustment.

Why does conflict have more impact on children in stepfamilies than children in nuclear families? Perhaps the nature of conflict has different meanings for children who have experienced parental divorce and remarriage. For these children, family relationships are more tenuous, so that children are sensitized to the negative impact that conflict plays in marital transitions and family breakups. Thus, they respond to conflict by acting out and other externalizing behaviors. Furthermore, conflict in families can interfere with effective parenting, which is also directly related to poorer child outcomes (Forgatch, Patterson, & Ray, 1995). Given that Gottman (1994) found certain types of marital conflict and disagreements may have positive benefits for resolving problems over time in first-marriage couples, it is important to determine what, if any types of family conflict may be useful for stepfamilies. Families may then learn to manage conflict effectively so that it does not a have detrimental impact on children.

Nonresidential Parent Issues

The relation between children's adjustment and contact with their nonresidential parents depends on several factors. Some studies find direct correlations among more contact, a better relationship between nonresidential parents and children, and better adjustment for children and adolescents. Others find that the correlations are mediated by such factors as interparental conflict and parenting (Emery, 1988; Hetherington, 1993; Hetherington et al., 1982; Johnston et al., 1989; Kline et al., 1991). The role of the nonresidential father following divorce and remarriage and the impact on children is a central area of study in the DIS Research Project. Enduring anger and animosity from the divorce may re-emerge after remarriage. Any remaining fantasies or desires that the original couple will reunite are usually dealt a final blow after the remarriage. However, even years after the remarriage, some children still want their divorced parents to reunite (Bray & Berger, 1992). After a remarriage some children may begin to treat their stepparents with animosity and hostility, despite good relationships before the remarriage. These changes indicate that the emotional divorce has not been resolved completely or that ongoing interparental conflict continues to take its toll on children in stepfamilies.

Although relationships with nonresidential fathers are important to the concurrent behavioral adjustment of children in the early months after remarriage, this impact is less after several years in a stepfamily (Bray & Berger, 1990, 1993b). More contact and better relationships between fathers and children were related to better behavioral adjustment for both boys and girls after 6 months in stepfather families. For girls, a positive impact was also found after 2½ years of remarriage. After 4½ years of living in a stepfather family, however, there was no concurrent relation between either the amount of contact or the quality of the nonresidential father–child relationship and the child's behavioral adjustment (Bray & Berger, 1990, 1993b). Given the limited amount of time children spend with their fathers and their older ages in the longer remarried families these results are not entirely surprising. During adolescence, children are often influenced more by their peer relationships than family relationships (Baumrind, 1991).

Cross-sectional analyses showed no differences in the amount of contact and quality of the relationships between nonresidential fathers and children in stepfamilies remarried 6 months, 2½ years, and 5 to 7 years. However, the longitudinal assessments reflected gender differences and changes over time in the father–child relationship (Bray, Berger, Touch, & Boethel, 1993). At the longitudinal follow-up, girls tended to have less contact with their nonresidential fathers but maintained similar quality in the father–child relationship as at the initial assessments. Boys and their fathers tended to continue the same amount of contact; however, boys reported improvements in the quality of the relationships with their nonresidential fathers over time. Although these differences may be due to the smaller sample size or a sampling bias in the cross-sectional study, they may also reflect developmental changes as children progress through adolescence. It is probable that a nonresidential father–child relationship may affect other areas of a child's life, such as happiness, sex role, or identity development, which were not examined in our study. Given the complex relationships in stepfamilies, it is important to identify other factors that may mediate or moderate these relationships rather than making assumptions, either good or bad, about the impact of contact between nonresidential fathers and their children.

Stepparent Roles

Role ambiguity seems to be a hallmark of stepfamilies. The lack of socially prescribed roles contributes to the ambiguity (Schwebel, Fine, & Renner, 1991). The lack of social norms and legal rights are often blamed for the increased stress and unrealistic expectations experienced by many stepfamilies. The most common socially prescribed family model in the United States is the two-parent nuclear family. Stepfamilies often attempt to replicate this family structure, only to find that the nuclear family myth does not work for them. As one stepparent reported, "it's like trying to force a square peg in a round whole. No matter how you try, it just doesn't fit right."

Consensus between spouses in stepfather families was found concerning step-family roles and relationships (Bray, Berger, & Boethel, 1994). First-marriage and remarried spouses had differences of opinion regarding stepparent roles and the continuing relationship between divorced spouses. Spouses in stepfamilies felt it was more appropriate for stepfathers to assume a parental role than did spouses in first-marriage families. Adults in first-marriage families were more likely to agree and to feel that it was appropriate for divorced spouses to communicate about their children than did adults in stepfamilies.

The similarity in remarried adults' attitudes at varying periods following remarriage suggests that attitudes about stepfamily roles remain stable over time. These findings indicate that, at least within stepfamilies, there are normative expectations about appropriate roles for adults who have experienced divorce and remarriage, or perhaps adults who do not agree on role expectations do not remarry.

Functional and Dysfunctional Stepfamilies

The family processes that contribute to problem formation in stepfamilies are not clear and may be related to the lack of established norms for stepfamilies (Bray & Berger, 1992). Thus, it is important to identify the characteristics that distinguish functional and dysfunctional stepfamilies. Clinical or dysfunctional stepfamilies have less involvement between stepfathers and their stepchildren and stronger tendencies toward the development of parent–child coalitions or triangled relationships (Anderson & White, 1986; Bray, 1992). Parent–child coalitions are even more extreme in dysfunctional stepfamilies than other families and are related to more problematic family processes. This is a common clinical problem in which the stepparent is excluded while the biological parent and children side together against the stepparent.

Dysfunctional or clinical stepfamilies have more conflict, less emotional expressiveness, less effective problem solving, less spousal individuation, poorer marital adjustment, and more negative and less positive child–parent interactions than members of nonclinical or functional stepfamilies (Bray, 1992; Brown, Green, & Druckman, 1990). More negative (i.e., more hostility, coercion, conflict) and less positive (i.e., less warmth, assertiveness, self-disclosure) child-to-parent interactions, less effective problem solving, and less spousal individuation are related to more behavior problems and less prosocial behavior for children in stepfamilies.

Both first-marriage families and stepfamilies may seek treatment because of increased conflict and communication problems; however, the types of conflict, number of conflict areas, and issues that affect communication can be different in the two family types (Bray, 1992). Stepfamilies may have conflict over the parental authority of stepparents or over relationships with the noncustodial parents or their families, whereas first-marriage families may have conflict about parenting practices or marital problems. Similarly, children's problems with relationships in stepfamilies may be related to loyalty conflicts or to unrealistic expectations, such as instant love, whereas children in first-marriage families may have problems as a result of rebellion or anger at parents. Thus, it is important to identify both the similarities and the differences in family processes and content that affect the adjustment of family members in stepfamilies.

CONCLUSIONS AND FUTURE DIRECTIONS

Marital transitions and especially remarriage create many new issues and challenges for modern stepfamilies. The remarriage process entails a number of risk factors for children in stepfamilies, such as increased stress, diminished parenting practices, disrupted family roles, and increased conflict. Warm, supportive relationships between children and custodial parents and stepparents; cooperative, understanding relationships between custodial and noncustodial parents; and authoritative parenting by custodial parents and later by stepparents are all important factors that contribute to children's adjustment in stepfamilies.

Although there are still important areas to study with stepfamilies, the DIS Research Project and others demonstrate that children of divorce and remarriage can grow and develop into well-functioning adolescents and that certain patterns of stepfamily relationships facilitate their adjustment. As the field evolves and matures, it is critical that these findings are used to develop prevention and intervention programs to help children and adults cope with and adjust to the stress and upheaval caused by marital transitions (Bray & Jouriles, 1995). Unfortunately, there are very few empirically based programs that have been developed or evaluated for effectiveness. The longitudinal research on divorce and remarriage strongly indicates that programs need to focus on both the short-term and the long-term adjustment issues that stepfamilies face in order to prevent or minimize some of the problems and enhance the positive adjustment for family members.

ACKNOWLEDGMENTS

This chapter is based in part on a Division 43 Presidential Address, American Psychological Association Annual Convention, New York. The research reported in this chapter was supported by NIH grants HD 18025 and HD 22642 from the National Institute of Child Health and Human Development. I would like to thank my collaborator, Sandra Berger, and all the staff and students who have worked on this project.

REFERENCES

Achenbach, T. M., & Edelbrock, C. S. (1983). *Manual for the Behavior Checklist and Revised Child Behavior Profile.* Burlington, VT: University of Vermont.

Amato, P. R., & Booth, A. (1996). A prospective study of divorce and parent–child relationships. *Journal of Marriage and the Family, 58,* 356–365.

Amato, P. R., & Keith, B. (1991). Parental divorce and the well-being of children: A meta-analysis. *Psychological Bulletin, 110,* 26–46.

Anderson, J. Z., & White, G. D. (1986). An empirical investigation of interactional and relationship patterns in functional and dysfunctional nuclear and stepfamilies. *Family Process, 25,* 407–422.

Baumrind, D. (1991). Effective parenting during the early adolescent transition. In P. A. Cowan & E. M. Hetherington (Eds.), *Family transitions* (pp. 111–164). Hillsdale, NJ: Lawrence Erlbaum Associates.

Block, J. H., Block, J., & Gjerde, P. F. (1986). The personality of children prior to divorce: A prospective study. *Child Development, 57,* 827–840.

Borrine, M. L., Handal, P. J., Brown, N. Y., & Searight, H. R. (1991). Family conflict and adolescent adjustment in intact, divorced, and blended families. *Journal of Consulting and Clinical Psychology, 59,* 753–755.

Bray, J. H. (1988a). Children's development during early remarriage. In E. M. Hetherington & J. Arasteh (Eds.) *The impact of divorce, single-parenting and step-parenting on children* (pp. 279–298). Hillsdale, NJ: Lawrence Erlbaum Associates.

Bray, J. H. (1988b). *Developmental issues in stepfamilies research project: Final report (Grant Number RO1 HD18025).* Bethesda, MD: National Institute of Child Health and Human Development.

Bray, J. H. (1992). Family relationships and children's adjustment in clinical and nonclinical stepfather families. *Journal of Family Psychology, 6,* 60–68.

Bray, J. H. (1994, February). *Longitudinal impact of parenting on adolescent adjustment in stepfamilies.* Paper presented at the Society for Research on Adolescence, San Diego, CA.

Bray, J. H., & Berger, S. H. (1990). Noncustodial parent and grandparent relationships in stepfamilies. *Family Relations, 39,* 414–419.

Bray, J. H., & Berger, S. H. (1992). Stepfamilies. In M. E. Procidano & C. B. Fisher (Eds.), *Contemporary families: A handbook for school professional* (pp. 57–79). New York: Teachers College Press.

Bray, J. H., & Berger, S. H. (1993a). Developmental issues in stepfamilies research project: Family relationships and parent–child interactions. *Journal of Family Psychology, 7,* 76–90.

Bray, J. H., & Berger, S. H. (1993b). Nonresidential family–child relationships following divorce and remarriage. In C. E. Depner & J. H. Bray (Eds.), *Noncustodial parents: New vistas in family living* (pp. 156–181). Newbury Park, CA: Sage.

Bray, J. H., & Berger, S. H. (1997). *Length of remarriage, conflict, stress, and children's adjustment in stepfather families and nuclear families.* Manuscript submitted for publication.

Bray, J. H., Berger, S. H., & Boethel, C. L. (1994). Role integration and marital adjustment in stepfather families. In K. Pasley & M. Ihinger-Tallman (Eds.), *Stepfamilies: Issues in research, theory, and practice* (pp. 69–86). New York: Greenwood.

Bray, J. H., Berger, S. H., Boethel, C., Maymi, J. R., & Touch, G. (1992, August). *Longitudinal changes in stepfamilies: Impact on children's adjustment.* Paper presented at the annual meeting of the American Psychological Association, Washington, DC.

Bray, J. H., Berger, S. H., Silverblatt, A., & Hollier, A. (1987). Family process and organization during early remarriage: A preliminary analysis. In J. P. Vincent (Ed.), *Advances in family intervention, assessment and theory, Vol. 4* (pp. 253–280). Greenwich, CT: JAI.

Bray, J. H., Berger, S. H., Touch, G., & Boethel, C. L. (1993, March). *Nonresidential parent-child relationships following divorce and remarriage: A longitudinal perspective.* Paper presented at the biennial meeting of the Society for Research in Child Development, New Orleans, LA.

Bray, J. H., & Harvey, D. M. (1995). Adolescents in stepfamilies: Developmental and family interventions. *Psychotherapy, 32,* 122–130.

Bray, J. H., & Hetherington, E. M. (1993). Families in transition: Introduction and overview. *Journal of Family Psychology, 7,* 3–8.

Bray, J. H., & Jouriles, E. (1995). Treatment of marital conflict and prevention of divorce. *Journal of Marital and Family Therapy, 21,* 461–473.

Brown, A. C., Green, R. J., & Druckman, J. (1990). A comparison of stepfamilies with and without child-focused problems. *American Journal of Orthopsychiatry, 60,* 556–566.

Bumpass, L. L., Sweet, J. A., & Castro-Martin, T. (1990). Changing patterns of remarriage. *Journal of Marriage and the Family, 52,* 747–756.

Carter, B., & McGoldrick, M. (1988). *The changing family life cycle: A framework for family therapy* (2nd ed.). New York: Gardner.

Cherlin, A. J., Furstenberg, F. F., Chase-Lansdale, P. L., Kiernan, K. E., Robins, P. K., Morrison, D. R., & Teitler, J. O. (1991). Longitudinal studies of effects of divorce in children in Great Britain and the United States. *Science, 252,* 1386–1389.

Demo, D. H., & Acock, A. C. (1996). Family structure, family process and adolescent well-being. *Journal of Research on Adolescence, 6,* 457–488.

Emery, R. E. (1988). *Marriage, divorce, and children's adjustment.* Newbury Park, CA: Sage..

Forgatch, M. S., Patterson, G. R., & Ray, J. A. (1995). Divorce and boys' adjustment problems: Two paths with a single model. In E. M. Hetherington & E. A. Bleckman (Eds.), *Stress, coping, and resiliency in children and families* (pp. 67–105). Hillsdale, NJ: Lawrence Erlbaum Associates.

Ganong, L. H., Coleman, M., & Mapes, D. (1990). A meta-analytic review of family structure stereotypes. *Journal of Marriage and the Family, 52,* 287–297.

Garbarino, J., Sebes, J., & Schellenbach, C. (1984). Families at risk for destructive parent–child relations in adolescence. *Child Development, 55,* 174–183.

Glick, P. C. (1989). Remarried families, stepfamilies, and stepchildren: A brief demographic profile. *Family Relations, 38,* 24–27.

Gottman, J. M. (1994). *What predicts divorce?* Hillsdale, NJ: Lawrence Erlbaum Associates.

Hetherington, E. M. (1987). Family relations six years after divorce. In K. Pasley & M. Ihinger-Tallman (Eds.), *Remarriage and stepparenting today: Current research and theory* (pp. 185–205). New York: Guilford.

Hetherington, E. M. (1993). An overview of the Virginia longitudinal study of divorce and remarriage. *Journal of Family Psychology, 7,* 35–56.

Hetherington, E. M., Bridges, M., & Insabella, G. M. (1998). What matters? What does not? Five perspectives on the association between marital transitions and children's adjustment. *American Psychologist, 53,* 167–184.

Hetherington, E. M., & Clingempeel, W. G. (1992). Coping with marital transitions: A family systems perspective. *Monographs of the Society for Research in Child Development, 57* (2–3, Serial No. 227).

Hetherington, E. M., Clingempeel, W. G., Eisenberg, M., Hagan, M. S., Vuchinich, R., & Chase-Lansdale, L. (1986). *Manual for the family interaction coding system.* Department of Psychology, University of Virginia, Charlottesville, VA.

Hetherington, E. M., Cox, M., & Cox, R. (1982). Effects of divorce on parents and children. In M. E. Lamb (Ed.), *Nontraditional families: Parenting and child development* (pp. 233–288). Hillsdale, NJ: Lawrence Erlbaum Associates.

Hetherington, E. M., & Jodl, K. M. (1994). Stepfamilies as settings for child development. In A. Booth & J. Dunn (Eds.), *Stepfamilies: Who benefits? Who does not?* (pp. 55–79). Hillsdale, NJ: Lawrence Erlbaum Associates.

Johnston, J. R., Kline, M. & Tschann, J. M. (1989). Ongoing postdivorce conflict: Effects on children of joint custody and frequent access. *American Journal of Orthopsychiatry, 59,* 1–17.

Kline, M., Johnston, J. R., & Tschann, J. M. (1991). The long shadow of marital conflict: A model of children's post-divorce adjustment. *Journal of Marriage and the Family, 53,* 297–309.

Kurdek, L. A., & Sinclair, R. J. (1988). Adjustment of young adolescents in two-parent nuclear, stepfa-ther, and mother-custody families. *Journal of Consulting and Clinical Psychology, 56,* 91–96.

McGoldrick, M., & Carter, E. A. (1988). Forming a remarried family. In E. A. Carter & M. McGoldrick (Eds.), *The changing family life cycle* (pp. 399–429). New York: Gardner.

Perkins, T. F., & Kahan, J. P. (1979). An empirical comparison of natural-father and stepfather systems. *Family Process, 18,* 175–183.

Santrock, J. W., Warshak, R. A., Lindberg, C., & Meadows, L. (1982). Children's and parent's observed social behavior in stepfather families. *Child Development, 53,* 472–480.

Schwebel, A. I., Fine, M. A., & Renner, M. A. (1991). A study of perceptions of the stepparenting role. *Journal of Family Issues, 12,* 43–57.

Vemer, E., Coleman, M., Ganong, L. H., & Cooper, H. (1989). Marital satisfaction in remarriage: A meta-analysis. *Journal of Marriage and the Family, 51,* 713–725.

Visher, E. B., & Visher, J. S. (1988). *Old loyalties, new ties: Therapeutic strategies with stepfamilies.* New York: Brunner/Mazel.

Whiteside, M. F. (1982). Remarriage: A family developmental process. *Journal of Marital and Family Therapy, 4,* 59–68.

Zill, N., & Schoenborn, C. A. (1990). Developmental, learning, and emotional problems: Health of our nation's children, United States, 1988. *Advance data from vital and health statistics; no 190.* Hyatts-ville, MD: National Center for Health Statistics.

12

A Social Constructionist
Multi-Method Approach to
Understanding the Stepparent Role

Mark A. Fine
Marilyn Coleman
Lawrence H. Ganong
University of Missouri

THERE HAS BEEN a growing consensus in the clinical and conceptual literatures that many of the challenges, opportunities, and issues facing members of stepfamilies revolve around the role of the stepparent (Crosbie-Burnett, 1989; Visher & Visher, 1996). One of the primary reasons why the stepparent role is so salient is that few societal norms provide guidelines for how stepparents should act toward their stepchildren (Cherlin, 1978). Nevertheless, relatively few empirical studies have examined stepfamily members' views of the role of the stepparent, how clear family members are in their views of the stepparent role, and the adjustment correlates of various aspects of stepparent role perceptions. In this chapter, we provide an overview of a programmatic line of inquiry into these dimensions of the stepparent role.

CONCEPTUAL ORIENTATION

A Social Constructionist Perspective on the Stepparent Role and its Adjustment Correlates

According to our social constructionist perspective on the stepparent role, stepfamily members, based on their interpretations of cultural norms, their experiences within their stepfamilies, and their idiosyncratic characteristics, construct their notions of various aspects of the stepparent role. Consistent with the multi-dimensional cognitive developmental model proposed by Fine and Kurdek (1994a), we believe that stepfamily members' constructions of the stepparent role influence not only interactions within the stepfamily but also the adjustment of stepfamily members and the family as a whole. Furthermore, we suggest that adjustment in stepfamilies is facilitated to the degree that family members agree with each other about the nature of the stepparent role.

Within a risk and resiliency perspective, we have been interested in whether some ways of viewing the role of the stepparent add to the risk of negative outcomes for stepfamily members and whether some constructions of the stepparent role lead to positive outcomes and increase resiliency. In addition, our constructionist approach suggests that risk in stepfamilies is increased when family members have different views of the stepparent role and resilience is enhanced to the extent that their role constructions are similar.

Dimensions of the Stepparent Role

We define the stepparent role as the set of cognitions and resulting behaviors pertaining to how stepparents should and do act towards their stepchildren. As we have proposed elsewhere (Fine, Ganong, & Coleman, 1997), we posit that the cognitive dimension of the stepparent role has two elements: *content* and *clarity*. Content refers to beliefs about how stepparents should and do carry out their role, whereas role clarity refers to one's level of confidence that these beliefs are appropriate for the stepparent role. These two cognitive aspects of the role are conceptually independent, as one's beliefs about how a stepparent should behave are distinct from how confident one is in the appropriateness of those beliefs. It is also useful to distinguish between societal and individual role clarity (Kahn, Wolfe, Quinn, Snoek, & Rosenthal, 1964). Societal role clarity refers to social consensus on what is appropriate role behavior for stepparents, whereas individual role clarity refers to a person's (whether stepparent, parent, or stepchild) experience of certainty about how the stepparent should behave.

In addition, content and clarity about the stepparent role influence the manner in which the stepparent role is performed. Thus, we posit that there are three primary dimensions of the stepparent role: role content, role clarity, and perceived role behavior. Few studies have simultaneously investigated these three aspects of the stepparent role.

FOCI OF OUR RESEARCH ON THE STEPPARENT ROLE

Our research has focused on the following four questions: What do stepfamily members perceive to be the content of the stepparent role? To what extent do stepfamily members have clear perceptions of the stepparent role? How do stepparents act toward their stepchildren? What are the adjustment correlates of role content, role clarity, and perceived role behavior?

Stepfamily Members' Perceptions of the Content of the Stepparent Role

The first focus of our research program is on the content of the stepparent role. In this chapter, findings pertaining to five distinct dimensions of role content are reviewed: the labels that stepfamily members assign to the current and ideal stepparent role, stepfamily members' perceptions of how much warmth stepparents do and should show to their stepchildren, perceptions of how much stepparents do and should discipline and monitor their stepchildren's behavior, leadership and influence in the stepfamily, and the extent to which family members believe that the stepparent has obligations to his or her stepchildren.

With respect to labels assigned to the role of the stepparent, previous research has suggested considerable variability in how stepparents define their role. For example, Erera-Weatherly (1996) found that some stepparents tried to function as parents, some tried to act as friends to their stepchildren, some had not defined a role, and some were minimally involved with residential stepchildren.

With respect to perceptions of how actively stepparents should show warmth toward their stepchildren and engage in disciplinary behaviors, we expected that we would find some differences among stepfamily members. In particular, we predicted that parents and stepparents would be more likely to believe that stepparents should be active in parenting (Marsiglio, 1992) than would stepchildren (Visher & Visher, 1988).

With respect to stepparents' obligations to their stepchildren, Ganong, Coleman, and Mistina (1995) found that many adults believed that stepfathers were at least partly responsible for financially supporting their stepchildren's educational needs. Ganong et al. (1995) concluded that participants believed that a residential stepfather essentially assumed the role of father while married to the child's parent, at least with respect to financially supporting stepchildren. In the present study, we built upon this research by asking members of stepfamilies about their perceptions of the stepparent's general obligations toward his or her stepchildren.

Given the relative lack of previous research, we approached the remaining issue pertaining to the content of the stepparent role—leadership and influence—in an exploratory manner.

Stepfamily Members' Perceptions of the Stepparent Role

Our second focus is on stepparent role clarity. A number of scholars have argued that the stepparent role is less clear than the role of the biological parent (Crosbie-Burnett, 1989). Our interest was in the clarity of different stepfamily members' perceptions of the stepparent role.

The few studies that have been conducted in this area have generally assessed the extent of societal rather than individual role clarity. For example, Schwebel, Fine, and Renner (1991) asked college students to rate how likely it was that a parental figure *would* engage in a designated parental behavior relevant to a case scenario and to what extent the parental figure *should* engage in the parental behavior. There was generally greater variability in ratings of what stepparents would do and should do than there was in ratings of what parents would and should do. Similarly, Fine and Kurdek (1994b) found greater variability in stepparents' ratings of how much they should show warmth toward their stepchildren than in parents' ratings of how much they should show warmth. Finally, Marsiglio (1992) found a great deal of variability in the extent to which stepfathers in the National Survey of Families and Households agreed with seven statements (e.g., "a stepparent is more like a friend than a parent to stepchildren") pertaining to the stepparent role. These findings support the notion that there is less agreement about how stepparents do and should act than there is in reference to parents.

However, two studies have found that adults in stepfamilies tend to agree on the role of the stepparent. Bray, Berger, and Boethel (1994) found that mothers and stepfathers in stepfamilies tended to agree on the relative extent to which each spouse was responsible for childrearing. Similarly, Ganong and Coleman (1994) found that stepparents and parents of adolescents tended to agree on how much responsibility the stepparent had in raising the stepchild. These studies raise the possibility that, at least within stepfamilies, there is some agreement on the appropriate stepparent role (Bray et al., 1994).

How Stepparents Act Toward Their Stepchildren

Our third focus is on perceived stepparent role behavior. In this chapter, we examine two aspects of this dimension of the stepparent role—affinity-seeking and affinity-maintaining behavior and the nature of stepparent–stepchild interaction. In terms of the former, we explored through semistructured interviews the extent to which stepfamily members perceived the stepparent as trying to elicit and maintain liking from his or her stepchild(ren). In terms of the latter, we coded a number of different interaction dimensions from a behavioral observation task.

The Adjustment Correlates of Role Content, Clarity, and Perceived Role Behavior

The fourth focus of our work is the relation between the way that the stepparent role is constructed and the adjustment of various units within the stepfamily system. We examined three distinct issues.

Links Between Consistency in Role Perceptions Among Family Members and Adjustment. Based on Fine and Kurdek's (1994a) model, we predicted that greater consistency in role perceptions between stepfamily members is related to better adjustment. Role consistency was examined for the stepparent–parent and the stepparent–stepchild dyads. Adjustment was examined broadly in three overlapping areas: the individual, dyads within the stepfamily, and the entire family system.

Relations Between Perceptions of Stepparent Role Clarity and Adjustment. Evidence suggests that greater stepparent role clarity is associated with some dimensions of adjustment. Kurdek and Fine (1991) found that high levels of stepparent role clarity were related to mothers' reports of family/marital/personal life satisfaction and stepfathers' reports of parenting satisfaction. Similarly, Fine, Kurdek, and Hennigen (1992) found that adolescents who saw the role of their stepmothers as clear also tended to report high levels of self-competence. Thus, consistent with Fine and Kurdek's (1994a) model, we predicted that greater role clarity is positively related to individual, marital, and family adjustment.

Relations Among Stepparents' Affinity-Seeking and Affinity-Maintaining Strategies and Closeness of Stepparent–Stepchild Relationships. Using semistructured interviews, we explored whether some affinity strategies are more successful than others in facilitating closeness in the stepparent–stepchild relationship. Given the lack of previous research, we posed no hypotheses about the nature of this relation.

METHODS: SURVEYS, INTERVIEWS, AND OBSERVATIONAL INTERACTIONS

Sample

Participants were stepparents, parents, and at least one stepchild (between the ages of 10 and 19 years) from 40 stepfamilies in a midwestern state. Thirty-four were stepfather–mother–stepchild triads, and 6 were stepmother–father–stepchild triads. Twenty-two target children were girls and 18 were boys. The mean ages of the stepparents, parents, and stepchildren were 39.8, 38.2, and 13.6 years, respectively. Ninety percent were White. The sample was generally of middle socioeconomic status.

The stepparents and parents had been married for a mean of 5.3 years and had been living together for a mean of 5.6 years. All parents and most stepparents (78%) had been married before; almost all remarried parents (95%) and all remarried stepparents had divorced their former spouses. More details on the sample can be found in Fine, Coleman, and Ganong (1998).

To estimate the extent to which these stepfamilies were representative of the population of stepfamilies, we compared them on selected demographic characteristics to stepfamilies in the nationally representative National Survey of Families and Households (NSFH; Sweet, Bumpass, & Call, 1988). Compared to the NSFH sample, these stepfamilies were somewhat older, better educated, had slightly higher family incomes, and had been remarried for a longer period of time. These differences may be partially attributed to one of our inclusion criteria—the stepfamily had to have a stepchild between the ages of 10 and 19 years living in the home. Our sample was also similar to normative samples in their scores on those instruments that have published norms (see Fine et al., 1997, for comparisons with stepfathers in this project).

Interview and Behavioral Observation Subsample. In 16 of these families, family members also participated in extensive semistructured interviews and were videotaped completing a problem-solving task. Both adults in the home as well as almost all stepchildren between the ages of 10 and 19 years were interviewed, resulting in completed interviews with 32 adults and 22 children. Of the 16 stepfamilies, 14 were stepfather–mother households and 2 were complex households in which both adults were stepparents to residential children. Comparisons between the subsample of 16 stepfamilies that participated in the interviews and observational task and the 24 stepfamilies that did not revealed no significant demographic differences, suggesting that the subsample was representative of the sample as a whole.

Procedure

Methods used to recruit stepfamilies included: advertisements placed in a local newspaper, announcements placed in payroll envelopes at the university and on the office doors of the principal investigators, contact with individuals thought to be living in stepfamilies, and requests that participants in the study recommend other stepfamilies. Potential participants were told that the study was designed to examine how stepparents and stepchildren relate to one another. If there were two or more stepchildren between the ages of 10 and 19, the oldest one was selected as the target child for completion of the quantitative surveys.

Measures

Consistent with an approach referred to as methods triangulation (Patton, 1990), survey, interview, and behavioral observation data were collected.

Surveys. Surveys were administered individually to the stepparents, parents, and target stepchildren in the 40 stepfamilies. These measures assessed perceptions of numerous aspects of the stepparent role and multiple dimensions of adjustment. On all multi-item measures, Cronbach's alphas for the individual family members' scores were satisfactory to excellent, ranging from .66 to .96.

Measures of Content and Clarity of the Stepparent Role.   Labels assigned
to the role of the stepparent were assessed by the Stepparent Role Questionnaire
(SRQ), which was developed for this study. Stepparents were asked, "Which relationship best describes your IDEAL way to relate to your stepchildren?" Response
options were: distant relative, teacher, friend, stepparent, acquaintance, advisor,
boss, parent, aunt (or uncle, depending on the sex of the stepparent), enemy, or
other. Parallel questions were asked of parents and stepchildren. All family members also were asked, with the same response options, to describe the current relationship between the stepparent and stepchild.

Role perceptions were measured by the Stepparent Behavior Inventory (SBI),
an instrument developed for this study. The two sections, actual and ideal, contained the same set of 18 items but different directions. Nine items tapped the
warmth (or acceptance) dimension of parenting (e.g., "compliment your stepchild,"), and nine assessed the control (or supervision) parenting dimension (e.g.,
"make sure that your stepchild does his or her homework").

In the actual section, stepparents were asked to "rate how often you *actually*
behave in these ways toward your stepchild" on a 1 (*rarely or never*) to 7 (*extremely
often or always*) scale. In the ideal section, stepparents were asked to "rate how often
you *personally believe that you should* behave in these ways." Similar questions were
asked of parents and stepchildren about the stepparent role.

Eight composite role discrepancy scores were computed at the dyadic level to
assess consistency in role perceptions of the ideal and actual stepparent role. For all
discrepancy scores, absolute values were used because differences in either direction were considered to have similar theoretical meaning. For each of the four SBI
subscales, discrepancy scores were calculated between the stepparents' and parents'
scores and between the stepparents' and stepchilds' scores.

Role clarity was assessed by the Stepparent Role Clarity Inventory, a seven-item
instrument developed for this study. On each item (e.g., "I have few doubts about
how I should act to be a good stepparent"), respondents rated their levels of agreement on a 1 (*strongly disagree*) to 7 (*strongly agree*) scale. Parents and stepchildren
responded to parallel items that tapped their perceptions of clarity regarding the
stepparent role.

Adjustment Measures.   Mental health symptoms were assessed by the 53-item
Brief Symptom Checklist (DeRogatis, 1993), and life satisfaction was assessed by
the 5-item Satisfaction With Life Survey (Diener, Emmons, Larsen, & Griffin, 1985).

Stepparents' satisfaction with stepparenting was measured by 12 items, 6 of
which were chosen from the National Survey of Families and Households (Sweet et
al., 1988). Higher scores were indicative of greater satisfaction.

Closeness of stepparent–stepchild relationship was measured by one item that
was asked of all participants. Stepparents were asked, on a 1 (*not at all close*) to 5
(*extremely close*) scale, "In the last 6 weeks, how close has your relationship to your
stepchild been?" Similar items were administered to parents and stepchildren re-

garding their perceptions of the closeness of the stepparent–stepchild relationship. Similarly, perceived success of stepparent was assessed by one item that was asked of stepparents and parents. Stepparents were asked, on a 1 (*not at all*) to 7 (*very much*) scale, "How successful do you think you've been as a stepmother/stepfather?" Parents responded to a similar item regarding their perceptions of how successful the stepparent has been in his or her role.

Marital satisfaction was assessed by the 3-item Kansas Marital Satisfaction Scale (Schumm et al., 1986). Family strengths were measured by the 12-item Family Strengths Scale (Olson, Larsen, & McCubbin, 1982).

Interviews. In-depth, semistructured interviews were conducted using an approach developed by Buehlman, Gottman, and Katz (1992). The interview was designed to tap the process by which the stepparent role is constructed and how a good stepparent–stepchild relationship is developed and maintained. Among the areas covered were stepparents' affinity-seeking and affinity-maintaining strategies (an aspect of perceived role behavior) and family members' views of the nature of the obligations that stepparents have toward their stepchildren (an aspect of role content). The interview protocol was chronologically based, beginning when the stepparent and parent first met and continuing with their courtship, the early years of their stepfamily, and the events of their lives together up to the time of the interview.

The transcribed interviews were read independently by all three authors. A similar process was used to code and analyze the interview data for both topics presented in this chapter—affinity-seeking and affinity-maintaining strategies and stepparent obligations toward stepchildren. In both cases, instead of using an a priori coding scheme, we used an inductive approach (Patton, 1990). Each author developed a coding scheme. We then met to compare the independently developed coding schemes, and minor differences and discrepancies in coding or definitions of coded categories were resolved via discussion. A revised set of codes was developed as a result of this discussion. The interviews were read and coded again using the revised coding scheme. Subsequent to this reading, we again met, discussed our analyses, and resolved the few minor discrepancies in coding. More detail on the analysis of the coding pertaining to the affinity strategies can be found in Ganong, Coleman, Fine, and Martin (in press).

Behavioral Observation. The behavioral observation task involved the following procedure. First, family members were brought to a room with several comfortable chairs and a sofa and were asked to sit wherever they wanted. Then, each individual was given the Stepfamily Unrevealed Differences Questionnaire (Ganong & Coleman, 1989), a 7-item measure adapted from Borduin's (1990) Unrevealed Differences family assessment. Each person was asked to rank the responses provided for each question according to their relative importance. When the family members were finished completing their individual ratings, the researcher gave to the family (any member could take the sheet) a page containing three of the seven questions that they had just completed. For example, one question was "There are often differences in opinions about how children should be disciplined. How do you think discipline should be handled?" Options were "the biological parent should decide," "the stepparent and biological parent should decide together," "the whole family as a unit should decide," "the stepparent should decide," and "the person who is upset with the child should decide." The family was then given the following instructions, "Your task now is to reach a family *consensus* on rankings to each of these 3 items. While you work on this task, we will leave the room, but will leave the camcorder on to record your deliberations."

Thus, we have three pieces of data from this task: each family member's individual rankings, the family unit's consensual ranking, and the videotaped family interaction while the group decisions were being reached. Using these three data elements, we derived a coding system that integrated items from several existing coding systems, including those developed by Borduin (1990), Thomas and Olson (1993), and Beavers, Hampson, and Hulgus (1985). For the purposes of this chapter, we focus on the following ratings: the family member(s) who assumed leadership for completing the task; parent–child relationship quality and stepparent–stepchild relationship quality in the areas of affect, amount of interaction, cooperation, conflict, and dominance; the family's consensus rating of how discipline should be performed in the family; and the family member whose responses were most consistent with the family's consensual responses.

EMPIRICAL FINDINGS PERTAINING TO THE STEPPARENT ROLE

In this section, we present results from our three primary types of data—survey, interview, and behavioral observation—in each of four areas: the content of the stepparent role; the clarity of the stepparent role; perceived stepparent role behavior; and the adjustment correlates of role content, clarity, and perceived role behavior.

Content of the Stepparent Role

Labels Assigned to the Role of the Stepparent. What labels do stepfamily members assign to the role of the stepparent, and how consistent are they in these assigned labels? Table 12.1 shows that about half the parents and stepparents identified "parent" as the ideal stepparent role; "stepparent" and "friend" were generally chosen by less than 20% of parents and stepparents. The parents' and stepparents' responses were not significantly different. In contrast, 40% of stepchildren identified "friend" as the ideal descriptor; only 47% identified either "stepparent" or "parent." The stepchildren's responses were significantly different from those of their parents and their stepparents.

TABLE 12.1
Parents', Stepparents', and Stepchildrens' Perceptions
of the Ideal and Actual Stepparent Role

	Parent	Stepparent	Stepchild
Ideal			
Stepparent	10 (26%)	7 (18%)	7 (18%)
Parent	20 (51%)	21 (52%)	11 (29%)
Friend	7 (18%)	7 (18%)	15 (40%)
Other	2 (5%)	5 (12%)	5 (13%)
Actual			
Stepparent	12 (31%)	10 (25%)	10 (28%)
Parent	15 (38%)	19 (48%)	10 (28%)
Friend	3 (8%)	4 (10%)	9 (25%)
Other	9 (23%)	7 (18%)	7 (19%)

Table 12.1 also shows that parents and stepparents again had similar perceptions of the actual stepparent role. Most identified the current role as either that of
stepparent or parent. In contrast, stepchildren were significantly more likely to
view the current stepparent role as friend than were their stepparents and their
parents.

Parental Warmth.   We used the SBI to explore how similar stepfamily members were in their perceptions of how actively stepparents should and do engage in
warm parenting behaviors. Stepparents', parents', and stepchildren's composite
scores on the ideal and actual warmth subscales of the SBI (see Table 12.2) were
compared with two one-factor (stepfamily member) repeated-measure ANOVAs.
Significant effects were found on both subscales, with post hoc tests revealing that
stepparents reported believing that stepparents should and do engage in more
warm parenting behaviors than did stepchildren.

Discipline and Control Parenting Behaviors.   To determine how consistent
stepfamily members' perceptions were in the area of control or monitoring parenting behaviors, stepparents', parents', and stepchildren's composite scores on the
ideal and actual control subscales of the SBI (see Table 12.2) were compared with
two one-factor (stepfamily member) repeated-measure ANOVAs. Significant effects were found on both subscales, with post hoc tests revealing that, compared to
stepchildren, stepparents reported believing that stepparents should and do engage in more control parenting behaviors.

Interviews with stepchildren provided some insights into why they believed
that stepparents should be less active in discipline than did either parents or stepparents. The following two quotes were illustrative of stepchildren's views. A 12-
year-old stepson, when asked what advice he would give a stepparent about how to
deal with his stepkids, stated:

Wait a few months before you start laying on the rules and telling them there will be different ones, but not right away start doing them. You can't have too many adjustments at once when you're still getting to know them pretty much.

A 16-year-old stepson, when asked what advice he would give a stepparent, stated:

The stepparent first would be to give room to the children, but still on the same spectrum, keep control basically, keep disciplining but I wouldn't say that you should make them, kinda let them ease into it. You shouldn't jump into something right away which is completely new.

On the behavioral observation task, one question that family members responded to was "How do you think discipline should be handled?" To capture the family's consensual responses in quantitative terms, the family's first, second, and third responses were assigned scores of 3, 2, and 1, respectively. The most popular response was "the stepparent and biological parent should decide together" (46 points; identified by 14 of 16 families as their first choice), followed by "the whole family as a unit" (19 points), "the biological parent" (18 points), and "the person who is upset with the child" (11 points). "The stepparent should decide" was by far the least popular response.

These rankings suggest that most of these stepfamily members may have adopted a nuclear family model of how to discipline children, because the top two choices—the parent and the stepparent and the whole family—each reflect the belief that both parents should decide how to discipline children, sometimes with input from other family members. Furthermore, the nuclear family model is also reflected in the "biological parent and stepparent" option being more popular than the "biological parent" choice.

However, members of these stepfamilies seemed somewhat aware of the unique aspects of stepfamilies and the role of stepparents, as they uniformly reported that

TABLE 12.2

Means and Standard Deviations on Stepparents', Parents', and Stepchildren's Scores on the Subscales of the Stepparent Behavior Inventory (SBI) and the Stepparent Role Clarity Inventory (SRCI) ($N = 40$)

Measure	Stepparents		Parents		Stepchildren	
	M	SD	M	SD	M	SD
SBI—Ideal Warmth	5.75	.67	5.54	.86	5.07	1.22
SBI—Actual Warmth	5.01	.87	4.63	1.39	4.51	1.39
SBI—Ideal Control	6.02	.73	5.65	1.06	4.89	1.57
SBI—Actual Control	5.47	.94	4.98	1.35	4.86	1.46
SRCI	4.47	1.01	5.04	.88	5.26	1.06

Note. On all of the SBI subscales, stepparents' mean scores were significantly ($p < .05$) higher than stepchildren's mean scores. On the SRCI, stepparents' mean score was significantly lower than their stepchildren's mean score.

the stepparent should not engage in discipline alone. In interpreting these results, readers should keep in mind that these are stepfamilies that generally have been together for a reasonably long period of time, which may mean that they have determined what does and does not work for them. Taken as a whole, these responses reflect a stance that stepparents should help discipline stepchildren but their role should be complimentary (or secondary) to that of the parent.

Leadership and Influence. Two codes from the behavioral observation task were relevant to leadership and influence. First, we coded leadership during the family interaction according to whether an individual, dyad, or a subgroup within the family assumed primary leadership for helping the family reach its consensual response. Among the 16 stepfamilies, the parent was identified as the leader in 10 instances, the parent–stepparent dyad in 4 families, the stepchild in 1 family, and the stepparent in 1 family. These results are noteworthy because the wife was a parent in all 16 families, although in two of these families, she was also a stepmother of residential stepchildren. Given findings suggesting that men are more likely to take control of conversations than are women (Anderson & Sabatelli, 1995), one might expect the stepfather to assume the primary leadership role more often. However, wives may have exhibited more leadership than husbands partly because the task was verbal and interpersonally oriented (Tannen, 1990). In addition, our findings are consistent with the notion that the parent (i.e., the mother) often mediates and tries to negotiate harmony between people she loves (i.e., her children and her new husband) but who often do not have strong positive feelings toward each other. Being invested in the greatest number of relationships in the family, she may feel the need to ease tensions between her spouse and children. Thus, particularly given the sex of the stepparents and parents, these results are consistent with the inference that stepparents generally do not assume a leadership or managerial role in the stepfamily and, when they do, it is typically in conjunction with the parent.

Second, as an index of influence in the stepfamily, we examined which individual's rankings most closely resembled the family's consensus rating. Our criterion for identifying an individual as having the greatest influence on the group decision was that he or she had the individual responses that most resembled the family consensus on at least 2 of the 3 questions to which the family responded. Among our 16 families, the stepparent was the most influential individual in 7 families, the parent in 5, the stepparent and the parent in 3, and no clear influential individual in the remaining family. Thus, in contrast to parents providing the most leadership in these families, the stepparents were slightly more influential than the parents in the process of influencing a family decision. Perhaps males have more influence in affecting the group decision-making process than in leading the group interaction, or perhaps mothers, in their role as mediators, acquiesced to their husbands when they disagreed and influenced their children to go along as well. Clearly, more work needs to be done to explain these potentially discrepant findings pertaining to leadership and influence, including an examination of the verbal communication that took place during the family interactions.

Obligations of Stepparents Toward Stepchildren. In the interviews, we asked stepparents, parents, and stepchildren about the obligations and responsibilities they had to their stepchildren. Their responses were coded into four categories: the stepparent has the same obligations to stepchildren as a parent has to children; the stepparent should play a secondary role to the parent, such as friend, helper, or financial provider, but should not be a parent; the stepparent has obligations that are similar to a parent in most ways but not all; and the stepparent has no obligations to his or her stepchild(ren).

Some quotes may shed light on the meaning assigned to these categories of responses. A code of 1 (i.e., the nuclear family model) was assigned to the response of a stepfather who stated, ". . . try to remember and realize that they shouldn't be treated any different from your own child. I am obligated to treat them like one of my own." A mother coded 1 said, "The same basic obligations as the biological parent." For a code of 2 (i.e., secondary, supportive role), a stepfather said, "I am obligated to be honest with her (the stepdaughter), to be there for her, to be trustworthy. I owe them respect." A mother stated, "Be there for emergencies. Child care, when I'm not available. Fix meals when I'm not around. He's free to say that doesn't work for me." A stepdaughter indicated, "I look at him as just someone that's there for my mom. He has some say in . . . family activities and financial stuff . . . I guess stepparents are just friendship and support." For a code of 3 (i.e., almost a parent), a stepmother stated, "Pretty much to be the parent. Give them as much respect and love as possible." A stepfather said, "They're my kids. I'm not their father, never will be, but as far as I'm concerned, all things given, I feel like I owe them." A stepdaughter reported, "I think they should be just like the regular parent, but also keep in mind that they're not. They're just not the biological parent." For a code of 4 (i.e., the stepparent has no obligations), a mother said, "I don't think he has that obligation because they're not his kids." A stepson in the same stepfamily declared, "Nothing, because they're not related, they're not theirs. It's nice if they do take care of them, but they shouldn't have to."

The results indicated that almost one half (47%) of the stepparents' responses were coded as 1 (i.e., the nuclear family model), whereas only 27% of both parents' and stepchildren's responses were assigned this code. Only one fourth (23%) of stepparents' responses were coded as 2 (i.e., secondary, supportive role), in contrast to 40% and 45% of parents' and stepchildren's responses, respectively. There were no differences among stepfamily members in the two remaining codes; 23% to 29% of all three family members' responses were coded as 3 (i.e., almost a parent) and 0% to 7% were coded as 4 (i.e., no obligations to stepchildren).

These results suggest that, even among a sample of fairly long-term stepfamilies, the members of the oldest dyad in a stepfamily—the parent and the child—have views of the stepparent's obligations that differ from those of the stepparent.

In particular, stepparents were more likely to proclaim that their obligations were no different than they would be if the child were their "own" than were either parents or stepchildren. Perhaps the parent and stepchild, because of their shared history together and experiences adapting to life in a single-parent family, feel that they do not need much from the stepparent. In addition, parents and children also know that another parent outside of the immediate household may assume some obligations to meet the children's needs. By contrast, stepparents, perhaps because they may have the unrealistic expectations that stepkin can and should instantly love one another and that the stepfamily is functionally equivalent to a first-marriage family (Visher & Visher, 1988), feel that it is important that they assume all obligations for the stepchild that one has for a biological child. A stepparent, while knowing that the nonresidential parent is a potential support to the child, may still believe that it is his or her responsibility, as the residential adult, to meet the child's needs.

Gender differences in perceptions of what it means to be a parent may also be a factor in explaining this difference between parents and stepparents. Men may be more likely than women to define being a parent in terms of providing financially for their stepchildren. Thus, although stepfathers and mothers were equally likely to label the ideal stepparent role as that of a parent, stepfathers may have defined the term *parent* in a narrower, more financial way than mothers.

Clarity of the Stepparent Role

As shown in Table 12.2, ratings of role clarity were generally in the middle range on the 1–7 scale of the SRCI, suggesting that family members were moderately clear about the role of the stepparent. In addition, two sets of analyses were conducted to compare family members' role clarity scores. First, a one-factor (stepfamily member) repeated-measure ANOVA was conducted on the composite SRCI score. As shown in the table, parents and stepchildren reported having a clearer perception of the stepparent role than did stepparents. Stepchildren's perceptions did not differ from those of their parents. Second, correlations were computed between each pair of stepfamily members' SRCI scores. Whereas stepparents' and parents' scores were significantly correlated ($r = .59$), stepchildren's scores were not correlated with either their parents' or their stepparents'.

A quote from one of the stepfathers nicely illustrates the lack of role clarity that many stepparents felt. A stepfather in a long-term stepfamily, when asked if there was a change in his thinking regarding the best way to be a stepparent, stated:

> I probably never did know how to be one (stepparent). You know, no one ever told me that, "Hey, you're a stepparent, and it's ABC now, and that's your responsibility, that's your role, these are the things you should do, these are the things you shouldn't do, and these are the things that you should look out for. So, nobody gave me that advice. As a matter of fact, I don't remember anybody giving me any advice at all about that. But it's like, "Wait a minute. There are some things here that somebody should

have told me somewhere, that you have to look out for this" or "This is just a natural part of being a stepparent."

Perceived Stepparent Role Behavior

Affinity-Seeking and Affinity-Maintaining Behaviors. Using our interview data, we explored the nature of the stepparents' attempts to elicit liking from the stepchildren and the success of these efforts in developing and maintaining close stepparent–stepchild relationships (Ganong et al., 1997). There were three relatively distinct patterns of affinity-seeking and affinity-maintaining strategies among the stepparents in our sample.

First, *nonseeking* (NS) stepparents did not do anything intentionally to elicit liking from their stepchildren and seldom thought much about this issue. These stepparents were not unfriendly to their stepchildren; in fact, usually in group outings and activities, they were often quite nice to the children who would later be their stepchildren. However, the primary goal of these friendly interactions was to solidify the romantic relationship with the child's parent, not the relationship with the child. These stepparents did not seem to think that eliciting liking from stepchildren was an important goal for them.

Second, *early affinity-seeking* (EAS) stepparents were motivated and tried to elicit liking from the stepchildren early in the relationships (typically while they were also trying to achieve other goals, such as courting the children's parents), but they stopped doing so relatively early in the relationships (usually after they began to share residences). These stepparents generally thought of themselves as the children's new parents and they identified their role as that of being a parent (not a stepparent) to the child. Our sense was that these stepparents stopped trying to elicit liking from their stepchildren primarily because they did not believe that parents should have to actively try to get their children to like them.

Third, *continuous affinity-seeking* (CAS) stepparents deliberately sought to elicit liking from their stepchildren-to-be, and they persisted in these efforts (although at a decreased frequency) after the stepfamily was formed. These stepparents thought about how they could get their stepchildren to like them, they did things with their stepchildren that the stepchildren wanted to do (as opposed to what the stepparent wanted to do or thought the stepchildren should do), and they seemed genuinely interested in establishing close relationships with the stepchildren. It is not surprising that these stepparents also were more likely to have stepchildren who themselves tried to elicit liking from their stepparents.

Quality of Stepparent–Stepchild Interaction. From the behavioral observation tapes, we compared our global ratings of the quality of stepparent–stepchild interaction (on the dimensions of affect, amount of interaction, cooperation, and conflict) with those of the parent–child interaction. Across the 16 families, we consistently rated parent–child interaction more positively than that between stepparents and stepchildren on the dimensions of affect, amount of interaction, and cooperation, although there were no differences in conflict between the two types of dyads. Thus, the most salient difference was not that stepparent–stepchild interaction was more antagonistic than parent–child interaction but rather that it was characterized by less positive affect, interaction, and cooperation.

Adjustment Correlates of Role Constructions

We examined the adjustment correlates of three aspects of stepfamily members' role constructions by correlating the dyadic-level consistency scores with the adjustment scores, correlating scores from the SRCI with the adjustment scores, and comparing our independently assessed levels of closeness in the stepparent–stepchild relationship (from the interviews) across the three categories of stepfathers derived from the affinity-seeking and affinity-maintaining data.

Adjustment Correlates of Consistency in Content of the Stepparent Role. To examine whether there was a link between the extent to which stepfamily members had consistent role perceptions and adjustment, we correlated the ideal and actual warmth and control role discrepancy scores (stepparent–parent and stepparent–stepchild) with the adjustment scores. Because of the large number of correlations, an alpha level of .01 was used. Tables presenting these correlations can be found in Fine et al. (1998).

All significant correlations were in the expected direction (i.e., larger discrepancy scores were related to poorer adjustment). Higher stepparent–parent ideal discrepancy scores were related to lower levels of stepparents' satisfaction with stepparenting (only on the warmth discrepancy score), parents' reports of less close stepparent–stepchild relationships, parents' (only on warmth) and stepparents' perceptions of less success as a stepparent, and parents' and stepparents' reports of fewer family strengths (only on warmth). Few of the correlations between the stepparent–stepchild ideal role discrepancy score and the adjustment measures were significant.

With respect to correlations between the actual warmth and control discrepancy scores and the adjustment scores, the actual stepparent–parent discrepancy score was related in the hypothesized direction to many of the interpersonal and family-level adjustment measures. Smaller discrepancy scores were related to stepchildren's reports of fewer mental health symptoms (only on the control discrepancy score), greater life satisfaction (for stepparents on control and for parents on warmth), stepparents' greater satisfaction with stepparenting, closer stepparent–stepchild relationships, perceived success as a stepparent, greater marital satisfaction (only for stepparents on warmth), and more family strengths. The correlations between the actual stepparent–stepchild discrepancy scores and the adjustment measures were generally nonsignificant.

Adjustment Correlates of Role Clarity.   Several patterns were found in the correlations between the role clarity and adjustment scores (see Fine et al., 1998). First, stepparents' and parents' role clarity scores, but not stepchildren's, were related to the perceived closeness of the stepparent–stepchild relationship and perceived success as a stepparent. Second, stepparents' role clarity scores were related to all three family members' perceptions of greater family strengths. Finally, stepparents' and parents' role clarity scores were related to greater satisfaction with stepparenting. In sum, there was moderate support for the notion that stepparent role clarity is positively linked to the interpersonal dimensions of adjustment in stepfamilies.

Adjustment Correlates of Affinity-Seeking and Affinity-Maintaining Strategies.   The three groups of stepparents defined by differences in affinity-seeking and affinity-maintaining behaviors differed substantially in the ratings we assigned to the closeness of the stepparent–stepchild relationship. In all but one instance, continuous affinity-seeking (CAS) stepparents had warm and close bonds with their stepchildren. The early affinity-seeking (EAS) stepparents had relationships with their stepchildren that varied in closeness. Those who had close bonds with their stepchildren—as did the CAS stepparents—had stepchildren who themselves recognized and reciprocated the stepparent's affinity-seeking efforts. EAS stepparents who were not close to their stepchildren generally had stepchildren who did not know that their stepparents had tried to get them to like them. In addition, the early disciplinary attempts of some EAS stepparents were often resented by stepchildren, particularly older ones, and seemed to reduce closeness in the stepparent–stepchild relationship. It is not surprising that stepchildren of nonseeking (NS) stepparents were consistently not close to their stepparents, nor did they acknowledge or reciprocate the stepparent's infrequent attempts to elicit liking from them.

DISCUSSION

Our inquiry into the way that the stepparent role is socially constructed by stepfamily members was enhanced because we used three different sources of information: quantitative surveys, qualitative semistructured interviews, and behavioral observation. Few studies of stepfamilies have used all three of these approaches, and to our knowledge, previous researchers studying the stepparent role have not tried to integrate findings across these diverse methods.

Constructions of the Content of the Stepparent Role

What have we learned about how the content of the stepparent role is constructed by stepfamily members? First, consistent with the notion that there is a lack of social consensus related to the role of the stepparent (Cherlin, 1978; Crosbie-Burnett, 1989), we found considerable variation in perceptions of the appropriate label for the actual and the ideal stepparent role. Although nearly half the parents and stepparents labeled the ideal and current role of stepparents to be that of a parent, the remaining half assigned varying labels—including stepparent, friend, and a variety of other labels—to both the ideal and current stepparent role.

Second, our results converged toward the conclusion that stepparents generally believe that they should play a more active role in parenting than do their stepchildren and, on some dimensions, than their spouses. For example, stepparents (and parents) were more likely to report that the actual stepparent role or ideal stepparent role was that of parent or stepparent than were stepchildren, and stepparents reported that they should engage in warmth and control parenting behaviors more often than did stepchildren. Similar results were obtained from the interview data pertaining to perceptions of stepparents' obligations to their stepchildren. Stepfathers were more likely than either parents or stepchildren to report that they had the same obligations as did fathers, which is partially consistent with Ganong et al.'s (1995) finding that stepparents are believed to have financial obligations to their residential stepchildren as long as they are married to the children's parents.

Collectively, our results suggest that the adults in a stepfamily often attempt to recreate their families in the image of a first-marriage, nuclear family. Rather than constructing an image of how the stepparent should function that is tailored to the unique aspects of the stepfamily situation, most adults believe that the stepparent should function as a parent or as a parent-like figure to the stepchild. Our findings further indicate that the stepparent is the family member most likely to adopt the nuclear family model and that the stepchild is the least likely to do so. This conclusion is strengthened by a finding not reported previously in this chapter; almost 40% of the stepparents reported that they did not consider themselves to be stepparents, despite the fact that only one of the stepparents had legally adopted her stepchildren. Although a number of stepfamily scholars have speculated that this construction of the stepfamily as a nuclear family may be maladaptive (Visher & Visher, 1988), our results do not directly address this issue.

In terms of leadership and influence, we found some tentative evidence that the parent assumes the major responsibility for leadership, serving as a manager of family activities, but that both the stepparent and parent have influence on the family decision-making process. In the behavioral observation task, we rated the mother as the leader in facilitating the group process the majority of the time but also found that the stepfather and the mother both had influence in the decision-making process.

Constructions of the Clarity of the Stepparent Role

Stepfamily members reported having moderately clear perceptions of the stepparent role. Stepparents reported being less clear about the stepparent role than did parents and stepchildren. Because stepparents live the role of the stepparent on a daily basis and must continually make decisions about how to behave towards their stepchild(ren), it makes sense that they would be more aware of their uncertainties concerning how they should behave than would other family members. In addition, because the stepparent–parent dyad is most likely to discuss the stepparent role and how it should be enacted, it is not surprising that their role clarity scores would be highly intercorrelated. By contrast, stepchildren's views appear to be unrelated to those of their parents and stepparents, which may be developmentally characteristic of children in a variety of family structures.

When roles lack clarity, family members can redefine the role in a way that attempts to increase role clarity to them or they can creatively construct role definitions out of family discussions. About half the adults in our sample may have chosen the former method to resolve a lack of clarity surrounding the stepparent role. By defining the role of stepparent as that of a parent, family members may hope to increase family consensus regarding the role, thereby reducing interpersonal difficulties. The remaining half of the adults and the majority of stepchildren, however, chose other labels to describe the stepparent's current and ideal role.

Perceived Stepparent Role Behavior

As noted earlier, many stepparents reported that they believed that they should act as a parent to their stepchildren. However, we noted from the interviews that many did so in a more limited way than did the parent. This lesser involvement by some of the stepparents was reflected in a number of ways: Some reported that they had not made much of an effort to be involved in their stepchildren's lives, with some regretting this choice later. A sizeable minority made no deliberate attempts to elicit liking from their stepchildren, and several others made initial attempts but did not continue these efforts after the remarriage. Our behavioral observation data also showed that stepfathers and stepchildren had interactions that were characterized by less positive affect, engagement, and cooperation than were interactions between parents and children.

The apparent discrepancy between constructions of the content of the stepparent role and perceived role behavior may be due to variations in constructions of what it means to be a parent. If stepparents thought of being a parent primarily in terms of financially supporting their stepchildren, then their behavior was not inconsistent with their reported role construction. However, if they thought of a parent as someone who provides emotional support and disciplines stepchildren, in addition to financially providing for them, then the discrepancy takes on greater salience.

Relations Between Role Content, Clarity, and
Perceived Behavior and Adjustment in Stepfamilies

Our results provide some initial, moderate support for the notion that consistency among stepfamily members in perceptions of the stepparent role is related to a number of interpersonal dimensions of adjustment in stepfamilies. In particular, perceptions of how the role is currently being enacted were more strongly related to adjustment in stepfamilies than was consistency in perceptions of the ideal step-parent role. Because the stepparent's behavior affects family members on a regular basis, family members more likely are aware of, express, and discuss their perceptions of how the stepparent is currently behaving than they are aware of their perceptions of how the stepparent should behave, which increases the salience of consistency in these perceptions.

As predicted, the more confident stepparents were about how to interact with their stepchildren and the more sure parents were about how their spouse should relate to their child, the more satisfied they were with a number of interpersonal aspects of stepfamily life. Stepchildren's perceptions of the clarity of the stepparent role, in contrast, were unrelated to their satisfaction, suggesting that they are less bothered by the lack of clarity regarding the stepparent role than are adults. Clarity about the stepparent role may have less relevance for stepchildren than for adults because the stepchildren have less control over how the stepparent role is per-formed than do parents and stepparents.

In aggregate, these studies suggest that constructions of the stepparent role are related to the risk the family members face for poor adjustment and to their resi-lience in adapting to the challenges of stepfamily life. In particular, our findings suggest that consistent views of the stepparent role, role clarity, and active and con-tinuous affinity-seeking and affinity-maintaining efforts by the stepparent serve to reduce risk and enhance resiliency to the inevitable stresses of living in a stepfam-ily. In the next section, we present suggestions for future research that we believe will extend our knowledge of factors that lessen risk and enhance resilience.

DIRECTIONS FOR FUTURE RESEARCH
ON THE STEPPARENT ROLE

Our findings provide some direction for future research into the manner in which the stepparent role is constructed. First, investigators need to gather richer and more detailed information about perceptions of the stepparent role. For example, because one common theme that emerged from our project was that stepchildren have perceptions of the stepparent role that are quite different from those of their parents and stepparents, future researchers could profitably examine these differ-ing perceptions in greater depth, perhaps with qualitative interviews. In addition, it could be fruitful to examine what men mean when they state that they should treat the stepchild as their own. What kinds of responsibilities and obligations does that entail for these men?

Second, with longitudinal designs, we would be able to determine if and how perceptions of various aspects of the stepparent role change over the life course of the stepfamily. This is a critical issue to examine because some ways of construing the stepparent role may be growth producing at one stage of the family life course, whereas a different role construction may be necessary at a later stage or as circumstances change.

Third, although we touched on this tangentially in the semistructured interviews, future researchers would do well not only to include the nonresidential parent in data collection efforts but also to explore how this parent and his or her role perceptions and behavior affect functioning within the stepfamily household. Our sense was that the nonresidential parent often influenced the nature and quality of the stepparent–stepchild relationship and, thus, the manner in which the role of the stepparent is constructed.

Finally, and perhaps most important, if subsequent studies document both concurrent and prospective relations between role perceptions and adjustment in stepfamilies, researchers need to turn their attention to trying to identify the mechanisms underlying these relations. To what extent do stepfamily members discuss their perceptions of the stepparent role, and what are the outcomes and consequences of these discussions, if they occur? How do constructions of the stepparent role and changes in these constructions affect later adjustment? In what ways do these constructions affect role behaviors?

REFERENCES

Anderson, S. A., & Sabatelli, R. M. (1995). *Family interaction: A multigenerational developmental perspective.* Needham Heights, MA: Allyn & Bacon.

Beavers, W. R., Hampson, R. B., & Hulgus, Y. F. (1985). The Beavers systems approach to family assessment. *Family Process, 24,* 398–405.

Borduin, C. M. (1990). *Observational coding system: University of Missouri-Columbia Delinquency Project.* Unpublished manuscript.

Bray, J. H., Berger, S. H., & Boethel, C. L. (1994). Role integration and marital adjustment in stepfather families. In K. Pasley & M. Ihinger-Tallman (Eds.), *Stepparenting: Issues in theory, research, and practice* (pp. 69–86). Westport, CT: Greenwood.

Buehlman, K. T., Gottman, J. M., & Katz, J. F. (1992). How a couple views their past predicts their future: Predicting divorce from an oral history interview. *Journal of Family Psychology, 5,* 295–318.

Cherlin, A. (1978). Remarriage as an incomplete institution. *American Journal of Sociology, 84,* 634–650.

Crosbie-Burnett, M. (1989). Application of family stress theory to remarriage: A model for assessing and helping stepfamilies. *Family Relations, 38,* 323–331.

DeRogatis, L. R. (1993). *Brief Symptom Inventory: Administration, scoring, and procedures manual.* Minneapolis, MN: National Computer Systems.

Diener, E., Emmons, R. A., Larsen, R. J., & Griffin, S. (1985). The satisfaction with life scale. *Journal of Personality Assessment, 49,* 71–75.

Erera-Weatherly, P. I. (1996). On becoming a stepparent: Factors associated with the adoption of alternative stepparenting styles. *Journal of Divorce and Remarriage, 25,* 155–174.

Fine, M. A., Coleman, M., & Ganong, L. H. (1998). Consistency in the perceptions of the stepparent role among stepparents, biological parents, and stepchildren. *Journal of Social and Personal Relationships, 15,* 811–829.

Fine, M. A., Ganong, L. H., & Coleman, M. (1997). The relation between role constructions and adjustment among stepfathers. *Journal of Family Issues, 18,* 503–525.

294   FINE, COLEMAN, GANONG

Fine, M. A., & Kurdek, L. A. (1994a). A multidimensional cognitive-developmental model of stepfamily adjustment. In K. Pasley & M. Ihinger-Tallman (Eds.), *Stepparenting: Issues in theory, research, and practice* (pp. 15–32). Westport, CT: Greenwood.

Fine, M. A., & Kurdek, L. A. (1994b). Parenting cognitions in stepfamilies: Differences between parents and stepparents and relations to parenting satisfaction. *Journal of Social and Personal Relationships, 11,* 95–112.

Fine, M. A., Kurdek, L. A, & Hennigen, L. (1992). Perceived self-competence and its relations to stepfamily myths and (step)parent role ambiguity in adolescents from stepfather and stepmother families. *Journal of Family Psychology, 6,* 69–76.

Ganong, L. H., & Coleman, M. (1989). *Stepfamily Unrevealed Differences Questionnaire.* Unpublished instrument, University of Missouri, Columbia.

Ganong, L. H., & Coleman, M. (1994). Adolescent stepchild–stepparent relationships: Changes over time. In K. Pasley & M. Ihinger-Tallman (Eds.), *Stepparenting: Issues in theory, research, and practice* (pp. 87–104). Westport, CT: Greenwood.

Ganong, L. H., Coleman, M., Fine, M. A., & Martin, P. (in press). Stepparents' affinity-seeking and affinity-maintaining strategies with stepchildren. *Journal of Family Issues.*

Ganong, L. H., Coleman, M., & Mistina, D. (1995). Normative beliefs about parents' and stepparents' financial obligations to children following divorce and remarriage. *Family Relations, 44,* 306–315.

Kahn, R. L., Wolfe, D. M., Quinn, R. P., Snoek, J. D., & Rosenthal, R. A. (1964). *Occupational stress: Studies in role conflict and ambiguity.* New York: Wiley.

Kurdek, L. A., & Fine, M. A. (1991). Cognitive correlates of adjustment for mothers and fathers in stepfather families. *Journal of Marriage and the Family, 53,* 565–572.

Marsiglio, W. (1992). Stepfathers with minor children living at home: Parenting perceptions and relationship quality. *Journal of Family Issues, 13,* 195–214.

Olson, D. H., Larsen, A. S., & McCubbin, H. I. (1982). Family strengths. In D. H. Olson, H. I. McCubbin, H. Barnes, A. Larsen., M. Muxen, & M. Wilson (Eds.), *Family inventories: Inventories used in a national survey of families across the family life cycle* (pp. 121–134). St. Paul, MN: University of Minnesota, Department of Family Social Science.

Patton, M. Q. (1990). *Qualitative evaluation and research methods.* Newbury Park, CA: Sage.

Schumm, W. R., Paff-Bergen, L. A., Hatch, R. C., Obiorah, F. C., Copeland, J. M., Meens, L. D., & Bugaighis, M. A. (1986). Concurrent and discriminant validity of the Kansas Marital Satisfaction Scale. *Journal of Marriage and the Family, 48,* 381–387.

Schwebel, A. I., Fine, M. A., & Renner, M. A. (1991). An empirical investigation of perceptions of the stepparent role. *Journal of Family Issues, 12,* 43–57.

Sweet, J. A., Bumpass, L. L., & Call, V. R. A. (1988). *The design and content of the National Survey of Families and Households* (Working Paper NSFH-1). Madison, WI: University of Wisconsin, Center for Demography and Ecology.

Tannen, D. (1990). *You just don't understand: Women and men in conversation.* New York: Ballentine.

Thomas, V., & Olson, D. H. (1993). Problem families and the Circumplex Model: Observational assessment using the Clinical Rating Scale (CRS). *Journal of Marital and Family Therapy, 19,* 159–175.

Visher, E., & Visher, J. S. (1988). *Old loyalties, new ties.* New York: Brunner/Mazel.

Visher, E. B., & Visher, J. S. (1996). *Therapy with stepfamilies.* New York: Brunner/Mazel.

13

The Dynamics
of Parental Remarriage
Adolescent, Parent, and Sibling Influences

Edward R. Anderson
Shannon M. Greene
Arizona State University

E. Mavis Hetherington
University of Virginia

W. Glenn Clingempeel
Francis Marion University

THIS CHAPTER is concerned with the transition of parental remarriage and its implications for children's well-being. We start by examining adolescent adjustment in remarried families, focusing on externalizing, which includes acting out, antisocial behavior, noncompliance, and aggression. Consistent with many other studies of remarriage, we demonstrate that adolescents living in stepfamilies are at higher risk for these problematic behaviors than those living in nondivorced households.[1] We then examine possible reasons for why the higher levels of externalizing occur in stepchildren, including the role of stressful life events for adolescents and the quality of family relationships. A major theme from these analyses is the reciprocal relation between adolescent adjustment and family process measures. Said another way, adolescents in stepfamilies are important products of and contributors to the stepfamily experience.

---

[1] We use the term *nondivorced families* to refer to families where the two residential parents are in an original marriage.

THE LONGITUDINAL STUDY OF REMARRIAGE

The data presented here come from the Hetherington and Clingempeel Longitudinal Study of Remarriage (LSR; Hetherington et al., 1992), an intensive study of 202 families with a child between the ages of 9 and 13. Approximately one third of the families were those in which the mother had divorced, retained custody of her children, and was in the first few months of a remarriage. Another third of the families consisted of divorced mothers who had not remarried. They had been divorced for approximately the same length of time as the remarried mothers. The remaining group of families contained couples who were not divorced. All families were Caucasian, and parents had at least a high school education. Families were assessed three times over the course of a 2-year period, corresponding to 4, 17, and 26 months after their remarriages.

The LSR used an intensive battery of instruments designed to yield comparable information across multiple informants, derived from structured interviews and standardized assessments. For example, perceived quality of the stepfather–stepchild relationship was obtained from each adolescent, stepfather, and mother. In addition, family members were videotaped in dyads and triads, and these tapes were rated by trained observers across various aspects of global family functioning. Family functioning was derived from composites formed from observational measures and self-report measures from multiple informants. Adolescent externalizing behavior was derived from mothers, (step)fathers, teachers, adolescents, and videotaped observations of adolescents interacting with family members. A composite measure of externalizing was created by aggregating these measures in standard score form.

ADOLESCENT ADJUSTMENT IN REMARRIED FAMILIES

Do adolescents in stepfamilies fare less well than adolescents living in continuously married families? An estimate of the total effect of remarriage on adolescents' externalizing behavior is made by using the multimethod, multi-informant measure of externalizing and creating an effect code (Aiken & West, 1991) representing the classification of remarried versus nondivorced. Using the composite measure assessed at 4 months after remarriage, the effect code represents the total average difference in initial level of externalizing across remarried and nondivorced groups. In addition, because the study was longitudinal, we can examine the influence of remarriage on change in externalizing. This latter question is addressed through the use of growth curve analysis (e.g., McArdle & Anderson, 1990). For each subject, a linear growth curve is calculated based on available data. This procedure provides a slope score for each adolescent, which indicates the rate of change in externalizing across the 2 years of the study. An effect code for remarriage that significantly predicts this slope score indicates that adolescents in remarried families increase in externalizing at significantly faster rates than counterparts in nondivorced families.

The correlation between the effect code and outcome was .36, meaning that the experience of remarriage explains 13% of the variance in adolescent externalizing behavior 4 months into the remarriage. The longitudinal relation of $\beta = .23$ indicates that adolescents in remarried families grow at faster rates in externalizing than adolescents in nondivorced families, even after controlling for the initial level of behavior. Thus, differences in externalizing between adolescents in stepfamilies and nondivorced families are apparent in the first months after remarriage, and on average, externalizing increases at a faster rate for adolescents in remarried families.

WHAT ACCOUNTS FOR ADOLESCENT ADJUSTMENT IN STEPFAMILIES?

The primary theoretical question, then, is to identify those factors that account for the differences in adolescent externalizing behavior between remarried and nondivorced families. In this section, we address how co-occurring stressful life events and distressed stepfamily relationships may account for these differences in adolescent adjustment. First, we examine whether life events and relationship quality are associated with adolescents' externalizing behavior within remarried families. The focus is to identify those factors that explain externalizing behavior for adolescents across remarried families. Next, we examine whether life events and relationship quality account for differences in externalizing between remarried and nondivorced families. These factors are examined in an attempt to remove the between-group difference identified by the effect code described previously. It is possible, however, to identify a factor that leads to improved functioning for stepfamilies but without enough of a boost to close the gap between remarried and nondivorced families completely. The role of co-occurring stressful life experiences and distressed relationships (i.e., parent–child, current marital, former marital, and sibling) in explaining children's externalizing behavior each are considered in turn.

Stressful Life Events and Adolescent Adjustment

In addition to establishing relationships with stepparents, adolescents whose custodial parent remarries often encounter a variety of significant other transitions. In order to assess these transitions, we asked adolescents to identify which of 57 possible events or relationship changes had occurred since the remarriage (or since the last interview in later waves) and to rate their corresponding reactions on a 7-point scale from −3 (*extremely negative*) to +3 (*extremely positive*).

Perhaps the most telling finding lies in adolescent responses to a single item on this inventory, "parent remarried." The mean stress rating was a positive 1.55,

298 ANDERSON ET AL.

meaning that, on average, an adolescent experiences the custodial parent's remarriage as moderately positive. Individual responses ranged from −3 to +3, indicating a wide diversity in adolescent reactions to this transition. Overall, though, 65% of adolescents scored remarriage at or above +2, whereas only 12% gave a negative rating (−1, −2, or −3) to this event. Because this question was asked only once, we cannot tell if ratings would have changed over time.

It is not surprising that the event most commonly associated with parental remarriage involved relocation, with about half (52%) moving to a new residence. For many, the move required an additional transition: starting a new school. Yet only about 20% of adolescents in remarried families perceived these experiences as negative, with the average rating for both moving and starting a new school at +1.5 (i.e., a moderately positive event).

Additionally, important differences between adolescents in nondivorced and remarried families emerged. As opposed to counterparts in nondivorced families, adolescents in remarried families reported more arguments with their parents 4 months after the remarriage. This difference may reflect in part increases in stresses and challenges that the parents themselves encounter early in remarriage. In contrast, one year later the adolescents in the *nondivorced* families reported an increase in such arguments. Figure 13.1 shows this change in frequency of family arguments.

Perhaps adolescents in remarried families were merely experiencing the normative increase in difficult parent–adolescent relationships earlier than other adolescents because of the reorganization required by the remarriage. An analysis of this

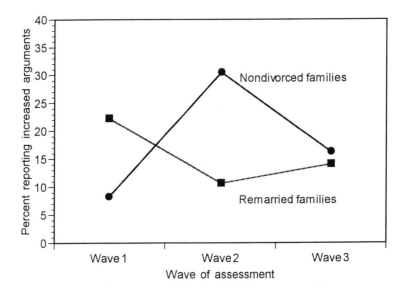

FIG. 13.1. Change in frequency of arguments between parents and adolescents.

idea of accelerated development has been described previously (Anderson, Hetherington, & Clingempeel, 1989). In that paper, we demonstrated that associations commonly found in nondivorced families between the child's pubertal status and parent–child relationship quality did not occur for stepfamilies in the first months after remarriage. It is possible that the reorganization required by the remarriage temporarily disrupted this normative developmental process. Alternatively, the decrease in arguments could be a sign of increasing disengagement from the stepfamily, as has been found in other stepfamily studies (e.g., Hetherington, Cox, & Cox, 1985).

As opposed to counterparts in nondivorced families, by the end of the first year, adolescents in remarried families were more commonly reporting fewer money problems for their families, an undoubtedly welcome experience. Several of the adolescents in remarried families reported the birth of a sibling to the new family, an experience less likely to have occurred in nondivorced families. Interestingly, the new sibling arrival was universally positive; none of the adolescents in the sample who had this experience rated it negatively. By 2 years into the remarriage, many adolescents also reported that their parents started school, again an experience less likely to occur in nondivorced families. Only a small proportion (15%) viewed this change as negative. Finally, as compared to nondivorced families, 2 years into the remarriage, adolescents reported more frequent dates, a positively rated experience offset by a negative—more frequent fights with boyfriends or girlfriends.

Further analyses of the LSR provide continued support for adolescents viewing their custodial parent's remarriage positively. As part of the LSR, adolescents could identify from a list of adjectives any that described their reactions to remarriage, such as "happy," "angry with mother," "hurt," or "pleased." The most frequent were all positive: "happy," checked by 82% of adolescents, "satisfied" (75%), and "pleased" (66%). The most frequently checked negative item was "jealous," experienced by only 18% of adolescents.

Mothers provide additional evidence for the generally positive adolescent reactions to remarriage. Using the same list of adjectives, mothers described their children's responses to the remarriage as well as to the earlier divorce. Although mothers generally rated adolescent reactions to the divorce as negative (i.e., "sad," "hurt," and "fearful"), reactions to remarriage corroborated views expressed by adolescents—"happy," "satisfied," and "pleased."

In summary, the vast majority of adolescents view their custodial parents' remarriages as positive events. Only a small minority (15–20%) expressed negative attitudes. How might these relatively positive attitudes toward remarriage be reconciled with the significantly higher levels of behavior problems shown by adolescents in stepfamilies?

Adolescents entering stepfamilies have experienced many transitions before the legal remarriage: conflict in the previous marriage, parental separation and divorce, cohabitation of the biological mother and stepfather or other partners before remarriage (experienced by most of the adolescents in the LSR stepfamilies), and transition into a stepfamily. Additionally, many custodial mothers in the LSR had dated extensively prior to remarriage, and earlier analyses of this data set showed that a history of frequent dating related to less positive adolescent adjustment and more difficult parent–adolescent relationships after the remarriage (Montgomery, Anderson, Hetherington, & Clingempeel, 1992). Moreover, some adolescents in the study had also experienced the remarriage of their noncustodial father. The cumulative impact of these transitions was evident. The lowest levels of adolescent social competence were observed when all three marital transitions had occurred—divorce, the custodial parent's remarriage, and the noncustodial parent's remarriage (Fig. 13.2).

To examine how the experience of transitions accompanying remarriage related to an adolescent's adjustment in the LSR, we developed indicators of the general level of stress experienced by adolescents. We distinguished between life events typically experienced as negative by the majority of children, such as getting sick, damage to home, and death of a family member, and events that related to adjusting to new situations and family members (i.e., more commonly experienced by children in stepfamilies). These latter events included moving to a new home, starting at a new school, birth of a new sibling, and the stepparent moving in. To create an indicator of stress, we simply counted the number of events that occurred within these two categories. Adolescents in remarried and nondivorced families

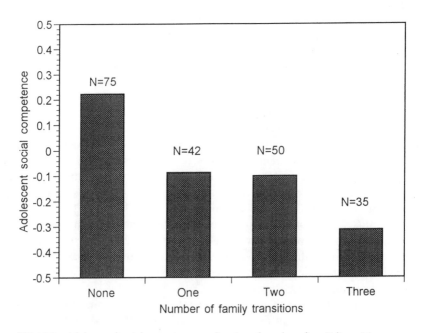

FIG. 13.2.   Adolescents' social competence as a function of number of marital transitions.

TABLE 13.1
Effect of Stressful Life Events on Initial Level
and Change in Adolescents' Externalizing

| | Regression Coefficients | | | |
| | Initial Level | | Change | |
	Without Remarriage	With Remarriage	Without Remarriage	With Remarriage
Predictors				
Negative stresses	.41***	.38***	.05	.06
Transition events	.14+	.01	.12	.02
Parental remarriage	—	.31***	—	.22*
Initial level of externalizing	—	—	−.45***	−.51***
R^2	.19	.26	.19	.22
d.f.	2,124	3,123	3,103	4,102
F	14.1***	14.4***	7.9***	7.3***

Note. $^+p < .10$; $^*p < .05$; $^{**}p < .01$; $^{***}p < .001$.

did not differ in the total number of negative stresses experienced, but adolescents in remarried families had significantly higher levels of transition events.

As shown in Table 13.1, the number of negative stresses was significantly related to adolescent externalizing behavior. The number of transitions experienced, however, was only marginally related to externalizing. In longitudinal analyses, neither transition events nor negative stresses predicted change in externalizing beyond what was accounted for by initial level.

When the effect code for parental remarriage was entered, negative stresses continued to relate significantly to externalizing problems. More important, the number of negative stressful events did not diminish the effect of parental remarriage. In other words, the negative impact of life stress on adolescent externalizing problems was independent of any effect of parental remarriage. In longitudinal analyses, parental remarriage continued to predict increases in adolescent externalizing after initial levels of externalizing and measures of stressful events were entered.

How can this finding be explained? First, the number of stressful events clearly matters for adolescent adjustment. Figure 13.3 shows the level of externalizing problems for adolescents with low (0, 1, or 2) and high (3 or more) numbers of stresses. In stepfamilies, those with more stresses fared less well than those with fewer stresses. This finding was also true for adolescents in nondivorced families. Importantly, though, the difference between family context remains. Adolescents in remarried families with low stress were approximately equivalent to adolescents in nondivorced families with high stress. Stress mattered, but it did not close the gap in functioning.

In summary, adolescents experiencing their custodial parents' remarriages encounter a number of co-occurring life transitions, such as moving to a new home,

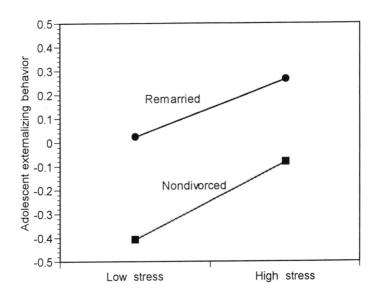

FIG. 13.3.   Adolescents' externalizing behavior in nondivorced and remarried families as a function of low and high numbers of stressful life events.

starting a new school, or adjusting to living with new siblings. Most adolescents, however, do not perceive these events as negative, although a minority, perhaps 15%, do. Importantly, it is not the cumulative experience of transitions that explains the elevated levels of conduct problems for adolescents in remarried families compared to nondivorced families. Adolescents who experience more negative events do show more problems, but the difference in adjustment between types of households remains. In the next section, we examine aspects of parent–adolescent relationships that might account for differences in adolescent adjustment between stepfamily and nondivorced households.

Parent–Adolescent Relationships

General Parenting Style.   Prior research provides ample support for the benefits to children of authoritative parenting (i.e., high levels of warmth and responsiveness, effective monitoring and control of children's behavior, enforcing and following through on rules, low levels of coercion and conflict). A common explanation for why children show elevated problems in remarried families is that such parenting-related processes become disrupted, particularly during the period of adjustment to remarriage. Many studies, in fact, find temporary increases in conflict and negativity during the first year of adjustment to remarriage (e.g., Bray, 1988; Hetherington, 1988, 1989). We have reported elsewhere (Hetherington et al., 1992) that the most difficult interpersonal challenge for remarried families is the development of constructive relationships between parents and their children. Over time, custodial mothers in remarried stepfather families seemed to negotiate this task effectively with their adolescent children. Initial high conflict and low monitoring and control gave way to levels similar to those in nondivorced families by 26 months after remarriage.

Relationships between stepfathers and their nonbiological stepchildren follow an opposite pattern, with difficulty increasing over time. Early after the remarriage, stepfathers themselves felt a lack of affection and rapport with their stepchildren but were acting toward their stepchildren in ways that appeared overtly positive or friendly, attempting to engage them in discussion and interaction—a pattern we have described previously as "polite strangers" (Hetherington et al., 1992). The responses of adolescents to these initiations, however, were frequently negative. As a consequence, stepfathers showed a relatively disengaged style of parenting, reporting little control or awareness of their stepchildren's activities and attempting to exert little discipline.

Previous studies of remarriage with younger children (Hetherington et al., 1985) have found that positive, supportive relationships with stepfathers are related to decreases in externalizing for boys. In prior analyses of the LSR, when the relation between parenting style and adolescent behavior was examined in stepfamilies, a clear, positive effect of authoritative parenting was found relative to other parenting styles, a finding that held across both custodial mothers and residential stepfathers (Hetherington et al., 1992). Figure 13.4 shows this relation. Adolescents in both family types benefited from the presence of an authoritative parent. As was found in the analyses for life stress, however, adolescents in stepfamilies reared by authoritative parents still showed higher levels of externalizing than those in nondivorced families who were reared by authoritative parents. In other words, offspring in stepfamilies under favorable parenting conditions fared about as well as those in nondivorced families under unfavorable parenting conditions.

Why do these differences in externalizing remain even after accounting for parenting style? It may be that particular aspects of parenting, such as coercive discipline or ineffective monitoring, are more salient in affecting adolescent behavior in stepfamilies than in nondivorced families. For example, the relative reluctance of stepfathers to engage in discipline may provide adolescents with opportunities to exploit any inconsistency in discipline between residential parents. This situation may provide the adolescent more frequent opportunities to engage in antisocial activities or fewer consequences for doing so. Thus, the next sections address parental contributions in more detail by examining first the role of monitoring and control and then the role of conflict, coercion, and punitiveness. Although authoritative parenting combines several broad dimensions (i.e., effective monitoring and control, low coercion, conflict, and punitiveness, together with involved and nurturant parenting), we have found in other analyses (Anderson, Lindner, & Bennion, 1992; Hetherington et al., 1985) that indices of parental warmth and involvement relate most strongly to positive outcomes of social and scholastic compe-

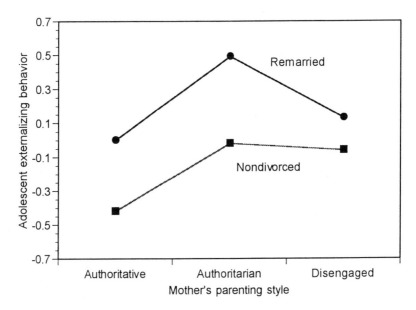

FIG. 13.4. Relation between adolescents' externalizing behavior and parenting type across nondivorced and remarried families. Authoritative parenting combines high nurturance with high control; authoritarian-conflictual parenting combines high conflict, coercion, and negativity with high control; and disengaged parenting combines low nurturance and involvement with low control and monitoring. Data from Anderson et al. (1992). Used with permission.

tence. Instead, this chapter focuses on adolescent externalizing problems, so the two dimensions of parenting most closely related to externalizing in adolescence, low parental monitoring and inept, coercive, conflictual discipline (Loeber & Stouthamer-Loeber, 1998; Patterson, 1982), are focused on.

Monitoring and Control. When a stepfather is introduced into the family, he may have limited knowledge and awareness about the child's life and activities, as compared to the custodial mother. The child, then, is likely to be exposed to inconsistent parental monitoring and control attempts between the residential mother and the stepfather, as well as between the residential and nonresidential parents. In fact, the adolescent may be keenly sensitive to what each parent knows and expects. In the LSR, adolescents reported on monitoring and control received from as many as three parents (i.e., custodial mothers, [step]fathers, nonresidential fathers), making possible a direct comparison of perceived consistency between different authorities in an adolescent's life.

To assess parental monitoring and control, adolescents used a 5-point scale to rate the extent of each parent's awareness and control over behavior in seven areas, such as choice of friends, school interests, and activities away from home. Cronbach alpha coefficients for a scale created from averaging these seven areas were above .79 for each parent at all three waves.

Mean level differences in parental control and monitoring are presented in Fig. 13.5. It is not surprising that adolescents view mothers as better monitors than fathers. This difference is smallest in nondivorced families and largest when comparing custodial mothers and nonresidential biological fathers. Parental differences are more marked for monitoring than for control.

Within stepfamilies, we can compare mean level differences across three different parents, as in Fig. 13.6. Again, mothers are rated highest, nonresidential fathers are rated lowest, and these parental differences are more marked for monitoring than for control. Parental differences are more apparent for girls than boys, primarily because of the greater degreee of involvement of nonresidential fathers in the lives of boys. Level of control is equivalent across parents for boys, whereas girls rate nonresidential fathers as less strict than residential parents.

The important question becomes whether variation in parental consistency relates to adolescent adjustment. Here, we focus on parental monitoring because the degree of parental differences was greater in this dimension. Parents were classified as either good monitors (i.e., usually or always knowing about their adolescent's behavior) or poor monitors (i.e., sometimes, rarely, or never knowing about their adolescent's behavior), based on the average score of the seven monitoring areas.

Mothers who were classified as good monitors at 4 months into the remarriage had adolescents who were consistently lower in externalizing throughout the 2 years of the study. Importantly, there were no interactions by family type for mothers, but there was an interaction of father's monitoring with family type, shown in Fig. 13.7. Although adolescents in stepfamilies evidenced more externalizing than adolescents in nondivorced families, those whose stepfathers started out as poor

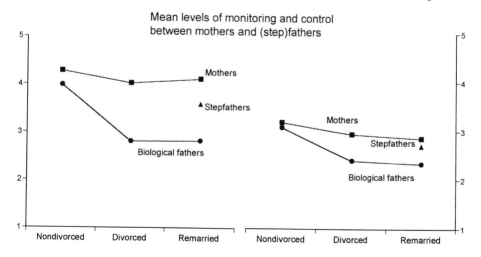

FIG. 13.5.   Mean differences between parents in monitoring and control in different family structures.

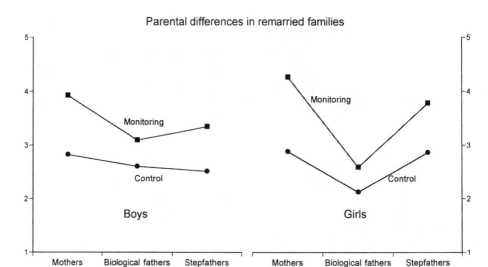

FIG. 13.6. Mean differences between parents in monitoring and control in remarried families.

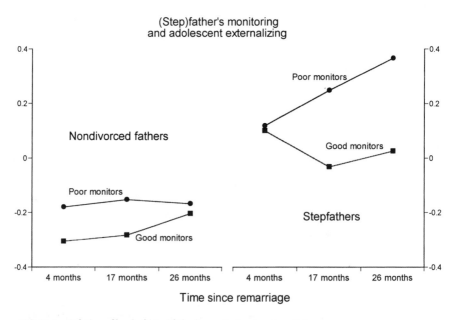

FIG. 13.7. Relation of level of (step)father's monitoring to externalizing.

monitors increased their externalizing over time. Thus, when stepfathers were good monitors in the first few months of remarriage, adolescents did not show higher levels of externalizing problems later.

Variation in knowledge among parents also has special significance for stepfamilies. The greater number of parental relationships within and across households provides adolescents with more opportunities for inconsistency in monitoring to develop. Discrepancy in knowledge among the parents involved in a remarried family is associated with higher levels of externalizing behavior in the adolescent. This effect on externalizing is obtained whether discrepancy occurs within ($r=.18$) or across ($r=.19$) households.

We examined whether consistency of monitoring explains the differences in externalizing between remarried and nondivorced families. Inconsistency across households was used for remarried families to obtain the greatest possible effect of remarriage; inconsistency was measured within households for adolescents in nondivorced families. From the adolescent's ratings, parents were classified as either consistent (i.e., identical scores were given to both parents on all seven areas) or inconsistent (i.e., different scores were given to parents). Inconsistency was related to externalizing, but only to initial differences ($r = .20$, $p < .05$), not change ($r = .03$). Similar to the previous analyses, inconsistency in parental awareness, even across households, did not explain the differences in problem behavior between remarried and nondivorced families.

In summary, similar to the findings presented thus far we find that inconsistent monitoring is a risk factor for stepfamilies; adolescents who receive poor monitoring from either residential parent or whose parents have discrepant knowledge of their activities evidence higher levels of externalizing problems. Even when adolescents in remarried families benefit from effective parental monitoring, a significant difference in externalizing problems remains, as compared to adolescents in nondivorced households receiving comparable levels of monitoring.

Negativity and Conflict. The second aspect of authoritative parenting considered in this chapter is the presence of negativity—coercive, conflictual, and punitive styles of parenting. In our analyses, within remarried families, respective levels of maternal and paternal negativity were correlated .53 and .42 with initial externalizing. Furthermore, prior work with this dataset shows higher levels of remarried mothers' but not stepfathers' negativity in comparison to mothers and fathers in nondivorced families (Hetherington et al., 1992). Thus, parental negativity, especially when involving mothers, might explain the deleterious effect of remarriage on externalizing. Yet when we entered these parenting variables in a regression along with the effect code of remarriage, remarriage remained significant. Similar to other variables explored thus far, negativity in parenting related to adolescent adjustment within stepfamilies but failed to explain adjustment differences between adolescents in nondivorced families and stepfamilies. In addition, neither mothers' nor (step)fathers' negativity predicted change in externalizing independent of parental remarriage or initial level of externalizing.

Adolescent-Driven Effects. Thus far we have found that although differences in parenting style between remarried and nondivorced households are quite marked, they fail to explain differences in adolescents' externalizing behavior across family type. One reason for this continued difference is the possibility that parents in remarried families are more reactive to their adolescents' externalizing behavior rather than proactive in preventing externalizing behavior. In an earlier analysis of the LSR that used cross-lag regression models (Hetherington et al., 1992), we found that parenting was unrelated to adolescent adjustment over time in remarried families but that the adolescents' behavior led to later changes in parenting for both mothers and stepfathers (Fig. 13.8). In contrast, for nondivorced families, parental behavior (i.e., negativity) predicted later levels of adolescent externalizing problems. When offspring are early adolescents at the time of remarriage, their parents react to rather than direct the adolescents' behavior in stepfamilies; adolescents are also unlikely to respond to parental attempts at socialization. Thus, the differences between remarried and nondivorced families in parent–adolescent negativity may well be due to the existing levels of problem behavior rather than the reverse.

We have found support for this notion of adolescent-driven effects in other analyses of the LSR (Deal, Anderson, Ratliff, Hetherington, & Clingempeel, 1990) in

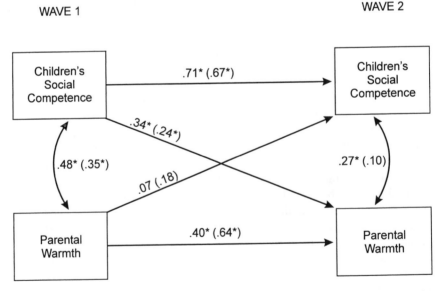

FIG. 13.8. Cross-lagged regression model with parental negativity and adolescents' externalizing for remarried families. From Anderson et al. (1992). Values for stepfathers in parentheses. Used with permission.

TABLE 13.2
Means (Standard Deviations) and Significant Effects
for Family Members' Actor and Partner Effects

| Effect | Nondivorced | | Remarried | | |
	Boys	Girls	Boys	Girls	Contrasts
Mother Actor	.79 (.32)	.79 (.32)	.88 (.43)	.88 (.35)	
Father Actor	.72 (.35)	.80 (.36)	.76 (.38)	.74 (.47)	
Child Actor	1.2 (.44)	1.2 (.39)	1.3 (.67)	1.5 (.52)	Rem > Non
Mother Partner	.65 (.27)	.68 (.29)	.66 (.30)	.70 (.30)	
Father Partner	.46 (.29)	.55 (.29)	.57 (.30)	.54 (.32)	
Child Partner	.84 (.33)	.89 (.33)	.91 (.42)	1.0 (.30)	Rem > Non

Note. Rem > Non = Family Type main effect; remarried higher than nondivorced.

which we conducted a social relations analysis (Kenny & LaVoie, 1984) using a round-robin interaction design. This analysis allowed us to partition behavior into a series of independent components: the average behavior for a group of persons; the actor effect, or the core behavior a person exhibits regardless of context; the partner effect, or the behavior that a person elicits from others; and the relationship effect, or the behavior that is unique to the particular relationship being observed.

For example, the adolescent's behavior toward the mother comprises the adolescent actor effect, the mother's partner effect, and the mother–adolescent relationship effect.[2] The adolescent's actor effect is observed in the adolescent–mother and adolescent–stepfather scores, but the mother partner effect is observed in the adolescent–mother and stepfather–mother scores; thus, each component is identified by a unique combination of scores.[3]

In this earlier analysis, we calculated actor and partner effects and found significant family type differences for negativity (see Table 13.2). Remarried families had significantly higher levels of adolescent actor and partner negativity. There were no family type differences with respect to parental actor and partner effects. Put simply, not only were adolescents in remarried families acting significantly more negatively toward their parents than were counterparts in nondivorced families, they also elicited more parental negativity. Thus, the higher levels of negative behavior displayed by mothers and stepfathers in remarried families compared to nondivorced families appeared to result primarily from children eliciting or provoking that negative behavior, rather than differences in the general dispositions of parents in remarried families.

In summary, the quality of parent–adolescent relationships does not account for most of the differences in externalizing across family types in part because of

[2] The Social Relations Model also includes a random error term for each score.
[3] In a round-robin design with only three individuals, the relationship effect in the Social Relations Model cannot be uniquely separated from the error term.

these adolescent-driven effects. There is also prior evidence that (step)parents in remarried families may be reactive to their adolescents' behavior, rather than active socializers of their offspring. Additionally, the LSR sample involved children entering adolescence, who were dealing with the developmental issues of self-regulation and interpersonal intimacy in relationships outside the family and becoming autonomous while maintaining attachment to the family. The combination of adaptation to parental remarriage and entry into adolescence, with its related developmental tasks, may be particularly difficult on adjustment, with adolescent-driven effects perhaps most prominent in these families.

We have found that stressful life events, parental negativity, and inept, inconsistent parental monitoring all contribute to adolescent externalizing within stepfamilies. None of these factors, however, provides an explanation for the observed initial differences in externalizing behavior between nondivorced families and stepfamilies. Moreover, none of the variables thus far have explained change in externalizing, independent of the remarriage. In the next sections, marital relationships between the custodial mothers and stepfathers, ongoing tensions between the divorced spouses, and sibling relationships are examined as possible mechanisms to explain between-family differences in adolescent conduct problems.

Current and Former Marital Relationships

Remarriages dissolve at higher rates and more quickly than first marriages, so perhaps the quality of the marital relationship informs about differences in adolescent adjustment. Using the LSR, we created a multirater, multimeasure variable of marital negativity to examine this possibility. Although marital negativity is unlikely to account for the initial level of externalizing (i.e., earlier analysis of the LSR showed no differences between first and second marriages on this measure at the initial wave of assessment; Hetherington et al., 1992), it may account for the effect of remarriage on change in externalizing.

Across remarried and nondivorced families, marital negativity is a significant predictor of initial level of adolescents' externalizing behavior ($r = .28, p < .01$), but does not predict change in externalizing ($\beta = .03$). With the effect code for remarriage entered, marital negativity remains a significant predictor of adolescents' behavior ($\beta = .27, p < .001$), but does not reduce the effect of remarriage. Parallel to findings for negativity in parent–adolescent relationships, marital negativity contributes to adolescent externalizing within the remarried sample. It does not, however, account for why adolescents in remarried families score higher than adolescents in nondivorced families.

One aspect of the marital relationship that is unique to stepfamilies is the relationship between divorced spouses. We can consider the degree of animosity present prior to the divorce as well as ongoing tensions between divorced parents, especially concerning the adolescent. Exposure to high levels of negativity between divorced parents may affect an adolescent's willingness to accept socialization from biological parents.

TABLE 13.3
Effect of Former Spouse Negativity on Initial Level
and Change in Adolescents' Externalizing

| | Regression Coefficients | | | |
| | Initial Level | | Change | |
Predictors	Without Remarriage	With Remarriage	Without Remarriage	With Remarriage
Number of separations	.24**	.23**	.03	−.02
Arguments over adolescent	.24**	.01	.17$^+$	.05
Parental remarriage	—	.29*	—	.19
Initial level of externalizing	—	—	−.47***	−.50***
R^2	.15	.18	.21	.22
d.f.	2,128	3,127	3,107	4,106
F	11.2***	9.4***	9.5***	7.5***

Note. $^+p < .10$; $^*p < .05$; $^{**}p < .01$; $^{***}p < .001$.

Because remarriage occurred long after the divorce for many stepfamilies in the LSR, we did not attempt to collect multi-informant measures of the former spousal relationship and obtained only a few retrospective responses concerning family life prior to divorce. Nonetheless, we asked about the number of separations that predated the actual divorce, a reasonable albeit crude measure of the degree of animosity and upheaval in the dissolving marital relationship. We find that the total number of separations positively correlates ($r = .38$) with adolescent externalizing in remarried families.

We assessed the current level of conflict in the relationships between divorced spouses from maternal perceptions of four items (i.e., custody, visitation, child support, and childrearing) ranging from 1 (*no disagreement*) to 3 (*much disagreement*). Cronbach alpha for this measure was .63. Because this variable was meant to reflect experiences unique to adolescents in remarried families, scores for non-divorced families were set to the lowest possible score. Similarly, for the analyses, adolescents in nondivorced families were assumed to have zero separations.[4]

As shown in Table 13.3, each of the measures of the former spouse relationship significantly predicted adolescent externalizing. More important, although the effect is marginal, frequency of arguments concerning the adolescent predict growth in externalizing—the only variable thus far besides the effect code for remarriage to show such an effect. When the effect code is entered, number of separations continues to predict initial differences in externalizing, but current arguments do not. As in other analyses, remarriage continues to be an independent predictor. In lon-

---

[4]Children in nondivorced families may have experienced separations but not divorce. Unfortunately, this information was not obtained for nondivorced families.

gitudinal analyses, though, entering both variables of the former spouse relation-ship reduces the effect of remarriage on change in externalizing to nonsignificance. Although no single predictor (besides initial level of externalizing) is significant, some shared variance is being captured by the variables assessing ex-spouse rela-tions to explain this change to nonsignificance. It is not simply due to adding addi-tional variables; remarriage remained a significant predictor of change even after mothers' and fathers' negativity were both entered. The addition of marital func-tioning in the divorced couple appears to account for the effect of remarriage on change in externalizing.

Thus, stressful transitions, parent–adolescent negativity, inept, inconsistent monitoring, and current marital negativity all contribute to adolescent antisocial behavior. These factors also affect adolescent adjustment in nondivorced families and hence do not explain differences between remarried and nondivorced families. Former spousal relationship quality, whether of a historical or contemporary na-ture, also explains adolescent externalizing, and when considered, reduces the overall impact of remarriage on change in adolescent externalizing. Nonetheless, the initial differences in adjustment still need to be explained. Perhaps one expla-nation lies in sibling relationships.

Sibling Relationships

Most adolescents in the LSR had a sibling within 4 years of their own age. The LSR also allowed for developing multimethod, multi-informant measures of sibling functioning. Prior analyses show adolescents in remarried families scoring higher on measures of negativity in sibling relationships (Hetherington et al., 1992). In addition, we found sibling relationships to be a significant longitudinal predictor of externalizing and social competence. This finding was replicated in a larger na-tional sample of same-sex adolescent sibling pairs (Anderson, 1998).

When sibling relationships are considered in the LSR, both initial and longitu-dinal effects emerge (see Table 13.4). These findings are based on a reduced set of families, however, because not all adolescents in the LSR had siblings within four years of age. With the exception of the quality of the relationship between former spouses, the sibling relationship is the only other variable considered thus far that provides an independent prediction of change in externalizing behavior. As before, the effect of parental remarriage holds even when considering sibling relation-ships.

Putting It All Together

Although no factor by itself reduced the effect of remarriage, each factor discussed thus far—stressful life events, negativity in parent–adolescent relationships, in-consistent monitoring, marital and ex-spousal animosity, and conflictual sibling relationships—may contribute some part in explaining the differences in exter-

TABLE 13.4
Effect of Sibling Negativity on Initial Level
and Change in Adolescents' Externalizing

| | Initial Level | | Change | |
	Without Remarriage	With Remarriage	Without Remarriage	With Remarriage
Predictors				
Sibling's negativity	.49***	43***	.30**	.27*
Parental remarriage	—	.25**	—	.26**
Initial level of externalizing	—	—	−.52***	−.59***
R^2	.24	.30	.22	.28
d.f.	1,105	2,104	2,87	3,86
F	25.4***	24.1***	12.0***	11.0***

Regression Coefficients

Note. $*p < .05; **p < .01; ***p < .001.$

nalizing between adolescents in remarried and nondivorced homes. Taken together, rather than individually, they may reduce the impact of parental remarriage on adolescent externalizing.

After entering all variables, 53% of the variance in initial level of externalizing and 33% of the variance in change was explained by the entire set (see Table 13.5). Significant independent effects on level were noted for mothers' and siblings' negativity.[5] Importantly, initial differences in adjustment between stepfamilies and nondivorced families were not accounted for by the entire set of predictors. Sibling and (step)father negativity predicted change in externalizing beyond initial level of externalizing, and, as in previous analyses, the effect of parental remarriage on increases in externalizing was accounted for by this array of predictors.

In a further attempt to explain between-group differences in conduct problems, we dichotomized the domains of stressful events; negativity with mothers, (step)-fathers, and siblings; and negativity between current spouses and used the presence of high risk factors as a predictor. Figure 13.9 shows the level of externalizing for nondivorced families and stepfamilies by number of high risk factors. As shown, the presence of these factors clearly matters for both family types, but the difference between the two households remains. Adolescents in remarried families who had healthy scores in all five domains were functioning at a level of externaliz-

[5]The negative coefficient for ex-marital arguments about the child was unexpected and in the opposite direction of findings from previous analyses. This is a case of classic suppression (Tzelgov & Henik, 1991), indicating that some combination of variables was serving to reduce extraneous variance in number of arguments. Because this finding was not expected, follow-up analyses were not undertaken.

TABLE 13.5
Combined Effect of all Predictors on Initial Level
and Change in Adolescents' Externalizing

	Regression Coefficients			
	Initial Level		Change	
	Without Remarriage	With Remarriage	Without Remarriage	With Remarriage
Predictors				
Negative stresses	.05	.07	.06	.06
Transition events	.06	−.06	.03	−.01
Mother's negativity	.28*	.23*	−.16	−.14
(Step)father's negativity	.15	.20*	.33*	.35*
Inconsistency	.10	.07	−.00	−.01
Marital negativity	.12	.13$^+$	−.13	−.11
Number of separations	.13	.13	.19	.16
Arguments over adolescent	.04	−.30*	.08	−.05
Sibling negativity	.31***	.31***	.34**	.35**
Parental remarriage	—	.48***	—	.21
Initial level of externalizing	—	—	−.62***	−.67***
R^2	.53	.59	.33	.34
d.f.	9,92	10,91	10,75	11,74
F	11.6***	13.0***	3.7***	3.5***

Note. $^+p < .10$; $^*p < .05$; $^{**}p < .01$; $^{***}p < .001$.

ing comparable to adolescents in nondivorced families with one of these risk factors. Overall, this difference remains—it takes but one risk factor in stepfamilies to approximate the effects of two risk factors in nondivorced families, and two risk factors in stepfamilies equal three risk factors in nondivorced families, and so on. The average level of externalizing in remarried families was equivalent to having about 2.5 of these risk factors in nondivorced families. Thus, all of these risk factors contribute to adolescent well-being in remarried families, but something else about living in a stepfamily must explain the difference in externalizing that remains between the groups.

Exploring Initial Differences

The previous analyses indicated that within-family processes are important for explaining adolescent behavior, but none, either singly or taken together, is enough to explain the effect of parental remarriage on externalizing. What, then, accounts for initial differences in externalizing between adolescents in remarried and nondivorced households? A final analysis provides some potential clues.

It is possible that the initial differences between remarried and nondivorced households can be explained by processes occurring prior to the remarriage that

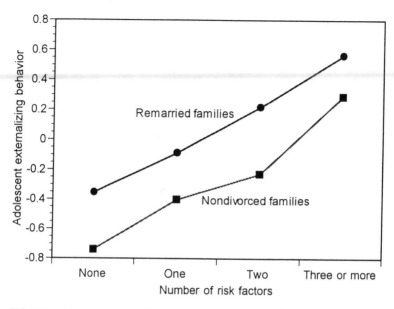

FIG. 13.9.   Adolescents' externalizing behavior in nondivorced and remarried families as a function of the number of risk factors present.

were not captured by the risk factors presented thus far. Because continuing conflict between divorced spouses explained (in part) the greater increase in externalizing found in remarried families, other aspects of the divorce process may explain the initial differences in externalizing. Stepfamilies in the LSR were all formed after divorce rather than from another pathway such as parental death. As such, we cannot test directly whether the experience of divorce accounts for the higher initial levels of externalizing in remarried families. Because the LSR also contained single-mother families who had experienced divorce but not remarriage, we can compare whether adolescents in these families differ from divorced-and-remarried families by entering a second effect code representing divorce status and using the entire sample from the LSR. When an effect code for divorce was entered (see Table 13.6), the effect of remarriage disappeared from the cross-sectional and longitudinal analyses. This finding indicates that adolescents in either context involving divorce differ from adolescents in nondivorced households, but those traversing the pathway of a prior parental divorce (i.e., remarried and remained-single families) do not differ. Implied in these analyses is that all initial differences between adolescent in stepfamilies and nondivorced families are attributed to the experience of parental divorce or some set of factors associated with the divorce process. Some of this effect was captured by the variables of marital instability (i.e., number of separations) and current arguments, but other aspects of the divorce must be considered.

TABLE 13.6
Effect of Parental Divorce and Remarriage on Initial Level
and Change in Adolescents' Externalizing

	Regression Coefficients	
	Initial Level	Change
Predictors		
Parental divorce	.34***	.09
Parental remarriage	−.01	.10
Initial level of externalizing	—	−.47***
R^2	.11	.21
d.f.	2,199	3,160
F	12.2***	13.9***

Note. ***$p < .001$.

It can be speculated that the experience of parental divorce and its concomitant disruptions in family process (e.g., living with diminished economic resources; experiencing changes in residence, neighborhood, and peer groups; exposure to marital conflict; involvement of the child in marital disputes; escalating cycles of coercion between parents and children) changes children in fundamental ways that make the transition to parental remarriage more difficult. Witnessing parents demean and criticize one another in an environment of hostility may diminish the capacity of parents in two ways, as effective role models for and as socializers of their children. Furthermore, in a climate where a parent uses the child to gain advantage over the other spouse, a child may learn readily the skills necessary to be an effective manipulator of his or her parents. It should be kept in mind that the children in the LSR were in early adolescence at the time of the remarriage and thus were socially advanced enough to take advantage of the lessons unwittingly offered by their parents. Other studies with younger children find more positive effects of stepfathers on boys' adjustment (Hetherington et al., 1985). Thus, for early adolescents, the experience of divorce may provide an arena to hone skills in aversive control. Later, when encountering parental remarriage, these skills serve to shape the behavior of the custodial and residential (step)parent, and thus, the remarried family system may be driven more strongly by characteristics of the adolescent rather than the parent.

There is a great deal of support for the notion that adolescents become involved in family conflict under conditions of marital distress (see Davies & Cummings, 1994, for a review). A recent microanalytic study of family negativity finds that boys with maritally distressed parents—whether formed from first or second marriages—were drawn into family conflict (Greene & Anderson, 1998). When behavioral contingencies were examined (i.e., the likelihood that negativity by one person would be followed by negativity from another), this group was at a clear disadvantage. Elder sons tended to escalate the negativity they received from their parents, and (step)fathers escalated negativity from their sons. These contingent ways of responding to negativity were not found in families with girls, nor in families with boys when marriages were not distressed. Thus, boys may be particularly vulnerable to effects of marital conflict.

We speculate that the processes that put children most at risk in remarried families are likely formed during the marital dissolution. Active involvement in escalating family conflict may provide extended trials for children to learn aversive mechanisms for dealing with conflict. The echoes of these trials appear later in remarried families when we see the continuing role of parent–adolescent, sibling, and marital negativity in maintaining conduct problems. Especially under times of stress, overlearned use of negativity may maintain and exacerbate conduct problems in adolescents. If marital dissolutions and its associated processes are in fact largely responsible for externalizing problems in remarried families, we expect that stepfamilies formed with a previously single nondivorced mother would not be associated with the same pattern of externalizing as that with divorced mothers. Stress and family factors are clearly important for adolescents in remarried families, but these factors alone cannot explain why adolescents in stepfamilies start the remarriages at a disadvantage. Just as relationships between divorced family members continue long after the legal decree, many of the processes at work in stepfamilies begin before the decision to remarry. Potential stepparents evaluate the likelihood of establishing and maintaining satisfactory relationships with their stepchildren, and the circumstances under which those relationships begin may determine to a large extent whether or not a remarriage takes place at all.

SUMMARY

By the majority of adolescent accounts, parental remarriage and the accompanying transitions of moving to a new home, starting at a new school, and dealing with new siblings are not inherently negative circumstances. Nevertheless, when the average level of adolescent externalizing behavior in remarried families is compared to that in nondivorced families, significant differences are found, and the experience of parental remarriage predicts increasing problems over time. In this chapter, a variety of potential explanations for this effect were examined.

The frequency of negative stressful events was significantly related to adolescent problem behavior, in accord with previous research. Moreover, negative relationships within a family, whether between adolescents and (step)parents, the new marital partners, or siblings, were associated with adolescents' conduct problems. In addition, qualities of the relationship between former spouses, such as number of separations prior to divorce and frequency of current child-related arguments, predicted the level of externalizing in the adolescent. None of these variables, taken together or individually, accounted for the differences in externalizing behavior between nondivorced and remarried families. Only the experience of parental divorce itself appeared to account for these initial differences. Additionally, characteristics of the divorced couple relationship accounted for the effect of remarriage on increasing externalizing problems over time. Whatever initial differences were found between adolescents in remarried and nondivorced families, at least with respect to conduct problems, could be attributed to factors associated with the experience of parental divorce. It is likely that involvement in parental hostility provides adolescents with opportunity to engage in coercive interchanges and to learn aversive ways of handling conflict and disagreement. These patterns may not only increase adolescent conduct problems but make it more difficult for parents to exert effective socialization. Other analyses suggest that adolescent problem behavior not only leads to negativity from parents (Hetherington et al., 1992) but may make the transition to remarriage less likely to occur (Montgomery et al., 1992).

It should be kept in mind that a great deal of variation in adolescent adjustment to remarriage remains. Many stepfamilies were able to establish warm, involved, supportive relationships across all household members. Adolescents in such situations fared much better than when family relationships were characterized by more coercive, punitive, and conflictual exchanges. For the typical early adolescent, living in a remarried family appears equivalent to living in a moderately stressful nondivorced family. This evidence suggests lasting influence from the cumulative effect of experiencing multiple family transitions (i.e., divorce, life in a single-parent household, cohabitation, and entry into a remarriage). Future research and theory on adolescent adjustment to remarriage needs to be guided by further understanding the critical processes that are set into motion by a dissolving parental marriage.

ACKNOWLEDGMENTS

This research was supported by a grant from the John D. and Catherine T. MacArthur Foundation to E. Mavis Hetherington and W. Glenn Clingempeel. Support for the writing of this chapter was provided by NIMH 5P30MH39246 and 2T32MH18387.

REFERENCES

Aiken, L. S., & West, S. G. (1991). *Multiple regression: Testing and interpreting interactions.* Newbury Park, CA: Sage.
Anderson, E. R. (1998). *Sibling, half-sibling, and stepsibling relationships in remarried families.* Manuscript under review.
Anderson, E. R., Hetherington, E. M., & Clingempeel, W. G. (1989). Transformations in family relations at puberty: Effects of family context. *Journal of Early Adolescence, 9,* 310–334.
Anderson, E. R., Lindner, M. S., & Bennion, L. D. (1992). The effect of family relationships on adolescent development during family reorganization. *Monographs of the Society for Research in Child Development, 57* (2–3, Serial No. 227).

Bray, J. H. (1988). Children's development during early remarriage. In E. M. Hetherington & J. D. Arasteh (Eds.), *Impact of divorce, single parenting and stepparenting on children* (pp. 279–298). Hillsdale, NJ: Lawrence Erlbaum Associates.

Davies, P. T., & Cummings, E. M. (1994). Marital conflict and child adjustment: An emotional security hypothesis. *Psychological Bulletin, 116,* 387–411.

Deal, J. E., Anderson, E. R., Ratliff, D., Hetherington, E. M., & Clingempeel, W. G. (1990, November). *A social relations model analysis of family behavior in remarried families.* Paper presented at the meetings of the National Council on Family Relations, Seattle, WA.

Greene, S. M., & Anderson, E. R. (1998). *Behavioral contingency in tetradic family interactions.* Manuscript under review.

Hetherington, E. M. (1988). Parents, children, and siblings six years after divorce. In R. Hinde & J. Stevenson-Hinde (Eds.), *Relationships within families* (pp. 311–331). Cambridge, England: Cambridge University Press.

Hetherington, E. M. (1989). Coping with family transitions: Winners, losers, and survivors. *Child Development, 60,* 1–14.

Hetherington, E. M., Clingempeel, W. G., Anderson, E. R., Deal, J. E., Stanley Hagan, M., Hollier, E. A., & Lindner, M. S. (1992). Coping with marital transitions: A family systems perspective. *Monographs of the Society for Research in Child Development, 57* (2–3, Serial No. 227).

Hetherington, E. M., Cox, M. J., & Cox, R. (1985). Long-term effects of divorce and remarriage on the adjustment of children. *Journal of the American Academy of Child and Adolescent Psychiatry, 24,* 518–530.

Kenny, D. A., & LaVoie, L. (1984). The social relations model. In L. Berkowitz (Ed.), *Advances in experimental social psychology* (Vol. 18, pp. 141–182). New York: Academic.

Loeber, R., & Stouthamer-Loeber, M. (1998). Development of juvenile aggression and violence: Some common misconceptions and controversies. *American Psychologist, 53,* 242–259.

McArdle, J. J., & Anderson, E. R. (1990). Latent variable growth models for research on aging. In J. E. Birren and K. W. Schaie (Eds.), *Handbook of the psychology of aging* (3rd ed., pp. 21–44). San Diego: Academic Press.

Montgomery, M. J., Anderson, E. R., Hetherington, E. M., & Clingempeel, W. G. (1992). Patterns of courtship for remarriage: Implications for child adjustment and parent–child relationships. *Journal of Marriage and the Family, 54,* 686–698.

Patterson, G. R. (1982). *Coercive family process.* Eugene, OR: Castalia.

Tzelgov, J., & Henik, A. (1991). Suppression situations in psychological research: Definitions, implications, and applications. *Psychological Bulletin, 109,* 524–536.

PART V

Intervention

14

Psychological Interventions
for Separated and Divorced Families

Robert E. Emery
University of Virginia

Katherine M. Kitzmann
University of Memphis

Mary Waldron
University of Virginia

THREE OBSERVATIONS serve as points of departure for the present overview of interventions with divorcing families. First, demographic data clearly indicate that both children and adults from divorced families are two to three times as likely to receive psychological treatment as are members of married families (Howard et al., 1996; Zill, Morrison, & Coiro, 1993). Divorced family members are overrepresented in the treatment population in part because psychological disorders are more common among children and parents from divorced families. At the same time, resilience is the normative psychological outcome following divorce, and the proportion of children and parents who receive treatment exceeds the proportion with demonstrable psychological disorders (for a review, see Emery, 1998). Many members of divorced families likely seek treatment, not for a psychological disorder but for help in dealing with the subclinical distress caused by the family disruption (Laumann-Billings & Emery, 1998). Treatment also may be initiated for other reasons, such as a custody dispute. Regardless of how one interprets the data, however, epidemiogical evidence underscores the importance of research on psychological intervention in divorce from the perspective of service utilization if for no other reason.

The second point concerns the wide range of potential targets and timings of intervention in divorce. Divorce involves social, legal, and economic consequences as well as psychological ones, and various societal controls have been implemented and continue to be considered as means of regulating divorce (Eekelaar, 1991). Moreover, longitudinal research has clearly demonstrated that divorce is best conceptualized as a process of adaptation and change over a period of several years (Hetherington, 1989, 1991, 1993), and interventions may take place at various points in time before the divorce (e.g., laws designed to promote marriage), during the divorce (e.g., mediation or family therapy), or long afterwards (e.g., individual or group psychotherapy). All these interventions are of potential interest not only for their intended impact but also because of their potential indirect psychological consequences in preventing, treating, or possibly exacerbating psychological problems among family members.

The third observation concerns the tremendous disparity between how frequently intervention in divorce is discussed in the applied literature (in psychology, law, and other fields) and how infrequently divorce interventions are subjected to methodologically sophisticated studies, particularly randomized trials. For example, a *Psychlit* search conducted for this chapter revealed over 500 articles and chapters published with the keywords *divorce* and *therapy* or *treatment*. As reviewed here and elsewhere (Emery, 1998; Grych & Fincham, 1992; Lee, Picard, & Blain, 1994), few of these published accounts are empirical reports; only a handful are randomized trials.

The present review focuses on research on divorce intervention with an emphasis on the psychological consequences for children's well-being, including both their psychological disorders and their subclinical distress. The review also includes interventions designed to affect family relationships or individual parents' mental health because these factors are critically important to children's mental health following divorce. The review pays special attention to those few studies that have used experimental or quasi-experimental designs, although selected empirical studies or clinical reports are also included when they suggest creative directions for future research on assessment or intervention. Finally, the review is divided into three major sections based on the target of intervention: the individual child, parents and parenting, and the co-parenting relationship. It should be noted at the outset that systematic research on treatments for individual children is limited exclusively to school-based interventions. Controlled trials of therapy for postdivorce parenting are limited to group therapy, and methodologically adequate research on co-parenting interventions is limited to divorce mediation. Other interventions are frequently used for individual children (e.g., play therapy), parents and parenting (e.g., individual psychotherapy), and coparenting (e.g., family therapy), but we discuss these treatments only briefly here due to the absence of research.

CHILD-FOCUSED TREATMENTS:
SCHOOL-BASED DIVORCE INTERVENTIONS

As noted, children from divorced families are overrepresented in the mental health treatment population, but there are no systematic data on what types of treatment these children typically receive. Many children likely are in individual psychotherapy, including but not limited to play therapy (see Hodges, 1991, for a clinical overview), and others may be involved in group therapy in the community. In addition, a number of children from divorced families probably are treated in family therapy, which is discussed in the next section on parenting interventions. It is surprising, however, there have been no systematic attempts to evaluate the effectiveness of individual psychotherapy with children from divorced families, a treatment that is likely to be recommended when lack of commitment or intractable problems prevent family therapy (Hodges, 1991). Rather, research on child-focused intervention in divorce is limited to group therapy and more specifically, school-based treatment groups.

Group therapy is the most common format for various school-based divorce interventions, as most schools do not have adequate resources to address divorce-related difficulties in a child-specific manner (Grych & Fincham, 1992; Kalter & Schreier, 1993; Pedro-Carroll, 1993). The primary benefit of a group format is contact with other children who have had similar experiences (Pedro-Carroll, 1997; Stolberg & Cullen, 1983). Supportive peer groups may help to lessen feelings of isolation and loneliness, foster feelings of support and trust, and offer opportunities to clarify divorce-related misconceptions, such as feelings of responsibility or blame for their parents' break-up (Pedro-Carroll, 1997; Stolberg & Cullen, 1983). In contrast to individual therapy with an adult clinician, groups made up of peers may also offer a more open, natural, and comfortable environment in which to disclose sensitive experiences (Grych & Fincham, 1992; Pedro-Carroll, 1997; Stolberg & Cullen, 1983).

Although techniques and materials vary across specific programs, school-based divorce interventions share many goals and strategies (Grych & Fincham, 1992). Most incorporate both educational and therapeutic activities in the attempt to foster feelings of support, clarify divorce-related misconceptions, and develop effective coping skills to deal with the challenges and stressors associated with parental divorce. In addition, school-based divorce interventions are typically time-limited, ranging from 6-week sessions (Bornstein, Bornstein, & Walters, 1988) to 16-week sessions (Alpert-Gillis, Pedro-Carroll, & Cowen, 1989). The shorter duration of the interventions is advantageous given limited resources as well as concerns expressed by some parents that children not miss out on other school activities for extended periods of time (Kalter & Schreier, 1993).

There are many advantages of school-based interventions for children of divorce. The number of children served in school-based groups is much larger than is possible within individual therapy; indeed, many children of lower income could not afford such services on an individual basis (Grych & Fincham, 1992; Pedro-Carroll, 1997). Schools are also a natural context for providing support given the number of both peers and teachers present (Cowen, Hightower, Pedro-Carroll, & Work, 1989; Grych & Fincham, 1992). In addition, children of divorce are more likely than children from married families to experience behavior problems in the classroom (Emery, 1982; Guidubaldi, Perry, & Cleminshaw, 1984) resulting in difficulties in concentration and compromised academic performance (Kalter & Schreier, 1993). Consistent with the educational goals of the school (Hodges, 1991), school-based programs may help to reduce both behavioral and academic problems.

Evaluation of School-Based Interventions

Although school-based intervention programs for children of divorce are frequently implemented, empirical evaluation of such programs is limited (see Grych & Fincham, 1992). The two exceptions include Pedro-Carroll and colleagues' Children of Divorce Intervention Project and Stolberg and colleagues' Divorce Adjustment Project, both of which have been subjected to one or more replication studies. In the following sections, we review research on these two programs as well as several smaller scale studies evaluating various school-based divorce programs.

Children of Divorce Intervention Project (CODIP). CODIP is a school-based, child-focused, supportive group intervention designed to be a preventive intervention. Five specific objectives include: providing a supportive group environment, helping children identify and express appropriate feelings, clarifying divorce-related misconceptions, enhancing coping skills, and enhancing children's perceptions of self and family (Cowen et al., 1996). Various CODIP programs targeting children of different ages and backgrounds have been evaluated since the program was first implemented in the early 1980s.

In the initial evaluation (Pedro-Carroll & Cowen, 1985), 75 fourth- through sixth-grade children from four suburban schools were randomly assigned to either an immediate 12-week intervention or a delayed intervention control group matched for sex, grade, and length of time since their parents' separation. According to teacher report, children in the intervention group exhibited significantly greater reductions in shy–anxious behavior, learning problems, and overall school-related problems, and they improved significantly more on measures of total competence and more specific competencies including peer sociability, frustration tolerance, rule following, and adaptive assertiveness as compared to children in the control group. Similarly, the reports of parents and group leaders indicated significant decreases in feelings of self-blame and increases in personal problem-solving abilities. Children in the intervention reported feeling less anxious and having less negative self-attitudes and perceptions of divorce than did controls; however, no differences were found between children in the intervention and control groups on perceived self-competence. A replication of this initial study with different group leaders and different schools, but without random assignment to conditions, revealed similar findings (Pedro-Carroll, Cowen, Hightower, & Guare, 1986).

CODIP was subsequently adapted for urban children with diverse ages, ethnicities, and socioeconomic backgrounds (Pedro-Carroll & Cowen, 1985; Pedro-Carroll et al., 1986). For example, in the revised program the concept of "divorce" was extended to include not only legal marriages but also long-term live-in partnerships. In an evaluation of a 16-session adaptation, intervention and comparison groups of second- and third-grade urban children were recruited separately through school announcements, resulting in 52 program participants, 52 comparison children from divorced families, and 81 demographically matched comparison children from intact families (Alpert-Gillis et al., 1989). Pre- to post-intervention statistics indicated that CODIP children reported greater improvements on measures assessing coping abilities in problem situations and feelings about self and family than did children from either divorce or intact comparison groups. Parents reported more gains in children's ability to deal with feelings, behave appropriately, and solve problems. In addition, teachers reported more improvement for CODIP children in school competencies including peer social skills, assertiveness, and frustration tolerance but not school-related problem behaviors. An evaluation of CODIP for fourth- through sixth-grade urban children revealed similar results (Pedro-Carroll, Alpert-Gillis, & Cowen, 1992). Additional evidence of CODIP's effectiveness across ages can be found in evaluations of seventh- and eighth-grade children (Pedro-Carroll, Sutton, & Black, 1993, cited in Cowen et al., 1996).

Finally, in a recent study of 105 kindergarten and first-grade children (Pedro-Carroll & Alpert-Gillis, 1997), teacher ratings indicated that CODIP children displayed significantly more gains in school-related competencies, as well as exhibited less anxious, withdrawn, and disruptive behavior than demographically matched control children from divorced families. In contrast to children in the comparison group, children in the program reported feeling less worried about changes that had taken place in their family and more positive about themselves, their families, and their experience in the group. They also reported talking more with their parents and in general, said they enjoyed talking about their feelings. Parents reported improved parent–child communication; increased ability to share feelings, display appropriate behavior, and cope with problems; and decreased moody and anxious behavior (Pedro-Carroll, Sutton, & Wyman, 1996, cited in Pedro-Carroll & Alpert-Gillis, 1997).

Divorce Adjustment Project (DAP).   DAP is a structured primary intervention program consisting of two components: a two-part school-based Children's Support Group (CSG) and a community-based Single Parents' Support Group (SPSG; Stolberg & Garrison, 1985). Because the present focus is treatments for children, SPSG is discussed in a later section on parenting. CSG is a 12- to 14-week psychoeducational support group designed to provide emotional support for 7- through 13-year-old children of divorce and to teach cognitive behavioral skills including problem solving, anger control, impulse control, communication, and relaxation.

In the first of the DAP evaluations (Stolberg & Garrison, 1985), 82 children aged 7 through 13 years old and their custodial mothers were assigned to either a no-treatment control group or to one of three 12-week treatment groups, including CSG alone, SPSG concurrent with CSG, or SPSG alone. In comparison to both the control and combined intervention groups, children in the CSG alone group improved in self-concept as measured immediately after the program and at a 5-month follow-up. At follow-up, children in the CSG alone group also exhibited greater increases in adaptive social skills. Surprisingly, the combined CSG and SPSG intervention group did not result in expected adjustment gains, but this finding may reflect nonrandom assignment and preexisting demographic differences between the groups. Mothers in the combined intervention were separated longer, had lower employment status, and reported less frequent visitation with fathers, whereas children in the combined group were better adjusted prior to the intervention.

In a more recent evaluation, Stolberg and Mahler (1994) supplemented the existing DAP by adding adjustment measures tapping clinical ranges, teacher reports of child adjustment, and more game-like activities to engage the interest of the families. Participating schools were randomly assigned to a no-treatment divorce control group or one of three 14-week treatment groups, including support only, support with skill building, or support, skill building, skill transfer (i.e., therapeutic home workbooks for children and parents designed to facilitate transfer of in-class adjustment gains), and parenting training. Third- through fifth-grade children of separated and divorced parents were recruited, resulting in a sample of 103 children from divorced families. In contrast to the controls with divorced parents, children in both skill-building groups displayed significant improvement immediately following intervention and at a one-year follow-up. Greater reductions in both internalizing and externalizing behavior, total pathology, and clinical symptomatology were observed for children in the skills and support group immediately following intervention. Children in the skill-building condition with skill transfer and parenting training exhibited less trait anxiety post-intervention; however, behavioral gains were not observed until follow-up. Children in the support-only condition exhibited greater reductions in clinical symptomatology at follow-up, with the impact greatest for those children entering the group with significant preexisting clinical problems.

Additional Evaluation Studies.   In addition to these two programs, several smaller scale group interventions with children have been studied empirically. In one of the earliest reports, Anderson, Kinney, and Gerler (1984) evaluated a school-based group intervention targeting children's attitudes toward divorce, classroom behavior, and academic performance in mathematics and language arts. Third to 6th grade children were recruited through school announcements: 52 were randomly assigned to one of seven 8-week divorce groups, and 32 children served as a control group. Groups included role playing new behaviors, discussing feelings about divorce, puppet activities to aid in understanding and acceptance of divorce, and learning new relationships skills. Pre–post comparisons indicated adjustment gains for those children in the treatment group significantly exceeded those of control children on measures of attitudes toward divorce and classroom conduct. No significant improvement in language arts or mathematics was found for either the treatment or the control group.

Roseby and Deutsch (1985) evaluated a school-based program to determine whether skill training in social role-taking and assertive communication result in improved divorce adjustment. In this study, 57 children 9 through 11 years old participated in one of two 10-week intervention groups: experimental or placebo control. The experimental condition provided training in cognitive social role taking and assertive communication skills, whereas the placebo control group provided no skill training, focusing instead on identification and discussion of divorce-related feelings. Following the intervention, children in the experimental group were less likely to blame their mothers, fathers, or themselves for the divorce, to fear peer ridicule or parental abandonment, to hold unrealistic hopes for reconciliation, or to deny feelings of pain as compared to those children in the placebo condition. In contrast, no differences between children in the experimental and placebo conditions were observed on measures of classroom behavior, specifically aggressive behavior, or on measures of depression following the intervention; that is, both the experimental and placebo groups exhibited improved classroom behavior and decreases in depression.

Gwynn and Brantley (1987) investigated the effectiveness of an 8-week educational support group designed to educate children of divorce about divorce-related concepts and issues, encourage expression of feelings, and promote adaptive problem-solving skills. Participants included 30 children aged 9 through 11 years whose parents had been separated for at least 1 year. Thirty children matched for gender and time since parental separation served as a control group. Pre–post comparisons indicated adjustment gains for those children in the treatment group significantly exceeded those of control children on measures of depression, anxiety, negative feelings about divorce, and knowledge about divorce.

Omizo and Omizo (1987) evaluated the efficacy of a 12-week school-based group on children's self-concept and locus of control. Sixty fourth- through sixth-grade children were randomly assigned to either treatment or control groups. Treatment activities involved group discussion of divorce-related feelings, role playing, and relaxation and assertiveness training. Post intervention, children in the treatment group scored higher on measures of locus of control and two of four indices of self-concept.

Bornstein, Bornstein, and Walters (1988) examined a 6-week school-based support group for 7- through 14-year-old children of divorce. Thirty-one children were randomly assigned to either an experimental group, emphasizing identification and clarification of divorce-related feelings, anger management, training in communication skills, problem solving, and group support, or a delayed treatment control group. A positive effect was found for only one of seven outcomes measured. Children in the experimental group exhibited greater decreases in school-related behavior problems measured at follow-up, but no pre–post differences were found in children's attitudes about divorce, parent–child conflict, and additional measures of child adjustment, including child anxiety, self-esteem, or other behavior problems. It is also important to note that this group was shorter than many other such groups, and the assessment tools focused solely on adjustment and not on children's communication or problem-solving skills.

Kalter, Schaefer, Lesowitz, Alpern, and Pickar (1988) found no differences in internalizing and externalizing behaviors for girls who participated in a group designed to normalize the divorce experience, clarify divorce-related issues, provide a safe place to express and discuss feelings, develop coping strategies, and teach parents about children's concerns. However, parents reported significant reductions in boys' externalizing and overall aggression compared to controls. Furthermore, both girls and boys reported more positive perceptions of divorce 6 months following program completion.

Burke and Van de Streek (1989) evaluated an 8-week school-based divorce intervention targeting children's self-concept. In this study, 39 children in fourth through sixth grades were randomly assigned to either treatment or delayed treatment control groups. Treatment exercises were designed to facilitate group discussion and included films, stories, and games with divorce-related themes. Pre–post comparisons in self-concept indicated significant gains for only those children in the experimental treatment group. No outcome other than self-concept was reported.

Crosbie-Burnett and Newcomer (1990) evaluated the effectiveness of a school-based group intervention on children's beliefs about divorce, depression, and self-esteem. Eleven sixth-grade students were randomly assigned to one of two conditions, experimental or wait-list control groups. Following intervention, the experimental group exhibited greater improvement in post-divorce adjustment. Children in the experimental group reported less problematic beliefs about their parents' divorce, increased scholastic competence, and lower scores for depression as compared to controls.

Summary and Evaluation

The findings reviewed are generally consistent and support the utility of school-based divorce interventions, but there nevertheless is much room for improvement (see also Grych & Fincham, 1992; Lee et al., 1994). Most studies are wrought with methodological problems—few employed random assignment; raters of children's adjustment were aware of the treatment, and a placebo treatment was used in only one study; and assessments were completed soon after the intervention, an obvious limitation given the preventive rationale for the treatments. Exceptions include a 2-year follow-up conducted by Pedro-Carroll, Sutton, and Black (1993) and a 1-year follow-up of the DAP (Stolberg & Mahler, 1994). In addition, few attempts have been made to isolate the active components of change, and potential moderating variables such as age, gender, ethnicity, socioeconomic status, time since divorce, remarriage, and child temperament have rarely been considered.

In addition to these methodological issues, an important substantive concern is the nature and the magnitude of change produced by school-based groups. In a review of child and parent-focused interventions, Lee, Picard, and Blain (1994) noted that child interventions, including most of the studies reviewed here, generally produced modest results as measured by an average effect size of .27 standard deviation units. This effect is considerably smaller than the commonly reported effect sizes for psychotherapy in general (e.g., Smith & Glass, 1977). It appears, moreover, that child-focused interventions may be more successful in alleviating children's distress or altering their beliefs about divorce than in eliminating disturbances such as conduct disorders in school. In short, school-based groups appear to be a helpful but limited intervention for children coping with parental divorce.

PARENT AND PARENTING INTERVENTIONS

Although parent-focused programs are less common than are child- and school-based programs, they appear to be more effective in helping parents adjust to divorce. Lee et al. (1994) found that evaluations of parenting programs yield an average effect size of .80, comparable to the average effect reported for psychotherapy in general. However, the greater effectiveness appears to be limited to parents. As summarized in the next section, improved parent adjustment typically is not related to improved child adjustment in these intervention studies.

Goals, Format, and Content

Divorced adults are overrepresented in individual psychotherapy patient populations, but most parent-focused interventions designed specifically for divorce and all research evaluations of parent-focused divorce interventions involve group therapy. These groups have three implicit goals: improved psychological adjustment of the parent, improved parenting, and improved family relationships. In practice, most place a primary emphasis on improving adult adjustment, with less emphasis on parenting skills and family relationship issues. More specific topics may include coping with the lack of a support system, having to run a household independently, task overload, emotional overload, and perhaps other issues including communication skills, financial planning, social support, dating, feelings of isolation and rejection, parenting and coparenting, self-esteem, depression, relaxation skills, interpersonal skills, legal issues, and career planning. Members typically are custodial parents so many groups have a single-parent focus. Programs vary in the number of contact hours participants have with the treatment and typically meet in schools (often in coordination with child-focused groups), community mental health centers, or churches or synagogues (Cantor & Drake, 1983; Lee et al., 1994).

Review of Empirical Studies

A handful of studies of parent-based programs have been conducted using a comparison or control group. Four of the more sophisticated studies include the Colorado Separation and Divorce Project, the Divorce Adjustment Project, the Children of Divorce Parenting Intervention, and the Parenting Through Change program. A few smaller studies also used comparison groups and are included in the following review.

Colorado Separation and Divorce Project.   This 6-month intervention program addressed newly separated (but not divorced) adults, 43% of whom were parents. By random assignment, 100 adults participated in treatment, and 50 were part of a no-treatment control group. The program provided general support as well as specific skills-related training in order to reduce or control stress in several key areas of relevance to the newly separated. Paraprofessionals contacted participants on a regular basis to promote social interaction and to make referrals to other parts of the program. Optional study groups were also available; participants could meet with an expert who provided information and guidance related to one of the stress areas targeted by the program. Of the 100 participants, 59 chose to make use of a study group. The groups most utilized by the participants were groups related to socialization, childrearing and single parenting, and financial planning (Bloom, Hodges, & Caldwell, 1982; Bloom, Hodges, Kern & McFaddin, 1985; Hodges & Bloom, 1986).

Comparisons were made both of pre–post scores within each group and of differences between the intervention and control groups (using pretest scores as covariates). Compared to initial scores, scores at 6 months indicated that all participants (experimental and control) had more legal and financial stresses. However, the intervention group showed a significant drop in overall distress and maladjustment, in psychological distress, and in anxiety, whereas the control group showed a significant increase in psychological symptoms. Comparisons of the two groups using pretests as covariates showed that the control group also had significantly more problems with housing than did the intervention group.

Interestingly, improvement in the intervention group was not related to extent of use of specific study groups. In fact, participants who made use of the study groups were those with more problems initially, and these participants continued to have more problems at the end of the program. Bloom and colleagues concluded that the immediate benefits of the intervention program were general rather than specific and that knowing that services were available was enough to promote better functioning in the intervention group 6 months later (Bloom et al., 1982).

The sample was reevaluated at 18, 30, and 48 months. Over time, virtually all participants (intervention and control) showed improved functioning, but the intervention group maintained its better adjustment. At 30 months, the benefits of intervention were more apparent than they were at 6 or 18 months. By 4 years, more than half of the previously demonstrated significant effects were no longer apparent, but the intervention group showed new improvements not seen in the control group, related to psychological functioning, quality of life, and job satisfaction (Bloom et al., 1985).

The Divorce Adjustment Project—Single Parent Support Group (SPSG) (Stolberg & Garrison, 1985).   Participants in the SPSG were 82 pairs of single, custodial mothers (separated less than 33 months) and their 7- to 13-year-old children. Each mother and child was assigned (although not randomly) to one of four treatment conditions: the Children's Support Group (CSG) alone; the CSG and the Single Parents' Support Group (SPSG); the SPSG alone; or a nontreatment control group. As described earlier, the CSG alone condition was associated with benefits that were not apparent when the CSG met in parallel with the SPSG (combined condition).

Like the Children's Support Group, the SPSG met for 12 one-hour sessions. Based on the assumption that improved adjustment of the mothers would lead to better parenting, the parent group was designed as a psychoeducational support group and did not attempt to modify parenting behaviors directly. Some parents participated in the SPSG alone condition, and their children were part of the control group; other parents participated in the SPSG in parallel with their children's participation in the CSG. In the latter case, parent–child pairs assigned to the combined treatment condition were not working together in treatment.

The SPSG did not produce any significant changes in parent or child adjustment relative to the no-treatment control group. On the other hand, involvement in the single-parent support group may have prevented deterioration in parent adjustment that was seen in control-group parents. This was only the case, however, for mothers in the SPSG-alone condition. Mothers involved in the combined SPSG/CSG condition not only did not show any evidence of prevention but showed drastic reductions in adjustment. As Stolberg and Garrison noted (1985), this finding could reflect preexisting demographic differences that were not controlled for during or after assignment to groups.

Children of Divorce Parenting Intervention (Wolchik et al., 1993).   Wolchik and colleagues developed an intervention program that targeted five parenting practices hypothesized to mediate the relation between divorce and child adjustment: parent–child relationships, interparental conflict, discipline, contact with and support for nonparental adults, and contact with the noncustodial parent. Participants were mothers who had divorced within the past 2 years and who had at least one child between 8 and 15. Because the primary purpose of this intervention program was prevention, the researchers excluded both low- and high-functioning families from their sample, hoping to target those families who would most benefit from the program. The final sample consisted of 70 families. By random assignment, 36 mother–child pairs were enrolled in treatment, and 34 were put on a waiting list, with treatment to follow 6 months later.

As part of the intervention program, mothers participated in 10 weekly sessions with a group of about 6 to 8 mothers and in 2 individual sessions (after the third and sixth groups). Groups were led by a male–female team and strongly emphasized skills training related to discipline, listening skills, anger management, and the quality of the mother–child relationship. The researchers were careful to make ongoing "quality control" assessments, ensuring full participation and consistent application of the program plans by group leaders.

Mothers and children completed parallel versions of the same questionnaires, assessing the mother–child relationship, mothers' parenting, and other aspects of family functioning more specific to the divorce. Evidence for positive change in family functioning was more notable based on mothers' reports than on children's reports. Children whose mothers participated in the program reported slightly fewer divorce-related negative events and significantly more acceptance of their mothers. However, these children did not differ from control-group children in their descriptions of other areas of family life, such as the openness of communication, positive routines, the consistency of mothers' discipline, or extent of contact with fathers. In addition, contrary to expectations, children in the intervention group reported receiving less support from outside adults. By contrast, pre- and posttest scores indicated several program-related changes in family functioning according to mothers' reports. Intervention mothers reported significantly more open communication and more positive routines after treatment and described themselves as slightly more accepting of their children than they were before the program. Mothers who had described themselves as showing very inconsistent discipline before the program showed gains in this area. Finally, mothers in the program reported fewer negative events related to the divorce and a more positive attitude about changing fathers' visitation schedules.

Program involvement by mothers was associated inconsistently with benefits in children's mental health outcomes, according to mothers' ratings of child behavior on the Achenbach Child Behavior Checklist. Overall, children whose mothers participated in the program showed drops in aggression but were no different than control children in their anxiety, behavior problems, or depression. Children with the most preprogram problems showed significant gains, however, in their mothers' Achenbach ratings of total behavior problems.

Parenting Through Change (Forgatch & DeGarmo, 1998). This intervention program grew out of the Oregon Divorce Study, a longitudinal study of recently separated families. Based on Patterson's (1982) model of coercive family processes, this program is geared specifically toward improving children's outcomes at home and in school by altering mothers' discipline practices in the early stages of divorce. The researchers noted that it may be more effective to intervene with mothers rather than within the school setting because parents are more constant in the lives of their children than are teachers and school programs. The researchers also hypothesized that changes in maternal parenting practices would effectively improve children's behavior without intervening with children directly.

Participants were mothers who had been separated within the last 24 months and their sons, who were in first to third grade. By random assignment, 153 families were enrolled in the intervention program, and 85 families served as experimental controls. Parents met in a series of 14 parent group sessions, made up of 6336to 16 members, held at the Oregon Social Learning Center. The groups were designed to provide training in parenting practices (e.g., discipline, contingent encouragement, monitoring, and problem solving) and in other issues relevant to divorcing women (e.g., regulating negative emotions, managing interpersonal conflict). Staff (who were all women, both professionals and paraprofessionals) also made mid-week telephone calls to mothers, encouraging use of the procedures and troubleshooting problems, and provided individual sessions as needed. A manualized treatment approach (Forgatch, 1994) and ongoing quality control assessments were used to ensure the integrity of the intervention program.

The effectiveness of the Parenting Through Change program was assessed with multiple measures and by multiple informants, with assessments made every 6 months (i.e., baseline, treatment termination, and follow-up). Mothrs' ratings indicated a high degree of consumer satisfaction. More important, the program was associated with significant improvements in maternal discipline (i.e., reductions in negative reinforcement, observed in structured mother–child problem-solving tasks) and significant improvements in teachers' ratings of children's behavior at school. Improvements in school behavior were in turn related to gains in reading achievement scores on the Woodcock–Johnson Psychoeducational Battery, although path analysis showed that the intervention did not have a direct effect on achievement scores.

Smaller Control-Group Studies of Parent-Focused Treatments. In this section, several smaller studies are reviewed because they made use of comparison groups to assess effectiveness. In general, the interventions studied are more brief and focused, and research shows mixed evidence of effectiveness.

The Children First program was designed with the narrow focus of alerting parents to the adverse consequences that poorly managed conflict has for children and was limited two 90-minute group sessions. Parents heard a local judge discuss the negative impact of divorcing parents' behavior on children, they viewed six videotaped vignettes depicting maladaptive interactions among divorced family members, and a group leader then moderated discussion (Kramer & Washo, 1993). In a study of the program, outcome was assessed by comparing 168 parents who were mandated to participate in Children First to a group of 43 divorcing parents from a nearby area. The results showed high consumer satisfaction but no evidence of improvements in parenting, parent–child relationships, or the coparental relationship among the parents involved in the Child First program. Over time, participants reported more involvement in other divorce-related programs.

No evidence of effectiveness was found in another study of a series of weekend workshops designed to assist family members to cope emotionally with divorce and to improve contact and communication between ex-spouses and between noncustodial parents and children (Woody, Colley, Schlegelmilch, & Maginn, 1985). By contrast, some effectiveness was demonstrated in a psychoeducational program for divorced fathers (Devlin, Brown, Beebe, & Parulis, 1992). The experimental group comprised the first 15 fathers to enroll in the community-based program, and the waiting list comprised the next 15 fathers who called. Fathers met as a group for 90 minutes in 6 weekly sessions, typically led by two male facilitators, with a female leader present for sessions focused on coparenting. Fathers in the treatment group showed more satisfaction with parenting and reported greater effectiveness in talking with and listening to their children. However, there were no program-associated changes in child support payments, contact with children, or number of child-related problem situations reported by the fathers.

Lee and Hett (1990) demonstrated increases in general adult adjustment associated with a program designed to teach coping skills to recently separated and divorced adults. Their sample of 24 adults (mostly women) were randomly assigned to a treatment group or to a waiting list control group. The eight group sessions focused on helping group members cope with divorce-related trauma through stress management, communication skills, and discussion of divorce-related problems. The adults in the program showed program-related drops in depression and anxiety and gains in general adjustment and ability to form meaningful relationships.

Several other studies have used control-group comparisons to assess the effectiveness of divorce-related intervention programs (Kessler, 1978; Malouff, Lanyon, & Schutte, 1988; Salts & Zongker, 1983; Thiessen, Avery, & Joanning, 1980). However, because these programs targeted general adult adjustment without a focus on parenting, they are not described here (for a review, see Lee et al., 1994).

Summary and Evaluation

Parent-based intervention programs for families of divorce are commonly used by the community and even are court-mandated in some areas. Although parents in these programs consistently report high consumer satisfaction, the quality of these programs in terms of objective gains is quite variable. Some programs show gains in parent adjustment, but these gains generally do not have the beneficial impact on child adjustment that researchers might hope. Studies that reported improvements in child adjustment showed that the quality of the mother–child relationship and parenting skills were important mediators of change (Wolchik et al., 1993). Community enthusiasm for parenting programs offers investigators an opportunity to develop more effective means of service delivery, to use a stronger theoretical and empirical foundation, to include a stronger developmental focus, and to develop alternative formats for delivering different interventions.

COPARENTING: DIVORCE MEDIATION

Troubles in the ongoing coparenting relationship between separated and divorced parents are the focus of treatment in family therapy and increasingly in court-mandated or voluntary parent education programs such as Children First. Unfortunately, there are no empirical evaluations of family therapy for improving coparenting following divorce (except as a part of ongoing mediation and arbitration), and studies of parent education to date have been limited to poorly controlled evaluation research. Thus, research on intervention in coparenting following divorce is limited to the investigation of divorce mediation. Mediation is intended primarily to be a dispute resolution technique, but the process also can be viewed as a preventive intervention that may improve the coparenting relationship and thereby affect children's well-being following divorce (Emery & Wyer, 1987b).

Characteristics and Goals

Divorce mediation offers divorcing parents a forum for dispute settlement at a time when communication between them obviously is very difficult. Mediation is based on the assumption that cooperative negotiation will both facilitate short-term dispute settlement and promote continued cooperation in the ongoing relationship between former spouses who remain parents. The process may take place in courts, social service agencies, or private practices, and it typically involves a limited number of sessions ranging from 1 up to 15 or perhaps 20 hours total. However, most mediation, and most research on mediation, has focused on structured, short-term intervention offered in a court setting. The clients seen in the court setting are an unrepresentative sample of the divorcing population, namely, those people who are contesting various aspects of their settlements and are requesting court involvement. In short, mediators and mediation research deals with the most acrimonious divorces.

Divorce mediators come from many different professions, but they primarily are attorneys, psychologists, and social workers. The mediator's professional background may influence how much the process addresses relationship issues, but in all cases, the overriding focus of mediation is on negotiating a divorce settlement, not on improving family relationships (Emery, 1994).

Research on Mediation

Mediation has been compared with litigation in a handful of controlled studies. As such, mediation has been evaluated in terms of its success in resolving disputes, the durability of mediated agreements, and client satisfaction with the process. The focus of the present review is on mediation as a preventive intervention, although the success of the procedure in meeting other goals is also noted.

Dispute Resolution. In an initial study and in a replication, where families were randomly assigned to mediate or litigate their custody disputes, mediation clearly promoted parental agreement and reduced the need for court hearings (Emery, Matthews, & Wyer, 1991; Emery & Wyer, 1987a). Only 4 of the 35 families assigned at random to mediation proceeded to court, in contrast to 26 of 36 families in the litigation control group. Disputes also were resolved more quickly in mediation than in adversary settlement (Emery et al., 1991). Two other studies that used random assignment also found that mediation reduced court hearings (Irving, Benjamin, Bohm, & MacDonald, 1981; Pearson & Thoennes, 1984). In one study of private mediation, 59% of the partners reached a complete divorce agreement, and an additional 15% reached a partial agreement (Kelly & Duryee, 1992).

Beyond encouraging initial settlements, compliance with agreements may be somewhat higher following mediation than litigation. In randomized trials, compliance with child support was higher following mediation than litigation, and evidence indicated that fathers otherwise stayed more involved in their children's lives (Dillon & Emery, 1996; Emery, Matthews, & Kitzmann, 1994). Other controlled studies also have found lower rates of relitigation following mediation, at least under certain circumstances (Kelly, 1990; Margolin, 1973; Pearson & Thoennes, 1989).

The assessment of parental satisfaction following mediation and litigation has been another major dispute resolution focus of mediation research. Evidence is consistent in finding more satisfaction with mediation than with adversary settlement in studies using random assignment or comparison group designs (Emery & Wyer, 1987a; Emery et al., 1991; Emery et al., 1994; Irving et al., 1981; Kelly, 1990; Pearson, & Thoennes, 1984). Some controversy has been generated about whether fathers are more satisfied with mediation than are mothers, but gender differences appear to be more attributable to the changing background of litigation (which is moving toward gender neutrality) than of mediation (Emery, 1994).

Coparenting and Psychological Adjustment. In the most extensive research on the topic, no differences were found for most measures of parents' and children's mental health following mediation or litigation (Emery & Wyer, 1987a; Emery et al., 1991; Emery et al., 1994). On a more positive note, fathers who participated in mediation reported less coparenting conflict one year after dispute settlement, but the difference fell just short of statistical significance (Emery et al., 1994). Furthermore, a more positive coparenting relationship and more father involvement in childrearing was reported in a 9-year follow-up pilot study (Dillon & Emery, 1996). Finally, a decline in parental conflict over time was associated with improved child mental health when the mediation and litigation groups from this study were combined (Kitzmann & Emery, 1994).

The data available from other studies also have failed to indicate differences in mental health between family members using mediation and adversary settlement. No differences in child outcomes were found in a brief assessment in one study (Pearson & Thoennes, 1984), and detailed assessments of the former partners in another study similarly found no differences in adults' psychological adjustment (Kelly, 1990; Kelly, Gigy, & Hausman, 1988).

One interesting direction for intervention and research on the effect of mediation on mental health and family relationships is increasing the duration of mediation, particularly by including intermittent contact following dispute settlement or even ongoing supervision or arbitration. Johnston and Roseby (1997) found that "therapeutic mediation," which included rather extensive assessment and individual prenegotiating counseling, produced considerable agreement among families who had repeatedly litigated divorce disputes. Of particular interest, more cooperative and less conflictual coparenting relationships were produced by group intervention methods (i.e., seeing several disputing families in a group), whereas better parent–child relationships came from family- rather than group-focused intervention.

Summary and Evaluation

The failure to demonstrate differences in adults' and children's mental health following mediation might be due to any number of substantive and methodological problems. Mediation typically is very brief, and the parents seen in mediation are highly acrimonious. In addition, only a few studies of possible psychological outcomes have been conducted, and many possible targets of change have not been measured in research conducted to date. Furthermore, the duration of follow-up has been short in almost all research, and more differences may emerge in long-term follow-up studies (Dillon & Emery, 1996). At the same time, some documented effects, such as the success in resolving disputes, client satisfaction, and the increased involvement of nonresidential fathers following mediation rather than litigation, are important outcomes regardless of their relation with measures of children's or adults' mental health. Clearly, more research is needed on the psychological and relationship consequences of mediation and adversary settlement, and such research obviously is of considerable social importance.

SUMMARY AND DIRECTIONS FOR FUTURE RESEARCH

Taken as a whole, the empirical evidence on the success of intervention with children, parents, and coparents during or following separation and divorce is far from compelling. Data from controlled studies indicate that school-based groups for children have beneficial effects, but the positive outcomes are generally small in magnitude and focused on subclinical distress rather than disordered emotions, cognitions, or behaviors. Parenting groups are viewed positively by adults and aid in facilitating their adjustment to divorce, but the eased parental transition produces few demonstrable benefits for children. Moreover, divorce mediation settles many disputes, produces higher levels of consumer satisfaction than adversary settlement, leads to somewhat better coparenting relationships, and helps to encourage nonresidential parents' continued economic and parenting responsibilities, but mediation has not been shown to improve parents' or children's psychological functioning.

The limited benefits demonstrated in intervention research to date must be acknowledged squarely. At the same time, there are several important reasons for tempering the conclusion that the programs produce only modest benefits. First, most research conducted to date was based on brief, focused intervention that is often offered in a group format with no follow-up sessions. Given the number and range of disruptions that predate and follow separation and divorce, it would be surprising if eight sessions in a children's group, six weeks in a parenting class, or four sessions in mediaton produce substantial psychological improvements in family members in the short or the long run. The extensive body of descriptive research on divorce indicates that the transition involves substantial psychological, social, and economic stressors over a prolonged period of time. Although various brief interventions are helpful, it would be unrealistic to expect any of them to offer a quick fix for separated and divorced families. Clearly, there is a need for more research on divorce interventions that offer a range of services to children, parents, and divorced families and include or at least offer occasional follow-up or "booster" sessions over a period of perhaps a year or more.

Second and more broadly, there simply is a need for more research on divorce interventions. Given the limited research conducted to date, it would be premature to conclude that intervention in divorce produces limited benefits, that is, to accept the null hypothesis. This is especially true because only a few styles and forms of intervention have been studied systematically. A plethora of programs have been developed to help divorcing families. Too often, these interventions are developed—and often mandated by courts—without empirical support or evaluation, especially evaluation involving random assignment or adequate comparison groups. Both for clinical and research purposes, moreover, intervention programs would benefit if they systematically incorporated both the empirical findings and the theoretical perspectives that can be gleaned from the rich body of descriptive research on divorce (Barber, 1995; Grych & Fincham, 1992; Lee et al., 1994).

In addition to research on divorce programs, epidemiological data make it clear that children and adults from divorced families are significantly overrepresented in the outpatient mental health treatment population. Unfortunately, there is no research on the outcome of outpatient psychotherapy directed at divorce, and little research has been conducted on whether traditional therapies (e.g., parent training) are more or less effective with divorced parents (for a review, see Emery, 1998). Both of these psychotherapy issues merit detailed investigation, even in an era where psychotherapy research is dominated by studies of single mental disorders (which often are co-morbid with life events with divorce as well as with other emotional difficulties).

Third and even more broadly, it must be recognized that the social and legal culture of divorce has changed rapidly in recent decades, and our societal views and laws continue to evolve. Interventions in divorce must be viewed against this evolving backdrop because the social, legal, and cultural context makes it more or less easy (or appropriate) to normalize divorce for children, support single parents, or encourage cooperative coparenting. For example, differences found between women's relative satisfaction with mediation or litigation in two studies, one in Virginia (Emery, Matthews, & Wyer, 1991; Emery & Wyer, 1987a) and another in California (Kelly, 1989, 1990), appear to be due to the contrasting social and legal background of litigation, not mediation, in the two states (Emery, 1994). Indeed, with the exception of child support enforcement, the law appears to have been a weak intervention in divorce, as changes in divorce law in recent decades appear to have followed rather than preceded changes in the public's attitude and behavior (Emery, 1998). For example, the passage of no-fault divorce laws seems to have been a consequence, not a cause, of increasing rates of divorce in the United States (Glenn, 1997). Such observations draw attention to the importance of culture in affecting the behavior of individuals, and the limited effectiveness of psychological interventions in divorce also seems more significant when viewed against the backdrop of the limited influence of the law.

REFERENCES

Alpert-Gillis, L., Pedro-Carroll, J., & Cowen, E. (1989). The children of divorce intervention program: Development, implementation, and evaluation of a program for young urban children. *Journal of Consulting and Clinical Psychology, 57,* 583–589.

Anderson, R., Kinney, J., & Gerler, E. (1984). The effects of divorce groups on children's classroom behavior and attitudes toward divorce. *Elementary School Guidance and Counseling, 19,* 70–76.

Barber, B. (1995). Preventive intervention with adolescents and divorced mothers: A conceptual framework for program design and evaluation. *Journal of Applied Developmental Psychology, 16,* 481–503.

Bloom, B. L., Hodges, W. F., & Caldwell, R. A. (1982). A preventive program for the newly separated: Initial evaluation. *American Journal of Community Psychology, 10,* 251–264.

Bloom, B. L., Hodges, W. F., Kern, M. B., & McFaddin, S. C. (1985). A prevention program for the newly separated: Final evaluations. *American Journal of Orthopsychiatry, 55,* 9–26.

Bornstein, M., Bornstein, P., & Walters, H. (1988). Children of divorce: Empirical evaluation of a group-treatment program. *Journal of Clinical Child Psychology, 17,* 248–254.

Burke, D., & Van de Streek, L. (1989). Children of divorce: An application of Hammond's group counseling for children. *Elementary School Guidance and Counseling, 24,* 112–118.

Cantor, D., & Drake, C. (1983). *Divorced parents and their children: A guide for mental health practitioners.* New York: Springer.

Cowen, E., Hightower, A. D., Pedro-Carroll, J., & Work, W. (1989). School-based models for primary prevention programming with children. In R. Lorion (Ed.), *Prevention in human services* (Vol. 7, pp. 133–160). Binghamton, NY: Haworth Press.

Cowen, E. Hightower, A. D., Pedro-Carroll, J., Work, W., Wyman, P., & Haffey, W. (1996). *School based prevention for children at risk: The primary mental health project.* Manuscript submitted for publication.

Crosbie-Burnett, M., & Newcomer, L. (1990). Group counseling children of divorce: The effects of a multimodel intervention. *Journal of Divorce, 13,* 69–78.

Devlin, A. S., Brown, E. H., Beebe, J., & Parulis, E. (1992). Parent education for divorced fathers. *Family Relations, 41,* 290–296.

Dillon, P., & Emery, R. (1996). Divorce mediation and resolution of child custody disputes: Long-term effects. *American Journal of Orthopsychiatry, 66,* 131–140.

Eekelaar, J. (1991). *Regulating divorce.* New York: Oxford University Press.

Emery, R. (1982). Interparental conflict and the children of discord and divorce. *Psychological Bulletin, 92,* 310–330.

Emery, R. E. (1994). *Renegotiating family relationships: Divorce, child custody, and mediation.* New York: Guilford.

Emery, R. (1998). *Marriage, divorce, and children's adjustment* (2nd ed.). Thousand Oaks, CA: Sage.

Emery, R. E., Matthews, S., & Kitzmann, K. (1994). Child custody mediation and litigation: Parents' satisfaction and functioning a year after settlement. *Journal of Consulting and Clinical Psychology, 62,* 124–129.

Emery, R. E., Matthews, S., & Wyer, M. M. (1991). Child custody mediation and litigation: Further evidence on the differing views of mothers and fathers. *Journal of Consulting and Clinical Psychology, 59,* 410–418.

Emery, R. E., & Wyer, M. M. (1987a). Child custody mediation and litigation: An experimental evaluation of the experience of parents. *Journal of Consulting and Clinical Psychology, 55,* 179–186.

Emery, R. E., & Wyer, M. M. (1987b). Divorce mediation. *American Psychologist, 42,* 472–480.

Forgatch, M. S. (1994). *Parenting through change: A training manual.* Eugene, OR: Oregon Social Learning Center.

Forgatch, M. S., & DeGarmo, D. S. (1998). *Promoting boys' academic outcomes: An effective parent training program for divorcing mothers.* Unpublished manuscript, Oregon Social Learning Center, Eugene, OR.

Glenn, N. D. (1997). A reconsideration of the effects of no-fault divorce on divorce rates. *Journal of Marriage and the Family, 59,* 1023–1025.

Grych, J., & Fincham, F. (1992). Intervention for children of divorce: Toward greater integration of research and action. *Psychological Bulletin, 111,* 434–454.

Guidubaldi, J., Perry, J., & Cleminshaw, H. (1984). The legacy of parental divorce. In B. Lahey & A. Kazdin (Eds.), *Advances in child clinical psychology* (Vol. 7, pp. 109–151). New York: Plenum.

Gwynn, C., & Brantley, H. (1987). Effects of a divorce group intervention for elementary school children. *Psychology in the Schools, 24,* 161–164.

Hetherington, E. M. (1989). Coping with family transitions: Winners, losers, and survivors. *Child Development, 60,* 1–14.

Hetherington, E. M. (1991). Presidential address: Families, lies, and videotapes. *Journal of Research on Adolescence, 1,* 323–348.

Hetherington, E. M. (1993). An overview of the Virginia Longitudinal Study of Divorce and Remarriage with a focus on early adolescence. *Journal of Family Psychology, 7,* 39–56.

Hodges, W. (1991). *Interventions for children of divorce: Custody, access, and psychotherapy.* New York: Wiley.

Hodges, W., & Bloom, B. (1986). Preventive intervention program for newly separated adults: One year later. *Journal of Preventive Psychiatry, 3*(1), 35–49.

Howard, K. I., Cornille, T. A., Lyons, J. S., Vessey, J. T., Lueger, R. J., & Saunders, S. M. (1996). Patterns of service utilization. *Archives of General Psychiatry, 53,* 696–703.

Irving, H., Benjamin, M., Bohm, P., & MacDonald, G. (1981). *A study of conciliation counseling in the family court of Toronto: Implications for socio-legal practice.* Toronto: Department of National Health and Welfare and the Ontario Ministry of the Attorney General.

Johnston, J. R., & Roseby, V. (1997). *In the name of the child: A developmental approach to understanding and helping children of conflicted and violent divorce.* New York: Free Press.

Kalter, N., Schaefer, M., Lesowitz, M., Alpern, D., & Pickar, J. (1988). School-based support groups for children of divorce. In B. Gottlieb (Ed.), *Marshaling social support: Formats, processes, and effects* (pp. 165–185). Newbury Park, CA: Sage.

Kalter, N., & Schreier, S. (1993). School-based support groups for children of divorce. In J. Zins & M. Elias (Eds.), *Promoting student success through group interventions* (pp. 39–66). Binghamton, NY: Haworth.

Kelly, J. B. (1989). Mediated and adversarial divorce: Respondents' perceptions of their processes and outcomes. *Mediation Quarterly, 24,* 71–88.

Kelly, J. B. (1990). *Final report. Mediated and adversarial divorce resolution processes: An analysis of post-divorce outcomes.* (Available from the author, Northern California Mediation Center, 100 Tamal Plaza, Suite 175, Corte Madera, CA 94925.)

Kelly, J. B., & Duryee, M. A. (1992). Women's and men's views of mediation in voluntary and mandatory mediation settings. *Family and Conciliation Courts Review, 30,* 34–49.

Kelly, J. B., Gigy, L., & Hausman, S. (1988). Mediated and adversarial divorce: Initial findings from a longitudinal study. In J. Folberg & A. Milne (Eds.), *Divorce mediation: Theory and practices* (pp. 453–474). New York: Guilford.

Kessler, S. (1978). Building skills in divorce adjustment groups. *Journal of Divorce, 2,* 209–216.

Kitzmann, K. M., & Emery, R. E. (1994). Child and family coping one year after mediated and litigated child custody disputes. *Journal of Family Psychology, 8,* 150–157.

Kramer, L., & Washo, C. A. (1993). Evaluation of a court-mandated prevention program for divorcing parents. *Family Relations, 42,* 179–186.

Laumann-Billings, L., & Emery, R. E. (1998). *Young adults' painful feelings about parental divorce.* Unpublished manuscript, University of Virginia.

Lee, J. M., & Hett, G. G. (1990). Post-divorce adjustment: An assessment of a group intervention. *Canadian Journal of Counseling, 24,* 199–209.

Lee, C. M., Picard, M., & Blain, M. D. (1994). A methodological and substantive review of intervention outcome studies for families undergoing divorce. *Journal of Family Psychology, 8,* 3–15.

Malouff, J. M., Lanyon, R. I., & Schutte, N. S. (1988). Effectiveness of a brief group RET treatment for divorce-related dysphoria. *Journal of Rational-Emotive and Cognitive-Behavior Therapy, 6,* 162–171.

Margolin, F. M. (1973). *An approach to resolution of visitation disputes post-divorce: Short-term counseling.* Unpublished doctoral dissertation, United States International Univerity, San Diego, CA.

Omizo, M., & Omizo, S. (1987). Group counseling with children of divorce: New findings. *Elementary School Guidance and Counseling, 22,* 46–53.

Patterson, G. (1982). *Coercive family process.* Eugene, OR: Castalia.

Pedro-Carroll, J., Sutton, J., & Black, A. (1993). *The Children of Divorce Intervention Program: Preventive outreach to early adolescence* (Final Report). Rochester, NY: Rochester Mental Health Association.

Pearson, J., & Thoennes, N. (1984). *Final report of the divorce mediation research project.* (Available from authors, 1720 Emerson St., Denver, CO 80218.)

Pearson, J., & Thoennes, N. (1989). Divorce mediation: Reflections on a decade of research. In K. Kressel & D. Pruitt (Eds.), *Mediation research* (pp. 9–30). San Francisco: Jossey-Bass.

Pedro-Carroll, J. (1993). *The children of divorce intervention program: A prevention program designed to foster resilience and enhance children's capacity to cope.* Unpublished manuscript.

Pedro-Carroll, J. (1997). The children of divorce intervention program: Fostering resilient outcomes for school-aged children. In G. Albee & Gullotta (Eds.), *Primary prevention works, Vol 6: Issues in children's and families' lives* (pp. 213–238). London: Sage.

Pedro-Carroll, J., & Alpert-Gillis, L. (1997). Preventative interventions for children of divorce: A developmental model for 5 and 6 year-old children. *Journal of Primary Prevention, 18,* 5–23.

Pedro-Carroll, J., Alpert-Gillis, L., & Cowen, E. (1992). An evaluation of the efficacy of a preventive intervention for 4th–6th grade urban children of divorce. *Journal of Primary Prevention, 13,* 115–130.

Pedro-Carroll, J., & Cowen, E. (1985). The children cope with divorce program: An investigation of the efficacy of a school-based prevention program. *Journal of Consulting and Clinical Psychology, 53,* 603–611.

Pedro-Carroll, J., Cowen, E., Hightower, A., & Guare, J. (1986). Preventive intervention with latency-aged children of divorce: A replication study. *American Journal of Community Psychology, 14,* 277–290.

Roseby, V., & Deutsch, R. (1985). Children of separation and divorce: Effects of social role-taking group intervention on fourth and fifth graders. *Journal of Clinical Child Psychology, 14,* 55–60.

Salts, C., & Zongker, C. (1983). Effects of divorce counseling groups on adjustment and self-concept. *Journal of Divorce, 6,* 55–67.

Smith, M., & Glass, G. (1977). Meta-analysis of psychology outcome studies. *American Psychologist, 32,* 752–760.

Stolberg, A., & Cullen, P. (1983). Preventative interventions for families of divorce: The Divorce Adjustment Project. In L. A. Kurdek (Ed.), *New directions in child development, Vol. 19: Children and divorce* (pp. 71–81). San Francisco: Jossey-Bass.

Stolberg, A., & Garrison, K. (1985). Evaluating a primary prevention program for children of divorce. *American Journal of Community Psychology, 13,* 111–124.

Stolberg, A., & Mahler, J. (1994). Enhancing treatment gains in a school-based intervention for children of divorce through skill training, parental involvement, and transfer procedures. *Journal of Consulting and Clinical Psychology, 62,* 147–156.

Thiessen, J. D., Avery, A. W., & Joanning, H. (1980). Facilitating postdivorce adjustment among women: A communication skills training approach. *Journal of Divorce, 4,* 35–44.

Wolchik, S. A., West, S. G., Westover, S., Sandler, I. N., Martin, A., Lustig, J., Tein, J., & Fisher, J. (1993). The Children of Divorce parenting intervention: Outcome evaluation of an empirically based program. *American Journal of Community Psychology, 21,* 293–331.

Woody, J. D., Colley, P., Schlegelmilch, J., & Maginn, P. (1985). Relationship between ex-spouses: Impact of a weekend educational workshop. *International Journal of Family Psychiatry, 6,* 99–115.

Zill, N., Morrison, D. R., & Coiro, M. J. (1993). Long-term effects of parental divorce on parent-child relationships, adjustment, and achievement in young adulthood. *Journal of Family Psychology, 7,* 91–103.

Author Index

A

Abidin, R. R., 49, *62*
Ablon, S., 48, 49, *62*
Achenbach, T. M., 49, *62*, 97, 103, *115*,
   185, *187*, 242, *249*, 259, *269*
Acitelli, L. K., 34, 35, *41*, *43*
Acock, A., 24, 40, *41*, 259, *270*
Adams, R. G., 169, *189*
Adelmann, P. K., 25, 27, *41*
Ahrons, C., 249, *249*
Aiken, L. S., 296, *318*
Alexander, K. L., 197, *219*
Alpern, D., 330, *343*
Alpert-Gillis, L., 325, 327, *341*, *343*
Amato, P. R., 23, 24, *41*, 47, *62*, 66, *88*,
   93, 94, 95, 114, *115*, 147, 148, 150,
   151, 153, 154, 161, *161*, *162*, 259,
   269
Anderson, E. R., 68, 85, *89*, 227, 229,
   249, *251*, 296, 299, 300, 302, 303,
   304, 307, 308, 310, 312, 316, 318,
   318, *319*
Anderson, J. Z., 261, 262, 267, *269*
Anderson, R., 328, *341*
Anderson, S. A., 284, *293*
Aquilino, W. S., 155, *162*
Arbuckle, J. L., 158, *162*
Arthur, J., 108, *116*
Aseltine, R. H., 66, *88*, 237, *249*
Astone, N., 119, *144*, 167, *189*
Avery, A. W., 336, *344*

B

Baerger, D. R., 25, 27, *41*
Baker, D., 51, *62*
Baldwin, A., 48, 49, *64*, 67, 68, *88*
Baldwin, C., 48, 49, *64*, 67, 68, *88*
Baldwin, W., 196, *219*
Bank, L., 229, *249*
Barber, B., 340, *341*
Barnard, K. E., 209, *219*
Barnett, R. C., 158, *162*
Barrera, M. J., 237, *249*
Barry, W. A., 11, *22*
Baruch, G. K., 158, *162*
Basham, R. B., 238, *251*
Bates, J. E., 48, 49, *63*, *64*, 68, *88*, 201,
   202, 220, 222
Baumrind, D., 67, 68, 72, *88*, 202, *219*,
   263, 266, *269*
Baydar, N., 174, *187*
Beaman, J., 229, 237, 238, *252*
Beardsall, L., 49, *63*
Beavers, W. R., 281, *293*
Beebe, J., 336, *342*
Belle, D. H., 238, *249*
Belsky, J., 18, *20*, 23, *41*, 148, *162*, 177,
   187, 237, 238, 239, *249*
Benjamin, M., 338, *342*
Bennett, T. L., 239, *250*
Bennion, L. D., 227, *249*, 303, 304, 308,
   318
Bensley, L., 180, *190*

Benson, P. R., 17, *21*
Berger, S. H., 227, *250*, 253, 254, 256, 257, 259, 260, 261, 262, 263, 264, 265, 266, 267, *269*, 276, *293*
Bergner, R. M., 108, *116*
Bianchi, S. M., 24, *43*, 161, *163*
Biederman, J., 48, 49, *62*
Biglan, A., 108, *116*
Billingsley, A., 24, 25, *41*, 166, *187*
Black, A., 327, 330, *343*
Black, M. M., 180, *187*
Blain, M. D., 324, 330, 331, 332, 336, 340, *343*
Blankenhorn, D., 117, *144*, 147, *162*
Blechman, E. A., 150, *163*, 237, *252*
Block, J., 93, 99, *115*, 205, *221*, 259, *269*
Block, J. H., 93, 99, *115*, 205, *221*, 259, *269*
Bloom, B., 332, *342*
Bloom, B. L., 332, *341*
Boethel, C., 257, 262, 264, 266, *269*, 276, *293*
Bohm, P., 338, *342*
Bolger, N., 238, *250*
Booth, A., 47, *62*, 93, 94, 95, *115*, 148, 151, 154, 161, *161*, *162*, 259, *269*
Booth, C. L., 209, *219*
Booth, K., 119, *145*
Borduin, C. M., 280, 281, *293*
Bornstein, M., 325, 329, *341*
Bornstein, P., 325, 329, *341*
Borquez, J., 217, *221*
Borrine, M. L., 259, 264, 265, *269*
Bos, H., 194, *222*
Bos, J. M., 194, 205, *222*
Bowman, P., 32, *41*
Bradbury, T. N., 3, *21*
Bradley, R. H., 180, *190*, 198, 202, 207, 211, *219*, *220*
Brantley, H., 329, *342*
Braun-Curtin, R., 119, 137, *145*
Bray, J. H., 227, *250*, 253, 254, 256, 257, 259, 260, 261, 262, 263, 264, 265, 266, 267, 268, *269*, *270*, 276, *293*, 302, *319*
Bridges, M., 259, *270*
Brillon, L., 86, *89*
Brody, G., 65, *88*
Brody, G. H., 227, *250*
Broman, C. L., 25, 26, 37, *41*
Bronars, S., 126, *144*
Bronfenbrenner, U., 67, *88*, 183, *187*, 197, *220*
Brooks-Gunn, J., 48, 49, *63*, 166, 167, 171, 172, 174, 177, 178, 179, 180, 181, 182, 183, 185, 186, *187*, *188*, *189*, *190*, *191*, 195, 196, *220*, *221*

Brown, A. C., 267, *270*
Brown, B., 194, *221*
Brown, B. B., 68, *90*
Brown, C. H., 169, *189*
Brown, E. H., 336, *342*
Brown, N. Y., 259, 264, 265, *269*
Brubaker, T. H., 23, *41*
Brunelli, S. A., 180, *191*
Buchanan, C. M., 47, *62*, 98, *115*
Buehlman, K. T., 5, 6, 16, 20, *20*, 280, *293*
Bugaighis, M. A., 280, *294*
Bumpass, L., 119,129, *144*, *145*, 166, *187*
Bumpass, L. L., 147, 153, *162*, 253, *270*, 278, 279, *294*
Burke, D., 330, *341*
Buriel, R., 66, 68 *89*
Burleson, B. R., 238, *250*
Burton, L. M., 49, *63*, 166, 169, 180, *187*, *188*
Bus, A. G., 202, *220*
Bushwall, S. J., 65, 66, 72, *88*, 108, *115*
Bryk, A. S., 232, *250*

C

Cain, V., 196, *219*
Caldwell, B. M., 198, 202, 207, 211, *219*, *220*
Caldwell, R. A., 332, *341*
Call, V. R. A., 278, 279, *294*
Campbell, L. E., 98, *116*
Cancio, J., 24, 40, *43*
Candell, K., 237, *251*
Cantor, D., 332, *341*
Capaldi, D. M., 227, 229, *250*
Carey, W. B., 53, *63*
Carlsmith, J. M., 65, 66, 72, *88*, 108, *115*
Carlson, 197, *220*
Carrere, S., 13, 14, 15, 16, 17, 19, 20, *20*
Carstensen, L. L., 23, *41*
Carter, B., 256, *270*
Carter, E. A., 265, 257, *271*
Casey, P. H., 180, *190*
Caspi, A., 25, *41*, 148, 154, *162*
Castro-Martin, T., 253, *270*
Cave, G., 194, *222*
Ceballo, R., 217, *221*
Chadwick, K., 25, 27, *41*
Chao, R. K., 68, *88*
Chao, W., 229, 237, 238, *252*
Chase-Lansdale, P. K., 93, *115*, 157, *162*, 166, 167, 171, 172, 176, 177, 178, 179, 180, 181, 182, 183, 184, 185, 186, *187*, *188*, *189*, *190*, *191*, 196, *221*, 227, *250*, 259, *270*

Chatters, L. M., 32, 37, *43*, 173, *189*
Cherlin, A. J., 93, *115*, 147, 157, *162*,
    178, *188*, 227, *250*, 259, *270*, 273,
    290, *293*
Chorost, A. F. 23, *42*
Christensen, A., 14, *21*
Cicchetti, D., 49, *63*
Clements, M., 23, *42*
Cleminshaw, H. K., 68, *89*, 325, *342*
Clingempeel, W. G., 24, *42*, 61, *63*, 94, 96,
    116, 178, *189*, 227, *251*, 255, 258,
    259, 260, 261, 262, 263, 264, *270*,
    269, 299, 300, 302, 303, 307, 308,
    310, 312, 318, *318*, *319*
Coan, J., 13, 14, 15, 16, 17, 19, 20, *20*
Cohen, S., 7, *21*,78, *88*, 237, *250*
Coiro, M. J., 195, 199, *221*, *223*, 227, *252*,
    323, *344*
Cole, R. E., 67, 68, *88*
Coleman, J., 139, *144*
Coleman, M., 254, *270*, 260, *271*, 274,
    275, 276, 277, 278, 280, 287, 289,
    290, *293*, *294*
Coley, R. L., 166, 175, 176, 185, *188*
Coll, C. G., 49, *63*
Colley, P, 336, *344*
Collins, P. H., 27, *41*
Comstock, G. W., 199, *220*
Conger, R., 160, *162*,
Conger, R. D., 229, 237, 238, *250*, *252*
Conger, K. J., 160, *162*
Conners, C. K., 49, *62*
Cook, J., 12, 19, *21*
Cooley, M., 180, *190*
Coon, H. M., 28, *41*
Cooney, T. M., 155, *162*
Coontz, S., 148, *162*
Cooper, H., 260, *271*
Copeland, J. M., 280, *294*
Corbin, S. B.,, 87, *90*
Cornille, T. A., 323, *342*
Costa, F. M., 48, *63*
Cowan, C.,23, *41*, 101, 103, *115*
Cowan, P., 23, *41*
Cowan, P. A., 101, 103, *115*
Cowen, E., 325, 326, 327, *341*, *342*, *343*
Cox, J. L., 52, *63*
Cox, M., 68, 85, 89, 254, 258, 259, 265,
    270
Cox, M. J., 238, *250*, 299, 303, 316, *319*
Cox, R., 68, 85, *89*, 254, 258, 259, 265,
    270, 299, 303, 316, *319*
Coyne, J. C., 49, *63*, 237, 239, *250*
Crawford, A. G., 167, *188*
Creighton, L. L., 166, *188*
Crockenberg, S., 179, *188*, 200, *220*
Crohan, S. E., 35, 36, *41*

Crosbie-Burnett, M., 273, 275, 290, *293*,
    326, 330, *342*
Crouter, A. C., 67, *88*
Cummings, M. E., 95, 96, 97, 103, *115*
Cummings, E. M., 154, *162*, 316, *319*
Cullen, P., 325, *344*
Custer, L., 23, 37, *42*
Cutrona, C. E., 238, 239, *250*

D

Darling, C., 27, *42*
Davies, P. T., 95, 96, 97, 103, *115*, 154,
    162, 316, *319*
Davis, J. E., 27, 31, *41*, *42*
Davis, T. J., 31, 32, *41*
Deal, J. E., 296, 302, 303, 307, 308, 310,
    312, 318, *319*
Deater-Deckard, K., 48, 49, 50, 52, 53,
    61, *63*, 68, *88*
DeGarmo, D. S., 227, 229, 238, 241,
    242, 244, 246, 247, 334, *342*
Demo, D. H., 24, 40, *41*, 148, *162*, 259,
    270
DeRogatis, L. R., 279, *293*
De Temple, J., 204, 205, *220*
Deutsch, R., 329, *344*
Devlin, A. S., 336, *342*
Dickerson, B. J., 166, 169, *188*
Diener, E., 279, *293*
Dillon, P., 338, 339, *342*
Dion, M. R., 199, 217, *220*
Dishion, T., 231, *251*
Dodge, K. A., 48, 49, *63*, 68, *88*, 201,
    202, *220*, *222*
Dornbusch, S. M., 47, *62*, 65, 66, 67, 68,
    69, 72, 74, 85, *90*, 98, 108, *115*
Douvan, E., 23, 25, 28, 33, 37, *41*, *42*, *43*
Douvan, L., 34, 35, *43*
Downey, G., 49, *63*, 237, 239, *250*
Drake, C., 332, *341*
Druckman, J., 267, *270*
Dubow, E., 196, 197, *220*
Duffy, M. E., 238, *250*
Dukes, L. J., 201, *221*
Duncan, G., 195, *220*
Dunkel-Schetter, C., 239, *250*
Dunn, J., 47, 49, 50, 51, 52, 61, *62*, *63*,
    64
Dunn, L. M., 185, *188*
Duryee, M. A., 338, *343*

E

Eddy, M. J., 230, *251*
Edelbrock, C. S., 97, 103, *115*, 185, *187*,
    242, 249, 259, *269*

Edmonston, B., 194, *221*
Edwards, J. N., 23, *43*, 148, 151, *162*
Eekelaar, J., 324, *342*
Egeland, B., 197, 202, 203, 204, 205, 217,
    220, 221, 222
Ekman, P., 4, *21*
Elardo, R. D., 202, *220*
Elder, G. H., 25, *41*, 148, 154, 160, *162*
Eldred, C. A., 204, 205, *220, 223*
Emery, R. E., 48, 49, *64*, 66, *88*, 93, *116*,
    136, *144*, 148, *163*, 181, *188*, 261,
    265, *270*, 323, 324, 325, 337, 338,
    339, 341, *342, 343*
Emmons, R. A., 279, *293*
Ensminger, M. E., 169, 180, *189*
Entwistle, d. R., 197, *219*
Epps, E., 32, *41*
Erera-Weatherly, P. I., 275, *293*
Erickson, M. F., 202, *221*
Estes, A., 231, *251*
Eyster, S. L., 23, 26, 27, 37, 38, 39, *42*

F

Faraone, S. V., 48, 49, *62*
Farres, A. M., 98, *116*
Featherman, D., 72, *88*
Feldman, S., 71, *90*
Fetrow, R. A., 229, 230, *249, 251*
Fincham, F., 324, 325, 326, 330, 340, *342*
Fincham, F. D., 97, 98, *116*
Fine, M. A., 27, *42*, 266, *271*, 274, 276,
    277, 278, 280, 287, 289, *293, 294*
Fink, B. L., 194, *222*
Finlay, B., 151, *163*
Fischel, J. E., 202, *223*
Fisher, J., 333, 336, *344*
Floyd, F. J., 23, *42*
Ford, M., 71, *90*
Forehand, R., 65, *88*, 227, *250*
Forgatch, M. S., 65, 66, *88*, 227, 229, 238,
    241, 242, 244, 245, 246, 247, *249*,
    250, 251, 263, 265, *270*, 334, 335,
    342
Foster, M., 126, *145*, 231, 238, *250, 251*
Fraleigh, M., 68, 69, 74, *88*
Frate, D. A., 166, 169, *190*
Friedman, L., 108, *116*
Friesen, W. V., 4, *21*
Fu, V. R., 68, *89*
Furakawa, S., 166, *188*
Furstenberg, F. F., 65, *89*, 93, *115*, 126,
    145, 156, 163, 166, 167, 175, 178,
    180, 185, 187, 188, 196, 220, 221,
    227, 250, 259, 270

G

Galco, F. L., 202, *223*
Ganong, L. H., 254, 260, *270, 271*, 274,
    275, 276, 277, 278, 280, 287, 289,
    290, *293, 294*
Garbarino, J., 261, *270*
Garcia Coll, C., 86, *89*
Garfinkel, I., 130, 143, *144*
Garmezy, N., 48, *63*, 149, *163*, 197, 198,
    221
Garrison, K., 327, 333, *344*
Ge, X., 229, *250*
George, S. M., 166, 169, *188*
Gerler, E., 328, *341*
Geronimus, A., 126, *144*
GiGy, L., 339, *343*
Gjerde. P. F., 93, 99, *115*, 259, *269*
Glass, G., 331, *344*
Glenn, N. D., 153, 157, *163*, 341, *342*
Glick, P. C., 61, *63*, 65, *89*, 253, *270*
Gold, M., 74, *89*
Golding, J., 48, 50, 51, 52, 61, *63*, *64*
Gonzalez, R., 98, *116*, 169, *188*
Good, E. S., 237, *251*
Goodman, R., 51, *63*
Gordon, L. U., 7, *21*
Gordon, R. A., 166, 171, 172, 177, 179,
    183, 184, *188, 189, 191*,
Gottman, J., 4, 12, 19 , *21*
Gottman, J. M., 5, 6, 7, 9, 10, 11, 12, 13,
    14, 15, 16, 17, 18, 19, 20, *20, 21*,
    23, 28, 38, *41*, *42*, 242, *250*, 265,
    270, 280, 293
Green, G. J., 267, *270*
Green, S., 179, *191*
Green, S. M., 316, *319*
Greenberger, E., 74, *89*
Greene, A. D., 185, *190*, 196, 200, 217,
    221
Griffin, S., 279, *293*
Grogger, J., 126, *144*
Gross, R. T., 65, 66, 72, *88*, 108, *115*
Grych, J., 324, 325, 326, 330, 340, *342*
Grynch, J. H., 97, 98, *116*
Guare, J., 326, *343*
Guerney, B. G., 14, *21*
Guidubaldi, J., 68, *89*, 325, *342*
Guite, J., 48, 49, *62*
Gwynn, C., 329, *342*

H

Haas, S. D., 5, *21*
Hacker, T. A., 238, *251*

Haffey, W., 327, *342*
Halverson, C. F., 183, *191*
Hampson, R. B., 281, *293*
Handal, P. J., 259, 264, 265, *269*
Hanson, T., 119, 130, 131, 136, *144*, *145*
Hao, L., 173, *190*
Hardy, J., 167, *189*
Harrington, G., 205, *221*
Harris, B. F., 166, *189*
Harris, K. M., 175, *188*
Harvey, D. M., 261, *270*
Haskey, J., 48, *63*
Hastorf, A. H., 65, 66, 72, *88*
Hatch, R. C., 280, *294*
Hatchett, S., 23, 25, 28, 33, 38, *42*, *43*
Hausman, S., 339, *343*
Haveman, R., 121, *145*
Hawkins, M. W., 17, *21*
Hawkins, N., 51, *64*
Heavey, C. L., 14, *21*
Helsing, K. J., 199, *220*
Henderson, V. K., 178, 184, *190*, 227, 229, 238, *250*, *251*
Henderson-King, D. H., 35, *42*
Hendrix, H., 10, 13, 14, 19, *21*
Henick, A., 313, *319*
Hennigen, L., 277, *294*
Hennighausen, K. H., 204, *222*
Hernandez, D. J., 65, *89*, 160, *163*, 166, *189*
Hertel, R. K., 11, *22*
Hetherington, E. M. 24, 40, *42*, 50, 61, *63*, *64*, 68, 85, 87, *89*, 94, 95, 96, 97, 108, 113, *116*, 148, 150, *163*, 178, *189*, 254, 255, 257, 258, 259, 260, 261, 262, 263, 264, 265, *270*, 296, 299, 300, 302, 303, 307, 308, 310, 312, 316, 318, *318*, *319*, 324, *342*
Hett, G. G., 336, *343*
Hightower, A., 326, *343*
Hightower, D., 325, 327, *341*, *342*
Hill, R. B., 166, *189*
Hinde, R., 177, *189*
Hobfoll, S. E., 238, *251*
Hodges, W., 325, 326, 332, *342*
Hodges, W. F., 332, *341*
Hoff-Ginsberg, E., 86, *89*
Hoffman, S., 126, *145*, 156, *163*
Hogan, D. P., 173, *190*
Holden, J. M., 52, *63*
Holmberg, D., 35, *43*
Hollier, A., 256, 260, 261, *269*
Hollier, E. A., 296, 302, 303, 307, 310, 312, 318, *319*
Hollingshead, A. B., 231, 247, *251*

Holloway, S. D., 237, *251*
Hops, H., 108, *116*
Hornyak, L. A., 17, *21*
Horton, C. B., 108, *116*
Horwitz, s. M., 180, 185, *189*
Hossain, Z., 37, *42*
House, J., 24, *43*
House, J. S., 23, *42*, 153, *163*
Howard, K. I., 323, *342*
Howe, G., 94, *116*
Howell, C. T., 49, *62*, 185, *187*
Hsdorf, H., 108, *115*
Huck, S., 160, *162*
Hughes, M. E., 185, *188*
Hughes, R., 237, *251*
Hulgus, Y. F., 281, *293*
Hunter, A. G., 27, 31, 37, *42*
Huston, A. C., 49, *63*
Huston, T. L., 23, *42*

I

Insabella, G. M., 259, *270*
Irving, H., 338, *342*

J

Jackson, J. S., 32, *43*
Jayakody, R., 173, *189*
Jayaratne, T. E., 217, *221*
Jekel, J. F., 180, 185, *189*
Jendrek, M. P., 166, *189*
Jenkins, C. L., 49, *62*
Jessor, R., 48, *63*
Joanning, H., 336, *344*
Jodl, K. M., 61, *63*, 259, *270*
Johnson, C., 237, 238, 239, *252*
Johnson, D. R., 151, *162*
Johnson, L. B., 25, 32, *42*, *43*
Johnson, P. L., 93, *116*
Johnston, J. 108, *116*
Johnston, J. H., 242, *251*
Johnston, J. R. 98, *116*, 265, *270*, 339, *343*
Jouriles, E. N., 98, *116*
Jouriles, E., 261, 268. *270*

K

Kahan, J. P., 261, *271*
Kahn, R. L., 274, *294*
Kalter, N., 325, 326
Kane, E. W., 27, *42*
Kaniasty, K., 238, *251*

Karney, B. R., 3, *21*
Katz, L. F., 6, 16, 20, *20*, 280, *293*
Kenney, D. A., 309, *319*
Keith, B., 24, *41*, 47, *62*, 66, *88*, 93, 95, 114, *115*, 147, 148, 150, *162*, 259, *269*
Keith, V. M., 151, *163*
Kellam, S. G., 169, 180, *189*
Kelleher, K. J., 180, *190*
Kelly, J. B., 339, 341, *343*
Kent, R. N., 231, *251*
Kephart, G., 25, *42*
Kern, M. B., 332, *341*
Kessler, R. C., 7, *21*, 237, *249*
Kessler, S., 336, *343*
Kibria, N., 158, *162*
Kiely, K., 48, 48, *62*
Kiernan, K. E., 93, *115*, 157, *162*, 227, *250*, 259, *270*
King, V., 167, 175, *189*
Kinney, J., 328, *341*
Kitson, G. C., 237, *251*
Kitzmann, K., 338, *342*
Kitzmann, K. M., 339, *343*
Klebanov, P. K., 195, *220*
Klepinger, D., 126, *145*
Klerman, L. V., 180, 185, *189*, 194, *221*
Kline, M., 265, *270*
Kochman, T., 35, 36, *42*
Korenman, S., 126, *144*
Kou, H. S., 180, 185, *189*
Kramer, K. B., 153, 157, *163*
Kramer, L., 335, *343*
Krein, S. F., 151, *163*
Krokoff, L. J., 5, 13, *21*
Kurdek,L. A., 259, 265, *271*, 276, 277, *294*

L

Ladner, J. A., 166, *189*, 205, *222*
La Gaipa, J. L., 238, *251*
Lahey, B., 179, *191*
Lamborn, S. D., 67, 68, 69, 72, 85, *90*
Lane, C., 238, *251*
Lanyon, R. I., 336, *343*
LaPoint, V., 166, *189*
Larkin, K., 198, *221*
Larsen, A., 198, *221*, 280, *294*
Larsen, R. J., 279, *293*
Lathrop, M., 242, *250*
Laumann-Billings, L., 323, *343*
Laundry, D. J., 25, *42*
Lavizzo-Mourey, R., 32, *43*
La Voie, L., 309, *319*
Lee, C. M., 324, 330, 331, 332, 336, 340, *343*

Lee, J. M., 336, *343*
Leiderman, H., 65, 66, 68, 69, 72, 74, *88*, 108, *115*
Leppin, A., 239, *251*
Lesowitz, M., 330, *343*
Levenson, R. W., 6, 7, 15, 19, 20, *21*, 23, *41*
Leventhal, 179, *191*
Lewis, E. 37, *43*
Lewis, J. M., 87, *90*, 238, *250*
Liaw, F., 48, 49, *63*
Lichter, D. 32, *42*
Lichter, D. T. 25, *42*
Lieberman, M. A., 209, 211, *222*
Lightel, J., 68, *89*
Lin, C. C., 68, *89*
Lin, S., 65, *89*
Lindberg, C., 261, *271*
Lindblad-Goldberg, M., 201, *221*
Lindner, M. S., 227, *249*, 296, 302, 303, 304, 307, 308, 310, 312, 318, *318*, *319*
Little, H. M., 166, *189*
Litteljohn-Blake, S. M., 27, *42*
Locke, H. J., 18, *21*
Loeber, R., 179, *191*, 304, *319*
Loomis, L. S., 95, *115*, 148, 161, *161*
Long, N., 65, *88*
Lonigan, C. J., 202, *223*
Lorber, M., 17, *21*
Lorenz, F. O., 160, *162*
Lueger, R. J., 323, *342*
Lundberg, S., 126, *145*
Luster, T., 196, 197, *220*, *221*
Lustig, J., 333, 336, *344*
Luthar, S. S., 197, *221*
Lyons, J. S., 323, *342*

M

Maccoby, E. E., 47, *62*, 67, *89*, 94, 98, *115*, *116*
MacDonald, G., 338, *342*
Machida, S., 237, *251*
Maclean, M., 151, *163*
Magenheim, E. B., 195, 199, *221*
Maginn, P., 336, *344*
Mahler, J., 328, 330, *344*
Malamuth, N. M., 14, *21*
Malouff, J. M., 336, *343*
Manski, C., 121, *145*
Mapes, D., 254, *270*
Margolin, F. M., 338, *343*
Margolin, G., 14, *21*
Markman, H., 5, *21*
Markman, H. J., 23, *42*

Marshall, N. L., 158, *162*
Marsiglio, W., 175, *189*, 275, 276, *294*
Martin, A., 333, 336, *344*
Martin, E. P., 166, *189*
Martin, J., 67, *89*
Martin, J. A., 194, *222*
Martin, J. M., 166, *189*
Martin, P., 280, 287, *294*
Martin, T. C., 153, *162*
Masheter, C., 94, *116*
Masten, A. S., 197, 198, *221*
Matas, L., 178, *190*
Matjasko, J. L., 166, 171, 172, *189*
Maton, K. I., 175, *191*
Matthews, S., 338, 341, *342*
Maurer, J. D., 194, *222*
Maymi, J. R., 257, 262, 264, *269*
Maynard, R., 126, *145*, 178, *189*, 194, *221*
McAdoo, H. P., 169, *190*, 197, *221*
McAdoo, J., 175, *190*
McArdle, J. J., 296, *319*
McCarthy, D., 185, *190*
McCubbin, H. I., 280, *294*
McDevitt, S. C., 53, *63*
McDonald, E., 147, *162*
McFaddin, S. C., 332, *341*
McGaughey, M. C., 49, *62*
McGoldrick, M., 256, *270*, 256, 257, *271*
McHale, J., 185, 186, *190*
McLanahan, S., 24, *42*, 61, 66, *89*, 95, 96, *116*, 119,121, 130, 131, 135, 136, 137, 143, *144*, *145*, 151, 161, *163*
McLaughlin, D. K., 25, *42*
McLeod, J. D., 151, 152, 157, *163*
McLoyd, V., 66, 68, *89*, 199, *221*
McLoyd, V. C., 49, *63*, 167, *190*, 201, 217, *221*
McNamara, G., 237, *252*
Meadows, L., 261, *271*
Meens, L. D., 280, *294*
Mekos, D., 50, *64*
Melby, J. N., 160, *162*
Menaghan, E. G., 209, 211, *222*
Mero, R. P., 23, *42*
Meyer, D., 130, 143, *144*
Meyer, E. C., 86, *89*
Mick, E., 48, 49, *62*
Milberger, S., 49, 49, *62*
Miller, C., 130, *144*
Miller, S. M., 195, 199, *221*
Miller, T., 167, *189*
Minkler, M., 166, *190*
Mistina, D., 275, 290, *294*
Mitchell, S. K., 209, *219*
Mitchell-Kernan, C., 25, *43*

Mnookin, R. H., 94, 98, *116*
Montgomery, M. J., 300, 318, *319*
Moore, K. A., 185, *190*, 194, 195, 196, 199, 200, 217, *221*, *223*
Moore, J. J., 183, *191*
Morgan, P. S., 167, 180, 185, *188*
Morris, S., 51, *62*
Morrison, D. R., 93, *115*, 185, *190*, 194, 196, *221*, 227, *252*, 259, *270*, 323, *344*
Mounts, N. S., 67, 68, 69, 72, 85, *90*
Mueller, C. W., 153, *163*
Mullan, J. T., 209, 211, *222*
Murphy, C. M., 98, *116*
Murray, J., 11, 12, 19, *21*
Musick, J. S., 205, *222*
Myers, D.,194, *221*

N

Nastasi, B. K., 68, *89*
Neubaum, E., 227, *250*
Newcomer, L., 326, 330, *342*
Nitz, K., 180, *187*
Ng, R., 238, *250*
Nord, C. W., 194, *221*
Norris, F. H., 238, *251*
Notarius, C. I., 5, 17, *21*
Nye, F. I., 66, *89*

O

Obiorah, F. C., 280, *294*
O'Connor, T. G., 50, 51, 52, 61, *63*, *64*
Ogawa, J. R., 204, 205, *222*
Ogbu, J. U., 68, *89*
O'Leary, D. K., 231, *251*
O'Leary, K. D., 93, *116*
Olson, D. H., 280, 281, *294*
Omizo, M., 329, *343*
Omizo, S., 329, *343*
Orbuch, T. L., 23, 24, 26, 27, 34, 35, 37, 38, 39, 40, *42*, *43*, 153, *163*
Osteem, V., 108, *116*
Owen, M. T., 178, 184, *190*, 238, *250*

P

Paff-Bergen, L. A., 280, *294*
Paikoff, R., 177, *188*
Parish, W. L., 173, *190*
Parke, R. D., 66, 68, *89*, 178, *190*
Parrot, L.,10, 13, *22*
Parulis, E., 336, *342*

Patterson, G., 72, *89*, 334, *343*
Patterson, G. R., 65, 66, *88*, 227, 229,
    238, 242, 244, 245, *249, 250, 251*,
    263, 265, *270*, 304, *319*
Patterson, J. R., 14, *22*
Patton, M. Q., 280, *294*
Pearlin, L. I., 209, 211, *222*
Pearson, J., 338, 339, *343*
Pedro-Carroll, J., 325, 326, 327, 330, *341*,
    342, 343
Pellegrine, D. S., 198, *221*
Pellegrini, A. D., 202, *220*
Pensky, E., 18, *20*, 148, *162*
Perkins, T. F., 261, *271*
Perry, J., 325, *342*
Perry, J. D., 68, *89*
Peters, K. D., 194, *222*
Peterson, L., 229, *252*
Pettit, G. S., 48, 49, *63*, 68, *88*, 201, 202,
    220, 222
Pianta, R., 202, *221*
Picard, M., 324, 330, 331, 332, 336, 340,
    343
Pickar, J., 330, *343*
Pickering, K., 52, 61, *63*
Pickett, M. O., 166, *189*
Pittman, L., 181, 182, 185, 186, *190, 191*
Pleck, J. H., 158, *162*
Plomin, R., 48, *64*, 94, *116*
Plotnik, R., 126, *145*
Polit, D. F., 194, 205, 210, 212, *222*
Pope, H., 153, *163*
Pope., S. K., 180, *190*
Popenoe, D., 117, *145*, 147, *163*
Powers, D., 121, *145*
Presser, H. B., 174, *190*
Price-Sparlen, T., 49, *63*
Prinz, R. J., 231, *251*

Q

Quay, H. C., 49, *62*
Quinn, R. P. 274, *294*
Quint, J. C., 194, 203, 205, 217, *222*

R

Radloff, L. S., 74, *89*, 209, 222, 231, 242,
    251
Rahe, D. F., 205, *222*
Raley, R. K., 166, *187*
Ratliff, D., 308, *319*
Raub, V. A., 180, *191*
Raudenbush, S. W., 232, *250, 251*
Raush, H. L., 11, *22*

Ray, J. A., 227, 229, 244, *250*, 263, 265,
    270
Reed, E., 48, 49, *62*
Reid, J. B., 230, *251*
Reiss, D., 50, *64*, 94, *116*
Rende, R., 49, *63*
Renick, M. J., 23, *42*
Renner, M. A., 266, *271*, 276, *294*
Rezac, S., 154, *162*
Richters, J. E., 98, *116*
Rickert, V. I., 180, *190*
Ritter, P. L.. 65, 66, 68, 69, 72, 74, *88*,
    108, *115*
Roberts, D., 68, 69, 74, *88*
Robertson-Beckley, R. J., 166, *190*
Robins, P., 130, *144*
Robins, P. K., 93, *115*, 259, *270*
Rodgers, R. R., 72, *89*
Rodgers, S. T., 23, *41*
Roe, K. M., 166, *190*
Rogosch, F. A., 49, *63*
Rook, K. S., 237, *251*
Roopnarine, J. L., 37, *42*
Roseby, V., 329, 339, *343, 343*
Rosenberg, D. M., 178, *190*
Rosenberg, M., 74, *89*
Rosenthal, R., 74, 77, *90*
Rosenthal, R. A., 274, *294*
Rosnow, R., 74, 77, *90*
Ross, C. E., 158, *163*
Rossi, A., 148, 158, *163*
Rossi, P., 148, 158, *163*
Rothbart, M. K., 48, *64*
Rovine, M., 23 *41*
Rowser, S. L., 194, *222*
Ruckstuhl, L., 16, 20, *20*
Rusby, J. C., 231, *251*
Rushe, R., 12, 19, *21*
Rutter, M., 48, *63*, 149, *163*, 197, *222*

S

Sabatelli, R. M., 284, *293*
Sagovsky, R., 52, *63*
Salem, D. A., 175, *191*
Salts, C., 336, *344*
Saluter, A., 194, *222*
Sameroff, A. J., 48, 48, *64*
Sandefur, G., 24, *42*, 66, *89*, 95, 96, *116*,
    119, 121, *145*, 151, 161, *163*
Sandler, I. N., 333, 336, *344*
Santrock, J. W., 261, *271*
Sarason, B. R., 238, *251*
Sarason, I. G., 238, 242, *251*
Saunders, S. M., 323, *342*

Schafer. E., 72, *90*
Schafer, M., 330, *343*
Schellenbach, C., 261, *270*
Schlegelmilch, J., 336, *344*
Schoenborn, C. A., 259, 260, *271*
Schreier, S., 325, 326, *343*
Schulz, M. S., 101, 103, *115*
Schumm, W. R., 280, *294*
Schutte, N. S., 336, *343*
Schwarzer, R., 239, *251*
Schwebel, A. I., 266, *271*, 276, *294*
Searight, H. R., 259, 264, 265, *269*
Sebes, J., 261, *270*
Seifer, R., 48, 49, *64*
Sellers, S. L., 27, 37, *42*
Seltzer, J., 130, 131, 143, *144*, *145*
Seltzer, J. A., 24, *43*, 175, *190*, 227, *250*
Shapiro, A. F., 18, 20, *22*
Shapiro, S., 167, *189*
Shaw, D. S., 48, 49, *64*
Sherman, L., 108, *116*
Shimkin, D. B., 166, 169, *190*
Shimkin, E. M., 166, 169, *190*
Shreshta, S., 156, *163*
Siegel, J. M., 242, *251*
Silverblatt, A., 256, 260, 261, *269*
Simmons, R. L., 93, 94, 96, 103, *116*
Simons, R. L., 160, *162*, 229, 237, 238, 239, *252*
Sinclair, R. J., 259, 265, *271*
Skinner, M. L, 65, 66, *88*
Skolnick, A., 117, *145*
Slaughter, D. T., 167, *190*
Sloane, D., 17, *21*
Slomkowski, C., 49, *63*
Smith, A. W., 32, *43*
Smith, D. A., 98, *116*
Smith, E. W., 195, *223*
Smith, M., 331, *344*
Smith, R., 197, *223*
Snoek, J. D., 274, *294*
Snow, C., 204, 205, *220*
Snyder, J., 229, *252*
Sorrentino, C., 65, *90*
Spain, D., 161, *163*
Spanier, G., 23, *41*
Speiker, S., 180, *190*
Spencer, M. B., 49, *63*, 167, *190*
Spenner, K., 72, *88*
Spieker, S. J., 209, *219*
Sroufe, L., 178, *190*, 197, *220*
Stack, C. B., 26, 32, 38, *43*, 166, *190*
Stacy, J., 117, *145*
Stanley, S. M., 23, *42*
Stanley-Hagan, M., 68, 85, *89*, 94, 95, 107, *116*, 229, *251*, 296, 302, 303, 307, 310, 312, 318, *319*

Staples, R., 25, *43*
Steinberg, L., 66, 67, 68, 69, 72, 74, 85, 89, *90*
Stevens, J. H., 179, *190*, 200, *222*
Stevenson-Hinde, J., 177, *189*
Stief, T., 195, *223*
Stolberg, A., 325, 327, 328, 330, 333, *344*
Stouthamer-Loeber, M., 72, *89*, 304, *319*
St. Peter, C., 229, *252*
Summers, K. J., 5, 16, *22*
Sutherland, L., 37, *43*
Sutton, J., 327, 330, *343*
Swain, M. A., 11, *22*
Swanson, C.,13, 14, 15, 17, 19, 20, *21*
Sweet, J., 129, *144*
Sweet, J. A., 153, *162*, 253, *270*, 278, 279, *294*

T

Tannen, D., 284, *294*
Tardif, T., 86, *89*
Taylor, H., , 51, *62*
Taylor, R. J., 32, 37, *43*, 173, *189*, *190*
Tein, J., 333, 336, *344*
Teitler, J. O., 93, *115*, 259, *270*
Tellegen, A., 197, 198, *221*
Thiessen, J. D., 336, *344*
Thoennes, N., 338, 339, *343*
Thomas, V., 281, *294*
Thomson, E., 119, 136, 137, *144*, *145*, 147, *162*
Thornton, A., 24, 40, *43*
Thorpe, K., 52, *64*
Thorpe, K. J., 51, *64*
Timmer, S. G., 23, 38, *43*
Tinsley, B. J., 178, *190*
Touch, G., 257, 262, 264, 266, *269*
Tschann, J. M., 265, *270*
Tsunematsu, N., 72, *88*
Tublin, S., 71, *90*
Tucker, M. B., 25, 37, *43*
Turbin, M. S., 48, *63*
Turner, R. J., 180, *189*
Tyron, A., 94, *116*
Tyson, R., 12, 19, *21*
Tzelgov, J., 313, *319*

U

Unger, D., 180, *190*, 200, *222*

V

Vaccaro, D., 237, *252*

Valleau, M. D., 108, *116*
Van Den Bos, J.,48, *63*
Vanderrym, J., 48, *63*
Van de Streek, L., 330, *341*
Van Ijzendoorn, M. H., 202, *220*
Van Ryn, M., 23, *43*
Van Widenfelt, B., 183, *188*
Vanzetti-Nelly, N. A., 17 , *21*
Vaux, A., 74, *89*
Vemer, E., 260, *271*
Ventura, S. J., 194, *222*
Veroff, J., 23, 25, 28, 33, 34, 35, 38, 39,
    41, *42, 43*
Vessey, J. T., 323, *342*
Vinokur, A. D., 23, *43*, 238, *250*
Visher, E. B., 263, *271*, 273, 275, 286,
    290, *294*
Visher, J. S., 263, *271*, 273, 275, 286, 290,
    294
Vondra, J., 237, 239, *249*
Vuchinich, S., 227, *252*
Vuchinich, R., 227, *252*

W

Wadsworth, M. E., 151, *163*
Waite, L. J., 158, *163*
Wakschlag, L. S., 179, 181, 182, 183, *191*
Wallace, K. M., 18, *21*
Wallerstein, J. S., 68, 85, 87, *90*
Walker, H. A., 25, 26, *43*
Walker, K., 18, 20, *22*
Walters, H., 325, 329, *341*
Walters, L. H., 173, *191*
Walper, S., 108, *116*
Wampler, K. S., 183, *191*
Wampold, B. E., 14, *21*
Wandersman, L. P., 200, *222*
Warburton, R., 48, 49, *62*
Warren, R. C., 32, *43*
Warshak, R. A., 261, *271*
Washo, C. A., 335, *343*
Wasserman, G., 180, *191*
Waters, E., 98, *116*
Webster, P., 24, *43*
Webster, P. S., 23, *42*, 153, *163*
Weinberger, D., 71, *90*
Weinfield, N. S., 204, 205, *222*

Weinmann, L., 66, *90*
Weiss, B., 202, *222*
Weiss, R. S., 108, *116*
Weiss, R. L., 5, 16, *22*
Wells, T., 121, *145*
Went, D., 37, *43*
Werner, E., 197, *223*
West, S. G., 296, *318*, 333, 336, *344*
Weston, S., 72, *90*
Weston, W., 72, *90*
Westover, S., 333, 336, *344*
Whitbeck, L., 160, *162*
White, G. D., 261, 262, 267, *269*
White, J., 12, 19, *21*
White, L., 23, *43*
White, L. K., 151, 155, 156, *162, 163*
Whitehead, B., 117, *145*, 147, *163*
Whitehurst, G. J., 202, *223*
Whiteside, L., 180, *190*
Whiteside, M. F., 256, 257, *271*
Williams, D. R., 32, *43*
Willie, C. V., 37, *43*
Wills, T. A., 237, *250, 252*
Wilson, L., 199, *221*
Wilson, M. N., 166, *191*
Wolchik, S. A., 333, 336, *344*
Wolfe, B., 121, *145*
Wolfe, D. M., 274, *294*
Wood, B., 227, *252*
Woody, J. D., 336, *344*
Work, W., 325, 327, *341, 342*
Wu, C., 158, *163*
Wyer, M. M., 338, 337, 341, *342*
Wyman, P., 327, *342*

Z

Zahn-Waxler, C., 48, *64*
Zamsky, E. S., 167, 178, 179, 180, *188*
Zaslow, M., 217, 195, 199, 204, *220*,
    221, 223
Zhang, X., 32, *43*
Zigler, E., 197, *221*
Zill, N., 195, 210, 212, *223*, 227, *252*,
    259, 260, *271*, 323, *344*
Zimmerman, M., 175, *191*
Zongker, C., 336, *344*

Subject Index

A

Adolescent mothers
 and child development
  protective factors, 197–198
  child characteristics, 197, 213
  external supports, 197
  measurement of, 198–201
  parenting, 201–202, 214, 218
  risk factors, 195–197
  poverty, 195
  role of father involvement, 217
 and parenting, 201, *see also*
  Multigenerational families
Adolescents
 adjustment to stepfamilies, *see*
  Stepfamilies, transition to
 externalizing behaviors
  and marital conflict, 310
  and parents' prior divorce, 311
Analysis of Moment Structures (AMOS)
 program, 158
Avon Longitudinal Study of Pregnancy and
 Childhood (ALSPAC), 50–62
 implications, 60–62
 measures, 51–53
 results, 53–60
 sample and procedure, 51

B

Baltimore Multigenerational Family Study
 (BMFS), 167–186

conclusion, 186
procedure, 168
results, 170–186
sample and design, 167–168
Behavior Problems Index, 210, 212
Bracken Basic Concept Scale School
 Readiness Component, 210, 212
Brief Symptom Checklist, 279

C

Carey Infant Temperament Scale, 53
Cascade Model of Marital Dissolution,
 6–9
Center for Epidemiological Studies De-
 pression Scale (CES–D), 74, 209,
 211, 231, 242
Child Behavior Checklist (CBCL), 97,
 185, 243, 259
Children First, 335
Children of Divorce Intervention Project,
 326–327
Children of Divorce Parenting Interven-
 tion, 333–334
Colorado Separation and Divorce Project,
 332–333
Conflict resolution
 gender differences in, 19
Couples Interaction Scoring System
 (CISS), 5
Cross-lag regression models, 308

D

Detroit Area Study, 151, 152
Developmental Issues in StepFamilies
    (DIS) Research Project, 254–268
    conclusion, 268
    goals, 255
    method, 254–255
    results, 257–268
Divorce Adjustment Project, 327–328, 333
Divorce
    and child adjustment, 95–96
    risk factors, 96
    long-term consequences in
    adulthood,
        model of, 158–159
        quality of marital relationships,
            151–154
        quality of relationships with
            parents, 155–156
        socioeconomic attainment,
            150–151
        subjective well-being, 156–157
    and parentification, 108
    perspectives on,
        life course, 148–149, 159
        risk and resiliency, 149–150, 159
    rates of, 147
    and self-concept, 330
    transmission across generations, 153
        explanatory mechanisms, 154
Divorce interventions
    and child outcome, 328–329
    for children, 324–331
    for fathers, 336
    for parents, 331–336
    mediation
        and litigation, 338
        and mental health, 339–340
    school-based, 325

E

Early Years of Marriage Project, 24, 28
Edinburgh Postnatal Depression Scale
    (EPDS), 52
Ekman and Friesen's facial action coding
    system, 4

F

Familial leadership, 284, 290
Family Events Checklist, 242
Family structure, transitions in
    and parenting, see Parenting in
        transition
Family systems theory, 177

Father absence
    consequences of,
        access to community resources,
            139–142
        diminished emotional
            attachment, 130
        income loss, 130–131
        parenting quality, 135–138
        poverty, 131–132
    implications for policy, 143
    vs. two-parent families, differences
        in child adjustment
        detachment from labor force,
            124–126
        school achievement, 120–124
        teenaged parenthood, 126
Four Horseman of the Apocalypse, 9–10

G

General Social Survey, 151
Georgia Family Q-Sort, 183
Group therapy, 325
Growth curve analysis, 296–297

H

Hetherington Parentification Inventory,
    109
High School and Beyond Study (HSB),
    118, 122, 126, 137, 141
HLM growth modeling, 232
Hollingshead Index of Social Status, 231
Home Observational for Measurement of
    the Environment (HOME) Inven-
    tory, 207, 208, 211

I

Interpersonal Process Code (IPC), 231
Issues Checklist, 231

K

Kansas Marital Satisfaction Scale, 280

L

Life events
    and child adjustment, 297
    and externalizing behaviors, 301
Life Experience Survey, 242
Linking Interests of Families and Teachers
    (LIFT) study, 230–237, 248

conclusion, 248
measures, 231
results, 231–237
sample and design, 230
Locke–Wallace Marital Adjustment Test
    (MAT), 18

M

Marital conflict
    and child adjustment, 96–98, 310
        age differences, 98
        following divorce, 101–102
        gender differences, 98, 101–102
        preceding divorce, 98–101
    and parentification, 108–114
        consequences for children,
            109–114
        types of, 108
    and parenting, 100–101, 103–104
Marital dissolution
    prediction of, 6–9
    stages of, 7–10
Marital Instability over the Life Course
    study (MIOLC), 151, 153, 154
Marital Interaction Coding System
    (MICS), 5, 8–9, 11
Marital interactions
    assessment of, 3–6
    mathematical modeling of, 11–13
    and negative affect, 14
        escalation of, 14
        initiation of, 14
        reciprocity of, 14
    and positive affect, 15
Marital satisfaction, 7
    during transition to parenthood,
        18–19
    in stepfamilies, see Stepfamilies,
        transition to
Marital stability
    cultural differences
    and cultural factors, 26–27
    and interactional factors
        integration with social networks,
            32, 37–38
        interpersonal compatibility, 31,
            35–36
        male achievement, 31–32, 36–37
        husbands' autonomy and control,
            32–33, 38
        role of supportive wives, 29, 34
    meaning of parenthood, 38–39
    and structural factors, 25–26
Marriage
    distance and isolation in, 10, 12, 17,
        19

functional and dysfunctional
    processes in, 13–15
    typologies of, 11–12, 19
McCarthy Scales of Intellectual Abilities,
    185
Method triangulation, 278
Mother-headed families
    adolescent mothers, see Adolescent
        mothers
Multigenerational families
    and child adjustment, 184–185
    and family functioning, 183–184
    parenting quality, 178–181
        adolescent mothers vs.
            grandmothers, 178–180
        effects of mother–grandmother
            co–residence on, 180–181
        effects of mother–grandmother
            relationship quality on,
            181–183
    residential arrangements, 171
        changes in, 173
    role of fathers, 172
        contact and exchange with,
            174–175
        correlates of father involvement,
            176
    role of grandmothers, 173
        contact and exchange with, 173
    socioeconomic contexts, 170
Multigenerational Family Q-Sort (MFQ),
    183

N

National Longitudinal Survey of Youth
    (NLSY), 118, 120–121, 124–125,
    126, 134, 141, 151
National Survey of Families and House-
    holds (NSFH), 118, 127, 129, 134,
    136, 150, 153, 278, 279
Negative Startup Model, 14
New Chance Observational Study, 194,
    203–219
    conclusion, 216–219
    measures, 206–212
    plan of analysis, 206
    results, 212–215
    sample and procedure, 203–205
Nonresidential parents, 293
Nonshared Environment and Adolescent
    Development (NEAD) project, 94

O

Oral History Interview, 5, 6, 16, 17, 18,
    19

Oregon Divorce Study (ODS), 240–248
    conclusion, 248
    measures, 242–243
    results, 243–248
    sample and procedure, 240–241

P

Panel Study of Income Dynamics (PSID),
    118, 121, 131–132, 134, 141, 151
Parenting
    by stepfathers, 303
    in multigenerational families, *see*
        Multigenerational families
    monitoring and control, 304–307
    negativity and conflict, 307–310
Parenting in transition
    changes in maternal parenting,
        234–235
    contextual factors associated with,
        232–234
    and child adjustment, 247
    social support, 237–239, 244–245
    predictors of, 243–244
Parenting styles
    across ecological contexts, 67–70
        ethnicity, 68
        family structure, 68, 75–77, 85
        socioeconomic background, 68
    and child adjustment, 67–70, 77–86
    measurement of, 72–74
Parenting through Change, 334
Peabody Picture Vocabulary Test (PPVT),
    168, 182, 185
Problem Solving System (PSS), 242, 243
Protective factors
    and child development, *see*
        Adolescent mothers
    operationalizing, 198–201

R

Rapid Couples Interaction Scoring System
    (RCISS), 5, 7–9, 11
Remarriage
    impact of, 315
    and school achievement, 129
    transition to, *see* Stepfamilies,
        transition to
Risk and resiliency, 167
    children in poverty, 195–198
    and divorce, *see* Divorce
Risk factors
    and child adjustment, 53–62
    definition of, 48

domains of,
    child characteristics, 48–49, 53
    home environment and
        parenting, 49, 52–53
    sociocultural, 49, 52
    and family type, 50, 55, 57–59, 61
models of,
    cumulative risk model, 49,
        55–58
    equifinality, 49, 58–60
    multiple risk, 49, 53–55
Rosenberg Scale of Self-Esteem, 74
Round-robin interaction design, 309

S

Satisfaction with Life Survey, 279
Scales of Intergenerational Relationship
    Quality (SIRQ), 182
Sentiment Override
    positive and negative, 16–17, 20
Sibling
    birth of, 299
    relationships with, 312
Single-parent families
    and child adjustment, *see* Father
        absence
Social constructionism, 273–274
Specific Affect Coding System (SPAFF),
    4–5, 7, 11, 16–17, 242
Stepfamilies, transition to
    and child adjustment, 257–259
    developmental issues during
        adolescence, 258
    effect of duration of remarriage,
        257–258
    gender differences, 259
    sleeper effect of divorce, 258
    family relationships,
        coalitions and triangles, 261
        conflict, 264–265
        mother–child relationships, 261,
            262
        stepparent–child relationships,
            261, 262
    functional and dysfunctional family
        processes, 267–268
    marital satisfaction, 260–261
        child effects, 260
    nonresidential parents, 256,
        265–266
        gender differences in children's
            contact with, 266
    parenting, 263–264
    risk and protective factors, 256
Stepparent Behavior Inventory, 279

Stepparent Role Clarity Inventory, 279
Stepparent Role Questionnaire (SRQ), 279
Stepparents
   affinity with stepchildren, 287, 291
   and discipline, 283
   obligations, 285
   roles of,
     and child adjustment, 277,
      288–289
     content and clarity in, 266–267,
      274, 290–291
     descriptors of, 281–282, 290
     interparental agreement in, 276
   vs. stepchildren's perceptions, 286,
     291, 292
Strengths and Difficulties Questionnaire
   (SDQ), 51
Structural Equation Modeling (SEM),
   7–10, 104, 158

T

Transition
   and parenting, *see* Parenting in
     transition
   to stepfamilies, *see* Stepfamilies,
     transition to

U

Unrevealed Differences assessment, 280

V

Virginia Longitudinal Study of Divorce
   and Remarriage, 94, 97